THE BLACK BOX SOCIETY

# THE
# BLACK BOX
# SOCIETY

The Secret Algorithms That Control Money and Information

FRANK PASQUALE

Harvard University Press

*Cambridge, Massachusetts*
*London, England*
*2015*

*Library of Congress Cataloging-in-Publication Data*
Pasquale, Frank.
    The black box society : the secret algorithms that control money and information / Frank Pasquale.
        pages cm
    Includes bibliographical references and index.
    ISBN 978-0-674-36827-9
    1. Power (Social sciences)    2. Elite (Social sciences)
3. Knowledge, Theory of.    4. Observation (Psychology)    I. Title.
    HN49.P6.P375 2015
    303.3—dc23
                                                            2014013480

For Ray


In Memory of my Parents

# CONTENTS

[T]here is one world in common for those who are awake, but [when] men are asleep each turns away into a world of his own.

—Heracleitus

Million-fuelèd, ' nature's bonfire burns on.
But quench her bonniest, dearest ' to her, her clearest-selvèd spark
Man, how fast his firedint, ' his mark on mind, is gone!
Both are in an unfathomable, all is in an enormous dark
Drowned.

—Gerard Manley Hopkins

# 1

## INTRODUCTION—THE NEED TO KNOW

Everybody knows the story about the man crawling intently around a lamppost on a dark night. When a police officer comes along and wants to know what he's doing, he says he's looking for his keys. "You lost them here?" asks the cop. "No," the seeker replies, "but this is where the light is." This bromide about futility has lately taken on a whole new meaning as a metaphor for our increasingly enigmatic technologies.

There's a noble tradition among social scientists of trying to clarify how power works: who gets what, when, where, and why.[1] Our common life is explored in books like *The Achieving Society*, *The Winner-Take-All Society*, *The Good Society*, and *The Decent Society*. At their best, these works also tell us why such inquiry matters.[2]

But efforts like these are only as good as the information available. We cannot understand, or even investigate, a subject about which nothing is known. Amateur epistemologists have many names for this problem. "Unknown unknowns," "black swans," and "deep secrets" are popular catchphrases for our many areas of social blankness.[3] There is even an emerging field of "agnotology" that studies the "structural production of ignorance, its diverse causes and conformations, whether brought about by neglect, forgetfulness, myopia, extinction, secrecy, or suppression."[4]

Gaps in knowledge, putative and real, have powerful implications, as do the uses that are made of them. Alan Greenspan, once the most powerful central banker in the world, claimed that today's markets are driven by an "unredeemably opaque" version of Adam Smith's "invisible hand," and that no one (including regulators) can ever get "more than a glimpse at the internal workings of the simplest of modern financial systems." If this is true, libertarian policy would seem to be the only reasonable response. Friedrich von Hayek, a preeminent theorist of laissez-faire, called the "knowledge problem" an insuperable barrier to benevolent government interventions in the economy.[5]

But what if the "knowledge problem" is not an intrinsic aspect of the market, but rather is deliberately encouraged by certain businesses? What if financiers keep their doings opaque on purpose, precisely to avoid or to confound regulation? That would imply something very different about the merits of deregulation.

The challenge of the "knowledge problem" is just one example of a general truth: What we do and don't know about the social (as opposed to the natural) world is not inherent in its nature, but is itself a function of social constructs. Much of what we can find out about companies, governments, or even one another, is governed by law. Laws of privacy, trade secrecy, the so-called Freedom of Information Act—all set limits to inquiry. They rule certain investigations out of the question before they can even begin. We need to ask: To whose benefit?

Some of these laws are crucial to a decent society. No one wants to live in a world where the boss can tape our bathroom breaks. But the laws of information protect much more than personal privacy. They allow pharmaceutical firms to hide the dangers of a new drug behind veils of trade secrecy and banks to obscure tax liabilities behind shell corporations. And they are much too valuable to their beneficiaries to be relinquished readily.

Even our political and legal systems, the spaces of our common life that are supposed to be the most open and transparent, are being colonized by the logic of secrecy. The executive branch has been lobbying ever more forcefully for the right to enact and enforce "secret law" in its pursuit of the "war on terror," and voters contend in

an electoral arena flooded with "dark money"—dollars whose donors, and whose influence, will be disclosed only *after* the election,
if at all.[6]

But while powerful businesses, financial institutions, and government agencies hide their actions behind nondisclosure agreements,
"proprietary methods," and gag rules, our own lives are increasingly
open books. Everything we do online is recorded; the only questions left are to whom the data will be available, and for how long.
Anonymizing software may shield us for a little while, but who
knows whether trying to hide isn't itself the ultimate red flag for
watchful authorities? Surveillance cameras, data brokers, sensor networks, and "supercookies" record how fast we drive, what pills
we take, what books we read, what websites we visit. The law, so
aggressively protective of secrecy in the world of commerce, is increasingly silent when it comes to the privacy of persons.

That incongruity is the focus of this book. How has secrecy become so important to industries ranging from Wall Street to Silicon
Valley? What are the social implications of the invisible practices
that hide the way people and businesses are labeled and treated?
How can the law be used to enact the best possible balance between
privacy and openness? To answer these questions is to chart a path
toward a more intelligible social order.

But first, we must fully understand the problem. The term "black
box" is a useful metaphor for doing so, given its own dual meaning.
It can refer to a recording device, like the data-monitoring systems
in planes, trains, and cars. Or it can mean a system whose workings
are mysterious; we can observe its inputs and outputs, but we cannot
tell how one becomes the other. We face these two meanings daily:
tracked ever more closely by firms and government, we have no clear
idea of just how far much of this information can travel, how it is
used, or its consequences.[7]

## The Power of Secrecy

Knowledge is power. To scrutinize others while avoiding scrutiny
oneself is one of the most important forms of power.[8] Firms seek
out intimate details of potential customers' and employees' lives,
but give regulators as little information as they possibly can about

their own statistics and procedures.[9] Internet companies collect more and more data on their users but fight regulations that would let those same users exercise some control over the resulting digital dossiers.

As technology advances, market pressures raise the stakes of the data game. Surveillance cameras become cheaper every year; sensors are embedded in more places.[10] Cell phones track our movements; programs log our keystrokes. New hardware and new software promise to make "quantified selves" of all of us, whether we like it or not.[11] The resulting information—a vast amount of data that until recently went unrecorded—is fed into databases and assembled into profiles of unprecedented depth and specificity.

But to what ends, and to whose? The decline in personal privacy might be worthwhile if it were matched by comparable levels of transparency from corporations and government. But for the most part it is not. Credit raters, search engines, major banks, and the TSA take in data about us and convert it into scores, rankings, risk calculations, and watch lists with vitally important consequences. But the proprietary algorithms by which they do so are immune from scrutiny, except on the rare occasions when a whistleblower litigates or leaks.

Sometimes secrecy is warranted. We don't want terrorists to be able to evade detection because they know exactly what Homeland Security agents are looking out for.[12] But when every move we make is subject to inspection by entities whose procedures and personnel are exempt from even remotely similar treatment, the promise of democracy and free markets rings hollow. Secrecy is approaching critical mass, and we are in the dark about crucial decisions. Greater openness is imperative.

## Reputation, Search, Finance

At the core of the information economy are Internet and finance companies that accumulate vast amounts of digital data, and with it intimate details of their customers'—our—lives. They use it to make important decisions about us and to influence the decisions we make for ourselves. But what do we know about them? A bad credit score may cost a borrower hundreds of thousands of dollars, but he will never understand exactly how it was calculated. A predictive analytics firm may score someone as a "high cost" or "unreliable" worker, yet never tell her about the decision.

More benignly, perhaps, these companies influence the choices we make ourselves. Recommendation engines at Amazon and YouTube affect an automated familiarity, gently suggesting offerings they think we'll like. But don't discount the significance of that "perhaps." The economic, political, and cultural agendas behind their suggestions are hard to unravel. As middlemen, they specialize in shifting alliances, sometimes advancing the interests of customers, sometimes suppliers: all to orchestrate an online world that maximizes their own profits.

Financial institutions exert direct power over us, deciding the terms of credit and debt. Yet they too shroud key deals in impenetrable layers of complexity. In 2008, when secret goings-on in the money world provoked a crisis of trust that brought the banking system to the brink of collapse, the Federal Reserve intervened to stabilize things—and kept key terms of those interventions secret as well. Journalists didn't uncover the massive scope of its interventions until late 2011.[13] That was well after landmark financial reform legislation had been debated and passed—*without* informed input from the electorate—and then watered down by the same corporate titans whom the Fed had just had to bail out.

Reputation. Search. Finance. These are the areas in which Big Data looms largest in our lives. But too often it looms invisibly, undermining the openness of our society and the fairness of our markets. Consider just a few of the issues raised by the new technologies of ranking and evaluation:

- Should a credit card company be entitled to raise a couple's interest rate if they seek marriage counseling? If so, should cardholders know this?

- Should Google, Apple, Twitter, or Facebook be able to shut out websites or books entirely, even when their content is completely legal? And if they do, should they tell us?

- Should the Federal Reserve be allowed to print unknown sums of money to save banks from their own scandalous behavior? If so, how and when should citizens get to learn what's going on?

- Should the hundreds of thousands of American citizens placed on secret "watch lists" be so informed, and should they be given the chance to clear their names?

The leading firms of Wall Street and Silicon Valley are not alone in the secretiveness of their operations, but I will be focusing primarily on them because of their unique roles in society. While accounting for "less than 10% of the value added" in the U.S. economy in the fourth quarter of 2010, the finance sector took 29 percent—$57.7 billion—of profits.[14] Silicon Valley firms are also remarkably profitable, and powerful.[15] What finance firms do with money, leading Internet companies do with attention. They direct it toward some ideas, goods, and services, and away from others. They organize the world for us, and we have been quick to welcome this data-driven convenience. But we need to be honest about its costs.

## Secrecy and Complexity

Deconstructing the black boxes of Big Data isn't easy. Even if they were willing to expose their methods to the public, the modern Internet and banking sectors pose tough challenges to our understanding of those methods. The conclusions they come to—about the productivity of employees, or the relevance of websites, or the attractiveness of investments—are determined by complex formulas devised by legions of engineers and guarded by a phalanx of lawyers.

In this book, we will be exploring three critical strategies for keeping black boxes closed: "real" secrecy, legal secrecy, and obfuscation. *Real secrecy* establishes a barrier between hidden content and unauthorized access to it. We use real secrecy daily when we lock our doors or protect our e-mail with passwords. *Legal secrecy* obliges those privy to certain information to keep it secret; a bank employee is obliged both by statutory authority and by terms of employment not to reveal customers' balances to his buddies.[16] *Obfuscation* involves deliberate attempts at concealment when secrecy has been compromised. For example, a firm might respond to a request for information by delivering 30 million pages of documents, forcing its investigator to waste time looking for a needle in a haystack.[17] And the end result of both types of secrecy, and obfuscation, is *opacity*, my blanket term for remediable incomprehensibility.[18]

Detailed investment prospectuses, for instance, can run to dozens or hundreds of pages. They can refer to other documents, and those to still others. There may be conflicts among the documents that the original source references.[19] Anyone really trying to understand the investment is likely to have to process thousands of pages of complicated legal verbiage—some of which can be quite obfuscatory. The same holds for accounting statements. When law professor Frank Partnoy and Pulitzer Prize–winning journalist Jesse Eisinger teamed up to explore "what's inside America's banks" in early 2013, they were aghast at the enduring opacity. They reported on the banks as "'black boxes' that may still be concealing enormous risks—the sort that could again take down the economy."[20] Several quotes in the article portrayed an American banking system still out of control five years after the crisis:

- "There is no major financial institution today whose financial statements provide a meaningful clue" about its risks, said one hedge fund manager.
- "After serving on the [Financial Accounting Standards] board [FASB]," said Don Young, "I no longer trust bank accounting."
- Another former FASB member, asked if he trusted bank accounting, answered: "Absolutely not."[21]

These quotes came five years after the financial crisis and three years after the Dodd-Frank Act, a gargantuan piece of legislation that comprehensively altered banking law. Financial crises result when a critical mass of investors act on that distrust, and their skepticism cascades throughout the system. And when governments step in with their "bailouts" and "liquidity facilities," they add new layers of complexity to an already byzantine situation.

In the case of technology companies, complexity is not as important as secrecy. However sprawling the web becomes, Google's search engineers are at least working on a "closed system"; their own company's copies of the Internet. Similarly, those in charge of Twitter and Facebook "feeds" have a set body of information to work with. Their methods are hard to understand primarily because of a mix of real and legal secrecy, and their scale. Interlocking technical and legal prohibitions prevent anyone outside such a company from understanding fundamental facts about it.

Activists often press for transparency as a solution to the black box issues raised in this book. In many cases, sunshine truly is the "best disinfectant." However, transparency may simply provoke complexity that is as effective at defeating understanding as real or legal secrecy. Government has frequently stepped in to require disclosure and "plain language" formats for consumers. But financiers have parried transparency rules with more complex transactions. When this happens, without substantial gains in efficiency, regulators should step in and limit complexity. Transparency is not just an end in itself, but an interim step on the road to intelligibility.

## The Secret Judgments of Software

So why does this all matter? It matters because authority is increasingly expressed algorithmically.[22] Decisions that used to be based on human reflection are now made automatically. Software encodes thousands of rules and instructions computed in a fraction of a second. Such automated processes have long guided our planes, run the physical backbone of the Internet, and interpreted our GPSes. In short, they improve the quality of our daily lives in ways both noticeable and not.

But where do we call a halt? Similar protocols also influence—invisibly—not only the route we take to a new restaurant, but which restaurant Google, Yelp, OpenTable, or Siri recommends to us. They might help us find reviews of the car we drive. Yet choosing a car, or even a restaurant, is not as straightforward as optimizing an engine or routing a drive. Does the recommendation engine take into account, say, whether the restaurant or car company gives its workers health benefits or maternity leave? Could we prompt it to do so? In their race for the most profitable methods of mapping social reality, the data scientists of Silicon Valley and Wall Street tend to treat recommendations as purely technical problems. The values and prerogatives that the encoded rules enact are hidden within black boxes.[23]

The most obvious question is: Are these algorithmic applications fair? Why, for instance, does YouTube (owned by Google) so consistently beat out other video sites in Google's video search results? How does one particular restaurant or auto stock make it to the top of the hit list while another does not? What does it mean when Internet retailers quote different prices for the same product to different buyers? Why are some borrowers cut slack for a late payment, while others are not?

Defenders of the status quo say that results like these reflect a company's good-faith judgment about the quality of a website, an investment, or a customer. Detractors contend that they cloak self-serving appraisals and conflicts of interest in a veil of technological wizardry. Who is right? It's anyone's guess, as long as the algorithms involved are kept secret. Without knowing what Google actually *does* when it ranks sites, we cannot assess when it is acting in good faith to help users, and when it is biasing results to favor its own commercial interests. The same goes for status updates on Facebook, trending topics on Twitter, and even network management practices at telephone and cable companies. All these are protected by laws of secrecy and technologies of obfuscation.

## The One-Way Mirror

With so much secrecy so publicly in place, it is easy for casual observers to conclude that there is a rough parity between the informational protection of individuals and civil associations and those of corporations and government. It is comforting to think that our personal bank records are as secure as the bank's own secrets. But I will attempt to overthrow this assumption. We do not live in a peaceable kingdom of private walled gardens; the contemporary world more closely resembles a one-way mirror. Important corporate actors have unprecedented knowledge of the minutiae of our daily lives, while we know little to nothing about how they use this knowledge to influence the important decisions that we—and they—make.

Furthermore, even as critical power over money and new media rapidly concentrates in a handful of private companies, we remain largely ignorant of critical ways in which these companies interact (and conflict) with public powers. Though this book is primarily about the private sector, I have called it *The Black Box Society* (rather than *The Black Box Economy*) because the distinction between state and market is fading. We are increasingly ruled by what former political insider Jeff Connaughton called "The Blob," a shadowy network of actors who mobilize money and media for private gain, whether acting officially on behalf of business or of government.[24] In one policy area (or industry) after another, these insiders decide the distribution of society's benefits (like low-interest credit or secure employment) and burdens (like audits, wiretaps, and precarity).

Admittedly, as Jon Elster has written in his book *Local Justice*, there is no perfectly fair way to allocate opportunities.[25] But a market-state increasingly dedicated to the advantages of speed and stealth crowds out even the most basic efforts to make these choices fairer. Technocrats and managers cloak contestable value judgments in the garb of "science": thus the insatiable demand for mathematical models that reframe subtle and subjective conclusions (such as the worth of a worker, service, article, or product) as the inevitable dictate of salient, measurable data.[26] Big data driven decisions may lead to unprecedented profits. But once we use computation not merely to exercise power over things, but also over people, we need to develop a much more robust ethical framework than "the Blob" is now willing to entertain.

## The Secrecy of Business and the Business of Secrecy

Today's finance and Internet companies feverishly sort, rank, and rate. They say they keep techniques strictly secret in order to preserve valuable intellectual property—but their darker motives are also obvious. For example, litigation has revealed that some drug companies have cherry-picked the most positive studies for publication, hiding those with serious health or safety implications.[27] Journalists are prying open Wall Street's pre-financial crisis black boxes to this day.[28] The Sunlight Foundation, Center for Effective Government, AllTrials.net, and Transparency International press for openness.

Politicians are responding, and try to improve disclosure here and there. But they must be cautious. When a gadfly proves too inconvenient, companies can band together in a super PAC, funding attacks on the would-be reformer without having to reveal what they are doing until well after the election.[29]

Asked about Google's privacy practices, former CEO Eric Schmidt once said that "Google policy is to get right up to the creepy line and not cross it." It is probably more accurate to say that he and other Silicon Valley leaders don't want to be *caught* crossing the creepy line.[30] As long as secrecy can be used to undermine market competition and law enforcement, they will be emboldened to experiment with ever creepier, more intrusive, and even exploitative practices.

## Looking Back

The quest for a more transparent society—more easily understood, and more open about its priorities—has animated leading reformers in the United States. Louis Brandeis's comment that "sunlight is said to be the best of disinfectants," so often cited today, is a century old, dating back to business scandals of the Gilded Age eerily similar to today's casino capitalism.[31] Muckraking journalists and trust-busters of the Progressive Era shamed robber barons by exposing their misdeeds.[32] They targeted politicians, too: the Publicity Act of 1910 mandated disclosure of campaign donations.[33]

Many states of the time took up similar reforms. Voters wanted politics and business subject to public scrutiny. After shady commercial practices surged again in the 1920s, the New Deal echoed and amplified Progressivism. Congress, disgusted by the hucksters who paved the way for the great crash of 1929, imposed sweeping new disclosure obligations in the Securities Act of 1933 and the Securities Exchange Act of 1934. New legislation created the Federal Communications Commission and gave it plenary power to investigate abuses in the telegraph and radio industries.[34] New Deal agencies revealed the inner workings of critical industries.[35]

Government balanced these new powers by opening itself up in important ways. For example, the Administrative Procedure Act (APA) of 1947 forced agencies to give the public notice and a chance to comment before they imposed important rules. Reformers built on the APA with the 1966 Freedom of Information Act, which opened up many government records.[36]

In the 1960s, a broad coalition of interests fought both government and corporate secrecy in the name of citizen empowerment and consumer protection.[37] Perhaps their most enduring legacy was the establishment of procedures of openness. For example, the National Environmental Policy Act required major federal projects to include Environmental Impact Statements that would reveal likely effects on air, water, flora, and fauna. Agencies ranging from the Food and Drug Administration to the Consumer Product Safety Commission now make daily activities less dangerous by revealing the risks of things we purchase.[38]

But there was always pushback. By the late 1960s, businesses were successfully challenging scrutiny from what they branded the "nanny state." When the Environmental Protection Agency wanted to release data on the composition of some pesticides, for example, Monsanto fought back. It won a Supreme Court ruling that prevented the disclosure on the grounds that the formulations were a "trade secret" (a form of intellectual property we'll explore in more detail later). Such rulings chilled many disclosure initiatives, including investigations of Philip Morris's cigarettes and frackers' chemicals.[39]

Confidence in government waned during the stagflation of the 1970s, and business lobbyists seized the opportunity to argue that journalists could do a better job at exposing and punishing corporate wrongdoing than bureaucrats. With zealous investigators ferreting out bad behavior, why bother to require reports? Establishment figures pooh-poohed complaints that banks were becoming too big, complex, and rapacious. "Sophisticated investors" could understand the risks, they insisted, and banks themselves would avoid duplicity to preserve their reputations.[40]

Companies tried to maintain an advantage over their competitors by classifying innovative work as "proprietary" or "confidential." As computerized exchanges made it possible to gain or lose fortunes within seconds, information advantage became critical throughout the economy. Some economists began to question the wisdom of regulating, or even monitoring, the fast-moving corporate world. Some failed to disclose that they were being paid for "consulting" by the same secretive corporations their writings supported. Business schools taught MBAs the basics of game theory, which stressed the importance of gaining an information advantage over rivals.[41]

Over the last decade, fortunes made via stealth techniques made secrecy even sexier. Google rose to the top of the tech pack while zealously guarding its "secret sauce"—the complex algorithms it used to rank sites. Investment banks and hedge funds made billions of dollars by courting sellers who didn't understand the value of what they were holding and buyers who didn't understand the problems with what they were purchasing.[42]

While neoliberals were vitiating the regulatory state's ability to expose (or even understand) rapidly changing business practices, neoconservatives began to advance a wall of secrecy for the deep state.[43] In the Nixon administration, Dick Cheney and Donald Rumsfeld were already chafing at the idea that Congress could force the executive branch to explain its foreign engagements and strategies. When they renewed their executive service in the George W. Bush administration, they expanded the executive branch's freedom to maneuver (and its power to avoid oversight).[44] After 9/11, they pressed even harder for government secrecy, claiming that the only way to win the "war on terror" was for the state to act as clandestinely as its shadowy enemies.[45]

The Obama administration embraced the expansion of executive secrecy, with far-reaching (and occasionally surreal) results. By 2010, leading intelligence agency experts could not even estimate the overall costs of the U.S. antiterrorism effort; nor could they map the extent of the surveillance apparatus they had built.[46] And their fumbling responses to questions were positively enlightening in comparison with the silence of defense officials funded by the "black budget," whose appropriations only a sliver of Congress and responsible officials are privy to understand.[47] Big government now stands together with security contractors to manage strategic surprise.

Thus the openness mantra of Progressive Era reformers has been neatly reversed in favor of a Faustian (and credulous) bargain: just keep us safe and we won't ask about the details. "Nanny state" takes on a very different connotation in this context.

Things weren't supposed to turn out this way. Little more than a decade ago, the Internet was promising a new era of transparency, in which open access to information would result in extraordinary liberty. Law professor Glenn Reynolds predicted that "an army of Davids" would overthrow smug, self-satisfied elites. Space physicist David Brin believed that new technology would finally answer the old Roman challenge, "Who will guard the guardians?" But the powerful actors of business, finance, and search did not meekly submit to the fishbowl vision of mutual surveillance that Brin prophesied in *The Transparent Society*. Instead, they deployed strategies of obfuscation and secrecy to consolidate power and wealth.[48] Their opaque technologies are spreading, unmonitored and unregulated.

## The Shape of the Book

In this book, I will explore the business practices of leading Internet and finance companies, focusing on their use of proprietary reputation, search, and finance technologies in our often chaotic information environment. In some cases, they enable great gains in efficiency. In others, however, they undermine both economic growth and individual rights.

The success of individuals, businesses, and their products depends heavily on the synthesis of data and perceptions into *reputation*. In ever more settings, reputation is determined by secret algorithms processing inaccessible data. Few of us appreciate the extent of ambient surveillance, and fewer still have access either to its results—the all-important profiles that control so many aspects of our lives—or to the "facts" on which they are based. Chapter 2 illustrates how broadly the new technologies of reputation have infiltrated society.[49]

The more we rely on search engines and social networks to find what we want and need, the more influence they wield. The power to include, exclude, and rank is the power to ensure that certain public impressions become permanent, while others remain fleeting.[50] How does Amazon decide which books to prioritize in searches? How does it ferret out fake or purchased reviews? Why do Facebook and Twitter highlight some political stories or sources at the expense of others?[51] Although internet giants say their algorithms are scientific and neutral tools, it is very difficult to verify those claims.[52] And while they have become critical economic infrastructure, trade secrecy law permits managers to hide their methodologies, and business practices, deflecting scrutiny.[53] Chapter 3 examines some personal implications of opaque search technology, along with larger issues that it raises in business and law.

Like the reputation and search sectors, the finance industry has characterized more and more decisions as computable, programmable procedures. Big data enables complex pattern recognition techniques to analyze massive data sets. Algorithmic methods of reducing judgment to a series of steps were supposed to rationalize finance, replacing self-serving or biased intermediaries with sound decision frameworks. And they did reduce some inefficiencies. But they also ended up firmly building in some dubious old patterns of credit castes and corporate unaccountability.[54] The black boxes of finance replaced familiar old problems with a triple whammy of technical complexity, real secrecy, and trade secret laws. They contributed to the financial crisis of 2008, according to the *Financial Times*'s John Gapper, because "the opacity and complexity . . . let deception, overpricing and ultimately fraud flourish."[55] Perhaps worse, by naturalizing these (avoidable) features of our social landscape, unregulated financial secrecy is starting to give them a patina of inevitability. Chapter 4 examines the role of opaque models and practices in financial markets, along with the challenges they present to citizens, to society, and to the law.

In his book *Turing's Cathedral*, George Dyson quipped that "Facebook defines who we are, Amazon defines what we want, and Google defines what we think."[56] We can extend that epigram to include *finance*, which defines what we have (materially, at least), and *reputation*, which increasingly defines our opportunities. Leaders in each sector aspire to make these decisions without regulation, appeal, or explanation. If they succeed, our fundamental freedoms and opportunities will be outsourced to systems with few discernible values beyond the enrichment of top managers and shareholders.

This book charts two paths of resistance. Chapter 5 recommends several legal strategies for checking the worst abuses by black box firms. Chapter 6 makes the case for a new politics and economics of reputation, search, and finance, based on the ideal of an intelligible society. It would be foolish to hope for immediate traction in today's gridlocked political environment. But agencies would need to make "all the right moves" within existing legal frameworks to cabin black box practices. Moreover, those concerned about the power of Silicon Valley and Wall Street need to do more than complain about the limited availability of crucial information. We can imagine a future in which the power of algorithmic authority is limited to environments where it can promote fairness, freedom, and rationality.

We do not have to live in a world where hidden scores determine people's fates, or human manipulations of the stock market remain as inscrutable as the "invisible hand." We should not have to worry that the fates of individuals, businesses, and even our financial systems are at the mercy of hidden databases, dubious scores, and shadowy bets. The same technological and legal revolutions that have so far eviscerated personal privacy can be used to protect it and to advance, rather than curtail, our freedoms and our understanding of the social world. Directed at the right targets, data mining and pervasive surveillance might even prevent the kinds of financial crises and massive misallocations of resources that have devastated the U.S. economy over the past decade.

We need to promote public values in Internet and finance companies, drawing on best practices in other, more regulated sectors. In health care, for example, regulators are deploying technologically savvy contractors to detect and deter fraud, abuse, and unnecessary treatments.[57] Similar techniques can and should be applied to keep banks, search engines, and social networks honest.

More transparency would help outside analysts check "irrational exuberance" in markets and uncover corporate misconduct that is now too easily hidden. It might expose unfair competitive or discriminatory practices. But as I propose regulatory measures, I will repeatedly make the point that transparency is not enough, particularly in the finance sector. When companies parry with complexity too great to monitor or understand, disclosure becomes an empty gesture. We need to put an end to the recursive games of "disclosure" and "tricks to defeat disclosure" that have plagued regulators. Transactions that are too complex to explain to outsiders may well be too complex to be allowed to exist.[58]

## The Self-Preventing Prophecy

We need to face the darker possibilities betokened by current trends. There is a venerable fiction genre known as the "self-preventing prophecy."[59] An author imagines a dystopia, plausibly extrapolating to the future some of the worst trends of the present. If enough readers are shaken from their complacency, they start to make the changes that can prevent the prophecy.[60] The author then avoids the fate of Cassandra, the prophetess of Greek myth whose warnings were fated to be disregarded. George Orwell's *1984* and Aldous Huxley's *Brave New World* could both be understood in this way, helping to mobilize resistance to the totalitarian futures they described.[61]

Films have also aimed for self-preventing prophecy. In Terry Gilliam's *Brazil*, things start to go downhill for protagonist Sam Lowry after a fly accidentally jams a printer at an antiterror agency. As he tries to fix the error, a sclerotic bureaucracy closes in around him, wrongly associating him with violent extremists. Gilliam depicted a state run amok, unaccountable and opaque. Its workings are as mindless and catatonic as the citizens whom it tortures into submission.[62]

We like to believe that we have escaped Gilliam's 1985 dystopia, just as the plausibility of *1984* was eroded by the Eastern Bloc revolutions of 1989. Most major decisions about our lives are made in the private sector, not by a state bureaucracy. State-of-the-art computers are a far cry from the dusty files of the Stasi or the Rube Goldberg contraptions of Gilliam's imagining.[63] The vibrant leaders of Wall Street and Silicon Valley are far more polished than the bumbling and brutal beadles of *Brazil*. Cornucopians urge citizens to simply get out of their way, and to rest assured that technology will solve problems ranging from traffic jams to freakish weather.

But complacency is unwarranted. Many of these companies make decisions affecting millions of people every day, and small mistakes can cascade into life-changing reclassifications. We cannot access critical features of their decision-making processes. The corporate strategists and governmental authorities of the future will deploy their massive resources to keep their one-way mirrors in place; the advantages conferred upon them by Big Data technologies are too great to give up without a fight. But black boxes are a signal that information imbalances have gone too far. We have come to rely on the titans of reputation, search, and finance to help us make sense of the world; it is time for policymakers to help us make sense of the sensemakers.

In their workplaces and in their homes, Americans are increasingly influenced—some might say bullied—by managers who keep their methods under wraps. Corporations depend on automated judgments that may be wrong, biased, or destructive. The black boxes of reputation, search, and finance endanger all of us. Faulty data, invalid assumptions, and defective models can't be corrected when they are hidden. This book exposes them, and proposes solutions.

# 2

# DIGITAL REPUTATION IN AN
# ERA OF RUNAWAY DATA

Tell us everything, Big Data croons. Don't be shy. The more you tell us, the more we can help you. It's like the Elf on the Shelf, whom Santa deputizes to do his holiday watching. It sits and reports— naughty or nice? It can move around, the better to see, but only when the kids aren't looking. If they touch the elf, its magic is lost. But for the obedient, Christmas presents await!

While most kids don't believe in the elf past the age of reason, policymakers are still buying into Big Data's myths. Too many consumers do, too. Eric Schmidt says that he wants Google users to be able to ask it, " 'What shall I do tomorrow?' and 'What job shall I take?'," and users barely raise an eyebrow about the implications of giving one company such intimate knowledge about their lives. Given optimal personalization and optimal data points, Big Data will plan for us an optimal life. And it costs us nothing!

Except that's the myth. For every discount or shortcut big data may offer, it's probably imposing other, hidden costs or wild goose chases. Your data is a source of huge profit to other people, but often at your expense. In the wrong hands, your data will cost you dearly.[1]

Data-intensive advertising helps generate over $150 billion a year in economic activity.[2] Boosters claim that it gives us an ever more personalized, user-friendly Internet. But advertising companies, and the people who pay them, aren't in business for their health. They're looking for profit. When we click on an ad promising a discount, there's probably a program behind the scenes calculating how much more it can charge us on the basis of our location,[3] or whether we're using a Mac or PC, or even court records.[4] It's not only the National Security Agency (NSA) that covets total information awareness; that's the goal of marketers, too. They want that endless array of data points to develop exhaustive profiles. Of us.

Pattern recognition is the name of the game—connecting the dots of past behavior to predict the future. Are you a fierce comparison shopper, or the relaxed kind who's OK spending a few extra dollars for a plane ticket or a movie if it saves some trouble? Firms want to know, and they can find out quite easily. Every business wants a data advantage that will let it target its ideal customers.

Sometimes the results are prosaic and predictable: your favorite retailer may pop up as an ad on every other website you visit. But that's the tip of an iceberg of marketing. What lies beneath are myriad unsavory strategies. One data broker sold the names of 500,000 gamblers over 55 years old for 8.5 cents apiece to criminals, who then bilked money from vulnerable seekers of "luck." Others offered lists of patients with cancer or Alzheimer's disease.[5] Firms can "refine" such lists, seeking out the gullible and the desperate. They aren't just the bottom feeders on the margins of the economy, either. Google is a "go-to" firm for digital marketing because it knows us so well—naughty or nice, wise or foolish, good credit or bad.[6] And a surprising proportion of digital marketing is about finding marks for dubious loans, pharmaceutical products, and fly-by-night for-profit educators.[7]

Businesses are looking for the cheapest, most cost-effective workers, too. They scrutinize our work records the way they scour our online data trails. This data analysis is usually framed as a way of rewarding high performers and shaming shirkers. But it's not so simple. Most of us don't know that we're being profiled, or, if we do, how the profiling works. We can't anticipate, for instance, when an apparently innocuous action—like joining the wrong group on Facebook—will trigger a red flag on some background checker that renders us effectively unemployable.

We also don't know much about *how* data from one sphere feeds into another: as the Federal Trade Commission has concluded, there is "a fundamental lack of transparency about data broker industry practices."[8] We do know that it does. Law enforcement, for example, can enlist the help of our bosses—and of Big Data—to keep an eye on us. The Fourth Amendment puts some (minimal) constraints on government searches of our records, but does not apply to employers. One woman, using a computer that belonged to her employer, searched for "pressure cookers" in the same time frame that her husband searched for "backpacks." Though she'd left the company, her employer was still reporting "suspicious activities" on its machines to local police. Six agents, two of whom identified themselves as members of the government's regional Joint Terrorism Task Force, came to visit her.[9]

As complaints, investigations, and leaks give us occasional peeks into the black boxes of reputation analysis, a picture of decontextualized, out-of-control data mining emerges. Data brokers can use private and public records—of marriage, divorce, home purchases, voting, or thousands of others—to draw inferences about any of us. Laws prevent government itself from collecting certain types of information, but data brokers are not so constrained. And little stops the government from *buying* that information once it's been collected. Thus commercial and government "dataveillance" results in synergistic swapping of intimate details about individual lives.[10]

America's patchwork of weak privacy laws are no match for the threats posed by this runaway data, which is used secretly to rank, rate, and evaluate persons, often to their detriment and often unfairly. Without a society-wide commitment to fair data practices, digital discrimination will only intensify.

## On (and beyond) Data

Even with that commitment, we can't forget that access to data is just the first and smallest step toward fairness in a world of pervasive digital scoring, where many of our daily activities are processed as "signals" for rewards or penalties, benefits or burdens. Critical decisions are made not on the basis of the data per se, but on the basis of data analyzed *algorithmically:* that is, in calculations coded in computer software. Failing clear understanding of the algorithms involved—and the right to challenge unfair ones—disclosure of underlying data will do little to secure reputational justice. Here a familiar concept from personal finance—the credit score—can help illuminate the promise and pitfalls of a "scored" world.

*From Credit History to Score: The Original Black Box.* Credit bureaus pioneered black box techniques, making critical judgments about people, but hiding their methods of data collection and analysis. In the 1960s, innuendo percolated into reports filed by untrained "investigators." They included attributes like messiness, poorly kept yards, and "effeminate gestures."[11] The surveillance could be creepy and unfair—virtually everyone has some habit that could be seized on as evidence of unreliability or worse. Combine the lax standards for reporting with a toxic mix of prejudices common at the time, and the flaws of this system are obvious.

News reports on credit bureaus were alarming enough that in 1970, Congress passed the Fair Credit Reporting Act (FCRA), which required that the bureaus make their dossiers both accurate and relevant.[12] Credit bureaus' files were opened to scrutiny, and consumers were given the right to inspect their records and demand corrections.[13] This dose of sunlight was a decent disinfectant as far as relevance was concerned; questionable characterizations of sexual orientation and housekeeping faded out of bureau reports as people gained access to their profiles.

However, the right to dispute credit bureau records did not, and does not, guarantee accuracy. In a report for *60 Minutes*, journalist Steve Kroft described a conversation with a "dispute agent" at one of the large credit bureaus. His informant bluntly admitted the prevailing attitude that "the creditor was always right."[14] Agents said their bureau asked them to review ninety cases a day, which averages out to less than six minutes per case. And even when they had the opportunity to get to the bottom of things, they had little power to resolve the matter in favor of the consumer. Little wonder, then, that Kroft's report exposed an avalanche of complaints against the industry.

Though bureaus complained *60 Minutes* was unfair, their track record is not exactly sterling. Reports show that credit bureaus have strived mightily to deflect minimal demands for accountability.[15] For example, after federal law required them to release to consumers an annual free copy of their credit histories via the site Annual-CreditReport.com, bureaus set up "FreeCreditReport.com" to lull the unsuspecting into buying expensive credit monitoring services.[16] Decoy websites proliferated.[17] To minimize the visibility of the real site, www.annualcreditreport.com, the bureaus "blocked web links from reputable consumer sites such as Privacy Rights Clearinghouse, and Consumers Union, and from mainstream news web sites."[18] Enforcers at the Federal Trade Commission had to intervene in 2005, but the penalties imposed (a tiny fraction of the revenues generated by the deceptive practice) could not possibly have a serious deterrent effect.[19]

The story gets even more depressing when we consider that, by the time the United States got relatively serious about making credit *reporting* transparent, credit *scores* were more important—and still largely black-boxed. Banks and credit card issuers use the scores to predict the likelihood of borrowers to default on their debts.[20] A bad score can mean significantly higher interest rates. But critics have called the scores opaque, arbitrary, and discriminatory, and there is little evidence scorers are doing much to respond to these concerns.[21]

That's an uncomfortable reality in a world where credit scores have escaped from their native financial context and established themselves as arbiters of general reliability in other areas, like car insurance.[22] An unemployed person with a poor credit history, not necessarily through his own fault, is likely to find it harder to find the work needed to earn the money to pay off his debts.[23] If he fails to, his credit history will further deteriorate, his interest rates will go up, and a vicious cycle ensues. The credit score is too powerful a determiner of success and failure to be allowed to do its work in secrecy.[24]

In 2010, in the aftermath of the subprime mortgage meltdown, many homeowners wanted to know who actually owned their mortgages,[25] and a website called "Where's the Note" offered information on how to force servicers to prove that they had legal rights to mortgage payments.[26] Given the unprecedented level of foreclosure fraud, sloppy paperwork, and "robo-signed" affidavits revealed during the crisis, one might think that a sensible credit scoring system would reward those who took the trouble to verify the status of their financing.[27] But participants in online forums worry that the opposite is the case.[28] A homeowner who followed the instructions on "Where's the Note" reported that he took a 40-point hit on his credit score after his inquiry.[29] In the Heisenberg-meets-Kafka world of credit scoring, merely trying to figure out possible effects on one's score can reduce it.

Scoring is just comprehensible enough to look like a fair game. But it's opaque enough that only insiders really know the rules. FICO and the credit bureaus promote their systems as models of fairness, but justify them with generalities.[30] They peddle bromides: pay your debts on time; don't push against the upper bounds of your credit limit, but don't eschew credit entirely; build up a record so your credit history can be scored.[31] There are dozens of self-help books and pamphlets on the topic.[32] Internet groups like "FICO Forums" discuss the practices of the credit card companies and try to reverse engineer their scoring decisions.[33] But even the most faithful student of these mysteries is never really going to be able to predict the exact consequences of his actions.

Three credit bureaus, Experian, TransUnion, and Equifax, routinely score millions of individuals.[34] But not always the same way. In one study of 500,000 files, "29% of consumers [had] credit scores that differ by at least fifty points between credit bureaus."[35] Fifty points can mean tens of thousands of dollars in extra payments over the life of a mortgage; unless the aims of the different bureaus diverge in undisclosed ways, so much variation suggests that the assessment process is more than a little arbitrary. The experience of the "Where's the Note" man is an egregious example of its unpredictability, but there are easier ways for responsible people to get into trouble when the rules aren't stated. A consumer might reduce his limit on a credit card with the intent of limiting his exposure to fraud or even his own spending. If he doesn't know that the bureaus tend to favor those who use a smaller proportion of their existing credit,[36] he may be surprised to see the resulting increase of the card's "debt-to-limit ratio" ding his score instead of rewarding his prudence.[37]

So while the public face of credit evaluation is a three-digit number, a marvel of concrete and compact clarity, beneath that appealing surface is a process that cannot be fully understood, challenged, or audited either by the individuals scored or by the regulators charged with protecting them. One expert observes that the inevitable subjectivity of these black box assessments is rendered "hidden and incontestable by the apparent simplicity of [that] single figure."[38] The number may *feel* as objective and real as the score on a math test. But a critical mass of complaints over the past twenty years has eroded credit assessors' claims to objectivity and reliability.[39]

*The Scored Society.* Many grievances arise out of the growing influence of secret credit scoring algorithms as an all-purpose reputational metric.[40] But at least the data and rough outlines of credit scoring procedures are regulated and disclosed. Another world of consumer profiling—ranging from ad networks to consumer scores—is barely touched by law. They revive some of the worst aspects of unregulated credit reporting, but well out of the public eye.

The credit bureaus aren't intuiting our sexual orientations anymore, or rating us by our housekeeping. Still, there's money to be made from knowing if someone is gay, or how well they keep their property up, or if they have property at all. Marketers crave that information, and the vacuum left by the bureaus has been filled by a behind-the-scenes cohort of unregulated data gatherers, brokers, sensor networks, and analysts who collect and scrutinize every bit of spoor, digital and otherwise, that we leave behind.

As far back as 2002, a digital video recorder (DVR) took it upon itself to save a number of gay-themed shows for its owner after he recorded a film with a bisexual character in it.[41] The owner persuaded it (that is, he sent the right signals to the algorithm encoded in its software) to revise its "opinion" by recording something from the Playboy Channel. Big Data partisans would doubtless argue that with *more* data the machine could have made more accurate predictions before. But the telling point for the rest of us is that the machine had that data at all—and power to make use of it.

That power has spread to many online contexts. One MIT study concluded that gay men "can be identified by their Facebook friends,"[42] and bots can plunder social networks for their wealth of clues to sexual orientation. One closeted user who left a positive comment on a story on gay marriage found himself targeted by a rainbow-underwear-emblazoned ad for a "Coming Out Coach."[43]

The United States is at last entering an era where being gay is less of a stigma than it has been; some might even laugh off the rainbow underwear as a welcome sign of inclusion. But imagine how the information might be used in Russia. Moreover, plenty of characterizations are indisputably damaging or sensitive in any context. OfficeMax once accidentally sent a mailing addressed to "Mike Seay, Daughter Killed in Car Crash." Seay's daughter had indeed died in a car accident less than a year before.[44] How or why this piece of creepiness could have been relevant to OfficeMax's marketing strategy is anybody's guess. The company is not telling. It's not revealing where it got its information from, either. Data brokers can oblige customers contractually not to reveal them as sources.[45] The shadowy masters of industrial data mining eviscerate personal privacy from behind a veil of corporate secrecy. We'll see this dynamic repeatedly: corporate secrecy expands as the privacy of human beings contracts.

RUNAWAY DATA isn't only creepy. It can have real costs. Scoring is spreading rapidly from finance to more intimate fields. Health scores already exist, and a "body score" may someday be even more important than your credit score.[46] Mobile medical apps and social networks offer powerful opportunities to find support, form communities, and address health issues. But they also offer unprecedented surveillance of health data, largely ungoverned by traditional health privacy laws (which focus on doctors, hospitals, and insurers).[47] Furthermore, they open the door to frightening and manipulative uses of that data by ranking intermediaries—data scorers and brokers—and the businesses, employers, and government agencies they inform.[48]

Even regulated health data can pop up in unexpected ways. Consider the plight of Walter and Paula Shelton, a Louisiana couple who sought health insurance.[49] Humana, a large insurer based in Kentucky, refused to insure them based on Paula's prescription history—occasional use of an antidepressant as a sleep aid and a blood pressure medication to relieve swelling in her ankles. The Sheltons couldn't get insurance from other carriers, either. How were they to know that a few prescriptions could render them pariahs? And even if they had known, what should they, or their doctor, have done? Indeed, the model for blackballing them might well still have been a gleam in an entrepreneur's eye when Mrs. Shelton obtained her medications. But since then, prescription reporting has become big business: one service claimed reports of "financial returns of 5:1, 10:1, even 20:1" for its clients.[50]

Chad Terhune, the journalist who in 2008 first reported on the Sheltons, detailed the many ways that prescription data was being used in the individual insurance market. Companies were gathering millions of records from pharmacies.[51] They then sold them on to insurers eager to gain a competitive advantage by avoiding people likely to incur high medical fees. Since 1 percent of patients account for over one-fifth of health care costs, and 5 percent account for nearly half of costs, insurers who can "cherry-pick" the healthy and "lemon-drop" the sick will see far more profit than those who take all comers.[52] Prescription data gave insurers the information they needed to tailor policies to exclude preexisting conditions and to impose higher charges for some members.

Ironically, this kind of data was originally gathered to help patients in emergency care settings—to assure access to a record of their medications. But when that plan failed, the records were quietly repurposed as a means of discriminating against the sick. If there's one thing Wall Street loves, it's a quick pivot to a winning business strategy.

*From Medical Record to Medical Reputation.* Given the passage of the Affordable Care Act (ACA), those with a long history of prescriptions do not have quite as much to worry about in the health insurance market: insurers cannot discriminate on the basis of pre-existing conditions now.[53] But other opportunities may be foreclosed. Moreover, the ACA also includes provisions promoting insurance discounts in exchange for participation in "wellness programs." Verifying that participation (in activities ranging from meditation to running) can only expand the market for bodily surveillance and quantified selves.

Medical reputations are being created in processes we can barely understand, let alone control.[54] And in an era of Big Data, companies don't even need to consult physicians' records to impute to us medical conditions and act accordingly. Do a few searches about a disease online, fill out an (apparently unrelated) form, and you may well end up associated with that disease in commercial databases.

An insightful reporter documented that process with a (healthy) friend who received a mystifying invite to a meeting of multiple sclerosis patients. Apparently the (non)patient had filled out a registration form, and the data was harvested and sold to a marketing company.[55] She still doesn't know exactly what they found on it, or whether the form warned her about this type of use (imagine trying to recall all the terms of service you've clicked through without reading). But the marketer sold it to MS LifeLines®, a support network owned by two drug companies. The first time she had any inkling of any of this was when she received the promotional materials for the MS event. How many of the rest of us are mysteriously "weblined" into categories we know nothing about?[56]

Even the partial exposure of such data transfers is unusual. In most cases, they stay well hidden. But reporters are beginning to open up the black box of consumer profiling, as Charles Duhigg did in his 2012 report on Target, the second-largest U.S. discount retailer and a company that prides itself on knowing when its customers are pregnant.[57] For a retailer of that size, the pattern recognition was easy. First, Target's statisticians compiled a database of "the known pregnant"—people who had signed up for baby registries. Then they compared the purchases of consumers in that data set to the purchases made by Target shoppers as a whole. (Every Target shopper has a "Guest ID" number, tied to credit card, e-mail address, and other such identifiers.) By analyzing where the pregnant shoppers diverged the most from the general data set, they identified "signals" of pregnancy-related purchases.

In the first twenty weeks, "supplements like calcium, magnesium and zinc" were a tip-off. Later in the pregnancy, "scent-free soap and extra-big bags of cotton balls" were common purchases. By the end of the analysis, the statisticians had incorporated a list of twenty-five products into a "pregnancy prediction score" and due-date estimator; if a twenty-three-year old woman in Atlanta bought "cocoa-butter lotion, a purse large enough to double as a diaper bag, zinc and magnesium supplements and a bright blue rug" in March, Target estimated an 87 percent chance that she was pregnant and due to give birth in late August. Not surprisingly, some customers found it creepy to start receiving pregnancy-related ads. Target responded, not by explaining to customers how it came to its conclusions, but by mixing more non-pregnancy-related ads into the circulars targeting expectant mothers.

We don't know what other health-related categories Target slices and dices its customers into. It stopped talking to Duhigg, and it probably considers its other methods (and categories) valuable trade secrets. But about two years later, Target suffered a data breach—one of the largest in retail history. It affected an estimated 110 million people. Hackers stole "mailing and email addresses, phone numbers or names, [and] the kind of data routinely collected from customers during interactions like shopping online."[58] Lots of customers found *that* creepy—and scary, too, given how much data retailers routinely collect. Imagine what sub rosa data brokers could do with comprehensive customer profiles.[59]

The growing danger of breaches challenges any simple attempts to justify data collection in the service of "consumer targeting." Even huge and sophisticated companies can be hacked, and cyber-criminals' data trafficking is, unsurprisingly, an obscure topic.[60] In at least one case, an established U.S. data broker accidentally sold "Social Security and driver's license numbers—as well as bank account and credit card data on millions of Americans" to ID thieves.[61] Until data companies are willing to document and report the precise origins and destinations of all the data they hold, we will never be able to estimate the magnitude of data misuse.

Big data enables big dangers. Are the present benefits worth the long-term costs? Perhaps. Some pregnant moms-to-be may be thrilled to get coupons tailored precisely to them. But not the teen who hadn't yet told her father that she was pregnant.[62] And probably not the people who type words like "sick," "stressed," or "crying" into a search engine or an online support forum and find themselves in the crosshairs of clever marketers looking to capitalize on depression and insecurity.[63] Marketers plot to tout beauty products at moments of the day that women feel least attractive.[64] There's little to stop them from compiling digital dossiers of the vulnerabilities of each of us.[65] In the hall of mirrors of online marketing, discrimination can easily masquerade as innovation.

These methods may seem crude or reductive, but they are beloved by digital marketers. They are fast and cheap and there is little to lose. Once the data is in hand, the permutations are endless, and somebody is going to want them. If you're a childless man who shops for clothing online, spends a lot on cable TV, and drives a minivan, we know that data brokers are going to assume you're fatter than the average person.[66] And we now know that recruiters for obesity drug trials will happily pay for that analysis, thanks to innovative reporting.[67] But in most cases, we don't know what the brokers are saying about us. And since a data breach could spill it open to the world at large, it would be nice if we did.

## Runaway Profiles

Where does all this data come from? Everywhere. Have you ever searched for "flu symptoms" or "condoms"? That clickstream may be around somewhere, potentially tied to your name (if you were signed in) or the IP address of your computer or perhaps some unique identifier of its hardware.[68] It's a cinch for companies to compile lists of chronic dieters, or people with hay fever. "Based on your credit-card history, and whether you drive an American automobile and several other lifestyle factors, we can get a very, very close bead on whether or not you have the disease state we're looking at," said a vice president at a company in the health sector.[69]

Other companies sell the mailing addresses and medication lists of depressed people and cancer patients. A firm reportedly combines credit scores and a person's specific ailments into one report.[70] The Federal Trade Commission is trying to nail down a solid picture of these practices, but exchange of health data is an elusive target when millions of digital files can be encrypted and transmitted at the touch of a button.[71] We may eventually find records of data *sales*, but what if it is traded in handshake deals among brokers? A stray flash drive could hold millions of records. It's hard enough for the agency to monitor America's brick-and-mortar businesses; the proliferation of data firms has completely overtaxed it.[72] Consider a small sample of the sources that can collect information about a person, in the table below.

Table 2.1 separates information-collecting sources into specific sectors, denoting only their *primary* activities, not all the inferences they make by way of the data they compile. For example, we already know that at least one credit card company pays attention to certain mental health events, like going to marriage counseling.[73] When statistics imply that couples in counseling are more likely to divorce than couples who aren't, counseling becomes a "signal" that marital discord may be about to spill over into financial distress.[74] This is effectively a "marriage counseling penalty" and poses a dilemma for policy makers. Left unrevealed, it leaves cardholders in the dark about an important aspect of creditworthiness. Once disclosed, it could discourage a couple from seeking the counseling they need to save their relationship.

*Table 2.1.*   A Glimpse of the Data Tracking Landscape

|  | Health | Finance | Retail |
|---|---|---|---|
| First Party (self-tracking) | Weight loss or exercise app on phone | Home finance software | Self-monitoring of purchases |
| Second Party (direct interaction) | Amazon logs purchase of diet books | Purchase of Turbotax® online | Target or Amazon logs purchases in company database |
| Third Party (intermediary logging data) | ISP or search engine logs queries about diabetes, cancer, other diseases | Credit card company analyzes transactions between first party (you) and sellers (second party) | Cookies from ad networks or social networks may be logging records of items reviewed |
| Fourth Party (broker buying data from any of the above) | *Data brokers increasingly try to integrate all of the aforementioned sources into profiles. They help create a competitive landscape where leading second- and third-party firms also feel the need to integrate data.* | | |

There doesn't have to be any established causal relationship between counseling and late payments; correlation is enough to drive action. That can be creepy in the case of objectively verifiable conditions, like pregnancy. And it can be devastating for those categorized as "lazy," "unreliable," "struggling," or worse. Runaway data can lead to *cascading disadvantages* as digital alchemy creates new analog realities. Once one piece of software has inferred that a person is a bad credit risk, a shirking worker, or a marginal consumer, that attribute may appear with decision-making clout in other systems all over the economy. There is little in current law to prevent companies from selling their profiles of you.[75]

Bad inferences are a larger problem than bad data because companies can represent them as "opinion" rather than fact. A lie can be litigated, but an opinion is much harder to prove false; therefore, under the First Amendment to the U.S. Constitution, it is much harder to dispute.[76] For example, a firm may identify a data subject not as an "allergy sufferer," but as a person with an "online search propensity" for a certain "ailment or prescription."[77] Similar classifications exist for "diabetic-concerned households." It may be easy for me to prove that I don't suffer from diabetes, but how do I prove that I'm not "diabetic-concerned"? And if data buyers are going to lump me in with diabetics anyway, what good does it do me even to bother challenging the record?

Profiling may begin with the original collectors of the information, but it can be elaborated by numerous data brokers, including credit bureaus, analytics firms, catalog co-ops, direct marketers, list brokers, affiliates, and others.[78] Brokers combine, swap, and recombine the data they acquire into new profiles, which they can then sell back to the original collectors or to other firms. It's a complicated picture, and even experts have a tough time keeping on top of exactly how data flows in the new economy.

*A Thousand Eyes.* Most of us have enough trouble keeping tabs on our credit history at the three major credit bureaus. But the Internet has supercharged the world of data exchange and profiling, and Experian, TransUnion, and Equifax are no longer the sole, or even the main, keepers of our online reputations. What will happen when we've got dozens, or hundreds, of entities to keep our eyes on?

We're finding out. They're already here, maintaining databases that, though mostly unknown to us, record nearly every aspect of our lives. They score us to decide whether we're targets or "waste," as media scholar Joseph Turow puts it.[79] They keep track of our occupations and preoccupations, our salaries, our home value, even our past purchases of luxury goods.[80] (Who knew that one splurge on a pair of really nice headphones could lead to higher prices on sneakers in a later online search?) There are now hundreds of credit scores for sale, and thousands of "consumer scores," on subjects ranging from frailty to reliability to likelihood to commit fraud. And there are far more sources of data for all these scores than there are scores themselves.[81]

ChexSystems and TeleCheck track bounced checks; Alliant Cooperative Data Solutions documents missed monthly payments for gym memberships; payday lenders report "deadbeats" to Teletrack. Datalogix has lists of dieters. The National Consumer Telecom and Utilities Exchange uses data from several large companies to set recommended deposits for cable and utility subscribers but would not reveal to a reporter the names of those data-gathering companies. Reporting agencies monitor our utility bills, our rent payments, and our medical debts. Any one of them could change our lives on the basis of a falsehood or a mistake that we don't even know about.

For example, one data broker (ChoicePoint) incorrectly reported a criminal charge of "intent to sell and manufacture methamphetamines" in Arkansas resident Catherine Taylor's file. The free-floating lie ensured rapid rejection of her job applications. She couldn't obtain credit to buy a dishwasher. Once notified of the error, ChoicePoint corrected it, but the other companies to whom ChoicePoint had sold Taylor's file did not necessarily follow suit. Some corrected their reports in a timely manner, but Taylor had to repeatedly nag many others, and ended up suing one.[82]

Taylor found the effort to correct all the meth conviction entries overwhelming. "I can't be the watchdog all the time," she told a *Washington Post* reporter. It took her four years to find a job even after the error was uncovered, and she was still rejected for an apartment. She ended up living in her sister's house, and she claims that the stress of the situation exacerbated her heart problems.

For every Catherine Taylor, who was actually aware of the data defaming her, there are surely thousands of us who don't know that there are scarlet letters emblazoned on our digital dossiers. It doesn't even occur to us that there might be anything to investigate. But even when the lies lead not to outright denials, but only to slightly worse credit rates or job opportunities, we suffer from them nonetheless.[83]

## Big Data at Work

Big Data dominates big workplaces, too, from the moment we make our first approach to an employer to the day we leave. Companies faced with tens of thousands of job applications don't want to deal with each one individually. It's easier and faster to let software programs crunch a few hundred variables first. There are online evaluation systems that score interviewees with color-coded ratings; red signals a candidate as poor, yellow as middling, and green as likely hires.[84] Some look at an applicant's life online,[85] ranking candidates on the creativity, leadership, and temperament evidenced on social networks and search results.[86] As with credit scoring, the new world of social scoring creates demand for coaching. (Better think twice about using three exclamation marks on a Facebook comment. But be sure to have *some* Facebook activity, lest you look like a hermit.)[87] Tools of assessment range from the obvious and transparent to the subtle and hidden. One company completed investigations for 4,000-plus employers, with almost no oversight from its clients or challenge from its subjects.[88]

Once we're in, firms like Recorded Future, partly funded by arms of Google and the CIA, offer more sophisticated techniques of data analysis to protect bosses from hirer's remorse.[89] "They're Watching You at Work," intoned *The Atlantic* in a compilation of examples of pervasive monitoring. (One casino tracks how often its card dealers and waitstaff smile.) Analysts mine our e-mails for "insights about our productivity, our treatment of co-workers, our willingness to collaborate or lend a hand, our patterns of written language, and what those patterns reveal about our intelligence, social skills, and behavior."[90]

Whatever prerogatives we may have had when we walked in the door, we sign many of them away just filling out the now-standard HR forms.[91] Workers routinely surrender the right to object to, or even know about, surveillance.[92] "Consent is the universal solvent," one employment lawyer told me matter-of-factly. Technology makes it easy for firms to record workers' keystrokes and telephone conversations, and even to translate speech into text and so, predictive analysts claim, distinguish workers from shirkers. Call centers are the ultimate embodiment of the panoptic workspace. There, workers are monitored all the time. Similar software analyzes callers simultaneously, matching them to agents via emotion-parsing algorithms. Sound furious as you talk your way through a phone tree, and you may be routed to someone with anger management training. Or not; some companies work extra hard to soothe, but others just dump problem customers. There's a fine line between the wooed and the waste.

"Data-driven" management promises a hyperefficient workplace. The most watched jobs are also the easiest to automate: a comprehensive documentation of everything a worker has done is the key data enabling a robot to take her place.[93] But good luck finding out exactly how management protocols work. If they were revealed, the bosses claim, employees would game the system. If workers knew that thirty-three-word e-mails littered with emoticons scored highest, they might write that way all the time. Thus a new source of tension arises: workers want and need to learn the rules of success at a new workplace, but management worries that if the rules are known, they'll lose their predictive value.

*The Fair, the Foul, and the Creepy.* Automated systems claim to rate all individuals the same way, thus averting discrimination. They may ensure some bosses no longer base hiring and firing decisions on hunches, impressions, or prejudices.[94] But software engineers construct the datasets mined by scoring systems; they define the parameters of data-mining analyses; they create the clusters, links, and decision trees applied; they generate the predictive models applied. Human biases and values are embedded into each and every step of development. Computerization may simply drive discrimination upstream.

Moreover, even in spheres where algorithms solve some problems, they are creating others. Wharton Business School professor Peter Cappelli believes firms are relying "too much on software to screen thousands of applications, which dooms promising candidates whose resumes lack the precise words that alert such programs."[95] Bewitched by matching and sorting programs, a company may treat ever more hires as "purple squirrels"—an HR term of art denoting the *exact* perfect fit for a given position. For example, consider a health lawyer qualified to work on matters involving Zone Program Integrity Contractors, but who does not use the specific acronym "ZPIC" on her resume. If automated software is set to search only for resumes that contain "ZPIC," she's probably not going to get an interview. She may never find out that this small omission was the main, or only, reason she never got a callback. Cappelli considers automated resume-sorting software an insurmountable barrier for some qualified persons looking for good jobs.[96]

Then there's the growing use of personality tests by retailers. In an era of persistently high unemployment, even low-wage cashier and stocking jobs are fiercely competitive.[97] Firms use tests to determine who is a good fit for a given job. Writer Barbara Ehrenreich encountered one of those tests when she applied for a job at Walmart, and she was penalized for agreeing "strongly" rather than "totally" with this statement: "All rules must be followed to the letter at all times."[98] Here are some other statements from recent pre-employment tests. There are four possible multiple-choice answers: strongly disagree, disagree, agree, and strongly agree.

- You would like a job that is quiet and predictable.
- Other people's feelings are their own business.
- Realistically, some of your projects will never be finished.
- You feel nervous when there are demands you can't meet.
- It bothers you when something unexpected disrupts your day.
- In school, you were one of the best students.
- In your free time, you go out more than stay home.[99]

How would you respond to questions like those? What on earth do they imply about a would-be clerk, manager, or barista? It's not readily apparent. Yet despite their indeterminacy, these tests have important consequences for job seekers. Applicants with a "green score" have a decent shot at full interviews; those in the "red" or "yellow" zone are most likely shut out.

One of these black box personality tests was used in 16 percent of major retail hiring in 2009, and at least one manager seemed to share Ehrenreich's view that it selected for soulless sycophants. "A lot of people who score green just figured out how to cheat the system, or are just the 'yes' people," she said. "I don't believe it makes them more capable than anyone else."

Profiling's proponents counter that there's no need to explain *how* the answers in a particular questionnaire correspond to performance, as long as we know *that they do*.[100] They aren't really trying to assess competence or overall job ability. The test is only one part of a multistep hiring process, designed to predict how likely a new hire is to succeed.[101] For example, a company might find that every applicant who answered "strongly agree" to all the questions above turned out to be a model employee, and those who answered "strongly disagree" ended up quitting or being fired within a month or two. The HR department would be sorely tempted to hire future applicants who "strongly agreed," even without knowing *how* such professed attitudes related to the job at hand.

However useful they may be to employers, black box personality tests are unsettling to applicants. Correctness aside, on what grounds do employers get to ask, "How nervous are you when there are demands you can't meet?" Why do nerves matter if an employee can flawlessly complete the given job nevertheless? We want and need reasons for the ways we are treated, even when they are curt or blunt.[102] Is the "reasoning" behind questions like this the kind of decision making that should decide people's fates?

Secret statistical methods for picking and assessing employees seem to promise a competitive edge. Whether these methods deliver or not is unclear, and they feel "creepy" to many workers, who fear having a critical aspect of their lives left to mysterious and unaccountable computer programs.[103] Employers invested in these technologies pooh-pooh the "creepiness" objection as a matter of taste or a regrettable lack of the toughness the work world requires. But the creepy feeling is world disclosive; it is an emotional reaction that alerts us to the possibility of real harm.[104] Employers and data analysts have become partners in the assembly of ostensible "realities" that have serious life consequences for the individuals they purport to describe. Yet these individuals have no idea how the "realities" are being constructed, what is in them, or what might be done with them. Their alarm is warranted.[105]

## The Specter of Racial Bias

Anyone may be labeled in a database as "unreliable," "high medical cost," "declining income," or some other derogatory term. Reputation systems are creating new (and largely invisible) minorities, disfavored due to error or unfairness. Algorithms are not immune from the fundamental problem of discrimination, in which negative and baseless assumptions congeal into prejudice. They are programmed by human beings, whose values are embedded into their software.[106] And they must often use data laced with all-too-human prejudice.

There are some partisans of the "reputation society" who acknowledge that all the data mining can get a little creepy sometimes. But, they promise, it's better than the alternative. They fault hiring and promotion decisions made the old-fashioned way—based on in-person interviews and human review of a resume—as more biased than automated judgments.[107] University of Chicago law professor Lior Strahilevitz thinks that "reputation tracking tools . . . provide detailed information about individuals, thereby reducing the temptation for decision makers to rely on group-based stereotypes."[108] He endorses the use of criminal background histories in hiring. But he does not adequately acknowledge the degree to which such sources can be based on biased data—for example, if police focus their efforts on minority communities, more minorities may end up with criminal records, regardless of whether minorities generally commit more crimes.[109] Researchers are revealing that online sources may be just as problematic. As the White House Report on Big Data has found, "big data analytics have the potential to eclipse longstanding civil rights protections in how personal information is used in housing, credit, employment, health, education, and the marketplace."[110] Already disadvantaged groups may be particularly hard hit.[111]

For example, consider one computer scientist's scrutiny of digital name searches. In 2012, Latanya Sweeney, former director of the Data Privacy Lab at Harvard and now a senior technologist at the Federal Trade Commission, suspected that African Americans were being unfairly targeted by an online service. When Sweeney searched her own name on Google, she saw an ad saying, "Latanya Sweeney: Arrested?" In contrast, a search for "Tanya Smith" produced an ad saying, "Located: Tanya Smith."[112] The discrepancy provoked Sweeney to conduct a study of how names affected the ads served. She suspected that "ads suggesting arrest tend to appear with names associated with blacks, and neutral ads or no [such] ads tend to appear with names associated with whites, regardless of whether the company [purchasing the ad] has an arrest record associated with the name." She concluded that "Google searches for typically African-American names lead to negative ads posted by [the background check site] InstantCheckmate.com, while typically Caucasian names draw neutral ads."[113]

After Sweeney released her findings, several explanations for her results were proposed. Perhaps someone had deliberately programmed "arrest" results to appear with names associated with blacks? That would be intentional discrimination, and Instant Checkmate and Google both vehemently denied it. On the other hand, let us suppose that (for whatever reasons) web searchers tended to click on Instant Checkmate ads more often when names associated with blacks had "arrest" associations, rather than more neutral ones. In that case, the programmer behind the ad-matching engine could say that all it is doing is optimizing for clicks—it is agnostic about people's reasons for clicking.[114] It presents itself as a cultural voting machine, merely registering, rather than creating, perceptions.[115]

Given algorithmic secrecy, it's impossible to know exactly what's going on here. Perhaps a company had racially inflected ad targeting; perhaps Sweeney's results arose from other associations in the data. But without access to the underlying coding and data, it is nearly impossible to adjudicate the dispute.

It would be easier to give tech companies the benefit of the doubt if Silicon Valley's own diversity record weren't so dismal. Google and other tech companies refused to reveal the demographic makeup for their own workforces for years, calling it a trade secret. When Google finally did reveal the numbers, critics were concerned: only 2 percent of its 46,000 or so U.S. employees were African American (compared with 12 percent of the U.S. workforce).[116] Might the lack of representation of minorities inside the company help explain its dismissive responses?

A similar controversy, involving Google's Gmail, is not encouraging. That service also aggregates information to target ads to users. Researcher Nathan Newman created a number of test Gmail accounts. He then compared the ad results delivered to different-sounding names when he sent e-mails about car shopping to and from the test accounts. He found that "all three white names yielded car buying sites of various kinds, whether from GMC or Toyota or a comparison shopping site. . . . Conversely, all three of the African-American names yielded at least one ad related to bad credit card loans and included other ads related to non-new car purchases."[117]

A Google spokesperson blamed "flawed methodology" for Newman's "wildly inaccurate conclusion," and claimed that Google would never "select ads based on sensitive information, including ethnic inferences from names."[118] The black box nature of reputation algorithms once again defeats any definitive resolution of the issue. Even if we could audit a company to assure ourselves that *intentional* discrimination is not affecting its methods, algorithmic negligence would remain a real concern.[119] It does not take an "ethnic inference" for an algorithm to start tracking "Latanyas" into one set of online opportunities and "Tanyas" into another. It could simply happen as a mechanical extrapolation of past evaluations of people with either of these names or similar ones. Without access to the underlying data and code, we will never know what type of tracking is occurring, and how the discrimination problems long documented in "real life" may even now be insinuating themselves into cyberspace.[120] As FTC chair Edith Ramirez has argued, we must "ensure that by using big data algorithms [firms] are not accidentally classifying people based on categories that society has decided—by law or ethics—not to use, such as race, ethnic background, gender, and sexual orientation."[121]

*Collateral Consequences:* The problem of collateral consequences is well known in the criminal justice system. Once someone has been convicted of a crime (or pleaded guilty), that stigma will often preclude him from many opportunities—a job, housing, public assistance, and so on—long after he has "paid his debt to society."[122] A similar dynamic is becoming apparent in finance. As they dole out opportunities for "prime" and "subprime" credit, automated systems may be silently resegregating racial groups in ways that would be clearly illegal if pursued consciously by an individual.[123]

"Data-driven" lending practices have hit minority communities hard. One attorney at the Neighborhood Economic Development Advocacy Project (now the New Economy Project) called subprime lending a systematic "equity stripping" targeted at minorities—even if they were longtime homeowners.[124] Subtle but persistent racism, arising out of implicit bias or other factors, may have influenced *past* terms of credit, and it's much harder to keep up on a loan at 15 percent interest than one at 5 percent.[125] Late payments will be more likely, and then will be fed into *present* credit scoring models as *neutral, objective, nonracial* indicia of reliability and creditworthiness.[126] Far from liberating individuals to be judged on their character rather than their color, credit scores in scenarios like these launder past practices of discrimination into a black-boxed score, immune from scrutiny.[127]

Continuing unease about black box scoring reflects long-standing anxiety about misapplications of natural science methods to the social realm.[128] A civil engineer might use data from a thousand bridges to estimate which one might next collapse; now financial engineers scrutinize millions of transactions to predict consumer defaults. But unlike the engineer, whose studies do nothing to the bridges she examines, a credit scoring system *increases the chance* of a consumer defaulting once it labels him a risk and prices a loan accordingly. Moreover, the "science" of secret scoring does not adopt a key safeguard of the scientific method: publicly testable generalizations and observations.[129] As long as the analytics are secret, they will remain an opaque and troubling form of social sorting.

Bias can embed itself in other self-reinforcing cycles based on ostensibly "objective" data. Police in the past may have watched certain neighborhoods more closely than others. Thus it's not surprising if such neighborhoods account for a disproportionate share of the overall number of crimes recorded, *even if crime rates are identical across neighborhoods*, because they happen to be where the police were looking. Once that set of "objective" data justifies even more intense scrutiny of the "high crime" neighborhoods, that will probably lead to more arrests—perhaps because of a real crime problem, but perhaps instead due to arrest quotas or escalating adversarialism between law enforcement and community members.[130] The *reasons* for data like arrest numbers matter.

In contexts like policing, there is often no such thing as "brute data," objective measures of behavior divorced from social context or the biases of observers.[131] When there is documented disparate impact in policing practices, the data gathered by law enforcers are scarcely a font of objective assessments of criminality.[132] Drug or gun possession is as likely among whites as it is among racial minorities, but in New York City, racial minorities comprise the vast majority of persons who are "stopped and frisked."[133] Disproportionately more nonwhites than whites, therefore, will end up with criminal records for gun or drug possession. That is one reason that ten states and fifty-one cities prohibit many employers from inquiring into job applicants' criminal histories.[134] But how many other suspect "data points" are silently working their way into automated decision making?

## The Birth of a Surveillance Nation

When the government gets into the reputation game, the stakes get very high very fast. It's not just that private corporations are using government records, like arrests, to make decisions. Police and intelligence agencies are using their databases, and private records, to revolutionize their own role in society.[135] The dark axiom of the NSA era says that you don't have to worry if you have nothing to hide. But if your political activities or interests deviate even slightly out of the mainstream, you do.[136]

In 2007, officers arrested law student and journalist Ken Krayeske while he took pictures of the Connecticut gubernatorial parade. He was identified as a potential threat on the basis of blog posts in which he encouraged protests of the governor's inaugural ball, his service as a Green Party candidate's campaign manager, and one arrest for a misdemeanor at an antiwar rally. He spent thirteen hours in jail before prosecutors dropped the charges.[137]

In Maryland, fifty-three antiwar activists, including two nuns and a Democratic candidate for local office, were placed on terrorist watch lists.[138] The false classification was shared with federal drug enforcement and terrorist databases, as well as with the NSA.[139] Like those wrongly tagged with wrongdoing by commercial data brokers, these victims will have to work hard to clear their names. And the hurdles will likely be more daunting. The post-9/11 "information-sharing environment (ISE)," as the government calls it, means that there are too many databases of suspicion even to know where to start.

In 2010, the ACLU published a report called "Policing Free Speech." It lists incidents in which police spied on Americans, or infiltrated their organizations, "for deciding to organize, march, protest, espouse unusual viewpoints, and engage in normal, innocuous behaviors such as writing notes or taking photographs in public." The Americans spied on included Quakers, vegans, animal activists, Muslims, and an individual who was handing out pamphlets critical of the FBI.[140]

We all know by now that the government has been taking a very keen interest in cultivating "intelligence" about its citizens.[141] There has been a world of outrage both over the NSA's overreach and the fact that it's gotten away with it. But I won't add to that here. My point is narrower: that the government's interest in intelligence gathering has led it into a pragmatic, powerful, and largely secret partnership with interests whose concern is not the public good, but private profit or personal advance.

The most visible and controversial example so far has been the cooperation in Manhattan between the Department of Homeland Security, the New York Police Department, and several major banks.[142] By 2009, the Lower Manhattan Security Coordination Center (LMSCC) was processing feeds from thousands of cameras run by Wall Street firms and the NYPD. One source identified Goldman Sachs, Citigroup, the Federal Reserve, and the New York

Stock Exchange as participants at the center. The exact composition of the staff is a closely guarded secret, but there are likely many other Wall Street firms with "on-site representatives."[143]

In the abstract, a post-9/11 partnership of this sort might seem like an efficient use of resources. But critics worried it would focus on protests like Occupy Wall Street, which was the target of other unusual federal involvements.[144] Homeland Security officials may have advised local police about others of the hundreds of Occupy encampments that arose in the fall of 2011.[145] According to documents obtained by the Partnership for Civil Justice, the Domestic Security Alliance Council described a "strategic partnership between the FBI, the Department of Homeland Security and the private sector" to closely monitor Occupy protests. Educational institutions were deputized by the Feds to spy on sympathetic members of their own communities; the FBI in Albany and the Syracuse Joint Terrorism Task Force sent information to campus police officials at SUNY–Oswego and followed the activity of students and professors there.[146]

What was actually happening in the Occupy villages to merit all this spying? Well, a golden calf was carried around. (It was later taken to Washington by a group called Catholics United, who petitioned House Speaker John Boehner to support a tax on financial transactions.) A debt jubilee was proposed to redress decades of rising inequality. Activists decried bank crimes and outsized bonuses. Yes, there were some confrontations (many of them initiated by police). But Occupy was an essentially peaceful protest, exemplifying freedoms specifically singled out by the First Amendment for protection.[147]

That being so, we can certainly ask whether the federal government should have been gathering intelligence on it at all. There's a more pointed question, though: Once it *did* get involved, should it have been partnering with banks whose managers made millions of dollars during the financial crisis of 2008 on the basis of ethically and legally dubious practices?[148] Even while Occupy was denouncing the failure of the Department of Justice and the FBI to prosecute the banks' lawbreaking, the Bank Fraud Working Group of the FBI's Denver field office "met and were briefed on Occupy Wall

Street in November 2011."[149] In its funding of the LMSCC, the government made Occupy's case for it by enacting the very corporate-state collusion that Occupy was protesting. How else, one indignant observer wanted to know, can we explain "$150 million of taxpayer money going to equip a government facility in lower Manhattan where Wall Street firms, serially charged with corruption, get to sit alongside the New York Police Department and spy on law abiding citizens"?[150]

*An "Information-Sharing Environment."* But for all its drama, Occupy was just one small corner of a very large picture. After 9/11, the government moved quickly to improve its surveillance capacities by establishing what it called an "information-sharing environment," or ISE. Out of this effort came two collaborative programs that I'll discuss here. One was called Virtual USA, "a pilot information-sharing initiative under the Department of Homeland Security . . . intended to facilitate disaster response by sharing technology, information, and data across federal, state, and local jurisdictions."[151] The other was the establishment of the *fusion centers*, which the Department of Homeland Security describes as "collaborative effort[s] of two or more agencies . . . with the goal of maximizing their ability to detect, prevent, investigate, and respond to criminal and terrorist activity." They are regional focal points for gathering and sharing government *and private* information related to "threats."[152] There are over seventy of them now, and with their generous federal funding, slick conferences, and firm corporate backing, they are beginning to unite the public and private monitoring of individual lives into unified digital dossiers.[153] They also keep track of their critics: as the *New York Times* has reported, "people connected to the [fusion] centers shared information about individual activists or supporters [during Occupy protests], and kept track of those who speculated in social media postings that the centers had been involved when police departments used force to clear Occupy camps."[154]

The guiding principle of the fusion centers is "the more information, the better."[155] Where do they get their information? They access public- and private-sector databases of traffic tickets, property records, identity-theft reports, drivers' licenses, immigration records, tax information, public health data, criminal justice sources, car rentals, credit reports, postal and shipping services, utility bills, gaming, insurance claims, and data-broker dossiers.[156] They monitor nonprofit contributions, political blogs, and home videos.[157] They mine footage from law enforcement, transportation, and corporate security cameras.[158] In Southern Nevada, they check out photos and videos from the local hotels and casinos.[159]

In short, fusion centers allow the government, in the name of "information sharing," to supplement its *constitutionally constrained* data-gathering activities with the *unregulated* collections of private industry. In return, the government amplifies the limited reach of local law enforcement, and sometimes even of private industry, with its greater power and larger scope.

*Data Mining and Law Enforcement.* Even many civil libertarians would not object to fusion centers if they restricted themselves to the responsible deployment of antiterrorist intelligence. But they do not. The Center for Investigative Reporting notes that "since so many states are unlikely to be struck by terrorists, fusion centers have had to expand their intelligence mission to cover all crimes and potential hazards, partly to convince local legislators they're worth financing with taxpayer money into the future."[160] Pork-barrel politics trumps sensible security policy.

When the Alabama Department of Homeland Security started working on a Virtual Alabama database collaboration with Google Earth, for example, local police departments weren't very supportive.[161] Surveillance researcher Torin Monahan says that the problem was solved when "DHS promised to include a GIS [geospatial information system] overlay for all registered sex offenders in the state, showing exactly where each of them are supposed to be residing."[162] What began as a national homeland security project expanded into state law enforcement. Expansion of the antiterror mission helped generate "buy in" from local and state agencies that did not themselves feel threatened by terrorism.[163] This is a common outcome in many fusion centers.[164]

Thus the combined resources of essentially unregulated industry data collecting, the close surveillance capacities of local law enforcement, and the massive power of the federal government are at each other's disposal, and largely free from their own proper constraints. Fusion centers are the door into a world where *all* data sources are open to law enforcement inspection and may be used secretly to generate probable cause for criminal investigation.[165]

The line between military and police action is also breaking down. Consider the following Orwellian collaboration, which Reuters reported in 2013. It began when the NSA gave "tips" (which it could have gotten, as we'll see presently, from absolutely anywhere, including Facebook or Google) to the Special Operations Division (SOD) of the Drug Enforcement Administration (DEA), which in turn gave them to the Internal Revenue Service. The legal status of such information sharing is murky at best; national security data is not supposed to be used for law enforcement purposes. But the SOD apparently sidestepped these niceties by creating criminal investigations in which they *retrospectively fabricated* alternative grounds for suspecting and investigating the targets.[166]

This is a black box arrangement of surpassing and appalling elegance. Separate and parallel "realities" are constructed and documented. One is the secret record of how the targets were actually selected; the other is specially invented for consumption by the courts. Two senior DEA officials defended this program and called it legal, but they disclosed neither their names nor any reasoning to support their contention. Michael Hayden, former head of the NSA and the CIA, has also generally defended these practices without offering any explicit legal arguments to support his position.[167] In the summer of 2013, five senators asked the Department of Justice to assess the legality of "parallel construction"; it has yet to respond.[168]

Traditionally, a critical distinction has been made between *intelligence* and *investigation*. Once reserved primarily for overseas spy operations, "intelligence" work is anticipatory; it is the job of agencies like the CIA, which gather potentially useful information on *external* enemies that pose threats to national security. "Investigation" is what police do *once they have evidence of a crime*. But the boundaries between the two are blurring.

This is another black box. State and federal law enforcement rarely shared information or intelligence before 9/11,[169] but since then, Congress has allocated over $500 million in grants to fusion centers to encourage such collaboration.[170] What police force wouldn't want such expanded powers? The possibility of preemptive "intelligence-led policing" (as opposed to the reactive after-the-fact sort) is tempting indeed.[171]

However, the sweeping techniques of post-9/11 surveillance and data gathering are of a scale appropriate to wholesale calamities like terror attacks and natural disasters, not to ordinary crime or protest. Thousands of people are being caught in data-driven dragnets for being activists, or just belonging to a suspect "identity" group.[172] Careful protection of the boundary between crime and dissent is not a high priority of the intelligence apparatus. One state official commented, "You can make an easy kind of a link that, if you have a protest group protesting a war where the cause that's being fought against is international terrorism, you might have terrorism at that protest. You can almost argue that a *protest* against [the war] is a *terrorist* act."[173] It would be nice to be able to dismiss this statement as an outlier, but FBI director Robert Mueller legitimized it all the way back in 2002, warning that "there is a continuum between those who would express dissent and those who would do a terrorist act."[174] That is a frightening expansion of the "threat matrix."

If mistakes were rare, we'd have less cause for worry. But a critical mass of civil liberties concerns is accumulating. The Virginia Fusion Center's 2009 *Virginia Terrorism Threat Assessment Report* urged that student groups be monitored on the grounds that they "are recognized as a radicalization node for almost every type of extremist group."[175] The Missouri Information Analysis Center's 2009 report to highway officers suggested that "violent extremists" typically associate with third-party candidates such as Ron Paul and Bob Barr, and that "potential threats" include anti-immigration and antitax advocates.[176] According to that report, violent extremists could also be identified by bumper stickers on their cars indicating support for libertarian groups.[177]

## The Fading Divide between "State" and "Market"

The mountains of data collected by private corporations make them valuable partners in "information sharing." There's plenty of room for dealing on both sides. Government agencies want data that they can't legally or constitutionally collect for themselves; data brokers have it and want to sell it.[178] Other kinds of companies can make other kinds of trades.[179]

For example, Daniel Solove documents a post-9/11 information exchange that confounds conventional distinctions between "market" and "state": "In violation of its [own] privacy policy, JetBlue Airlines shared the personal data of 1 million customers with Torch Concepts, an Alabama company contracting with the Defense Department to profile passengers for security risks. Torch combined the JetBlue data with SSNs, employment information, and other details obtained from Acxiom, Inc., a database marketing company."[180] While all these entities deserve the tools they need to deflect real terror threats, have they done enough to secure the data from hacks and other security threats? We may never know, given the veil of secrecy draped around "homeland security" matters.

Businesses may support the intelligence apparatus simply to gain a competitive edge. For example, in Washington, Boeing has enjoyed "real-time access to information from the fusion centers" thanks to its participation in the Washington Joint Analytical Center (WJAC).[181] According to a Boeing executive, the company hopes "to set an example of how private owners of critical infrastructure can get involved in such centers to generate and receive criminal and anti-terrorism intelligence." Starbucks, Amazon, and Alaska Airlines have expressed interest in placing analysts at the WJAC.[182]

After FedEx's CEO announced that his company would cooperate with the government, FedEx received a range of government perks including special access to government security databases, a seat on the FBI's regional terrorism task force—where it was the only private company so represented—and an exceptional license from the state of Tennessee to develop an internal police force.[183] Like the banks integrated into the Lower Manhattan setup, FedEx is sharing the privileges and immunities of the state, but not the accountability.

Google is also reported to have entered into deals with the NSA, but an effort by the Electronic Privacy Information Center (EPIC) to find out whether that was indeed the case was quashed by a federal judge.[184] The NSA neither confirms nor denies working with Google to develop its intelligence operations, even after the spectacular revelations of Edward Snowden in 2013.

Armies and spies have always relied on stealth; after all, loose lips sink ships. But secrecy also breeds conflicts of interest. Why should Google worry about potential antitrust violations if it's monitoring Internet access side by side with the DHS and the NSA?[185] Like the "too big to fail" banks, it may be "too important to surveillance" for the government to alienate the firm. In 2013, in fact, leaked documents showed that the NSA (or a British partner) targeted the official who was in charge of investigating Google's alleged violations of EU competition law.[186] As a growing literature suggests, privatization can be more than a transaction between government and business. It can be a marriage—a secret marriage—with a hidden economy of favors exchanged.[187]

Revolving-door issues loom especially large; government officials looking out for their futures may channel work to a company or industry they have their eyes on.[188] Many security officials go on to lucrative private-sector employment soon after leaving public service.[189] The manipulation of threat perception by the "homeland security-industrial complex" feeds corporate profits as well as government budgets.

## All Threats, All Hazards, All Information?

Though critics like James Bamford and Tim Shorrock have thoughtfully covered the intelligence beat for years, the full extent of the government's independent data-gathering practices exploded into public awareness in 2013, when NSA contractor Edward Snowden leaked material documenting extensive domestic surveillance. Snowden's files suggest that the NSA is working directly with (or hacking) our largest telecom and Internet companies to store and monitor communications; that the agency can seize and bug computers that have never been attached to the Internet; and that it can crack many types of encryption that had previously been thought secure.[190]

Very little of this relentless collecting is inspired by suspicion about any particular person or plot. It is done routinely, creating an ever-expanding haystack of stored information that may someday reveal a needle.[191] Not only telecom firms but also the largest Internet companies are either targeted by the NSA, working with it, or engaged in some combination of complicity and resistance. Google, Facebook, and Microsoft show up frequently in the Snowden slides; their data stores were apparently a rich resource for the surveillance state. Laws prevent the government from collecting certain kinds of information on citizens, but data brokers are not so constrained. *And once someone else has collected that information, little stops the government from buying it, demanding it, or even hacking into it.*

Our off- and online actions are logged in hundreds of private-sector databases. Aptly called "big brother's little helpers" by privacy expert Chris Hoofnagle, private-sector data brokers gather files that police would never be able to gather on their own, and then sell them to the police. This is not a "bug" in our surveillance system, but a "feature."[192] Note that the very definition of fusion centers includes their willingness to receive information from private parties. The Snowden leaks make the shared infrastructure of state and private data collection incontrovertible. Never again can data deregulationists claim that corporate data collection is entirely distinct and far less threatening than government surveillance. They are irreversibly intertwined.

## Enduring Opacity

Despite the leaks of Snowden (and Chelsea Manning and Julian Assange), the national surveillance apparatus is still opaque on many levels.[193] It enjoys both real and legal secrecy, hidden as it is in secure networks and protected by the heavy hand of the law. There's plenty of complexity, too, should secrecy fail. Intelligence agencies commission private defense contractors like SAIC, Northrop Grumman, Booz Allen, and Palantir to devise specialized software to monitor their data sources—which include social networks.[194] Their algorithms are complex enough by themselves, but the contractors are also bound to protect company trade secrets. Even oversight bodies that might—in principle—investigate purely governmental actions are hampered by a layer of commercial secrecy designed to maintain the value of private-sector spy methodology.

How could a firm exploit the full economic value of its intellectual property if some pesky oversight board (or, God forbid, journalist) could inspect it?

An unaccountable surveillance state may pose a greater threat to liberty than any particular terror threat.[195] It is not a spectacular danger, but rather an erosion of a range of freedoms.[196] Most insidiously, the "watchers" have the power to classify those who dare to point this out as "enemies of the state," themselves in need of scrutiny. That, to me, is the core harm of surveillance: that it freezes into place an inefficient (or worse) politico-economic regime by cowing its critics into silence. Mass surveillance may be doing less to deter destructive acts than it is slowly narrowing of the range of tolerable thought and behavior.

## No Exit

National security surveillance and corporate spying don't much resemble each other on the surface; the ostensible purposes, the techniques, and the scope are all very different. The stakes are different, too, at least theoretically. Private companies may object that regulation would reduce their profits, but the state can assert that without "total information awareness" we are all at risk for disastrous attack. In "national security matters," it's very hard to stop the government from doing exactly what it wants, even if what it wants isn't legal. For all these reasons, it can be harder to regulate a surveillance state than a surveillance corporation.

Still, in their black box structure, and in their developing collaboration, the two are more alike than otherwise. There are powerful bosses at the top, managers, analysts, and programmers in the middle, and a vast cast of outsiders watched at will. The same person may spend a few years at a tech firm, then serve in government, and then go back into business. Their activities ultimately raise similar questions. One is about the flow of information: Can we stop pervasive data collection? I think that the answer to that is probably no. The second question, therefore, is, What do we do?

*Self-Helpless.* Suggestions abound for digital self-protection; they range from the pedestrian to the fantastic, and from the obvious to the uber-arcane. There are personal security techniques, like strong passwords, restrictive privacy settings, "burner" phones, and vetting our online presence. Schools have begun to teach the basics of "cyberhygiene," a kind of preventive care for the digital self.[197] Not enough? The Electronic Frontier Foundation pushes for strong encryption. The Electronic Privacy Information Center wants web browsers to default to "do not track." Professor Helen Nissenbaum at NYU looks to creative obfuscation: her browser extension *TrackMeNot* floods your search engine with so many random queries that companies like Google can't compile an accurate psychological or marketing profile.[198] Presumably the same technology could be applied to Gmail by sending dozens of fake e-mails to dummy accounts. Other apps offer to watch our backs and tell us exactly who is sharing our data with others, and how.[199] There are "personal data vaults" in which we can store our information securely and then bargain, one-on-one, with anyone who wants access to it.[200]

But self-help can take us only so far. For nearly every "Privacy Enhancing Technology" (PET) developed, a "Privacy Eviscerating Technology" may arise. Week by week the PET recommendations of digital gurus are rendered obsolete by countermeasures. The best personal security in the world is nothing to a hacker with direct access to an account.[201] Huge databases of usernames, credit card numbers, and social security numbers already exist online, out of which a query as simple as "filetype:xls site:ru login" on a search engine will realize millions of passwords.[202] (*But before you try this, note that the search may be logged to your IP address and might tag you as a possible crook.*) We've talked about the gigabytes of sensitive consumer data that Target lost to hackers. The health care sector hosts a "Wall of Shame" that lists hundreds of data breaches.[203]

On social networks especially, cyberhygiene may be an exercise in futility. These sites have been known to change their default privacy settings without warning, opening "private" communications to general inspection. What if, as many states allow, a prospective employer asks for the password to your Facebook account? Give it, and you're exposed. Refuse, and you may have lost your chance at the job.[204] And let's say you actually do manage to track down an online calumny. In the United States, Google won't remove it from the sites it serves up when someone searches for your name; it just refers you to the sites themselves.[205] Unless you can prove falsehood in a court of law (or hire a "reputation manager" to drive the offending sites down in Google rankings), you're probably out of luck.

Furthermore, attempts to foil known privacy vulnerabilities and reputational threats can open up new ones. It would be nice to think that the "private browsing" setting will keep our Internet habits secret. But our ISPs, the websites we visit, and the ad networks present there all may be keeping track of our computers' unique IP addresses. The anonymization tool Tor, recommended by tech-savvy journalists to hide digital identities, may have been compromised. Even if it hasn't been, the very fact of using it may invite suspicion and closer surveillance. As soon as an encryption program gets too popular, it provokes rumors that it is a kind of honeypot, a promise of privacy that lures people into spilling their secrets in (what turns out to be) an intensively monitored environment.[206]

It's an endless cycle. When "device fingerprinters" begin to identify our computers and cell phones, journalists offer advice about masking their data trail. But even the scholars of surveillance have a tough time keeping up with all the new threats; the *Wall Street Journal*'s "What They Know" series has tracked dozens of privacy-diminishing technologies developed since 2010.[207] One thing is certain: "self-help" as a solution here fails on practical grounds for all but the most skilled (or wealthy) Internet users, and thus fails on moral grounds as well. A technological arms race will quickly leave most users behind.

Even nascent legal solutions may only delay, rather than deflect, invasive surveillance. For example, at least fourteen states have banned employers from requesting social network account passwords from current workers or applicants.[208] But what if competitive applicants start volunteering them? They may leave the privacy-concerned behind, regardless of their formal legal rights. Economists of information label this process "unraveling," and even well-intentioned protections are undermined by it.[209] Offering a password on an application may now seem like a desperate effort to stand out from the crowd. But the many people who make their posts "public" (rather than "friends only") are offering much of the information the password would grant. Where is the tipping point between "competitive advantage" and "what everybody does"? Until the *use* of sensitive information is prohibited (and audited), a full-disclosure future is foreordained.[210]

*A One-Percent Solution.* Contracting out reputation management to a private company is a growing "market solution" to the emerging traffic in data. Our brave new digital world is a much safer place for those with the time and money to hire lawyers to review terms of service, programmers to install layers of encryption on their computing systems, and reputation managers to tend to their online profiles. And it's a very lucrative place for those who can supply those services. Firms are already trading on the mysteries of Google rankings to nurture their clients' images online. It's only a matter of time before they extend their services to those looking to optimize the impressions they make on other data gatherers.

But is this how we want to handle the problem of invasive data collection? It hasn't worked well in the world of financial privacy.[211] Yes, with enough legal and accounting help, very wealthy people can hide their money from the taxman. But only the richest have the resources and time to develop foolproof versions of their own, personal black boxes. And the costs are very high to the global economy. Using multiple estimation methods, James Henry, a senior adviser to the Tax Justice Network, calculated the total amount of money hidden away from tax authorities as between $21 and $32 trillion.[212]

A report titled "Secrecy for Sale: Inside the Offshore Money Maze" reveals many of the grim details.[213] The techniques described work well for the possessors of investment income, who may well wish to extend them to their reputational affairs, adding a division of "reputation defense" to the wealth defense industry. But this Swiss Bank model would only entrench the divide between haves and have-nots. It will do more to stratify privacy protections than to guarantee them. It does not address the real problems of invasive data collection or unfair data use.

## Full-Disclosure Future

Even if absolute secrecy could somehow be democratized with a universally available cheap encryption tool, would we really want it? I don't think I want the NSA blinded to real terrorist plots. If someone developed a fleet of poison-dart drones, I'd want the authorities to know. I wouldn't want so-called "cryptocurrencies" hiding ever more money from the tax authorities and further undermining public finances.[214] Biosurveillance helps public health authorities spot emerging epidemics. Monitoring helps us understand the flow of traffic, energy, food, and medicines.[215]

So while hiding—the temptingly symmetrical solution to surveillance—may be alluring on the surface, it's not a good bet. The ability to hide—and to detect the hiders—is so comprehensively commodified that only the rich and connected can win that game. The help and the harm of information collection lies not in the information itself but in how it is used. The decisions we make about that have plenty to tell us about our priorities.

The digital economy of the moment prioritizes marketing over productivity. It's less likely to reward the builder of a better mousetrap than to fund start-ups that identify people likely to buy one. The critical point is no longer the trap or even the rodents, but the data: the constant streams of numbers that feed algorithmic systems of prediction and control. Profiling is big business in an economy like that. Cyberlibertarians used to brag that the Internet "reads censorship as damage and routes around it"; replace "censorship" with "privacy" and the statement would be just about as true.[216]

Much of the writing about the scored world focuses on how to outwit the evaluators—how to get an 800 credit score, how to "ace" job personality tests. But this vast and growing literature ignores the possibility of criticism, much less resistance. Economic models of the data can be even worse, complacently characterizing personalization as a mere matching problem (of, say, the riskiest borrowers to the highest interest rate loans). From a legal perspective, things can look very different: myriad penalties are imposed without even a semblance of due process.

If we're not going to be able to stop the flow of data, therefore, we need to become more knowledgeable about the entities behind it and learn to control their use of it. We need to hold business and government to the same standard of openness that they impose upon us—and complement their scrutiny with new forms of accountability. We need to enforce the laws that define fair and unfair uses of information. We need to equalize the surveillance that is now being aimed disproportionately at the vulnerable and ensure as best we can that critical decisions are made in fair and nondiscriminatory ways. We need to interrupt the relentless cascades of judgment that can turn one or two mistakes into a self-fulfilling prophecy of recurrent failure. And we need to plan for the inevitability that as soon as we open one black box, new modes of opacity will arise.

Thomas Jefferson once said that "he who receives an idea from me, receives instruction himself without lessening mine; as he who lights his taper at mine, receives light without darkening me."[217] To many of us this is an inspiring vision. But the total information dominance to which America's defense, police, and corporate institutions now aspire reflects a diametrically opposed mind-set. The black box society is animated by the belief that information is useful only to the extent that it is exclusive—that is, secret. Terrorists have to be kept in the dark because they're dangerous. Sick people have to be kept in the dark because they're expensive. To faceless algorithms, we might be terrorists, or sick. So we are kept in the dark, too.

It is time to reclaim our right to the presumption of innocence, and to the security of the light. It may be that we cannot stop the collection of information, but we can regulate how it is used. This is easier said than done; data collection has run so wild that it will take time and effort to purify reputation systems of inaccurate or unfair data points. But the alternative is worse. One of the best-known privacy blogs is entitled "Pogo Was Right," in honor of the old comic book tag "We have met the enemy, and he is us." The rebuke is obvious: we'd better stop being so careless about how technology creates reputations, and start to rein in arbitrary, discriminatory, and unfair algorithms. Chapter 5 suggests some initiatives for achieving that end. But to fully understand how they might work, and how needed they are, we need to turn from technologies of reputation (which increasingly mediate how we *are perceived*), to technologies of search (which mediate how *we perceive*). Search is the topic of the next chapter.

# 3

# THE HIDDEN LOGICS
# OF SEARCH

$S_{EARCH}$, IN THE VIEW of economic sociologist David Stark, is "the watchword of the information age."[1] Though most people associate the "search space" with Google, search is a far more general concept. Whether looking for information or entertainment, products or soulmates, we are relying more on dynamic searches than on stable sources. Search pervasively affects our view of the Internet and, increasingly, of "real life."[2]

Search engines host billions of queries per day. They "answer" more and more of them without the asker ever having to click through to another site. They keep track of our friends, real and virtual. They find our entertainment. They rank and rate everything for us, from movies to doctors to hotels. Search engines can be general, specialized, or social.[3] There are mammoth ones and tiny ones, public ones and encrypted ones, and the array is becoming more varied and more important as content offerings proliferate.[4]

These new masters of media are more than just conveniences. Thanks both to their competence and our inertia, they often determine what possibilities reach our awareness at all.[5] They are guides; they influence, sometimes quite profoundly, our decisions about what we do and think and buy (and what we don't). They are revolutionaries; Apple's and Amazon's portals have definitively reshaped commerce.[6] They are our agents: search for and "friend" a few dozen people on Facebook or follow them on Twitter, and the platforms deliver up a steady stream of content.

Search is a leveler. It lets us, the scrutinized, turn the tables and check out everyone else. It is our entrée to the pool of reputational data to which we all willy-nilly contribute, and at its best it lets us keep tabs on the "digital selves" that so often stand in for us at fateful junctures with bosses, bankers, and other decision makers.

Search gives anyone with a computer or a nearby public library access to resources that were once out of reach of all but the very few with unlimited funds and leisure time. It has the power to give each of us a perfect little world of our own, a world tailored so exquisitely to our individual interests and preferences that it is different from the world as seen by anyone else.

But like everything else in the digital age, search has a dark side, and that dark side has to do with trust. How does a platform decide on the coverage given a third-party mayoral candidate? Or how long to let a meme like Obama's leaden debate performance or Romney's 47 percent speech dominate campaign coverage? New media giants can tame information overload by personalizing coverage for us.[7] But how do those neat and compact presentations of a messy and sprawling world occur? Was a story selected for its statistical prominence among news organs, or because a personalization algorithm picked it out for us? If the selection was based on statistics, then *which* statistics—the number of mentions of the story, the authority of the news outlets promoting it, or something else entirely?

Businesses large and small worry over such matters daily. Hotels appear to be paying more or less stealthily for premium placement on Google's map and travel services.[8] How can we know whether news outlets or political campaigns are engaged in subtler manipulations, like routing readers and volunteers to Google+ to increase their salience in Google Search? At least with a dead-tree newspaper we know that everybody looking at it sees the same thing, and there are editors to write to when something doesn't smell right. But the decisions at the Googleplex are made behind closed doors or, as we'll see, within black boxes. How far can we trust the people who make them?

The power to include, exclude, and rank is the power to ensure which public impressions become permanent and which remain fleeting.[9] That is why search services, social and not, are "must-have" properties for advertisers as well as users. As such, they have made very deep inroads indeed into the sphere of cultural, economic, and political influence that was once dominated by broadcast networks, radio stations, and newspapers. But their dominance is so complete, and their technology so complex, that they have escaped pressures for transparency and accountability that kept traditional media answerable to the public.

There's a lot that we don't know about these services to which we hand over so much of our lives.[10] Despite their claims of objectivity and neutrality, they are constantly making value-laden, controversial decisions. They help create the world they claim to merely "show" us. I will explore four areas in which the behavior of the great search companies raises pressing issues of trust: transparency, competition, compensation, and control.

## Search and Transparency

"Better user experience" is the reason the major Internet companies give for almost everything they do. But surely their interests must conflict with ours sometimes—and then what?[11] Disputes over bias and abuse of power have embroiled most of the important Internet platforms, despite the aura of neutrality they cultivate so carefully. It would be reassuring to have clear answers about when conflicts happen and how they're handled. But the huge companies resist meaningful disclosure, and hide important decisions behind technology, and boilerplate contracts. What happens, happens out of our sight.[12]

*Sex and Politics in the Apple Store.* Apple remade the world of online music by designing a simple interface, cutting a Gordian knot of copyright conflicts, and providing instant access.[13] iTunes, iPod, and iPad unleashed a whole new ecosystem of music options and compensation.[14] The power of a well-maintained and popular platform like that is enormous.[15] Common standards let people share, cooperate, and play. As Amar Bhidé, finance expert and professor at

Tufts University's Fletcher School of Law and Diplomacy, has put it, those "innovations that sustain modern prosperity . . . are developed and used through a massively multiplayer, multilevel, and multiperiod game."[16]

But the rules of Apple's game can be pretty ambiguous. The company's business practices are notoriously secretive—so much so that legal scholars like Jonathan Zittrain and Tim Wu have worried that too much central control might be constraining the creativity of app developers.[17] More to my own point, users have sometimes had occasion to worry that all that invisible control is constraining *us*, as when Apple excludes popular programs from its app store, or prevents them from running on its products. Here are three disconcerting cases.

EUCALYPTUS. In 2012, developers were submitting about 10,000 apps per week to Apple. Quite a lot featured sexual subject matter. Apple's response has been pragmatic and efficient: an antiporn policy that purportedly reflects user demand and deflects spam.[18] The policy also allows Apple to process the flood of new apps efficiently.

But although the "objectionable content" guidelines at Apple are well publicized, the way they are applied is not. Take the veto of an app called Eucalyptus, which was intended for formatting and downloading public domain texts. Apple rejected Eucalyptus on the grounds that it could be used to access "a Victorian-era, text-only version of the *Kama Sutra*."[19] Yet Apple had previously approved apps that do precisely the same thing, and the *Kama Sutra* could be found on Apple's own Safari browser in illustrated (including some truly pornographic) editions. Until *Ars Technica*'s Chris Foresman highlighted this absurdity in a scathing column, Eucalyptus's creator knocked in vain against a "mysterious black box." Press coverage finally spurred Apple into action, and Eucalyptus's fate was reversed by higher-ups.[20]

In this case, a well-placed story provoked corrective action and a quick apology. But how many apps never attract the attention of journalists? We don't know. There's no census of app developers to poll, and Apple's not telling.

DRONES +. Eucalyptus seems to have been a victim of incompetent or arbitrary decision making.[21] Other rejections look less benign.

NYU graduate student John Begley developed Drones+ as U.S. drone warfare expanded. It aggregates news stories on drone targets, maps them, and delivers a pop-up notification whenever a new strike is reported. Begley included the real-time alerts to help users keep track of an underreported military initiative.[22]

Apple rejected Drones+ twice. The first reason given was that it was "not useful."[23] (Apple has, however, approved an app that does nothing but display a flame on the screen.) A second rejection letter called the app's content "objectionable and crude," a violation of the App Store Review Guidelines. But the content of Begley's app was news stories, quoted and plotted on a map.[24] Apple has approved plenty of apps that describe *and depict* the destruction reported in the news, so that rationale is hard to swallow.[25] Despite national publicity criticizing the decision, Apple held firm for two years.[26] After five rejections, Begley finally got the app included in the store in 2014 by removing the word "drone" from its name and description, rechristening it Metadata+.[27] Whether those interested in tracking drone strikes can find his app without its using the term "drone" is anyone's guess.

IN A PERMANENT SAVE STATE. Artist Benjamin Poynter submitted his In a Permanent Save State as a "persuasive gaming" app, a form of combined entertainment, provocation, and instruction.[28] It offered an interactive narrative inspired by the suicides of workers at Apple supplier Foxconn's plant, which had taken an enormous public relations toll on Apple the year before.[29] Poynter intended Permanent Save State to highlight the dark contrast between Apple's dream machines and nightmarish conditions in its supply chain.

Apple did not say why it removed the app shortly after it first appeared. It might have been Guideline 16.1, the catchall ban on "objectionable content," or 15.3, which forbids depictions of "a real government or corporation, or any other real entity." Or the topic might have just menaced the company's famous "reality distortion field."[30] Political speech is especially protected under the First Amendment, but Apple isn't bound by the Bill of Rights.[31]

Zittrain anticipated opportunistic behavior like this in his 2008 book *The Future of the Internet—And How to Stop It*. His work is a complex and nuanced call for technology companies to reflect public ılues in their decisions about what apps to make accessible. Technology scholar Rob Frieden has gone further, challenging the need for app approval at all. When we buy desktop computers we don't have to "phone home" for the manufacturer's permission before we can run a program on it.[32] Why does Apple insist on such control? Wouldn't free access to apps work better?[33]

In Apple's defense, some control may be necessary to ensure the smooth operation of their phones. Buggy, slow, or spammy apps do hurt its customer base. But Drones+? Since it clearly provides information that people want, why should Apple care? At the very least, it could tell users clearly which apps have been rejected, and why.[34]

*Google as the "Universal" Index.* Google is perhaps the most instructive case of how the black box culture developed, and why it matters. Before Google, web navigation for consumers often meant cluttered portals, garish ads, and spam galore. Google took over the field by delivering clear, clean, and relevant results in fractions of a second. Even Silicon Valley skeptics credit Google with bringing order to chaos. For the skilled searcher, Google is a godsend, a dynamic Alexandrian Library of digital content. But commercial success has given the company almost inconceivable power, not least over what we find online.[35]

Google does not reveal the details of its ranking methods. It has explained their broad outlines, and the process sounds reassuringly straightforward. It rates sites on *relevance* and on *importance*. The more web pages link to a given page, the more authoritative Google deems it. (For those who need to connect to a page but don't want to promote it, Google promises not to count links that include a "rel:nofollow" tag.) The voting is weighted; web pages that are themselves linked to by many other pages have more authority than unconnected ones. This is the core of the patented "PageRank" method behind Google's success.[36] PageRank's hybrid of egalitarianism (anyone can link) and elitism (some links count more than others) both reflected and inspired powerful modes of ordering web content.[37]

It also caused new problems. The more Google revealed about its ranking algorithms, the easier it was to manipulate them.[38] Thus

began the endless cat-and-mouse game of "search engine optimization," and with it the rush to methodological secrecy that makes
search the black box business that it is. The original PageRank patent, open for all to see, clandestinely accumulated a thick crust of
tweaks and adjustments intended to combat web baddies: the "link
farms" (sites that link to other sites only to goose their Google
rankings), the "splogs" (spam blogs, which farm links in the more
dynamic weblog format); and the "content farms" (which rapidly and
clumsily aggregate content based on trending Google searches, so as
to appear at the top of search engine result pages, or SERPs). Beneath
the façade of sleek interfaces and neatly ordered results, guerrilla war
simmers between the search engineers and the spammers.[39]

The war with legitimate content providers is just as real, if colder.
Search engine optimizers parse speeches from Google the way
Kremlinologists used to pore over the communiqués of Soviet pre-
miers, looking for ways to improve their showing without provoking the "Google Death Penalty" that de-indexes sites caught gaming the system. And just as wartime gives governments reasons (and
excuses) to hide their plans from the public, Google has used the
endless battle against spam and manipulation to justify its refusal to
account for controversial ranking decisions.[40]

Google is an ambitious company. Its stated goal, as cultural theorist Siva Vaidhyanathan noted in his thoughtful 2010 book *The
Googlization of Everything*, is to "organize the world's information."[41]
But faced with shareholder demands for ever-rising profits, it is also
angling for new sources of growth.[42] It is positioning Google Books
and Google Shopping to rival Amazon and eBay as marketplaces. It
has made YouTube a critical hub in the entertainment industry. To
shake up travel, Google acquired Zagat, the famed restaurant re-
viewer, and Waze, a leading traffic app.[43] As of 2013, it has been acquiring at least a company a month, often in spaces adjacent to its
core search business.[44]

Many welcome this expansiveness. Google brings user-friendly
design and scale to areas that sorely need them—in its free Gmail
and map services, for example. But it also gives cause for concern
about what Google's immensity means, both for us as searchers and
for the economy at large.

Google, for instance, has become a double-edged sword as web organizer and archivist.[45] Yes, its index dwarfs anyone else's. But that is precisely why it can no longer be relied upon as the "indexer of last resort." Virtually any needle can be "disappeared" into a haystack of that size; it is just too easy for the company to hide content it would rather we didn't see. Furthermore, pressing questions have arisen about whether Google is using its dominance in general purpose search to leverage undue power elsewhere. It cloaks its answers in layers of bureaucratic, technical, and contractual obscurity.

We pay no money for Google's services. But *someone* pays for its thousands of engineers, and that someone is advertisers. Nearly all the company's revenue comes from marketers eager to reach the targeted audiences that Google delivers so abundantly. We pay with our attention and with our data, the raw material of marketing. (You are not Google's client, Senator Al Franken once warned users of the World Wide Web. "You are its product."[46]) Sometimes we invest time and effort in a Google service (like arranging blog feeds in Google Reader), only to find the plug pulled abruptly when it isn't profitable enough.[47] We also pay in our ignorance of how the company operates, how it guides us through the web, and how it uses the data it collects on our activities there.

Secret algorithmic rules for organizing information, and wars against those who would defeat them, exist at Facebook and Twitter, too. Apple and Amazon have their own opaque technologies, leaving users in the dark as to exactly why an app, story, or book is featured at a particular time or in a particular place. The secrecy is understandable as a business strategy, but it devastates our ability to understand the social world Silicon Valley is creating.[48] Moreover, behind the technical inscrutability, there's plenty of room for opportunistic, exploitative, and just plain careless conduct to hide.

*Search, Transparency and Fairness.* We trust our search engines to play straight with us: to show us what's there; to put the best suggestions on top so that we don't have to click through thousands of pages to find them; and to rank by relevance unless they tell us otherwise. But do they?

*Foundem* is a UK-based firm that provides specialized "vertical search" for price comparisons. It is run by a team of husband and wife engineers with formidable CVs and a track record of innovation. Leading consumer and technology organs in the UK ranked Foundem extremely high in comparative studies of its niche.

But Foundem has not been able to convert this critical acclaim into a mass user base, and it blames Google. Less than six months after Foundem launched, Google appeared to block it from the front pages of its *organic* (that is, unpaid) search results when users queried for price comparisons.[49] The reason, according to Google, was that Foundem was a "low-quality" site, composed mainly of links to other sites. Downranking it could have been a direct result of Google's algorithmic procedure for protecting users from spammers and link farms.

But sometimes there's a legitimate reason for a site to sample other sites—in fact, that's exactly what search engines do, including Google. Google acknowledges this. So, it says, it distinguishes among such sites by downgrading any whose guesses about what a searcher wants are inferior to its own. But, it says, it allows *good* finding tools to make it into the top search results.[50]

Foundem favors another explanation. If Google has no interest in an area, it will let an upstart be. But once it enters (or plans to enter) the market of a smaller finding service, it downranks that service to assure the prominence of its own offerings. (Major incumbents are not displaced lest their users revolt, so they usually retain their access to prime real estate.)

If the smaller engine is a potential acquisition target, Google has another interest in suppressing traffic: to discourage its hope of succeeding independently. Like Pharaoh trying to kill off the baby Moses, it denies its rival the chance to scale.[51] When a would-be purchaser controls significant access to its target's potential customer base, overtures of interest are offers that can't be refused.[52]

The downranking of Foundem drastically reduced its visibility in Google's unpaid results. When the company tried to reach users with ads, Google cut off that option too. Foundem had been bidding five pence to participate in Google ad auctions, but now Google required a minimum bid of five *pounds*. This made the cost of advertising so prohibitive that, according to Foundem, for more than a year it was effectively eliminated from the view of those searching Google for price comparison websites.[53]

In September 2007, Google relented, "whitelisting" Foundem in its *paid* search results, and lifting its penalty. But the exclusion from *organic* search persisted until the tech press began to cover the story. Finally, in December of that year, Google "manually whitelisted" Foundem, assuring its owners that the algorithms that had branded Foundem as useless or spammy web junk would no longer act to penalize (and thus hide) the site.[54]

Google insists that "the system worked" with respect to Foundem; its algorithms for detecting low-quality sites had hurt it for a while, but eventually human intervention addressed the problem.[55] As Google's engineers like to say, "Search is hard." Evaluation and ranking protocols are as potentially controversial in search as they are anywhere else, and when controversies arise, users can't expect instantaneous resolutions.

But for Foundem and its supporters in the tech press, it's more sinister than that. Google must meet Wall Street's expectations and has demanding shareholders. They expect it to grow, and to do so it must expand. It has: with e-mail (Gmail), video (YouTube), social networking (Orkut and Google+), a blog platform (Blogger), and various specialized search technologies such as Image Search and Google News. Now it is venturing into the realms of shopping, travel, advice, reviews, and price comparisons.[56] Who will Google's system "work" for next? As Metafilter has found, a rapid decline in Google traffic can be a devastating and mysterious blow to even a well-known, well-respected site.[57]

Google counters that it is under no obligation to help other companies eat into its revenue. Its antitrust lawyers insist that what may look from the outside like self-serving bias is just a consistent commitment to customer service. If engineers know that Google Product Search works, why should they expend time and effort in due diligence on every untested alternative? YouTube has dedicated staff and an active user community that root out spam, porn, and other undesirable material. Is an upstart video service likely to be as well run as Google's own? The company frames its inexorable advance from text search into image, video, and who knows what next as a public service. That is one reason American courts have been so forgiving of Google in considering the copyright complaints against it; it has been seen as a benevolent force for order on the web.[58]

(The situation also highlights the limits of economic analysis. If competition law authorities decide to protect specialized services from domination by a general purpose search behemoth, they are effectively delineating a specialized market.[59] Their decision is not a *reflection* of market forces, but an engine shaping them.[60] The same can be said of the search engines themselves. Left to their own devices, they create the online marketplace at the same time that they participate in it.[61] There is no neutral ground here: the state either takes steps to protect the upstarts, or allows the giant platforms to swallow them. Like banks that, if allowed to grow too large, can effectively control commerce thanks to their power over its financing, massive internet platforms can similarly dominate because of their power over finding.)

Google's dominance is recognized in Europe, too, but differently. EU antitrust authorities recognize that Google is not really a competitor in numerous markets, but instead serves as a hub and kingmaker setting the terms of competition for others. To settle a long-standing antitrust investigation (requested by Foundem, among others), Google as of mid-2013 had offered to guarantee a place on its results page for at least three rival services whenever it offered a service of its own in response to a query.[62] This is a stark contrast with American antitrust authorities' minimalist approach.[63]

Was Foundem's exclusion really a side effect of Google's effort to protect searchers from spammy sites? Or was it an attempt to undermine a nascent competitor? The results are susceptible to either interpretation, but Google's "quality scoring" algorithms are so thoroughly black-boxed that we can't know which is correct. More on Google and competition shortly.

*Search, Transparency, and "Murketing."* "Stealth marketing" is another area of collision between search and trust. Like broadcast networks, search engines survive by offering unpaid content (in this case, *organic* search results) to sell advertising (*paid* search results).[64]

As search engines developed, most of them placed ads at the top and sides of result pages, but used the center for rankings that were free of commercial influence.

American law has long required the separation of editorial and paid content.[65] At first, Google honored those requirements in spirit as well as in letter. When it was just one of many search engines scrambling for market share, this was not only wise compliance but also good business. Google's transparency about advertising delivered high quality results and gained trust.[66] Early search leaders who succumbed to the siren song of ad-disguising drove their users away with irrelevant links while Google's audience grew. As more people signed into its system, Google learned more about them and became ever better at tailoring its search results.[67] Its ad income increased as its targeting improved. This triumph of "Don't Be Evil" is still a celebrated Silicon Valley success story. Patiently gathering data, the company entrenched its privileged position between advertisers, content providers, and audiences.[68]

But in 2012, as it moved from general purpose search into specialized fields like shopping, Google began to back away from strong separation of paid and editorial material.[69] The Federal Trade Commission strongly encourages search engines to label sponsored content,[70] and has reserved the right to file suit for unfair and deceptive practices against any search engine that fails to do so. Yet it has never actually filed such a suit. This passivity has emboldened small Internet players, and now Google itself, to weaken some of the visual distinction between paid and unpaid content.[71] Accordingly, it becomes harder to discern whether the inclusion, say, of a given hotel or florist shop in a page of search results reflects its quality or its willingness to pay for visibility.[72] And the secretiveness of Google's search ranking processes doesn't help. Even Danny Sullivan, a Silicon Valley journalist who has defended Google from many critics, was disappointed in the shift:

> For two years in a row now, Google has gone back on major promises it made about search. . . . In the past, Google might have explained such shifts in an attempt to maintain user trust. Now, Google either assumes it has so much user trust that ex-

planations aren't necessary. Or, the lack of accountability might be due to its "fuzzy management" structure where no one seems in charge of the search engine.[73]

And Google is not alone in arousing watchdogs. Blogs constantly speculate about what it might take to get one of the 500,000 or so apps in Apple's store to stand out. Paid-content issues also dog those seeking attention via Facebook.[74] Facebook doesn't disclose the "EdgeRank" methods it uses to sort the items in a user's news feed into the stream of links, pictures, and information from friends that makes the site so addictive.[75] But in 2012, it offered users a chance to pay to promote certain posts. Confusion and resentment ensued almost immediately, as some nonpayers noticed their sudden obscurity and interpreted it as Facebook's way of forcing them to pony up. Without knowing exactly how EdgeRank works, it is very difficult to assess how much substance there might have been in that particular concern.[76] But anyone with a critical mass of friends can see how unwieldly Facebook's "News Feed" has become: how hard it is, say, to be sure you see all your friends' posts, even when you choose to see "Most Recent" posts rather than "Top Stories." Facebook is increasingly a kingmaker for "digital content providers," but it's entirely unclear how it's choosing which sites to promote and which to doom to obscurity.

This confusion may be to Google or Facebook's advantage, but it is not to ours. Blending paid and editorial content creates a confusing world of "murketing" (murky marketing tactics).[77] Google founders Sergey Brin and Larry Page admitted in 1998 their expectation that "advertising funded search engines will be inherently biased towards the advertisers and away from the needs of the consumers."[78]

This situation comes up reliably enough in the communications context that there is a long-standing solution: require *both conduits and content providers* to disclose whether they are raising the profile of those who pay them.[79] Consumers and competitors alike suffer when sub rosa payments are permitted. Money confers an enormous advantage in the battle for mindshare, and fairness requires—at the very least—that when advantage has been bought, it be disclosed.[80]

The question now is whether regulators will adopt and enforce classic rules in a digital age, or let them wither into desuetude.

*Search, Transparency, and Judgment.* More complex trust issues come up in the ways that the Silicon Valley behemoths handle other disconcerting search surprises.

Google came under fire in 2012, for example, in an awkward situation regarding a prominent German woman, Bettina Wulff.[81] Users who typed her name into the search box were likely to see "bettina wulff prostituierte" and "bettina wulff escort" appear in the "autocomplete" list underneath. Those phrases reflected unfounded rumors about Wulff, who has had to obtain more than thirty cease-and-desist orders in Germany against bloggers and journalists who mischaracterized her past salaciously. Wulff feared that users would interpret the autocompletes (which Google offers as a convenience to users) as a judgment on her character rather than as an artifact of her prolonged and victorious legal battles against slanderers.[82]

Google's help pages say that the autocompletes are "algorithmically determined" and usually reflect "the search activity of users and the content of web pages indexed by Google."[83] The company maintained that Bettina Wulff's wrongful association complaint was none of its business—that it is the obligation of users to appraise the validity of what they read. Yet Google's own behavior refutes that position. The company is not generally indifferent to what its users think; on the contrary, it is constantly trying to educate us, to discern our intent, to give us "the right answer" in ever more contexts. It even corrects our spelling. Type in "lock ness monster" and we see the results for "*loch* ness monster," along with a small offer to "Search instead for 'lock ness monster'" underneath. Google makes at least *some* provisional judgments about what searchers are looking for. Given its interpretive activism about misspellings, one might think that it would lend a hand to a person defamed online, or otherwise dogged by unrepresentative and demeaning material.[84]

Not only autosuggestions, but also search results, can seem inappropriate or unfair. Consider what happened when politician Rick Santorum irked activist Dan Savage. Santorum had compared gay marriage to bestiality, and Savage led an outraged network of bloggers in retaliation. They linked so enthusiastically to a site associating *santorum* with anal sex that soon that site was the first result for most Google searches on the candidate's name. The online come-uppance of the ultraconservative candidate delighted many. Santorum supporters complained to Google to no avail. Only after he made a surprisingly strong showing in three GOP primaries in early 2012 did the anal sex association fade from the very top of the search results.[85]

In its public statements about such controversies, Google mostly characterized them as a reflection of the zeitgeist. Its defenders worried that Google would be "opening the floodgates" to political lobbying if it were to override its search algorithms in Santorum's favor. Google itself pointed out its great efficiency and speed are due to its automated search process; to call in human reviewers would likely slow response times. (An outsider might be forgiven for wondering whether it might also depress profit margins.) Above all, Google said, an override would contradict the culture of the company, which was committed to organizing and presenting information based on math, rules, and facts, not on opinion, values, or judgment.[86]

But Google has surrendered its "objectivity" position from time to time.[87] In 2004, anti-Semites boosted a Holocaust-denial site called "Jewwatch" into the top ten results for the query "Jew."[88] (Ironically, some of those horrified by the site may have helped by linking to it in order to criticize it; PageRank by and large looks only to linking itself, and not the reasons behind it, to determine a site's prominence.)[89] The Anti-Defamation League complained. Google added a headline at the top of the page entitled "An explanation of our search results."[90] A web page linked to the headline explained why the offensive site appeared so high in the relevant rankings, thereby distancing Google from the results.[91] It might want to consider doing the same at YouTube, where (according to a noted author) watching a few videos of old speeches on the Federal Reserve can quickly provoke a rabbit hole of anti-Semitic "suggested videos" on financial conspiracy theories.

There are principled grounds for a large Internet firm like Google to leave the Santorum results alone, while aggressively intervening to stop the spread of virulent discrimination. But we need to know more about how such decisions are made, given the power of large Internet firms, and the much harder issues on the horizon. A psychologist has conducted experiments suggesting that a "dominant search engine could alter perceptions of candidates in close elections."[92] Jonathan Zittrain spells out how known technology at a dominant social network could have an even more insidious effect:

> Consider a hypothetical, hotly contested future election. Suppose that Mark Zuckerberg personally favors whichever candidate you don't like. He arranges for a voting prompt to appear within the newsfeeds of tens of millions of active Facebook users. . . . Zuckerberg makes use of the fact that Facebook "likes" can predict political views and party affiliation, even beyond the many users who proudly advertise those affiliations directly. With that knowledge, our hypothetical Zuck chooses not to spice the feeds of users unsympathetic to his views.[93]

When Facebook tried the "vote prompt" in 2010, 0.39 percent more users notified by it voted—well more than enough to swing the outcome in contests like the 2000 U.S. presidential election. Note that Facebook is neither obliged by current law, nor by its terms of service, to announce such interventions.

Are tech titans' political preferences skewed enough to make such a plot tempting? Many Republicans have complained that Google[94] skews search results to mock or marginalize the right;[95] columnist Michelle Malkin charged that websites like hers weren't appearing in Google News results.[96] Later, after George W. Bush and Barack Obama were both subjected to "google bombs"[97] that linked their names to the words "miserable failure," Fox News reported conservative discontent that the manipulation involving Obama was resolved quickly, but it took Google almost four years to address the issue with respect to Bush.[98] Certainly its responses in these varied cases don't present a picture of a clear policy.

Moreover, Google *did* defuse the Bush and Obama g-bombs, although at different speeds. Why did they rate an override and Santorum didn't? Did the company learn enough from the response to the Bush prank to somehow respond faster when it was Obama's turn?[99] Did the difference reflect more years of practical experience? A new policy? Political views? We don't know. It's an odd thing to trust a search engine so much when we have no way of ascertaining whether or not it acts on a political agenda, or to what extent it will allow clear manipulation to go unchallenged.

Limited "rights of reply" would constitute one way of adding information to a digital platform; annotations could be permitted in certain instances of express or implied defamation, for example.[100] Google continues to maintain that it doesn't want human judgment blurring the autonomy of its algorithms. But even spelling suggestions depend on human judgment, and in fact Google developed that feature not only by means of algorithms, but also through a painstaking, iterative interplay between computer science experts and human beta testers who report on their satisfaction with various results configurations.[101] It's true that the policy for alternative spellings can be applied generally and automatically once the testing is over, while every situation like Wulff's or Santorum's would require a fresh independent judgment. Perhaps Google fears that reputational micromanagers would overwhelm it with requests. But would it really be so hard for the search engine to turn off autocomplete when it's causing unnecessary harm?

Google's repeated refusals even to entertain such reform proposals suggest that the companies' executives believe they've found one best way of ordering the web, outside input be damned. That is an ironic stance for a company that once accused critics (in the context of an FTC antitrust investigation) of a naïve, outdated, and overly rigid conception of search results as "ten blue links."[102] Google argued successfully at that time that certain prerogatives of malleability were due a company that has to make rapid and dramatic changes in its "product." Don't those prerogatives come with responsibilities, too?[103]

Unfortunately, technology firms tend to resist accountability. Consider how America's leading microblogging platform, Twitter, deflected concerns about its algorithms. Twitter hosts whatever short bursts of content (*tweets*) its users contribute. Their message varies widely: from the banal (@KimKardashian) to the profound (@SorenKQuotes), from networking to gibberish to satire (@KimKierkegaard). It can function as either a broadcaster or a narrowcaster, according to the predilections of individual users. It has also become a crowd-sourced democratic search engine for news and conversation. By putting a hashtag (#) in front of a term, users form an automatic "real-time" community around it; anyone who clicks on the term will see items tweeted about it in the past few seconds, hours, or days.[104]

The hashtag also serves to nominate some terms as "trending"— that is, interesting enough to be recommended *generally* rather than simply to the *followers* who subscribe to one's own tweets.[105] Trending topics are listed on Twitter's Home, Discover, and Search pages. Users tend to understand them as hot, fun, or particularly interesting news, and activists use the Trending Topics lists to assess their success in engaging a mass audience.[106]

In late September of 2011, Occupy Wall Street was starting to gain media attention. But although #OWS and #occupy seemed to be collecting more tweets than other terms on the official Trending Topics list, Twitter didn't show them there. Organizers and sympathizers began to accuse Twitter of overriding its trending topics algorithm to suppress those terms, and therefore of censoring their politically controversial movement.[107] @TheNewDeal (@ identifies a Twitter username) put it bluntly on October 1: "It is Official, @witter is Censoring #OccupyWallStreet There is No Way in Hell That it is Not the #1 Trending Topic in America."[108]

The response from the company was swift: no censorship was occurring. Sean Garrett, head of communications at Twitter, replied to @TheNewDeal that "Twitter is not blocking #OccupyWallStreet from trending. Trends are based on velocity not popularity." Twitter also pointed to a similar situation in 2010, when people had been complaining that #wikileaks did not appear prominently enough in Trending Topics. At that time, the company explained:

Twitter Trends are automatically generated by an algorithm that . . . captures the hottest emerging topics, not just what's most popular. Put another way, Twitter favors novelty over popularity. . . .

Topics break into the Trends list when the volume of Tweets about that topic at a given moment dramatically increases. . . . Sometimes, popular terms don't make the Trends list because the velocity of conversation isn't increasing quickly enough, relative to the baseline level of conversation happening on an average day; this is what happened with #wikileaks this week.[109]

The #wikileaks and #occupy controversies died down quickly after Twitter offered these explanations. But when a site called Thunderclap attempted to hold a trending topic in reserve until it could unleash its followers all at once, timing all their tweets for maximum impact, Twitter suspended Thunderclap's access to its API.[110]

Media studies scholar Tarleton Gillespie analyzed the company's position in a widely shared blog post titled "Can an Algorithm Be Wrong?" He observed that "as more and more of our online public discourse takes place on a select set of private content platforms and communication networks, and these providers turn to complex algorithms to manage, curate, and organize these massive collections, there is an important tension emerging between what we expect these algorithms to be, and what they in fact are."[111] For Gillespie, the problem is less one of fair platform practices than of media literacy. People were misunderstanding Trending Topics.[112]

But at what point does a platform have to start taking responsibility for what its algorithms do, and how their results are used? These new technologies affect not only how we are understood, but also how we understand. Shouldn't we know when they're working for us, against us, or for unseen interests with undisclosed motives?

Dizzying shifts in the ways Internet platforms characterize themselves amount to a form of regulatory arbitrage, evading the spirit of classic legal obligations.[113] When faced with copyright and defamation lawsuits, they claim not to be media companies (that is, producers of content), but only conduits (that is, pipelines for content).[114] A conduit does not enjoy the most robust First Amendment protection, but it gains freedom from liability in cases of defamation.[115] (For example, the phone company can't refuse to serve me on First Amendment grounds, but it also can't be sued by someone I defame using the phone.) Thus Google can argue that the very idea of suing it for its autocompletes is as nonsensical as a lawsuit against the phone company for enabling a slanderer to spread lies over its network.

But in other cases, Google has also maintained that its services *are* content and that it *is* entitled to the media's fullest First Amendment protections, which include not only the right to free expression but also the right not to be forced to express opinions not its own.[116] Expansive interpretations of the First Amendment could leave Google nearly unregulable. Fortunately, there is also plenty of legal doctrine suggesting the limits of opportunistic civil libertarianism.[117]

*Search, Transparency, and Personalization.* The secret workings of our search engines deeply inform our views of the world. That truth comes as a real shock to many of us. I don't know how often I've heard someone say, "I'm the top Google result for my name!" But if *I* searched for your name, would I see the same thing? Only Google knows, but very likely not. We can only guess at how our Google-mediated worlds differ.

We know that what we do while signed into Google services (like Gmail) will be reflected in our search results. This has been true for a long time. As far back as 2007, Google was investing heavily in customization technology.[118] By late 2009, it had changed its algorithms to deliver "personalized search" to all web users. Our locations, our search histories, our computers—all of these and more influence Google Search results, and therefore our view of the world.[119]

The basic outlines of similar processes are clearer on Facebook and Twitter, where users curate continuously scrolling feeds. But even there, judgments have to be made about what to do with, say, a sudden burst of content from one source, or the flagging of potentially "objectionable" content.

Personalization lets us hide annoying relatives on our Facebook feeds, list our favorite microbloggers, and get updates from crucial RSS feeds. It means that Google News might give pride of place to baseball, music, or left-wing politics according to the reputations we establish. It means that Google Search orders its results according to searches we've made before, through clicks collected by the

Google-owned ad network DoubleClick and through activity on other Google-related accounts.

Personalization makes for digital magic. Let's say that you've lost a favorite earring and want to replace it. And that when you first found the pair many years ago, you took a picture of it and sent it in an e-mail to your sister. When you next search Google Images for earrings, you may find an exact match at the very top. You wouldn't know that the critical data point was the picture in your e-mail; you don't even have to remember that there ever *was* a picture or an e-mail at all. This is just what happens when you've got a search engine (as aggressive about data aggregation as Google) attached to your own e-mail account. Multiply that experience by years of people, e-mail, and search—that's how powerful the dominant platforms really are as artificial intelligence aids for virtually any tasks we undertake.[120] They have unmatched abilities to advance users' data-dependent interests.

But personalization has unnerving effects, too. Google results have become so very particular that it is increasingly difficult to assess how much of any given subject or controversy any of us actually sees. We see what we have trained Google to show us and what Google gradually conditions us to expect. Entrepreneur Eli Pariser calls this phenomenon "the filter bubble" and worries that all this personalization has serious side effects, namely increased insularity and reinforced prejudice.[121] So intense is the personalization of search results, for instance, that when British Petroleum's (BP) massive oil spill was dominating cable news in the summer of 2010, searches for "BP" on Google led some users to fierce denunciations of the company's environmental track record, and others to investment opportunities in the company.[122] Only the search engineers at the Googleplex can reliably track who's seeing what and why. And they are bound by nondisclosure agreements not to tell us.[123]

Personalization means vulnerability as well as power. If a social network knows you love poker, it can prioritize posts about casinos. But it might also get you included on a "sucker's list" of problem gamblers for casino advertisers.[124] The same platforms on which Arab Spring protesters virtually assembled to overthrow corrupt rulers also generate intelligence for autocrats.[125] Data deployed to serve users one moment can be repurposed to disadvantage them the next. In contemporary American policy debates, these concerns are often framed as privacy issues. But they are equally concerns about search. Who are the men behind the curtain, and how are their black boxes sorting and reporting our world?

Shaping it, too. Personalization is critical to both buying and selling, and that is why reputation and search go hand in hand in the digital economy. How we are seen by websites in turn affects the choices they present to us. Businesses want to know how we search precisely so they can shape our view of the marketplace. We shape the marketplace too, in our search for the best prices and the widest choice. Accurately attuned search results attract users, and accurately targeted users attract advertisers. The most lucrative ads are those "narrowcast" on search result pages, because they reach niche audiences who have already volunteered information about what they want.[126] A florist is likely to pay more to advertise to people searching for "roses" than to any random group of computer users.[127] But it's better still when Google can tell it not only how often its searchers query "roses," but also the sites they go to in response. And what goes for Google is increasingly true of Facebook, Twitter, and so on.

As usual, there's danger here. The advantages of this sort of pinpointing are leading advertisers to abandon traditional, and even not-so-traditional, publishers in favor of the huge Internet platforms. Why? Because nobody else can approach either the granularity or the comprehensiveness of their data. The result is a revolution-in-process about who can afford to keep publishing, and concomitant alarm about the concentration of media clout into fewer and fewer hands.

## Search, Trust, and Competition

Neoclassical economists envision a direct and positive relationship on the Internet between privacy and competition. If a large online company is abusing its position, market-oriented scholars say, economic forces will solve the problem.[128] Can't find something on Google? There's always Bing. Don't like the new version of iTunes?

Subscribe to Rhapsody. Google not private enough? Try Duck-Duck-Go.[129] Users can select for a preferred level of privacy the way car buyers select for miles per gallon.[130] And if they choose services that *don't* provide privacy protection? Well, that just reveals the place of privacy in their priorities.[131]

It would be great if market forces really were directly promoting optimal levels of privacy. It would also be splendid if antitrust law were promoting them indirectly, by assuring that a diverse range of firms could compete to offer them.[132] But the plausibility of these desiderata is fading. Competitive striving can do as much to trample privacy as to protect it.[133] In an era where Big Data is the key to maximizing profit, *every* business has an incentive to be nosy.[134] What the search industry blandly calls "competition" for users and "consent" to data collection looks increasingly like monopoly and coercion.

Silicon Valley is no longer a wide-open realm of opportunity. The start-ups of today may be able to sell their bright ideas to the existing web giants. They may get rich doing so. But they're not likely to become web giants themselves. Silicon Valley promulgates a myth of constant "disruption"; it presents itself as a seething cauldron of creative chaos that leaves even the top-seeded players always at risk. But the truth of the great Internet firms is closer to the oligopolistic dominance of AT&T, Verizon, and Comcast.

In 2008, I testified before a congressional committee about Google's market power. Just about every representative who questioned me assumed that a clique of twenty-somethings could at that very moment be developing an alternative. They didn't know much about the Internet, but they knew that Larry Page and Sergey Brin had risen from grad students to billionaires by building a corporate colossus out of old servers and ingenuity. In their imaginations, Google's own rags-to-riches story foreshadowed its eventual displacement.[135] Even law professors who ought to know better buy into this myth. "No one's even going to care about Google in five years!" one heatedly told me. That was six years ago. Too many still believe that the digital economy is by its nature open, competitive, and subject to the disruption that it preaches for other fields.[136]

But how realistic is this? The electricity consumption of Google's data centers rivals that of Salt Lake City.[137] Technology historian and journalist Randall Stross estimated in 2008 that the company uses close to a million computers to index and map the web.[138] If he is within even an order of magnitude of the real number (a strictly protected trade secret), it's pretty hard to imagine how an alternative could be brewing in somebody's garage. Even with millions in venture capital funding, even with computing space leased from Amazon, a start-up with valuable new search technology is far, far more likely to be bought up by Google than to displace it.[139]

Well, then, maybe another giant could take Google on? So far Microsoft is losing $2.6 billion a year on Bing.[140] The government? They tried that in Europe, but the Quaero project sputtered out, perhaps because the $450 million or so allocated to it could not compete with Google's $100 billion in annual revenue. Anyway, it's a virtual certainty that any other Goliath that could seriously squeeze Google has its own secretive and restrictive black box carapace.[141]

It's not only prohibitive infrastructure costs that keep competitors from emerging in the general search space. Innovation in search depends on access to a user base that "trains" algorithms to be more responsive.[142] But the user base belongs to Google. Innovation in analysis depends on access to large quantities of data. But the data belongs to Google. And Google isn't sharing. As long as Google's search data store remains secret, outside innovation is dead in the water. Robert Merton called this the "Matthew Effect": to those who have much, more is given.[143]

Furthermore, what if someone *did* manage to come up with a terrific alternative? They'd often have to market it through the very channels they wish to displace. If Google, Apple, Amazon, and Facebook really don't want most of their users to see something—a competitor, an alternative, whatever—they are well able to make sure it won't be seen.

Restrictive terms of service are another deterrent.[144] Every user who types in a search query agrees not to copy, modify, distribute, sell, or lease any Google service for *any* reason, or attempt to reverse engineer one.[145] Advertisers have faced other restrictions.[146]

Finally, there's the black box itself. Google's secrecy not only keeps spammers from manipulating its results but also keeps rivals from building upon its methods or even learning from them. Unlike patented procedures, which must be disclosed and whose protection eventually expires, trade secrets need never be revealed, let alone released into the public domain of free reuse.

All of these factors undermine robust competition. Silicon Valley rushes to monetize and control access to information that would better be anonymized and licensed openly as the raw material of future innovation. Quantum leaps in technology sufficient to overcome such disadvantages are unlikely. Search now is as much about personalized service as it is about principles of information organization and retrieval.[147] Many more people use search now than when Google conquered the field in the early 2000s, and they are mostly Google's. So its current advantage is likely to be self-reinforcing.[148] There have been isolated consumer boycotts, but a company so dominant can do without the business of, say, hardcore Santorum supporters. Serious complaints lodged against the company are seldom loud enough to be noticed by ordinary searchers, let alone to provoke sympathy. Users lack both the ability and the incentive to detect manipulation as long as they are getting "good enough" results.

So we're stuck. And again the question arises: With whom? The exciting and radical Internet platforms that used to feel like playmates are looking more like the airlines and cable companies that we love to hate. "Don't Be Evil" is a thing of the past; you can't form a trusting relationship with a black box. Google argues that its vast database of information and queries reveals user intentions and thus makes its search services demonstrably better than those of its whippersnapper rivals. But in doing so, it neutralizes the magic charm it has used for years to fend off regulators. "Competition is one click away," chant the Silicon Valley antitrust lawyers when someone calls out a behemoth firm for unfair or misleading business practices.[149] It's not so. Alternatives are demonstrably worse, and likely to remain so as long as the dominant firms' self-reinforcing data advantage grows.

## Search and Compensation

At the 2013 Governing Algorithms conference at New York University, a data scientist gave a dazzling presentation of how her company maximized ad revenue for its clients. She mapped out information exchanges among networks, advertisers, publishers, and the other stars of the Internet universe, emphasizing how computers are taught by skilled programmers like herself to find unexpected correlations in click-through activity. To some extent the algorithms were machines that would go of themselves, freed from supervision. "That gives me more time to ride my horses," she joked.[150]

Intrigued by the idea of machines learning, one listener asked, "At what point do the algorithms do *your* job?" In other words, when does the computing process itself reach the third level of sophistication and start determining for itself which metrics are the best metrics for measuring past metrics, and recommending further iterations for testing?[151] The presenter brushed off the question. *She* remains indispensable, even as machine learning methods are said to render millions of other jobs obsolete.[152]

Maybe she's right. But to know, we'd need expert access to the interactions between humans and machines in her firm, and we don't have it. So some of us will keep wondering about the extraordinary returns that top CEOs, managers, and investors are deriving from the Big Data economy. Compensation, like competition, raises major legal and moral issues. The first step in approaching them is awareness, especially since the black box aspect of Internet infrastructure has been so notably successful in keeping its economic arrangements out of the public eye.[153]

There are two intertwined issues here. One has to do with concern about appropriate levels of compensation for executives, intermediaries, and investors. These questions do not apply uniquely to search firms; on the contrary, they are very common in other fields. They were central, for instance, in the struggle over the Affordable Care Act, which aimed to keep insurance premiums from being siphoned disproportionately out of health care proper and into insurer profits and CEO compensation. They will come up acutely in the next chapter, on Wall Street. They haunt other corners of the information world—for instance, the cable and telephone companies that benefit along with Silicon Valley firms from the massive increase in traffic engendered by the world of search. These companies have also been accused of capturing an unfair share of revenues. These are not new questions, but it's time to ask them in our new context.

The second issue has to do with appropriate recompense not for search firms and their investors, but for the innumerable contributors to the Internet who make search worthwhile. I will start with the second, and then circle back to the first.

If there were nothing on the net, no one would be looking for it. In their book *Unjust Deserts*, Lew Daly and Gar Alperovitz document the centuries of past endeavor on which today's technical progress rests. The top dogs of Webs 2.0 and 3.0 are enriched as surely by the millions of searchers who improve their services and attract their advertisers as they are by their own ingenuity. They are further enriched by the army of creative people without whom the web would be contentless. And they are enriched by all the old technologies that contribute to new ones. Without the communication and computing of the nineteenth and twentieth centuries, for example, search would not exist at all. Yet the revenue generated online goes more and more to the masters of search infrastructure, and less and less to support the culture that makes the infrastructure possible and meaningful.[154]

The retail dominance of Walmart offers a cautionary tale here. Walmart grew to be the largest retailer in the United States by attracting consumers and squeezing suppliers. As its customer base expanded, it forced its suppliers to accept ever smaller margins. Consumers had little loyalty to the sources of their shampoo, socks, and dog food; they were pleased to accept Walmart as the place to find ultracheap everything.[155]

Firms like Google and Apple are the Walmarts of the information economy.[156] They aggressively scheme to restrict their own workers' wages.[157] They squeeze content producers (for whom making it on a big platform may mean everything), and habituate users to value the finding service itself over the sources of the things found. The content contributors—the writers, musicians, filmmakers, artists, historians, scholars, photographers, programmers, journalists, activists, cooks, sailors, manufacturers, yoga teachers, knitting gurus, auto mechanics, dog trainers, financial advisers, Lego architects, and muckrakers in quest of whose output people use major internet platforms—may receive no share at all of the revenues that that vast user base occasions. The ones that do are often obliged under contract not to reveal what their share is.[158] That is an ingenious way for the platform to cripple any opportunity for them to unite to organize for better terms.[159]

Even some progressive voices trivialize the value of ordinary Internet users' work and play. When one gadfly called Google out as a parasite extracting value created by others, law professor and digital rights activist Lawrence Lessig answered: "In the same sense you could say that all of the value in the *Mona Lisa* comes from the paint, that Leonardo da Vinci was just a 'parasite' upon the hard work of the paint makers. That statement is true in the sense that but for the paint, there would be no *Mona Lisa*. But it is false if it suggests that da Vinci wasn't responsible for the great value the *Mona Lisa* is."[160]

This is a provocative but very puzzling metaphor. Is Lessig really implying that Google's organization of the web by query does for it what da Vinci did for some pots of paint? That it is not the content, but the *index*, that gives the web meaning? After all, the new economy preaches that "information" is just another commodity. From Google's perspective, content, data, and information are basically 1's and 0's and the ad payouts they generate. But to most of us, the value of a website lies in its meaning, not its salience. And real careers, real incomes, and real achievements are won and lost in the struggle for salience that platforms host daily.

This brings us back to our equestrienne presenter, to the lords of the cloud, and to the question that is really the theme of this chapter. Who are these people and these companies that wield so much power in our lives? What do we owe them? Are they really the Gandalfs of the digital world, wizards selflessly guiding us through digital brambles? Or is it time to reconsider some conventional views about technology, labor, and value in the information economy?[161]

Silicon Valley's top managers are well educated and technically skilled, but they are not great sages. They hide behind corporate operations so covert that their actual contributions are hard to assess, and it's hard not to wonder whether other firms or other individuals might make more constructive use of their data than they do. If not, why all the secrecy? Certainly they are beneficiaries of what is for them a wonderfully virtuous cycle. Thanks to the ingenuity and luck of company founders, they have acquired an audience. This allows them to offer data-driven targeting to advertisers, with whose handsome payments they can buy content, apps, and other enticements (the fruits of *other* people's ingenuity) that draw a bigger audience still, and so on. The well-realized technological vision that attracts the initial user base deserves recompense. But it does not entitle present corporate leaders to endlessly leverage past success into future dominance. What Thomas Piketty said of unlimited capital accumulation applies as well to untrammeled tech giants: "the past devours the future."[162]

The data advantage of the Silicon Valley giants may owe as much to fortuitous timing as to anything inherent in the firms themselves. Social theorist David Grewal has explained the "network power" of English as a lingua franca; it's not "better" than other languages; it's not easier to learn, or any more expressive. It just happened to be the language of an imperial power during an important period of globalization, and that of the world's dominant economic power from 1945 on. So it serves well now as a common standard for the communications of far flung elites. To have been prominent at a critical point in Internet development was a similar piece of luck. Google or Facebook were once in the right place at the right time. It's not clear whether they are still better than anyone else at online data science, or whether their prominence is such that they've become the permanent "default."

We also have to ask whether data *science* is still key here, or just the data itself. When intermediaries like Google and Facebook leverage their enormous databases of personalized information to target advertising, how much value do they add in the process? This is a matter of some dispute. Every so often we see an old-style advertising genius come up with a brilliant angle for introducing a new product to an unfamiliar audience. But that's not what Google and Facebook do. The frenzy of ad-matching described in books like

Joseph Turow's *The Daily You* is not a triumph of creative ingenuity.[163] Much depends on a store of personal and demographic information: who has the best list of single white women between 25 and 35; or wealthy, exurban gun-owning households. The matching game may simply rest on a catalog of crude correlations: who has the biggest set of past data on what X group of people (say, fathers under 30) does when Y appears (say, a Mother's Day ad for flowers). Some algorithmic expertise may be needed to infer telling characteristics from the websurfing habits of a particular IP address. But in some ways, the new media giants, for all their glamour, are glorified phone books, connecting message senders with message receivers. They just present businesses with a yellow pages of *people*, organized into audiences.

For all these reasons, it's time to recast the black box search culture as an occasion for skepticism, not for deference, adulation, or more fawning tech press profiles. But even though a more realistic assessment of the relative contributions of the search giants and the content makers, and the diversion of a fairer share of intermediary revenues to the latter, are necessary first steps toward a better online landscape, they are only first steps. There are other reasons to beware the concentration of so much power and money into so few hands, and they are not all economic.[164] They include the importance of media diversity, of independent gatekeepers, and of "distribution of communicative power and opportunities among private actors."[165] A series of laws passed over the course of the twentieth century ensures some basic ground rules for the communications infrastructure, but the new information environment raises new challenges at every turn.

Consider Google's breathtaking aspiration to scan millions of books, many still under copyright, into a searchable index of unprecedented proportions. Google Book Search has provoked storms of public controversy and private litigation.[166] The plan raises countless questions about fair compensation and transparent organization. The most highly publicized aspect of the debate centers on the rival property rights of Google and the owners of the copyrights of the books it wishes to scan and index.[167] But there are others just as important.

Journalistic narratives largely portray the Book Search project as an unalloyed advance in public access to knowledge, and Google has indeed established alliances with some of the leading libraries of the world. Its 2013 fair use victory also paves the way (in principle) for rival book search engines to arise. But here, again, competition may be illusory: it's hard to see the rationale (or investor or public enthusiasm) for subjecting millions of volumes (many of them delicate) to another round of scanning. Once again, Google reigns by default. The question now is whether its dictatorship will be benign.

Does Google intend Book Search to promote widespread public access, or is it envisioning finely tiered access to content, granted (and withheld) in opaque ways?[168] Will Google grant open access to search results on its platform, so experts in library science and information retrieval can understand (and critique) its orderings of results?[169] Finally, where will the profits go from this immense cooperative project? Will they be distributed fairly among contributors, or will this be another instance in which the aggregator of content captures an unfair share of revenues from well-established dynamics of content digitization? If the Internet is to prosper, *all* who provide content—its critical source of value—must share in the riches now enjoyed mainly by the megafirms that organize it.[170] And to the extent that Google, Amazon, or any other major search engine limits access to an index of books, its archiving projects are suspect, whatever public-spirited slogans it may adduce in defense of them.[171]

Philosopher Iris Murdoch once said, "Man is a creature who makes pictures of himself and then comes to resemble the picture. This is the process which moral philosophy must attempt to describe and analyse."[172] The large Internet firms make pictures of us and our world and enforce the resemblances between them. But they downplay the moral implications of their work, and the legal ones, too. In the next section, I will look back to earlier times when robust regulation was still being brought to bear on these processes.

## Search and Control

What if one of the big electric companies bought out Whirlpool and thereafter doubled its electricity rates for anyone using a different brand of refrigerator or washing machine?[173] I imagine there would be mass protest and a slew of lawsuits. The very possibility seems antique, the fever dream of a robber baron. But in the digital realm, monopolistic cable firms are angling to impose a similar arrangement: to make Internet access cheap if paired with their own content, and pricier if used to access others' work. Similarly, firms like Google and Amazon are in prime position to make money off both sides of a two-sided market: monetizing our data and purchases, while promoting to us their own products and services, or those of "partners" who let the larger platform share in their profits.

That's one reason we need to look back to the legal principles that animated Populists and Progressives in response to America's first Gilded Age. The great Internet companies and the physical networks that enable them are not the first private enterprises to achieve near monopolistic power over a key service, and to leverage that power into windfall profits and influence.[174] It happened in the nineteenth century with railroads and telegraphs.[175] Like today's search and cable companies, those firms controlled essential junctions of an emerging economic order. They were private businesses, but they controlled vital resources and enjoyed a power similar to that of a public authority.

Social, political, and legal conflicts arose around the exercise of this power, and demands to restrain it mounted. The most common and important grievances against these companies had to do with "discrimination," meaning both inequitable and unequal treatment of individuals, and complete refusals to serve.[176]

Litigants turned first to the ancient section of the common law that governed bridges, innkeepers, and other common carriers, and developed it into a comprehensive framework for governing the new entities that corporate industrialism had produced.[177] In a second stage, when court-based supervision alone proved insufficient, a statutory and administrative framework for regulation was gradually created. This became the foundation of the modern regulatory system, which over generations has established well-tested guidelines about how essential utilities can use their power.[178]

The telephone company, for instance, cannot oblige a business to pay rising shares of its revenue for service lest it be cut off. Telephone rates (or "tariffs") have to be publicly posted, and are often regulated. Utility firms may not discriminate: universal service rules keep carriers from connecting only to lucrative urban areas and ignoring others. This complex regulatory history profoundly shaped the U.S. communication landscape. The requirement that tariffs be fair and nondiscriminatory balanced the carriers' drive for profit against customers' need to be protected against exclusion or exploitation by a "must-have" service.[179] The requirement that networks include everyone established a level playing field among the different regions of the United States. And there are strict limits on the degree to which these essential companies can use their privileged access to communications for their own commercial advantage.[180]

Every time a new kind of infrastructure becomes critical to everyday life, regulators are challenged to strike the fairest balance they can between public and private good. It's time to situate the giants of Internet search and networking in this tradition. Time-honored principles underlie the regulatory framework of our other utilities.

Admittedly, these are complex issues. Even if we had a Federal Search Commission, we couldn't just transfer the current Federal Communications Commission Rules over to it.[181] A well-established rubric of accountability like the one for carriers does not yet exist for search technology. But the carriers' rules did not spring forth, fully formed, like Athena from the head of Zeus. They were crafted over decades, and we should commit ourselves to a similar project in the world of search.

One of the most enduring principles of communications regulation has been transparency. That's needed now more than ever. In the instantaneous and fluid world of apps and search engines, it's much harder to tell what actually goes on behind the scenes. Discrimination used to be as simple as flipping a switch and denying access to a network; everybody knew it was happening, and when, and where. But an ISP or search engine can slow down transmission speed or reduce a website's ranking in nearly undetectable ways.[182] Moreover, there are many points of control for both desktop and mobile Internet users.[183] Even when something suspicious is happening, it's easy for one player to shift responsibility to others.

Many communications mavens are ready to throw up their hands at the complexity, and hope that market pressures and bad press will deter bad behavior. But as we have seen, Big Data giants entrench their dominance over time.[184] They gain power in Washington and state capitals, too, and may well influence regulation in self-serving ways. It does not follow, however, that doing nothing is the preferable option. We need to revive regulation, not give up on it. Internet service providers and major platforms alike will be a major part of our informational environment for the foreseeable future. The normative concerns associated with their unique position of power are here to stay. A properly designed regulatory approach may do much to clarify and contain the situation; without one, will deteriorate.

## Content, Conduits, and Search:
## The Emerging Co-opetition

Once upon a time, we could imagine that scrappy Internet firms—Google among them—were doing battle on behalf of their users against old-line oligopolists like the record labels and cable companies. Silicon Valley firms fought for net neutrality and opened up troves of content. Business analysts hoped Google might even expand into "dark fiber" nationwide, to shake up the moribund Internet service market. But as Google has consolidated its own power, it is now more inclined to make common cause with these older giants than to resist them.[185] The implications are sobering. Competition is muted; cooperation accelerates; and the hoped-for dynamism of Internet economics is congealing into a static combination of the two, "co-opetition."[186]

*Strange Bedfellows.* The lifecycle of YouTube is a relatively straightforward example. Founded by a pair of young entrepreneurs, it grew explosively in the mid-2000s as a cornucopia of unauthorized videos: old films that had been MIA for decades; obscure gems of musical performance; early animations; political speeches. (Cats, too.)

Users uploaded millions of hours of their own content, and community members helped each other organize the material, developing a tagging "folksonomy" so clever that searchers could find even the most obscure content.[187]

The sale of YouTube to Google for over a billion dollars in 2006 was cheered as another of the great tech success stories. But YouTube was not universally adored. To many leading copyrightholders, it was an unrepentant enabler of infringement.

The Digital Millennium Copyright Act (DMCA) of 1998, while increasing the penalties for copyright infringement on the Internet, had immunized some providers of online services from direct responsibility for the content posted by their users. YouTube thus maintained that it was as innocent of infringement as, say, the phone company would be if one of its customers played a copyrighted recording over its lines. But the DMCA also suggested that a video search engine did have some responsibility for screening out pirated content. For example, an "information location service" could be liable for *secondary*, if not direct, copyright infringement if it ignored obvious red flags indicating illicit behavior.[188] And so the battle was joined.

Clearly, an account advertising "!!!Bootleg Movie Releases!!!" would be one of those obvious red flags. But what about a music video that is unavailable even to would-be purchasers? Or a three-minute clip from a two-hour film? These are issues that can be extensively litigated, and rulings on "fair uses" of copyrighted material come down on both sides.

Thus major content owners tolerate many questionably legal uses, but try to crack down on users who engage in many unauthorized downloads and uploads.[189] That uneasy truce sparked a business opportunity: a video or music search engine could grab a mass audience, as long most of its users only uploaded a few pieces of infringing content. YouTube grew to prominence on the back of the pirated content of millions of users. But as it consolidated its position as the dominant video search engine online, it began cleaning up its act.[190] It struck deals with major labels and independent artists, sharing ad revenue with them based in part on how many viewers and listeners they attracted. We can only know "in part" what the revenue share is, because Google keeps the terms of the contracts strictly under wraps.[191] But the basic industrial organization is pretty clear: like cable companies positioning themselves between subscribers and content providers, Google wants YouTube to be a broker, taking its cut of the ad revenue ultimately generated by the content it hosts.[192] And that ambition is reflected in its search results.

The recording industry has been targeting music-sharing sites for years.[193] Infringers pop up at a new address each time an old one is seized, a digital game of whack-a-mole. Content owners complained for years about Google's role in enabling infringement, especially after it bought YouTube. The search giant took its usual position with regard to most complaints: not our problem. Copyright holders could litigate against the offending sites themselves, but Google would not do more work than the DMCA required it to. This did not satisfy the copyright holders, who continued to demand that important search engines address the problem by automating punishment of the worst intellectual property scofflaws.[194]

In 2012, Google creatively capitulated to this demand. A comprehensive search engine makes it a cinch to find pirated materials— unless, of course, the search engine is trying to conceal them. Google decided to do so, agreeing to adjust its algorithm and systematically demote sites that collect multiple complaints of copyright infringement. Google's famously stubborn engineers acceded to Hollywood's demands.[195] Now that it is making serious money from copyrighted content on YouTube, it has an interest in assuring compensation for viewings.[196] It also has a brand (worth tens of billions of dollars, by some Wall Street estimates) and a business model to protect. Copyright-holders brought ad revenue to YouTube; Google had to return the favor with some takedowns of pirate havens and demotions of alleged infringers.[197]

In its public statements, Google denied that demoting sites for copyright infringement was a significant departure from existing policy. Like everything else at Google, it was framed as just another way of making results better.[198] But while it certainly did make for a change in user experience, the change was not, in many users' views, an improvement. Furthermore, Google justice was swift, secret, and arbitrary. Due process did not apply. Once a critical mass of copyright complaints accrued against a site, it just started to sink in the rankings.[199] Google didn't de-index it. But in an information environment where searches often result in thousands of results, being demoted to the ninety-ninth page of listings is tantamount to the same thing. And the demoted site might not even know that it had been demoted. If it looked for itself from its own IP address it might well appear near the top of the results, its own personalized signals for salience having locally overwhelmed the signals for demotion.

Google's draconian antipiracy practices also raised questions about collateral damage. For example, what happens if a site (whose intention is not infringement) accidentally or incidentally posts pirated material and loses prominence for that reason?[200]

Google's decision to serve as enforcer for the holders of intellectual property rights left unanswered many questions that are sure to arise about the laws of its secret "Googlement." But if its behavior in the past is any guide, it will address them behind closed doors. The public won't be privy to the considerations raised, the monetary interests involved, or the favors cut for one group or another. And as we'll all see the results through our own personalized search lenses, it will be well-nigh impossible for us to notice that a decision was even made, let alone assess the reasons or the effects.[201]

*Who Can Afford to Publish?* The power of the old media is waning. Traditional journalism is in crisis.[202] Some predict that investigative reporting will be sustainable only as a charity.[203] Broadcast media are in less serious financial trouble, but their political and cultural clout is declining, and their profit margins are threatened.[204] Broadcast radio too is culturally less relevant as younger listeners look online for music.[205]

All of these developments coincide with—and have in part been caused by—the rise of new media, which feature online video, text, and music. Users have abandoned old *sources* of content for new ways of *searching* for it. The huge user bases that result mean that both content providers and advertisers want to seize places at the top of Google's (or Facebook's or Apple's) users' front pages.[206] Not coincidentally, Google's U.S. advertising revenue is now greater than that of *all* newspapers.[207] If current trends continue, it will soon be larger than both newspaper and magazines combined. Current valuations of Facebook suggest it will capture 10 percent of global ad revenue by 2020.

Some web-based publishers feel empowered to use search engines and social networks to build audiences that would never have been possible in the analog world.[208] But others feel that the search intermediaries have done them ill. Microtargeted advertising by companies like Google has taken an ever-increasing share of the revenue that used to be spent directly at their sites. Google's tense relationship with many web-based political publications reveals these trends. In a provocative post titled "Has Google Destroyed the 4th Estate?," prominent progressive blogger Jane Hamsher attributes the decline of the fortunes of sites like hers to Google's rise to preeminence in key advertising markets. A *Washington Post* story confirmed that both Google and AOL played hardball during the election of 2012, negotiating portions of political campaign ad revenue that would have gone directly to sites like Hamsher's Firedoglake in past years. The ad buyers argued that it's not space on paper or pixels on a website that matters to them, but *audiences;* that's what they were looking to buy. In other words, the context of the advertisement was mere background: what really mattered was data on who was looking at the content, and Google had far more of that than anyone else. Google could connect advertisers to a precise demographic, and in an era of campaigns based on Big Data, that secret, proprietary information was the vital edge political campaigns needed.[209]

Though media is suffering now, campaigns themselves should also beware. Saving a bit now by avoiding wasted advertising may lead to huge costs down the road if data holdings further consolidate and become the key to finding undecided voters. The *Citizens United* decision is an open invitation to tech firms to escalate the prices they charge for audiences, as billionaire donors are eager to foot the bill.

Recall again Vaidhyanathan's title, *The Googlization of Everything.* For Big Data buffs, "Googlization" is ultimately a hopeful process: systematic use of analytics to squeeze maximum effectiveness out of any decision; maximum relevance from any search;

maximum risk-adjusted return from any investment. To para-phrase Jeff Jarvis, today's businesses should ask themselves, "What would Google do?" But the answer to that question is all too clear: use their data to outflank competitors and extract maximum prof-its from their customers.[210]

"Googlization" has an even darker meaning, too: that whole indus-tries stand to be taken over by Google itself.[211] Walmart (Walmart!) has said that it considers Google one of its most formidable com-petitors. Even Apple's greatest misstep—forcing Google off its iOS in favor of an incomplete and ill-conceived maps app of its own—was an (unsuccessful) attempt to compete with Google for the loca-tional data that Google's map services were collecting.[212] And what does "Googlization" mean to traditional publishers, booksellers, and educators, who don't have Google's opportunity to match individu-als to "optimal" sources of information based on their past predilec-tions, demonstrated abilities, and willingness to pay? That Silicon Valley engineers and managers are in charge of their fortunes.

Of course, Google isn't the only press baron on the horizon; Am-azonification, Facebookization, and Twitterification also beckon. Some will further hollow out once-hallowed properties. Others will invest, as venture capitalist Marc Andreessen recommends. Though he strikes fear into publishers, Amazon's Jeff Bezos has not yet re-duced writers at his newspaper (the *Washington Post*) to the status of Mechanical Turkers or warehouse pickers.[213] But we should not as-sume media independence as tech firms swallow more of the revenue that might have once gone to journalists. After Amazon inked a $600 million deal to provide the CIA with cloud computing services, 30,000 people petitioned the *Post* with the message "*Washington Post:* Readers Deserve Full Disclosure in Coverage of CIA."[214] Such inquiries will only become more common as Washington and Silicon Valley de-velop more partnerships for information dominance.

Of course, we can see why large firms want to keep their industry (and government) alliances under wraps. People want to feel like there is *someone* looking out for them. Google's decision to join forces with content industry leaders (regarding piracy) disappointed many of its users.[215] They had thought of Google as *their* agent, pushing for users' rights and a neutral, technical ordering of the

Internet against the usual corporate interests' efforts to exploit it. But as Google dominates more of the search space, and as its investors' demands remain pressing, its business focus has shifted from the need to *attract more users* to the need to *monetize what the viewers see*. Google found itself needing more compelling content, and that content would only materialize for a price.[216]

These are trust issues. In a classic example of what philosopher Langdon Winner called "technological somnambulism,"[217] we have given the search sector an almost unimaginable power to determine what we see, where we spend, how we perceive. Top legal scholars have already analogized the power relationships in virtual worlds and cloud computing to medieval feudalism.[218] Technological advance goes hand-in-hand with politico-economic regression.

## Toward a Digital New Deal

In the late 1990s, tech enthusiasts looked to search engines as an extraordinary democratization of the Internet. They permitted content creators from all over the world to reach far-flung audiences. Web 2.0 promised even more "democratization" by enabling self-organization of virtual communities. But recent commercial history suggests a different—even an opposite—effect. The very power that brought clarity and cooperation to the chaotic online world also spawns murketing, unfair competition, and kaleidoscopic distortions of reality.[219]

The first step toward reform is realizing the scope of the problem. Tim Wu, a prominent cyberlawyer and one of the intellectual architects of network neutrality, helps contextualize today's Internet disputes in a larger time frame. In his 2010 book *The Master Switch*, he animates a history of "industrial wars" over communications with strong moral judgments about the fairness or impropriety of the business strategies he investigates. The book is a tour de force of narrative. But it falls short, prescriptively. Wu acknowledges the coercive private power of an Apple or a Google but concludes that norms now restrain it: "Rare is the firm willing to assert an intention and a right to dominate layers of the information industry beyond its core business." However true that was then, it's outdated now: Google wants to expand to be a social network and military robot company; Facebook is not just a social network, but a kingmaker in online media; Amazon disrupts industry after industry. But Wu focuses more on the cultural and political impact of information-age giants than on the grubby economics that drives this rapid-scale expansion.[220]

I can understand why—people are far more interested in the outsized personalities of Silicon Valley than the complex money grabs that grant them their platforms. But we can't hope to reform the information economy without fundamentally changing the incentives at its core. Wu's postmaterialism would have been a good fit for the roaring nineties, when a rising tide of Internet firm profits seemed to be lifting many parts of the economy. But the economic crisis that has overtaken the United States since 2008 makes our time in many ways more similar to Franklin Roosevelt's era than Bill Clinton's. A small cadre of the lucky, the talented, and the ruthless are taking an enormous share of the revenues generated by new Internet technologies. They keep their methods strictly proprietary while reaping huge returns from content put out in the open by others.[221] Like the megafirms and CEOs that the New Deal helped bring to heel, the leaders of our largest tech firms have been very quick to misequate personal enrichment with the public good.

It is time to bring the substance and style of that era back into a progressive political economy of technology. In the first half of the twentieth century, the American lawyer, economist, and educator Robert Lee Hale studied the dominant firms of his day. Given their pervasive influence, he argued that personal freedom depended on responsible corporate conduct.[222] His theories were influential among FDR's advisers as they faced the economic catastrophe of the 1930s. Hale and Wu have both analyzed the "private coercive power" of large companies. But there are major differences between Hale's *Freedom through Law* and Wu's *The Master Switch*, and they speak volumes about changes in the American political climate over the past six decades.

Hale's work chronicles the gradual victory of democratic constraint over arbitrary and exploitative business practices. Hale discussed the "principles for determining how the wealth of the community should be distributed," patiently detailing the case law of ratemaking and taxation through the mid-twentieth century. He also made it clear that government couldn't just sit idly by as a "neutral party," in order to "avoid picking winners" in a time of technological change. If it failed to do so, there were other forces—such as finance—more than willing to step in and direct the economy. And we now see the results: monopolistic and manipulative behavior that has left many wary of a sector they once adored.

The search sector's profiteering is an effort to meet the demands of investors. Search firms may rank and rate the reputation companies that rank and rate people; but even search firms have to worry about how *they* are being rated by Wall Street. They can't keep swallowing up rivals unless investors keep betting on their enduring dominance. Opaque aspects of finance keep the leading Internet firms on their toes as surely as the Internet firms' mysterious ranking mechanisms keep everyone else alert and worried about any possible loss of standing. It is therefore to this final and most forceful aspect of the new political economy—finance—that we now turn our attention.

# 4

# FINANCE'S ALGORITHMS: THE
# EMPEROR'S NEW CODES

IN 2004, the Cato Institute awarded Peruvian economist Hernando de Soto the $500,000 Milton Friedman Prize for Advancing Liberty. Despite two assassination attempts by communists, de Soto had tirelessly proselytized market solutions for Peru's poor. American leaders loved his message, since he credited U.S. prosperity to rock solid financial markets and private property protections.[1]

By 2011, de Soto was lambasting the American economic system. He said that the financial crisis revealed a "staggering lack of knowledge" about "who owned and owed" in the United States. The "public memory systems" that America had exported to countries like Peru (such as "registries, titles, balance sheets, and statements of account") had become utterly unreliable at home. Incompetence and illegality clouded property records. Terms and conditions of billion-dollar deals were hidden. Behind the glass towers and computer networks of American finance lay ramshackle institutions and a declining respect for the rule of law.[2]

De Soto identified trends that continue to this day. Insiders craft deals that shift risk to unwitting investors and taxpayers while claiming enormous fees and bonuses for themselves. The strategies for hiding the risk are legion, ranging from murky accounting to proprietary models. From mortgage brokers to CEOs, finance's many workers rely on opaque complexity to generate profits. But much of the opacity is neither natural nor inevitable. Rather, it prevails in many critical transactions in order to give privileged insiders an advantage over their clients, regulators, and risk managers.[3]

Over the past few decades, more decisions in the finance sector have been computerized.[4] You would think that information technology would be making finance *clearer*, rather than more opaque. Algorithms were supposed to rationalize finance, replacing gut instinct and bias with sound decision frameworks. For example, credit scoring was to replace the biases and whims of local mortgage officers with expert, neutral, and consistent allocations of credit. But they've led to arbitrary assessments that can cost a family tens of thousands of dollars merely for making one late payment.[5] On the macro level, mortgage-backed securities (MBSes) promised to manage risk. But we all know about the financial crisis that sparked by their crash in 2007–2008. Cyborg finance executes complex trades faster than ever, but also delivers unfair advantages to well-positioned cliques.[6]

Many of my examples will be drawn from the financial crisis years, but no one should assume misuses of algorithms are unique to that time period. Bubbles and bad deals have recurred with increasing frequency in the U.S. financial system over the past few decades. Usually, small scams and hidden fees are scarcely contested or illuminated. But when very important investors lose vast sums—as they did from 2007 to 2009—litigation mushrooms, discovery ensues, and we get a peek into the darker recesses of finance's black box.

I am not going to go into the details of the crash and crisis here. That material is readily available elsewhere.[7] What I will do is describe the law and technology that fed them. My illustrations are not comprehensive, but they illustrate larger, troubling tendencies in financial markets. Moreover, I hope you'll agree by the end of the chapter that many involve "never events"—grotesque wastes of resources that should not be possible in a minimally functional financial system. In health care, a "never event" is an obvious, grave error—like a wrong-leg amputation or a sponge left in during surgery. Finance has "never events" aplenty—but, unlike the health sector, it has not taken this problem seriously.

Secret algorithms—obscured by a triple layer of technical complexity, secrecy, and "economic espionage" laws that can land would-be whistle-blowers in prison—still prevent us from understanding what is truly going on in many major financial firms. Algorithmic methods have supercharged classic forms of self-dealing. So-called "technologies of risk management" bedazzled gatekeepers both inside and outside the firm. The very software code that was supposed to render finance more of a science ended up being mere cover for speculation—or worse. Moreover, despite well-intentioned reform like the Dodd-Frank Act, many of the same black boxes persist to this day.[8]

This chapter tours two levels of black box finance: obfuscation in the service of illegality, and opacity resulting from complexity. Both create ample opportunities for self-serving or reckless behavior among finance's insiders. Many contemporary securities are complex; a firm is likely to model its value (as one might model the likely productivity of a worker, or the relevance of a website) on the basis of complex, secret calculations.[9] When those models are based on faulty, incomplete, or fraudulent data, instability and conflict result.

## Early Warning Signs

Banks effectively borrow from depositors and re-lend their funds out to others. A simple version of this relationship illuminates the risks involved. Your deposit in a savings account is effectively a loan to the bank in which you've deposited those funds. You probably get very low interest payments, but on the plus side, you can withdraw the funds at any time. The bank doesn't know exactly when you'll decide to do so—but it can estimate when that might happen. Let's say you are earning 3 percent in interest. If it is *certain* you won't withdraw the funds, and the bank can lend those funds out to someone else at a 6 percent rate for one year, and the bank is *certain* that person will repay, it's guaranteed a risk-free return of 3 percent per year. As the old saying goes, banking can be a 3-6-3 business: borrow at 3 percent, lend at 6 percent, hit the golf course at 3:00 p.m.

But certainty is more easily modeled than achieved. If a critical mass of depositors demands their money back immediately, a bank that lends unwisely could be overwhelmed. That happened at thousands of banks in the early 1930s, both reflecting and accelerating America's worst economic crisis. Unregulated banks are inherently unstable.

After the Great Depression, regulators decreed a firewall between depository institutions (which were supposed to invest very cautiously) and more freewheeling investment banks. A Federal Deposit Insurance Corporation (FDIC) was established to protect ordinary bank account holders.[10] Investment banks' customers weren't as protected, but could at least take comfort in the structure of the institution: the owners (partners) had their own capital on the line in case the bank failed. The leading financial institutions were smaller, too, and their balance sheets were easier for regulators to monitor and understand.

The post-Depression banking system was much more stable than what came before, but it ended up a victim of its own success. Having deregulated airlines, trucking, and other industries, a powerful laissez-faire movement questioned why banks still needed administrative training wheels. Investment banks also started "going public"—as corporations, not partnerships. This organizational change allowed management to shield its own fortunes from whatever losses the bank might incur.[11] Becoming a publicly traded company made some aspects of their books more open. However, it also created pressure to maintain the outward appearance of constant, steady growth.[12]

Given the business cycle and the natural instability of demand and supply, constant growth is an elusive target. Finance firms promised inventive ways to "smooth away" the risks from, say, interest rate hikes or volatile energy prices. Futures trading expanded as the less regulated world of "swaps" of risk. The 1990s witnessed the rapid growth of investment contracts called derivatives.[13] For example, the insurance company AIG established a Financial Products (FP) division to offer firms "interest rate protection": in exchange for a fee, AIGFP would pay in case rates rose or fell by a certain amount. Some of these "swaps" of risk lasted thirty years or more. The head of AIGFP kept these risks so hidden, and the CEO of the parent company grew so concerned about them, that AIG eventually hired a "covert operation of auditors, derivatives experts and other professionals to infiltrate" its own secretive unit.[14] A consulting firm estimated AIG lost $90 million on the bets.[15] (AIG went on to lose vastly more on risky bets in 2008, intensifying the financial crisis.)

While the contracts were marketed as a way to hedge risks, they could also create enormous losses. For example, in 1994, Orange County, California, became the largest municipality in U.S. history to go bankrupt after its treasurer lost $1.7 billion of its $7.4 billion investment portfolio in derivative bets.[16] (And the problem endures: cities to this day are spending enormous sums on bad derivative bets.) Former trader Frank Partnoy's book *F.I.A.S.C.O.* portrayed bankers who laughed about "ripping the face off" unsuspecting clients. Repeated crises provoked liberal Democrats in the House of Representatives to investigate these "products" in the early 1990s, but their legislative proposals were quickly blocked.[17]

The chair of the U.S. Commodity Futures Trading Commission (CFTC), Brooksley Born, renewed the call for more regulatory scrutiny of such transactions in 1997. She warned Congress that their rapid growth could menace "our economy without any federal agency knowing about it."[18] Born floated a "concept release," an agency document announcing the need for study of a given market practice. Note that Born had not proposed any specific regulation at the time— she was merely prodding agencies to learn more about this new and growing aspect of Wall Street trading. Then-assistant Treasury secretary Lawrence Summers quickly put the kibosh on her. He claimed, "I have thirteen bankers in my office, and they say if you go forward with this, you will cause the worst financial crisis since World War II."[19] Born backed down.

Many factors contributed to the deregulation of finance. Power and ideology matter: banks invested massively in lobbying, and the Reagan era primed politicians to see government as less a protector of markets than a pesky problem. Insiders shuttled between Washington and Wall Street. As information technology improved, lobbyists could tell a seductive story: regulators were no longer necessary. Sophisticated investors could vet their purchases.[20] Computer models could identify and mitigate risk. But the replacement of regulation by automation turned out to be as fanciful as flying cars or space colonization.

## Machine Dreams

Consider the role of computer models in a critical part of the housing crisis: mortgage-backed securities. While investors may not be interested in any one particular mortgagor's stream of payments, an aggregation of such payments can be marketed as a far more stable income source (or security) than, say, any one loan. Think, for instance, of the stream of payments coming out of a small city. It might seem risky to give any one household a loan; the breadwinner might fall ill, they might declare bankruptcy, they may hit the lottery and pay off the loan tomorrow (denying the investor a steady stream of interest payments). It's hard to predict what will happen to any given family. But statistical models can much better predict the likelihood of defaults happening in, say, a group of 1,000 families. They "know" that, in the data used, rarely do, say, more than thirty in a 1,000 borrowers default. This statistical analysis, programmed in proprietary software, was one "green light" for massive investments in the mortgage market.[21]

That sounds simple, but as finance automation took off, such deals tended to get hedged around by contingencies, for instance about possible refinancings or defaults. Furthermore, mortgage-backed securities were combined into ever larger and more diverse groupings.[22]

Despite their complexity, groupings of mortgage obligations could be marketed as a far more stable source of income (or security) than any single one. That analysis was a green light for the massive investments in the mortgage market. It was also a black box, programmed in proprietary software, with the details left to the quants and the computers.

For example, a proprietary "pricing tool" like INTEXcalc™, which could cost over $1.4 million a year to license,[23] offered a "computerized 'library' of the parameters of the underlying asset pools and the cash flow rules of more than 20,000 deals."[24] INTEXcalc™ analyzed scenarios "with control of interest rates, prepayments, defaults, delinquencies, loan modifications, triggers, deal specific variables, etc." Donald MacKenzie (an economic sociologist) noted how tractable such systems can make even extreme complexity seem.

A friendly banker showed me Intex in action. He chose a particular mortgage-backed security, entered its price and a figure for each of prepayment speed, default rate, and loss severity. In less than 30 seconds, back came not just the yield of the security, but the month-by-month future interest payments and principal repayments, including whether and when shortfalls and losses would be incurred.

"The psychological effect was striking," MacKenzie went on. "For the first time, I felt I could understand mortgage-backed securities. Of course, my new-found confidence was spurious. The reliability of Intex's output depends entirely on the validity of the user's assumptions."[25] But the alternative to the thirty-second computerized report was parsing "hundreds of pages of impenetrable legal prose," and presumably a great deal of calculation. The attraction of the black box isn't hard to understand. It promotes "automation bias," an assumption that a machine-driven, software-enabled system is going to offer better results than human judgment. And when the stakes are high enough, automation bias can degenerate into wishful thinking or worse: opportunistic misuse of models to validate sharp business practices.[26]

Let's grant for the sake of argument that under ideal circumstances, black boxes that are carefully programmed and responsibly used will work as they're supposed to, saving a lot of time, effort, and opportunity for error. But as Google knows all too well, as soon as there's a system, somebody will try to game it. What happens then?

## The Subprime Art Department

During the height of the housing bubble, the biggest subprime lender (Ameriquest) paraded its slogan, "Proud sponsor of the American dream," in countless television advertisements. It was less forthcoming about hidden fees embedded in loans. Nor did its ads feature its subprime boiler rooms, where salespeople equipped with white-out, exacto knives, and scotch tape could manipulate loan applications. If an applicant had a low income, a broker could simply forge a few zeroes on their paystubs or tax forms. Salespeople called one room where this occurred the "Art Department." The general attitude was summed up in an e-mail from one Ameriquest manager: "We are all here to make as much fucking money as possible. Bottom line. Nothing else matters."[27]

Top company managers may have suspected that frontline workers were pasting in higher figures from other W-2s that happened to be lying around. But controls were lax enough that they could plausibly deny specific knowledge of pervasive fraud.[28] Underwriting standards declined as convenient wishful thinking spread first through mortgage brokers, and then through banks. Assuming that housing prices could never decline, lenders could even justify no-income, no-job, no-asset (NINJA) loans. Even if the borrower turned out to be a deadbeat, the theory went, foreclosure would recapture an asset worth at least as much as the loan amount.[29]

Deceptive sales practices were ubiquitous. A parade of foreclosed upon homeowners has told familiar stories to judges, advocates, and the press. Brokers didn't disclose the real terms of the loan. Interest rates were higher in actuality than they appeared in documentation. Loans that were called fixed were in fact adjustable-rate, with payments spiking after two or three years. In case after case, the real costs were hidden or systematically understated. And the people who were supposed to be assessing the quality of securities built out of such loans were using models that blinded them to what was going on.[30]

## Statistical Legitimacy—The Failure of the Rating Agencies

It's no surprise that financial institutions jumped with both feet at the chance to broker deals between the sellers and buyers of structured securities like MBSes (and combinations of MBSes, often called collateralized debt obligations [CDOs]). They made money no matter what happened to the securities they sold. But why did buyers purchase them so readily? Why did the government not counsel caution? They were novel, untested, and complex in ways that might have made investors very nervous. Yet rating agencies managed to offer a reassuring seal of approval—thanks to their own, even more deficient modeling.[31]

There's a delicate balance between government and the market in America's investment landscape. The Securities and Exchange Commission (created during the Great Depression) wants to assure that investors understand how much risk they are taking on,[32] but the government itself does not want to be in the business of rating and ranking investments.[33] So the SEC registers private, *for-profit* credit rating agencies (CRAs) to make such judgments by designating them as Nationally Recognized Statistical Rating Organizations (NRSROs).[34] The CRAs Moody's, Fitch, and Standard & Poor's (S&P) are the leading NRSROs.[35] They rate investments from the super safe (AAA) to the more speculative, and even—less politely—junk.[36]

This "outsourcing" of regulation saved the government money and headaches as long as the CRAs maintained integrity and competence.[37] But both gradually eroded over time, accelerated by their need to compete for the business of the very entities they were rating.[38] When bankers crafting mortgage-backed securities began shopping around for the most pliable rater, the agencies' commitment to objective statistical analysis began to show some strain.[39] Before 2005, an AAA rating was a prized asset; only about 1 percent of AAA-rated investments incurred a default.[40] But a Senate report in 2011 found that "90% of the AAA ratings given to subprime residential mortgage-backed securities originated in 2006 and 2007 were later downgraded by the credit rating agencies to junk status."[41]

Rating agencies furiously competed to rate the flood of securities generated during the housing bubble. Like runaway "grade inflation" that cheapens straight A report cards, rating inflation has eroded the meaning (if not the value) of AAA ratings. There were plenty of convenient rationales at hand: the U.S. economy was remarkably strong, population rise meant housing prices could only go up, computer-driven productivity would lift all incomes.[42] The credit raters were soon in a race to the bottom in laxity. As sociologist Will Davies observes, those "tasked with *representing, measuring and judging* capitalist activity are also seeking to *profit from*" it, and there is little to connect probity in the former activities to prospering in the present.[43]

Their crudity eventually captured media attention, as various "gotcha" statements emerged. "Let's hope we are all wealthy and retired by the time this house of cards falters," one internal e-mail said. "It could be structured by cows and we would rate it," someone else quipped in an instant message.[44] The statements are entertaining, and they don't cover rating agency workers with glory. But it would be a mistake to pin the problem on flippant "bad apples" or unrepentant scammers. There are far bigger problems in finance than careless individuals—issues like statistical validity and mathematical modeling, for instance. And that's where the black boxes come in.

Standard & Poor's, for instance, used a model known as the loan evaluation and estimate of loss system (LEVELS) to rate mortgage-backed securities. The basic idea behind the model was simple: in 1999, it was using a database of about 166,000 fixed-rate, prime mortgage loans to estimate the probability that certain types of loans would default. Like Google using past click-data to predict what advertising will work and what will bomb, S&P could compare proposed securities with the database to figure out how likely it was that a certain percentage of loans in them would fail to be repaid.

One question for a database like this is, How relevant is the past to the future? Google can access real-time data to tell it from moment to moment how well a search ranking or advertisement is drawing clicks. S&P was trying to project performance over *years*. It designated a Global Surveillance/Servicer Evaluations Group to watch how rated securities actually performed, but it certainly had nothing as granular or immediate as the Internet platforms' data troves. As lenders started making riskier loans, some analysts began to wonder how robust the predictions based on LEVELS would be. In response to these concerns, S&P acquired a much larger and more representative data set, including 642,000 residential mortgages. This data was available by 2002.

But as late as 2004, S&P was still using a version of LEVELS that only included the original 166,000 loans. According to a Justice Department (DOJ) complaint, S&P repeatedly delayed integrating the better data set into LEVELS in order to keep giving high ratings to mortgage-backed securities. The DOJ also contends that S&P improved the LEVELS model in a hedged way, supporting truthful judgments about the state of the market only to the extent that they wouldn't scare away business. The case is pending, and its outcome should shed light on practices at the heart of the crisis.

There are two black box dynamics here beyond the alleged fraud. To the extent that S&P publicly stated that it was updating its models, but privately delayed any obvious improvement, it was keeping investors in the dark. But who was in the dark at S&P? The company says in its own defense that it carefully considered changes to its model, suggesting there were disagreements within the company about what constituted good rating practices.[45] Do those disagreements include letting profitability influence rating models? How many people there knew what was going on? How many did (or did not) want to know?

## Silencing Dissent in the Corporation

There can be problems with models *and* with the data entered into them. In well-functioning organizations, dissenters can air their worries. But as the stories of failed whistle-blowers emerge postcrisis, it's clear that many managers were about as open to internal critique as the U.S. government was to the intelligence agency whistle-blowers who tried to call out illegal actions in the decade after 9/11.

Consider the fate of concerned workers at subprime lender Countrywide. During the housing bubble, its CEO, Angelo Mozilo, prospered. He ended up one of the most punished executives in the wake of the subprime meltdown, paying massive fines—but he still walked away with hundreds of millions of dollars and no jail time. Why the leniency? In part, because Countrywide was structured in ways that made it difficult for the top brass to know exactly what was going on. Or, to be more precise about the ambiguities here: authorities considered the abuses at the lower levels of the firm not quite obvious enough to demonstrate to a jury that a criminal level of fraud prevailed at the top. America was supposed to have solved this problem after Enron. In that scandal, CEO Ken Lay presided over a company engaged in massive accounting fraud. But his defense lawyers characterized him as sincerely clueless, unable to understand the machinations of underlings who were hiding billions of dollars of debt. Enron-era accounting scandals shook the public's faith in markets sufficiently that Congress passed the Sarbanes-Oxley Act (SOX), which required CEOs to stand by their companies' financial statements and to maintain "internal controls" and other safeguards to assure their accuracy.[46] But SOX is rarely enforced in criminal prosecutions, and its civil fines are not much of a deterrent.[47] Barely plausible models and pliable auditors let managers help CEOs paint misleading pictures of their companies' futures and deny that they're doing it.

We may never know to what extent executives engineered their own ignorance during the housing bubble. But some troubling hardball tactics are emerging. Eileen Foster, a one-time senior vice-president for risk management at Countrywide, believed that fraud there was "systemic" and "intentional." After she complained to the mortgage lender's Employee Relations Department, *it investigated her* for allegedly unprofessional conduct.[48] Things got even worse after Countrywide was purchased by Bank of America [BofA], Foster said:

> In 2007, I found various levels of management working to circumvent fraud detection and disguise document doctoring by high-producing loan officers. . . . Since then, I've found there were scores of whistleblowers inside Countrywide and then BofA. Trumped-up investigations were widely used to discredit us. The inner circle at both corporations operated like the mob: company staff, including attorneys, often worked to silence employees, using weapons like blacklisting, hush money and confidentiality agreements. The upper echelons at BofA attempted to buy my silence with more than $200,000; I refused.[49]

Foster complained to OSHA, and ultimately settled her case confidentially. But she does not see her story as evidence that the system is working:

> The federal government . . . has done little or nothing to protect whistleblowers. Over the last 10 years, the Department of

Labor has found merit *in less than 2% of over 1200* whistleblowers cases brought under the Sarbanes Oxley Act. The vast majority have been dismissed on legal technicalities without any investigation into the potential crimes being reported.[50]

In 2013, six other employees alleged that Bank of America continued its deceptions into the post-bubble era.[51] Another would-be whistle-blower, Richard Bowen at Citigroup, went from supervising 220 employees to supervising two after he expressed concerns about risks. Risk managers were also swept aside at Lehman.[52] Sherry Hunter, a manager at Citigroup, found herself out in the cold when she reported that her bank was "buying mortgages from outside lenders with doctored tax forms, phony appraisals and missing signatures."[53] Unlike many other employees with reservations, Hunter managed to navigate the complex requirements for whistle-blowing and won millions of dollars when the government sued Citi based on information she provided. But the barriers to launching such lawsuits are high, and we have no idea how many other less principled and persistent individuals have been cowed by the pressure to adopt deceptive practices favored by key managers.[54]

## Risks and Regulation

I've painted a dark picture of the finance sector so far: one where dubious data can enter the manipulable models of opportunistic traders answering to clueless CEOs. You would think that after repeated crises, from the S&L crimes of the late 1980s to the accounting scandals of the early 2000s, the finance sector would have cleaned house by 2008. But rather than *improving* internal processes at companies they could not fully understand (let alone control), financiers started *insuring against* bad outcomes. "Financial engineers" crafted "swaps" of risk,[55] encouraging quants (and regulators) to try to estimate it in ever more precise ways.[56] A credit default swap (CDS), for instance, transfers the risk of nonpayment to a third party, which promises to pay you (the first party) in case the debtor (the second party) does not.[57] This innovation was celebrated as a landmark of "price discovery," a day-by-day (or even second-by-second) tracking of exactly how likely an entity was to default.[58]

As with credit scores, the risk modeling here was deeply fallible, another misapplication of natural science methods to an essentially social science of finance. "Value at Risk" models purported to predict with at least 95 percent certainty how much a firm could lose if market prices changed. But the models had to assume the stability of certain kinds of human behavior, which could change in response to widespread adoption of the models themselves. Furthermore, many models gave little weight to the possibility that housing prices would fall across the nation. Just as an unduly high credit score could help a consumer get a loan he had no chance of paying back, an overly generous model could help a bank garner capital to fund projects of dubious value. As ersatz insurance, CDSes further lulled investors into a false sense of security.

Some have compared CDSes to, say, home insurance on a residence. But this homely example begs many questions. Most people don't suddenly take a dangerous item into their house just because they know it's insured. The banks did. They used the new assurances to take on riskier bets.[59] Finance risk regulation is complex, but one simple principle is that a bank needs enough safe assets on hand to act as cushion against falls in the value of its portfolio. What could possibly be safer than a stream of payments that is not only a contractual obligation of mortgage debtors, but even insured against default (via a CDS)? That's the Holy Grail of today's Wall Street: guaranteed returns.[60]

The problem is that as this experiment got under way, a key insurer started doing the same thing—assuming it had a "sure thing" going. Recall that, in the 1990s, it was big news for AIG to lose less than a tenth of a billion dollars on swaps. By 2008, AIG had amassed a credit default swap portfolio of tens of billions of dollars and was happily collecting premiums from firms who wanted to insure their shaky securities.[61] It had nowhere near that amount of money at hand.[62] Those who had bought insurance from AIG confidently registered on their own balance sheets a guarantee that any lost revenue would be made up by AIG's credit default swaps.[63] The fantasy here was that a private entity like AIG could take on the essentially public function of an agency like the FDIC: to make the insured whole even after catastrophic failures of their counterparties.

Whenever a firm amasses such a large position, investors raise questions: Isn't that a great deal of risk? But AIG hid the risk by discounting it; there were quants happy to model the possibility of significant payouts as events that might occur "once in a million years," or even more rarely. One of its leading managers called the credit default swaps "gold" and "free money." In 2007, he assured investors that "it is hard for us, without being flippant, to even see a scenario within any kind of realm of reason that would see us losing one dollar in any of those transactions."[64] The firm ultimately needed $182 billion in bailout money.

The precariousness of AIG's financial situation emerged slowly. Through late 2007, the company's accountants tried repeatedly to discover the true risk involved in its transactions, and even they encountered black boxes. Managers within AIG aggressively underestimated the value of the commitments they had made. On February 11, 2008, the firm filed a "disclosure" form that one commentator says "remains legendary for its opacity and jargon-laden descriptions."[65] After months of trying to deflect collateral calls on its credit default swap portfolio, the firm disclosed it was a source of "material weakness."

Market players started to panic that AIG had no way of paying out anywhere near what it had promised.[66] Some had a right to demand collateral once their CDOs (which they had insured) dropped below a certain value. As mortgages started defaulting and the price of the CDOs backed by them plummeted, AIG had to post collateral repeatedly. And while AIG Financial Products was insuring CDOs against default, other parts of the firm were directly invested in the CDOs themselves, thus magnifying the impact of their decline: the firm was both directly exposed to losses from the subprime meltdown, and indirectly exposed via other firms' swap claims on it.

Rumors swirled around AIG throughout the summer of 2008. As markets crashed in September, the U.S. Treasury "saved" AIG, infusing the firm with capital—over $100 billion—and paying its obligations to firms like Goldman at 100 cents on the dollar, despite the fact that there was *no* government guarantee of the value of CDSes. Amazingly, the government did not use its leverage at the moment of crisis to penalize AIG counterparties. Deeply concerned about "moral hazard" in other situations, officials at Treasury and the Fed made the bettors whole rather than teaching them a lesson about overleveraging. For a real "learning moment," for example, Treasury could have imposed numerous conditions designed to assure the banks acted in the best interest of the citizens whose tax dollars rescued them. Instead, it allowed some of the worst actors in the crisis not only to keep their gains but to make even more afterwards pursuing similarly risky strategies.

The Treasury Department defended its actions by asserting that when the magnitude of the problem became clear, "the global economy was on the brink of collapse," and there was no time to make finely calibrated decisions about exactly how much of a boost AIG's counterparties needed to reassure jittery markets. Leading experts disagreed. By characterizing the situation as an emergency, they maintained, Treasury and Fed leaders were able to short-circuit the processes of investigation and deliberation that could have led to a fairer outcome—that is, to tuck the whole debacle into another black box of bureaucracy.

The federal government agreed to purchase a 79.9 percent stake in the firm—the highest ownership stake it could purchase without being required to blend AIG's woeful financial profile into its own balance sheet.[67] The bailout was renegotiated later, at terms more favorable to AIG. The harsh original terms helped both the government and the firm avoid the full brunt of criticism; the more lenient later ones came forward after press attention had moved on.

The government had a lot to learn about its new ward, especially as AIG's ostensible regulators had been clueless about its massive potential liabilities right up to the edge of the crisis. A former director of the Office of Thrift Supervision (OTS) stated that as late as September 2008, he had "no clue—no idea—what [AIG's] CDS liability was."[68] Another high-level regulator in the same department said that his primary concern had been "the safety and soundness of the FDIC-insured subsidiary of AIG."[69] Therefore, he had not questioned the positions taken by AIG Financial Products, the subsidiary that wrote most of the disastrous CDS contracts—and which was fully backed by the parent company. The "subsidiary" status would not have been able to hold off the creditors, whose claims could bring down the entire company. But it was more than enough to deflect the regulators.

How did they become so feckless? Recall that in the late 1990s, Brooksley Born was silenced when she tried to investigate the types of derivatives that would eventually transmogrify into things like CDSes. Bill Clinton's top finance policymakers deferred to Wall Street. George W. Bush's agency heads were even more sycophantic. In 2003, the head of OTS joined industry grandees for a "cut red tape" photo-op—complete with a real chainsaw and hedge trimmers.[70] In decision after decision, Bush-era regulators not only loosened federal restrictions on banks but also moved to preempt state regulation.[71] In some cases, they even boxed out international regulators.[72]

By 2008, finance law was honeycombed with loopholes, exceptions, and limitations, which simultaneously made OTS AIG's key regulator and left its inspectors unaccountable in the most likely collapse scenarios. Even the most obviously dangerous financial arrangements may escape the notice of sufficiently hamstrung or struthious regulators.

## Strategic Sloppiness

Even if regulators had scrupulously reviewed all of AIG's documents, they might not have been able to discover exactly what its liabilities were, or the true extent of its exposure. The obligations that ultimately sank the firm were not sold in an open exchange; they could not be priced on a real market. Rather than basing its calculations on current market prices for their assets (*mark to market accounting*), AIG "marked to model," which means that it assigned its assets the value that complex calculations estimated they *should* have, assuming normal conditions.

But what does "normal" mean? There is a narrow range of market prices for most real products. But there are countless models to value complex financial products. *Mark to model accounting* can obscure a firm's true financial situation as much as it reveals it.[73] The value of an asset is not determined by a market-based consensus but by the interaction of algorithms and byzantine legal classifications that outsiders cannot decode. Valuation here has more in common with the administered prices of Medicare than, say, an actual market for computers or cars. But at least Medicare has the benefit of decades of price trends in medicine. The modelers of new financial instruments have little more than (easily manipulable) math.

AIG was not the only firm to get creative about describing its financial position. For example, large investment banks were allowed to keep certain securities both on and off their books for different purposes with so-called special purpose vehicles (SPVs), creating a dual reality. To understand how this works, we need to step back from the world of finance specifically and review the complexity of corporate forms generally.

When we refer to, say, "Citigroup," we have some sense of that being a *single* company. But firms that large (it has over 250,000 employees) are really composed of hundreds of entities, over which the central office has varying degrees of control.[74] Citigroup has subsidiaries controlled via ownership of shares, the same way a majority stockowner may have voting rights over a firm. But stock ownership is not the only way to control a firm. Contracts may bind the directors of one firm to always obey instructions from directors of another firm, or to remit all their earnings to a "parent" company. In U.S. accounting, variable interest entities (VIEs) are any subsidiaries not controlled via voting shares.[75] They include special purpose vehicles (SPVs), which may just be contrived for a specific transaction.

Legal theorists have called the corporation a "nexus of contracts," and that's easy to understand on one level: some office has to make agreements with employees for the business to function. But it's harder to keep in mind all the varying interests a firm may have in other entities it has power or control over. Philosopher Graham Harman reminds us, "A black box allows us to forget the massive network of alliances of which it is composed, as long as it functions smoothly. . . . Call it legion, for it is many."[76] It took the massive malfunctioning of financial markets to call attention to just how complex megabanks had become.

In the run-up to the financial crisis, investment banks could package large numbers of mortgage-backed securities together into CDOs via variable interest entities that were essentially empty shells—little more than a collection of assets and liabilities rather than real business concerns.[77] Investment banks found that many potential buyers of CDOs wanted more than the backing of a shell corporation. So buyers were led to believe that the investment bank itself would step in to back the obligations of the special purpose vehicles that it sponsored. But these assurances would have been costly if they were publicized widely. Bond investors might have demanded higher interest rates; shareholders, higher dividends. They provided cheaper capital and debt than an informed market would have.[78]

The shell corporations served another dubious purpose: they helped insulate originators and sellers of mortgage-backed securities when an epidemic of dubious paperwork emerged in the wake of the crisis.[79] Banks had assured buyers of mortgage-backed securities that they, or their agents, had taken the many steps necessary for transferring ownership of mortgages. Foreclosure by foreclosure, state by state, we are learning that in many, many cases the proper paperwork was not filed.

Bank lawyers tried to rush proceedings through nonetheless, and often succeeded. But after seeing unfamiliar bank names on dunning notices, some scrappy debtors contested their foreclosures. In some states, this was a largely ineffective strategy—in Florida, for example, where a cadre of retired judges had been paid to rubber-stamp thousands of cases.[80] But in other jurisdictions, a more robust form of due process prevailed. Cases in Massachusetts and New York revealed widespread forgery of documents. The violations were so blatant they spawned a new term: *robo-signing*, denoting the repeated, systematic "signing" of documents by dead persons (whose signatures were forged) or of many persons signing the same signature. A company even began to specialize in "reconstructing" files needed for foreclosure for $149, a price that troubled those familiar with the effort required to do the job correctly.[81]

These scandals led to a series of state-level investigations. They revealed hastily concocted records meant to cover up the original negligence in documentation, and slapdash transfers that violated fundamental principles of property law. As Professor Christopher Peterson concluded, "For the first time in the nation's history, there is no longer an authoritative, public record of who owns land in each county."[82] By 2007, about two-thirds of the records were "held" at Mortgage Electronic Registration Systems, Inc. (MERS), whose implementation of "cloud computing" technology was meant to enable instantaneous transfers of ownership rights within the confines of a centralized database.[83] MERS aspired to remove recording responsibilities from the state to a private entity owned by parties (mortgage lenders) with an interest in ownership disputes. Legal scholars have criticized MERS as a biased privatization of key aspects of property recording.[84]

Maintaining paper based record systems may put some road bumps on the mortgage securitization superhighway. But what is that superhighway really accomplishing, except speedy speculation at scale for finance's insiders? Information-age mavens have long scoffed at the "primitive" state of paper based property recordation, but at least it provided an authoritative version of who owned what. Given the trillions of dollars of economic output destroyed in the wake of the financial crisis, getting the paperwork right is a small price to pay for mortgage securitization.[85]

Law enforcement did pay attention to the banks' illegal acts, but once again the response was belated and puny. Investigations culminated in a national "foreclosure fraud settlement," which was little more than a slap on the wrist for the entities involved. Though it was priced out at $25 billion, there are so many ways the banks can "pay" for the settlement (including "principal forgiveness" on loans that would never have been paid back in the first place) that experts estimate its true cost to them will be much lower. To add insult to injury, many states are now using the settlement money to plug budget gaps rather than to help families hurt by unfair foreclosure practices.

## Lies and Libor

The finance crisis revealed that large banks had plenty to hide: bad data, bad models, byzantine corporate structures, and ersatz insurance. The tensions of the crisis years exposed ever more cracks in the foundations of finance's reputational assessments. For example, one way banks' health was estimated was through their own daily reports of their estimated borrowing costs (for overnight, month-long, and other loans) to the British Bankers' Association (BBA). The BBA published the rates within an hour of submission. Just as a high credit card rate may indicate that a consumer is in financial distress, abnormally high borrowing costs could be a clue to a bank's ill health. By throwing out high and low numbers and averaging the rest, the BBA also set benchmarks like the London interbank offered rate (Libor). This rate was (and remains) the benchmark for hundreds of trillions of dollars of financial instruments and transactions.[86]

Banks reported estimated rates on an "honor system," approximating what they *believed their borrowing costs to be*.[87] That practice created opportunities for manipulative traders to push Libor higher or lower to benefit their own positions. Traders (whose profitability would often depend on the rates put forward by "submitters") were shameless in their manipulation. For example, the CFTC documented one trader stating to a submitter, "We have another big fixing tom[orrow] and with the market move I was hoping we could set [certain] Libors as high as possible." As the CFTC relates, many responses were positive:

> The traders' requests were frequently accepted by Barclays' submitters, who emailed responses such as "always happy to help," "for you, anything," or "Done . . . for you big boy," resulting in false submissions. . . . The traders and submitters also engaged in similar conduct on fewer occasions with respect to Yen and Sterling LIBOR.[88]

Press reports were even more salacious—an unintentionally hilarious picture of how cavalierly the bank employees took their duties:

> *Swiss Franc Trader:* can u put 6m [six month] swiss libor in low pls? . . .
> *Primary Submitter:* Whats it worth
> *Swiss Franc Trader:* ive got some sushi rolls from yesterday? . . .

*Primary Submitter:* ok low 6m, just for u
*Swiss Franc Trader:* wooooooohooooooo . . . thatd be awesome[89]

As former CFTC commissioner Bart Chilton has stated, "Given what we have seen in Libor, we'd be foolish to assume that other benchmarks aren't venues that deserve review."[90] The concern has spread to markets for gold, silver, jet fuel, diesel, electric power, coal, and municipal bond auctions. Britain's Financial Conduct Authority revealed that on the day after Barclays was fined $450 million for attempted Libor rigging, its lax internal controls allowed manipulation of gold prices. The latter infraction only cost the bank about $44 million—once more, a "cost of doing business" rather than a significant dent to its balance sheet. The interest rate at issue in many municipal swaps deals—known as ISDAfix—is under investigation, too.[91] At least two banks have already paid hundreds of millions of dollars in fines for rigging municipal bond auctions.

MIT finance professor Andrew Lo has stated that the Libor scandal "dwarfs by orders of magnitude any financial scam in the history of markets."[92] As Robert Peston of the BBC puts it, "It's quite hard to think of behaviour by a bank as shocking as this." The Libor scandal was big banking's "tobacco moment"—when informed commentators could no longer ignore or explain away the depredations of an industry. As journalist Jesse Eisinger and law professor Frank Partnoy point out, "Libor reflects how much banks charge when they lend to each other; it is a measure of their confidence in each other. Now the rate has become synonymous with manipulation and collusion. *In other words, one can't even trust the gauge that is meant to show how much trust exists within the financial system.*"[93] Investigations of energy and currency price benchmarks are also being pursued.[94] All but the most connected investors feel lost, unable to discern real value amid carefully orchestrated fakery.[95]

Even the beneficiaries of the system seem troubled by it in unguarded moments. Consider this e-mail from Fabrice Tourre, a twenty-something trader at Goldman Sachs, found liable in a trading scandal involving mortgage-backed securities:[96]

What if we created a "thing," which has no purpose, which is absolutely conceptual and highly theoretical and which nobody knows how to price? . . . Anyway, not feeling too guilty about this, the real purpose of my job is to make capital markets more efficient and ultimately provide the U.S. consumer with more efficient ways to leverage and finance himself, so there is a humble, noble and ethical reason for my job;) . . . amazing how good I am in convincing myself !!!![97]

Sometimes Wall Street workers' black boxes are so effective they even "fool" their creators. Or, worse, they foster cynicism that renders concepts like fairness or professionalism quaint relics, words to be forgotten as soon as they stand in the way of a profit.[98]

The raft of scandals could lead to a new era of compliance among financial professionals. But they could also provoke elaborate efforts to cover their tracks and hide what's going on. We have no idea how many classic stealth interactions—country club conversations, discreet drinks at out-of-the-way bars—take advantage of insider knowledge. It was rumored in 2013 that savvy traders will adopt Snapchat—a video and photo app promising self-destructing messages—to hide wrongdoing.[99] If the damning chatter quoted above were merely written down, "snapped" as a picture, messaged, and deleted, misdeeds from banks to rating agencies may have been left uncovered. The "smoking gun" would be ephemeral 1's and 0's. But by 2014, Snapchat itself ran afoul of the FTC for lying about how ephemeral its communications were. A "sandbox" feature stored many video chats; other apps grabbed pictures. So perhaps we can hope the Internet sector's dishonesty will provide some small check on finance's skulduggery.

On a more serious note, the Libor scandal helps show why we should beware "all pervasive encryption technology" pushed in the wake of NSA surveillance scandals. Ordinary citizens deserve a somewhat "erasable Internet": youthful indiscretions, for example, should not haunt people forever. But those in particularly crime-ridden or important fields should not be granted technological invisibility. It is an open invitation to bad behavior.

## Accounting for Self (and Others') Delusion

Accounting rules compound the difficulties, allowing both parties to a zero-sum bet to essentially assume each will win. For example, if one firm bets interest rates will rise, and another bets they will fall, each can create its own models to assess the probability it will need to pay out.[100] It is up to the firm to accurately record changes in those probabilities. As with LEVELS, sluggish updating of models can seriously exaggerate the financial health of a firm once things start to break against it.

What's the big deal, you may ask—gamblers suffer from biases all the time. But the scale and scope of large firms' bets is way beyond what we formally call "casinos." One financial writer observed, "Information-age tools allowed Lehman Brothers to assemble and manage a portfolio that contained 930,000 derivative transactions at the time of its bankruptcy."[101] Lehman had $738 billion in derivative contracts labeled as "off balance sheet arrangements" in its 2007 accounts.[102] In many derivatives contracts (as in bets), each side is expecting an opposing outcome, and each can base its accounting on some degree of wishful thinking.

That last point—that both parties could simultaneously claim a gain on what had to be zero-sum arrangements—is critical to understanding the risks posed by black box finance. It amplifies pie-in-the-sky modeling enabled by credit default swaps, leaving both the "insured" and the "insurers" capable of assuming away risk whenever it was convenient to do so. "We'll never need to pay," insurers told themselves and their creditors; "We'll always be paid," said the insured to themselves and their creditors. Fannie and Freddie's implicit guarantees encouraged similarly "double realities"—government never needed to budget for a bailout, while holders of bonds backed by these government-sponsored entities (GSEs) assumed they'd always get paid.[103]

Opportunistic modeling and accounting also explains why deal complexity is often pursued for its own sake, and not for a genuine economic or investment purpose. Technologist Jaron Lanier puts the matter starkly: "The wave of financial calamities that took place in 2008 was cloud-based. No one in the pre-digital-cloud era had the mental capacity to lie to himself in the way we are routinely able to now. The limitations of organic human memory and calculation put a cap on the intricacies of self-delusion."[104] Webs of credit and debt become a smoke screen for institutions rendered vulnerable (both individually and collectively) so that privileged parties within them can use leverage to multiply potential upside gains. The corporation absorbs losses (and, in the worst-case scenarios, bankruptcy or bailouts). Its leading managers and traders take a large share of the gains. Murky accounting lets a mountain of leverage and misallocated capital accumulate.

These dynamics persist. Consider, for instance, JP Morgan Chase's "London Whale" trades, which lost the bank billions of dollars. In 2012, the bank's Chief Investment Office (CIO) had about $350 billion in excess deposits to manage, and devoted some to a very risky synthetic credit portfolio (SCP). The CIO asserted that it had "five key metrics and limits to gauge and control the risks associated with its trading activities." But when several of those metrics indicated unacceptable losses, managers decided to change the metrics.[105] The Senate Report on the London Whale helpfully encapsulates just how suspect this practice was:

> The head of the CIO's London office . . . once compared managing the Synthetic Credit Portfolio, with its massive, complex, moving parts, to flying an airplane. The OCC [Office of the Comptroller of Currency] Examiner-in-Charge at JPMorgan Chase [said] that if the Synthetic Credit Portfolio were an airplane, then the risk metrics were the flight instruments.
>
> In the first quarter of 2012, those flight instruments began flashing red and sounding alarms, but rather than change course, JPMorgan Chase personnel disregarded, discounted, or questioned the accuracy of the instruments instead. The bank's actions not only exposed the many risk management deficiencies at JPMorgan Chase, but also raise systemic concerns about how many other financial institutions may be disregarding risk indicators and manipulating models to artificially lower risk results and capital requirements.[106]

This excerpt elegantly turns Wall Street's usual arguments for deregulation on their head. The airplane metaphor at first suggests the complexity of the CIO's work—and, by implication, warns pesky regulators away from trying to meddle in something too technical for them to fully grasp. But who would trust a pilot who ignored his own instruments? Regulators can't simply assume technical competence—much less, good faith—at behemoths like JP Morgan Chase.

The Whale trades imposed enormous risk on JP Morgan Chase—and had that massive bank failed, that would have triggered very dangerous knock-on effects. Assets are highly concentrated in about a dozen U.S. banks, and JP Morgan Chase has one of the largest balance sheets, exceeding the total assets of 5,400 community banks.[107] Financial regulators have recognized it as a "systemically important financial institution" (SIFI), but there is not much hope it will act responsibly if it can simply move the goalposts whenever it gets into trouble.

## Risk and Faith

The main stated purpose of the financial sector is price discovery. If there are only a few people buying and selling a given company's stock, it can be very difficult to determine what the right price is. Whatever haggling takes place between the buyers and sellers may reflect the bargaining power of either side or random conditions of the negotiations rather than the actual value of the equity.[108] Larger, impersonal markets are supposed to overcome this problem by spreading trades over multiple locations, involving diverse buyers and sellers. Sometimes the buyer may be desperate, and sometimes the seller might be. In the aggregate, this "noise" should cancel out as a clear price signal emerges.

The inventors of credit default swaps hoped that their derivative could achieve in debt markets what stock exchanges were (theoretically) realizing in equity markets.[109] The ultimate goal was to set exact prices on a wide array of financial risks. The financial engineers saw this as a great triumph of human ingenuity, a technology of risk commodification that would vastly expand societal capabilities to plan and invest. In the giddy days of the real estate bubble, investors who bought both a CDO and a credit default swap likely felt like Midas, guaranteed gains no matter how the future turned out.

As we now know, the price discovery function failed miserably. Complexity, malfeasance, and sometimes outright fraud made a mockery of the finely engineered financial future promised by quants. Instead, the crash generated enormous volatility, with individuals radically uncertain about the value of homes and retirement portfolios.

In the first months after the crisis, it seemed as though the failures of this price discovery system would lead to much greater regulation of finance. Sweden temporarily nationalized banks after a financial crash there in the early 1990s. The United States chose another path. Congress did not fundamentally alter banks' business practices. The Dodd-Frank Wall Street Reform and Consumer Protection Act was so long and cumbersome because only Rube Goldberg legislation could include enough loopholes and wiggle room to placate armies of lobbyists.[110] Its implementation by fragmented regulatory authorities is even more complex.

There is little chance of democratic demands for wholesale reform of finance. The sector's details are dull, but its promises are glamorous.[111] Middle-class Americans have begun to rely upon finance—including reverse mortgages, 401(k) plans, and other investments—to provide stable (if meager) streams of income.[112] Even if average voters have virtually no direct investment in private financial institutions, they still see the unquestioned integrity of the whole as vital to future possibilities.

Finance's black box also promises money in more pleasant and exciting ways than plain old government redistribution, infrastructure, or basic research. Evoking ballyhooed tech darlings or wonder drugs, the finance sector can raise the possibility of nearly unlimited gains, dwarfing the cost-of-living adjustments built into American social insurance. Financial intermediaries also spare small-time investors the trouble of actually understanding the business model and future prospects of what they invest in. "No need to worry if it's a bit of a black box," a broker may counsel about a hot tip. "It's our job to understand the details."

Sadly, many workers who earnestly contribute to 401(k) plans mistake the unglamorous realities of fixed-income arbitrage, algorithmic trading, and mind-numbing derivative contracts for the glitter of venture capital jackpots. Investors like to think of their money supporting brave innovators and entrepreneurs. But how many really know the ultimate destinations of their dollars? As Doug Henwood has shown, nearly all of the activity in the current stock market is transfers of existing shares.[113] The trading simply reallocates claims to the future productivity of existing firms. Short time horizons steer money away from long-term, risky, but potentially far more productive projects like green energy and nanotechnology. Finance's pervasive short-termism crowds out visionaries.[114]

Even for those used to the American solicitude for moneyed interests, finance debates are extraordinarily skewed toward the sector's insiders and away from broader social concern about what useful services they actually provide to the rest of the society. The trend toward self-reference reaches a reductio ad absurdum in an avant-garde form of black box finance: high-speed algorithmic trading.

## The Low Social Value of High-Frequency Trading

Modern equity markets are very complex.[115] For example, consider what happens when an investor logs into an account at a brokerage to place an order (all within a second, given automation). The broker will sometimes send the trade to wholesalers. As of 2012, these wholesalers could "internalize" about a fifth of trades, matching them with their own internal orders. The rest of the trades are sent out to two types of trading venues: public exchanges and dark pools.

Public exchanges must display prices openly and have other obligations to customers. As of early 2013, seven companies were operating thirteen public exchanges. Dark pools, by contrast, are more numerous and opaque. Handling about 13 percent of orders, they are favored by traders who do not want news of their activities to be disseminated (too quickly) to other traders.[116]

Why does secrecy matter? Consider, for instance, a trader who wanted to buy a sizeable portion of shares at each hour of the day, from 10:00 a.m. to 3:00 p.m. If rival traders learned of that strategy at 10:30 a.m., they might buy shares ahead of the sequential purchases, knowing the later purchases would drive up demand (and thus price). They could then make a quick profit by selling the shares to the sequential purchaser. Instead of seeing shares rise *after* his purchases, he'd see them rise *before*. His action may well be the primary reason for the rise, but the profits for it would go to the people who traded ahead of him. By contrast, imagine if the news of the sequential purchases breaks the next day. At that point, markets may interpret the buys as a sign of the strength of the company offering the shares. In that scenario, the sequential purchaser gets to keep the gains attributable to his own "vote of confidence" in the shares. It's all a matter of timing.

Computer programs now execute a sizeable portion of daily transactions.[117] The time frame has narrowed, and there are plenty of opportunities to gain a temporarily hidden advantage. The *Wall Street Journal* exposed a simple example involving sneak peeks at important reports. Algorithms parse major news stories the moment they "break" online, instantly dispatching buy or sell orders (when, say, the words "Pfizer" and "lawsuit" or "breakthrough drug" appear in the same paragraph). Reports can easily move markets. By paying for early access to the data, sometimes as little as two seconds, traders beat rivals who assumed they were all on a level playing field.[118]

Of course, buying early access to data streams is in some ways a self-defeating project—as soon as it is exposed, smart traders may stop using the data altogether as a prompt to trading. Or they may up the ante, and try to outwit the early-data buyers at their own game. How might that work? The key is the fragmentation of markets for stocks, and superfast communication technology. Let's say one trader's bots put in a buy order for 5,000 shares of Pfizer at $100 a share after parsing a report with the words "Pfizer" and "breakthrough" in it at 9:54:58 a.m. (58 seconds after 9:54 a.m., and two seconds before the story is made public). That order *itself* may be a kind of news to other traders, once it is transmitted to their terminals. If someone else's bots can process a trade before the early trader can, they can beat him to the punch. And just as the early trader paid for a peek at the news report before other saw it, a flash trader may pay the early trader's exchange to find out *immediately* when the order has been placed.

High-frequency trading (HFT) allows transactions to occur in fractions of a second.[119] In the example above, one trader may manage to grab the shares at 9:54:58:400 a.m. (58 seconds and 400 milliseconds (thousandths of a second) after 9:54 a.m.). HFT is a perfect match for a trading environment dominated by ever shorter time horizons. Equity markets are becoming ever less concerned with the real economy (e.g., questions like, Which company makes the most fuel-efficient cars? or even Which firm makes cars that customers will want to buy?) than with windows of opportunity for sudden arbitrage (e.g., How do we buy thousands of shares of Ford milliseconds before a major pension fund buys them and drives up their price, and then sell them milliseconds later?). The latter strategy depends entirely on information advantage—knowing something (or algorithmically decoding some signal) before everyone else does.[120]

The information arms race can get expensive. Traders worry about being "picked off" by a lurking algo. The more HFT activity occurs, the more other firms must invest in masking their own moves to avoid being "front run" (i.e., having news of their impending orders drive the market in ways that make their orders more expensive). HFT mavens effectively tax the rest of the market.[121]

If you ever wonder exactly what 401(k) "expense ratios" or other mysterious finance fees go toward, it may well be to help *your* fund manager anticipate and deflect HFT'ers arbitrage strategies. Armoring against HFT'ers (and all the other tricks and traps described in this chapter) takes expensive talent and software. The think tank Dēmos estimates that, over a lifetime, retirement account fees "can cost a median-income two-earner family nearly $155,000."[122] Investor John Bogle notes that a 2 percent fee applied over a 50-year investing lifetime would erode *63 percent* of the value of an average account.[123] Note, too, how the finance sector *as a whole* has little interest in stopping such wasteful activities. The more treacherous it becomes for outsiders to trade in the brave new world of computerized markets, the more they have to pay some knowledgeable insider a fee to fend off the piranhas.

Also note here how signals about value are being transmitted. HFT'ers merely anticipate and mimic what others are doing, without exploring the underlying *value* of the company whose shares are being traded. This bare signaling is another version of the black box problems illuminated in credit ratings or credit default swaps. The mere existence of an AAA rating, or insurance from AIG, led to a false sense of security for many investors. Here, buy and sell signals can take on a life of their own, leading to momentum trading and herding.[124]

Algorithmic trading can create extraordinary instability and frozen markets when split-second trading strategies interact in unexpected ways.[125] Consider, for instance, the flash crash of May 6, 2010, when the stock market lost hundreds of points in a matter of minutes.[126] In a report on the crash, the CFTC and SEC observed that "as liquidity completely evaporated," trades were "executed at irrational prices as low as one penny or as high as $100,000."[127] Traders had programmed split-second algorithmic strategies to gain a competitive edge, but soon found themselves in the position of a sorcerer's apprentice, unable to control the technology they had developed.[128] Though prices returned to normal the same day, there is no guarantee future markets will be so lucky.

## The Computerized Market

HFT is the ultimate in financial self-reference, where perceptions of value come entirely from signals encoded on trading terminals. Lately, the limiting factor in fast trading the speed of light in fiber optic cables. Thus firms are paying to construct ultrafast cables between financial centers.[129] Spread Networks spent over $200 million to lay a cable between Chicago and New York-area exchanges, estimating that firms could make $20 billion in a year exploiting price discrepancies (lasting less than a second) between the two cities.[130] Modelers have devised more extreme solutions to the time delay problem. An "optimal scheme" would "push trading firms to build new computers [at] the exact, optimal points in between markets"—even if that happened to be in the middle of an ocean.[131]

How does this minuscule speed advantage help? Consider "quote stuffing," strategy whereby a trader will flood the market with a large number of order quotes and then immediately—literally within fractions of a second—cancel the orders.[132] This causes congestion on an exchange and allows the stuffer to conceal its own trading strategy while less sophisticated traders are trying to process this flood of new information.[133] If those responding to the stuffer are likely to follow a certain pattern, and the stuffer successfully anticipates the pattern, he may be able to trade off that anticipated response.[134]

Similarly, "spoofing" (sometimes called "layering") involves a trader making a large number of buy orders with the intent to cancel.[135] The purpose of placing the orders is to create an impression of buy-side interest and drive the prices up.[136] Once prices have been driven up, the trader cancels its original purchase bids and sells to other traders who have been duped into buying at a higher price.[137] Again, this all occurs within fractions of a second.

Other trading practices involving rapid order and cancellation—and executed with the intent of deceiving other traders and making a profit—include "strobing,"[138] "smoking,"[139] and "last second withdrawal."[140] Runaway algorithmic interactions can have some humorous results. News-reading technology may cause "Berkshire Hathaway" stock to go up whenever actress Anne Hathaway is mentioned in the news.[141] But technology theorist Edward Tenner warns that the resulting intertwining of trading and text about trading can create dangerous feedback loops.[142] The dynamics resemble a videogame but have real-world consequences.[143]

## A Menace of Martingales

Self-dealing and waste is rampant in finance. But the sector need not be perfect in order to continue to attract massive amounts of capital; it need only surpass alternatives. In the public mind, it is beginning to do that with respect to the government. Individualized, privatized, financialized dreams are bouncing back, even after the crisis. Government debts are public, and campaigns from financiers cast aspersions on them and warn of impending collapse.[144] Meanwhile, financial firms can use all the techniques described above to hide their own debts, vulnerabilities, and risky bets. They can continually malign the government's fiscal foundations, all the while depending on the Fed to back them in case their own gambles fail.[145]

During Franklin Roosevelt's presidency, government tended to fight back, underscoring the need for public alternatives to private promises to store and build wealth. The Bush and Obama administrations have taken a fundamentally different course. They have backed cash infusions for the banks and quantitative easing (essentially, hundreds of billions of dollars of purchases of certain securities) that raised the price of stocks to record levels. The fundamental concern has been to rebuild public confidence in equity and debt markets as safe and reliable guardians of financial security. Social Security, by contrast, has become a target for "reform."

Like the alliances of business and law enforcement in fusion centers, the cooperation of big bank and big government leaders is supposed to reassure us. Experts at the commanding heights of business and government are in harmony, sharing a common vision. But, as Peter Boone and Simon Johnson have shown, the interconnections between the two can also erode confidence. Boone and Johnson foresee a "doom loop": as financial institutions are increasingly treated as too big to fail, they are empowered to take greater and greater risks, which will inevitably lead to greater stresses on the governments that effectively sponsor them.[146] These obligations foment worries about governments' ability to support both too-big-to-fail banks and the tens of millions who depend on health and welfare benefits. Meanwhile, as interest rates on sovereign debt are suppressed to spark a recovery, investors feel compelled to flee to the finance sector to gain more than nominal returns. Finance's black box is all the more appealing as ten-year Treasury bills flirt with rock bottom yields.[147]

The end result is a crippled state succoring a reckless finance sector prone to "martingale" strategies—the gambling term for a bettor who doubles down after each loss. As *Financial Times* columnist John Kay observes, if you are infinitely rich at the start, the martingale strategy is a sure winner, as long as each bet's chance of winning is greater than zero.[148] But infinite riches are a thing of fantasy, even in an era when the Federal Reserve can create billions of dollars digitally in a matter of hours.

## Black Swan or Black Box?

While some public intellectuals assure us that "no one could have foreseen" the financial crisis, many voices had called for the types of sensible regulation that may well have prevented it.[149] The FBI spotted rapid growth in mortgage fraud by 2003, and warned of dire consequences if it continued.[150] Law professor Lynn Stout predicted disruptive losses because "gamblers and derivatives traders

[are] tempted to try to exercise control over the future by manipulating the fate of the thing they were betting on." She foresaw chain reactions of failures as a natural consequence of radical deregulation.[151] Like Brooksley Born (the aforementioned CFTC chair silenced by "thirteen bankers"), Stout ended up a Cassandra, her work ignored as official Washington deferred to the "expertise" of financiers and the think tanks they supported.

Yet it would be too simplistic to blame mere shoddy regulation for the crisis. Bankers were adopting complexly structured finance that hid their risk taking from the last backdrop of restraint: the market.[152] Obligations would remain on balance sheets for some purposes, and off them for others. Byzantine agreements obscured who would be left holding the bag when a "credit event," triggering massive payments, occurred.[153] Derivatives slipped through numerous regulatory nets.[154]

The iconoclastic investor Nassim Taleb came to prominence by calling the financial crisis a "black swan," a freakish event both unpredicted and unpredictable.[155] But as more details emerge, it becomes apparent that it was less an unpredictable outcome of an unforeseen confluence of events than it was the natural consequence of a black box finance system. Even conscientious buyers of what turned out to be "toxic assets" couldn't understand their true nature. Many resulted, at least in part, from outright obfuscation: direct efforts to hide how they had been created.

The increasing role of legislators, judges, and regulators in helping large financial firms hide their dirty laundry is no accident. As technology has advanced, reporting transactions is easier than ever. Records that were once dispersed over millions of pieces of paper or thousands of computers can now be integrated in lightning-fast networks. Digital systems can be set to record, by default, nearly everything that happens on them, and storage keeps getting cheaper. Yet somehow, when billions of dollars are at stake, crisis-ridden financial institutions routinely lose or hide (or simply refuse to disclose) key information.

Critiques of Wall Street have a long and storied history. One hundred years ago, Louis Brandeis's *Other People's Money and How the Bankers Use It* lacerated the swindlers of his day. A few years ago, an ex-Goldman Sachs employee, Nomi Prins, reprised the complaint with a title of nearly the same name (and followed up with *It Takes a Pillage*.)[156] From Fred Schwed's wry and folksy *Where Are the Customers' Yachts?* to Matt Taibbi's coruscating outrage in *Griftopia*, the genre has reflected the manners and mores of the time. Journalists and legal scholars help the persistent to peer into finance's black box. They need a stronger voice in a regulatory process too often dominated by the few who profit from opacity.

To be sure, there are many conscientious souls working on Wall Street. But their voices and values matter little if they can be summarily overruled by their bosses. The aftermath of the housing crisis has exposed a critical mass of unethical and hugely costly deals. It has created a presumption of suspicion for large firms—particularly those that now enjoy "too big to fail" status.

Black box finance ranges from the crude to the cunning, the criminal to the merely complex. Countless narratives and analyses of the crisis have tried to pin down whether bankers, mortgage brokers, regulators, and insurers knew or should have known that the mortgage industrial complex was building a house of cards. Was the crash a result of fraud or mere incompetence? Regardless of how that debate plays out, all sides should agree on a deeper truth. Far too much of contemporary finance is premised on hiding information: from borrowers, lenders, clients, regulators, and the public.

## Money, Information, and Power

Money is a claim on future production, not a good in itself. The towering digital edifices of credit erected by advanced finance are increasingly disconnected from actual productivity.[157] Rather, they create illusions of prosperity. Behind all the reticulated swaps of risk and reward, the crash of 2008 boils down to a familiar story: leverage hidden in order to promote ever more bonuses and fee-generating deals.[158] One Wall Street bank paid out over $5 billion in bonuses in 2006, only to lose three times that amount by early 2009.[159] Virtually none of that bonus money has been recovered from individuals. To this day, the tax and accounting manipulations used to demonstrate that various institutions have or have not paid back government bailouts are confounding.[160]

Algorithmic methods also advance two of the most troubling aspects of contemporary finance: centralization and self-reference.[161] As economist Amar Bhidé has argued, the idea of "one best way" to rank credit applicants flattened the distributed, varying judgment of local loan officers into the nationwide credit score—a number focused on *persons* rather than *communities*.[162] Like monocultural farming technology vulnerable to one unanticipated bug, the converging methods of credit assessment failed spectacularly when macroeconomic conditions changed. Models' illusion of commensurability and solid valuation sparked a rush for what appeared to be easy returns, exacerbating both boom and bust dynamics.

In finance, algorithmic methods—reducing a given judgment or process to a series of steps—have long been billed as ways of leveling the playing field and reducing risk. They were supposed to replace, displace, or reduce the role of biased or self-serving intermediaries, ranging from mortgage loan officers to "specialist" traders. But all too often, new intermediaries arose, finding ways to extract even more from transactions than their predecessors.

Hidden conflicts of interest have long haunted Wall Street firms, so it would be foolish to argue that secret algorithms somehow hijacked or corrupted American finance.[163] But it would also be a mistake to pass over questions concerning technology in finance, because modeling methods and automation have vastly expanded the sector's capacity to bluff those who are supposed to manage risk and detect deception. As former trader Satyajit Das memorably puts it, "No trader making $1 million + a year is going to take questions from an auditor making $50,000 a year"—especially when the trader has myriad models to prove the wisdom of his position.[164]

Admittedly, my illustrations are not comprehensive. Some might say that they are unrepresentative, skewed toward go-go years of reckless speculation. Note, however, political scientist Daniel Carpenter's contention that "there is value in studying a singular process not because it stands in for so many others, but because it influences so many others."[165] Given how wealthy the boom years made so many in finance, and how unscathed the bust has left them, few aspiring traders and bankers would think of them as a cautionary tale. And trades like the London Whale indicate that years after the crisis, critical models are just as manipulable (and regulators as feckless) as they were in the bubble years. Until finance practices in general are *routinely* as scrutinized as those prevalent in the bubble years, we have little reason to think matters have changed all that much. Indeed, they may even be getting worse.

Moreover, it's hard to credit demands for representativeness in a field as opaque as contemporary finance. It is not only difficult to tell how much illicit activity is happening in finance; it's hard to even grasp the foundations of the main currents of indisputably legal activity. The point of black boxes is to *hide* critical facts about what is going on. They undermine any confident assertions about the precise nature of firms' investment, accounting, or documentation practices.

Journalist and anthropologist Gillian Tett has described the eerie "social silences" around exotic derivatives trades with a disarming observation: "Once something is labeled boring, it's the easiest way to hide it in plain sight."[166] And extreme complexity doesn't merely anesthetize the public. It also extends an open invitation for quants or traders or managers to bully their way past gatekeepers, like rating agencies, accountants, and regulators.[167] In so many situations leading up to the financial crisis, there was always some algorithmic wiggle room, some way for quants to tweak the numbers.

As French sociologist Bruno Latour has observed, "The world is not a solid continent of facts sprinkled by a few lakes of uncertainties, but a vast ocean of uncertainties speckled by a few islands of calibrated and stabilized forms."[168] A financial world built on exploiting information asymmetries amounts to an "ocean of uncertainties," but at least in the decades between the New Deal and wholesale deregulation, "calibrated and stabilized forms" like rating agencies, insurance firms, and investment bank partnerships (whose owners had their own money on the line) kept some semblance of order. Now, lightning-fast trades and ever more complex derivatives are supposed to maintain equilibrium. You can hedge against anything, and even hedge your hedges with reinsured insurance. But the frequency and severity of crises only seems to increase.

From the tech and telecom craze of the late 1990s to house price escalation from 2002 to 2006, asset bubbles are a predictable consequence of black box finance. Insiders who understand their true dynamics can sell at the top, reaping enormous windfalls. But their gains represent "a claim on future wealth that neither had been nor was to be produced."[169] By creating the illusion of enormous value in securities like CDOs and CDSes, black box financiers make their own fees (ranging from a fraction of a percent to over 30 percent in the case of some hedge funds) seem trivial in comparison. When the mirage dissipates, the desert of zero productive gains becomes clear. But in this harsh new economic reality, the money "earned" by the speculators has all the more purchasing power, arrayed against the smaller incomes of those who did not take advantage of the bubble.[170]

Thus the great paradox of contemporary finance: its premier practitioners are far better at creating need and demand for their "product" (price discovery) than they are at actually providing it. Their primary results are murk, darkness, volatility, and doubt. Matt Taibbi called Goldman Sachs a "vampire squid;" an ink-squirting octopus of obfuscation would be fitting, too.[171]

Theoretical justifications for finance's power focus on "free markets" generating fundamental knowledge about the economy. Without the great brokerages, and "bank holding companies," how would we price debt, equity, or the more exotic risks assimilated into derivatives?[172] Yet the rise of financialization has created enormous uncertainty about the value of companies, homes, and even (thanks to the pressing need for bailouts) the once rock solid promises of governments themselves. Recall Hernando de Soto's observation at the beginning of this chapter: when the basics of owing and ownership are in dispute, it's hard for real markets to operate. Finance thrives in this environment of radical uncertainty, taking commissions in cash as investors (or, more likely, their poorly monitored agents) race to speculate on or hedge against an ever less knowable future.

Like the employees scrambling to succeed on faceless companies' job scoring algorithms, or firms desperate for search engine optimization, now companies compete to use finance firms for just the right mix of bets and hedges. Algorithmic authorities govern these processes—conveniently tweaked to benefit their own guardians. Policymakers have barely begun to put in place necessary safeguards. The next chapter explains how they might do better under existing models of regulation. But the concluding chapter warns that an entirely new paradigm may be necessary to rein in black box finance.

# 5

# WATCHING (AND IMPROVING)
# THE WATCHERS

I'VE SPENT a good deal of the past decade thinking about how law could make our black box society more transparent. I've proposed "fair reputation reporting" to help people understand the stories data miners tell about them. I've promoted a "Federal Search Commission" to monitor how search engines are ranking and rating people and companies. I've contributed ideas to several meetings of finance transparency activists.[1]

Each of these movements has had some small victories over the years. But it's not enough just to *watch* the key firms controlling our information, our media, and our financial fates. We have to be able to *improve* them and the ways that they go about their business. Moreover, we need to build on successes in one area as models for the rest of the black box society. If credit scores can be regulated, why not the scoring systems used by digital advertisers and employers? If the HHS and SEC can require "audit trails" for high-tech companies, why not other regulators? Rather than reinventing the wheel each time Big Data–driven decision making changes a market, regulators could learn from best practices all around the government.[2]

The more the black boxes of corporate practices in these areas are revealed, the more pressure will mount to change them. What might real reform look like? When it comes to reputation, it would mean focusing less on trying to control the collection of data up front, and more on its *use*—how companies and governments are actually deploying it to make decisions. Nonviolent political views, for example, should never be a predicate for law enforcement investigation. And we need to assure that employers and banks are not basing key decisions on surreptitiously gathered health data. Far more of their algorithms should be open for inspection—if not by the public at large, at least by some trusted auditor.[3]

In the context of massive Internet firms, competition is unlikely. Most start-ups today aim to be *bought* by a company like Google or Facebook, not to displace them. (Stories like Foundem's serve as cautionary tales for the mavericks.) Data is the fuel of the information economy, and the more data a company already has, the better it can monetize it. Rather than merely hoping for competition that may never come, we need to assure that the *natural monopolization* now at play in fields like search and social networking doesn't come at too high a cost to the rest of the economy.

The same "rich get richer" dynamics afflict finance, where the largest entities tend to attract more capital simply because they are viewed as "too big to fail" and "too big to jail." Some reformers have fixated on "breaking up big banks" to restore competition in finance, reasoning that smaller institutions would be less likely to be bailed out if they got into trouble. But do we really want to enable "failure" in finance, and all the instability that that entails? Wouldn't it be better to assure that a few fixed points in our constellation of finance firms are stable *and* serve the public, too?

The first step toward improving reputation, search, and finance firms is to learn more about what they are doing. But that is only the beginning of reform. In many cases, business practices themselves need to change in order to preserve our basic commitments to due process and level commercial playing fields. As Internet and finance firms exercise more influence over the rest of the economy, they set the standards by which businesses and people are judged. It's time to set higher standards for them.

## The Who, When, What, and Why of Disclosure

Any transparency solution to black box problems should be specific about three main issues: How much does the black box firm have to reveal? To whom must it reveal it? And how fast must the revelation occur? Table 5.1 suggests the range of options:

*Table 5.1.*   A Spectrum of Disclosure

|  | Depth of disclosure | Scope of disclosure | Timing of disclosure |
|---|---|---|---|
| Preserving Secrecy | Shallow and cursory | To small group of outside experts | Delayed for years or decades |
| Providing Transparency | Deep and thorough | To the public generally | Immediate |

Most of the extremes here are unsatisfactory. For example, when a credit scorer gives "reason codes" of a few words to justify a bad score, it's a mere façade of an explanation. On the other hand, when a hacker spills the guts of an entire computing system onto open forums, there is collateral damage. We may learn a great deal about the target of the hack, but innocent people's secrets can be exposed as well. A fully transparent society would be a nightmare of privacy invasion, voyeurism, and intellectual property theft. Sometimes the route to orderly and productive investigation is to entrust the job to a small group of experts. For example, courts often need to have a deep knowledge about events leading up to a legal dispute. Even leading leakers seem to agree: both Julian Assange and Edward Snowden filtered their revelations though trusted news sources. I call this general trend "qualified transparency"—limiting revelations in order to respect all the interests involved in a given piece of information.

As time goes on, the negative impact of disclosure fades. Statutes of limitation run; power moves to other hands; technology that was once state-of-the-art becomes irrelevant. In the corporate context, at least, far more *should* eventually be revealed than we presently are privy to. It is hard to see how the story of our increasingly auto-mated age could even be written without a future historian having far more access to black box systems than we have now. And we should beware of pushing revelations too far into the future. Wall Street managed to keep gruesome details of the Fed's 2008 bailouts quiet until *after* critical financial reform legislation was passed. Legislators may have been more open to innovative reform if they had better understood the recent past.

To navigate between the extremes of full and immediate disclosures, and partial and delayed ones, we need to consider *why* we are making firms reveal what they are doing. The game must be worth the candle. For example, American regulators tend to set up elaborate monitoring regimes, but then are unable to (or fail to) impose meaningful fines for clear wrongdoing. Such regulation appears to be little more than a full employment program for compliance officers and attorneys. In their defense, toothless regulators point out that at least *consumers* can take into account the revelations in deciding whether to, say, buy an Apple or Samsung phone, or search using Google or Bing, or take out a mortgage via Citibank or Wells Fargo. But do people really hear about corporate wrongdoing? Do they care? Does action follow from revelation? Would it even matter if it did, or would more dubious firms take the place of shunned ones? These questions haunt virtually any disclosure regime. And they are particularly pointed in the black box contexts we've examined, where harm is often probabilistic and hard to measure—at least on the individual level.[4]

## Fictions of Privacy

The bulk of online privacy policies are a great example of a failed disclosure regime. They revolve around the fiction that consumers can and will bargain for privacy, or "opt out" of deals or jobs they deem too privacy invasive. But how can a job applicant even factor privacy considerations into the application process? Most firms don't advertise how they are monitoring workers. And what better way to mark oneself out as a "someone to watch" than to bargain with a boss for an unmonitored work computer?

Things are little better at home. Website terms of service are less "privacy policies" than contracts surrendering your rights to the owner of the service. If you read them carefully, you'll find capacious protection for companies, and little recourse for the consumer. People mechanically click "I agree" when confronted with "terms of service" agreements, fully aware that there's no chance they can modify the terms.[5] Moreover, it's not even clear that the terms themselves are worth perusing. Corporations' newest trick is to include a "unilateral modification" clause that lets them change the agreement later, with no notice to the persons affected.[6] It's market form, feudal substance: we all know who calls the shots in such "agreements."

Some scholars would double down on the notice strategy, requiring consumers to prove that they *really understood* what a company's privacy policies were before they could agree with them.[7] But who would want to jump through that hoop for the countless innocuous uses of data that happen each day? And even if something alarming came up, when was the last time a consumer actually renegotiated terms in his or her favor?[8] The prospect of altering the terms of service for an intermediary like Facebook or Google is beyond the ambition of almost all users.[9]

Informed consumers neither experience nor hope for meaningful protection in "privacy settings" that leading companies offer them.[10] It could take weeks to fully map the flow of data from something as simple as commenting on Facebook, and the payoff for doing so is vanishingly low.[11] Companies regularly push the envelope in online privacy, get caught lying about what they are doing, and treat the resulting fines as a (trivial) cost of doing business. From just one settlement (among many), here is a list of promises Facebook failed to keep to its users:

- Facebook told users they could restrict sharing of data to limited audiences—for example, with "Friends Only." In fact, selecting "Friends Only" did not prevent their information from being shared with third-party applications their friends used.

- Facebook had a "Verified Apps" program & claimed it certified the security of participating apps. It didn't.

- Facebook promised users that it would not share their personal information with advertisers. It did.

- Facebook claimed that when users deactivated or deleted their accounts, their photos and videos would be inaccessible. But Facebook allowed access to the content, even after users had deactivated or deleted their accounts.

- Facebook claimed that it complied with the U.S.–EU Safe Harbor Framework that governs data transfer between the U.S. and the European Union. It didn't.[12]

The monetary fines levied against Facebook for these violations were minuscule: less than a few hours of revenue. It's unclear if anyone was fired or even punished for what went wrong here. The same sad story can be told about numerous other firms.

Given well-documented failures of firms to keep meaningful privacy promises, regulators need to start forcing such firms to give consumers a sense of the sheer size of the data trove gathered about them—and its content. We cannot allow the lords of the cloud unfettered, secretive control over data use and profiling.[13]

## Fuller Disclosure: Toward Fair Data Practices

Some of the black boxes of reputation, search, and finance simply need to be pried open. For example, data brokers need to fess up about the data they are hoarding, trading, and selling. Individuals should have the right to inspect, correct, and dispute inaccurate data. We should also know the sources of the data, unless there are very good reasons to maintain their anonymity. Ironically, some data brokers now refuse to give out their data sources because of "confidentiality agreements" with them.[14] That chutzpah would not stand for consumer reporting agencies covered by the Fair Credit Reporting Act (FCRA), and it should not stand for data brokers. Of course, FCRA itself is far from a model—challenging information in a credit report can feel like an exercise in futility. But if there were proper penalties there—and they were extended to recalcitrant data brokers—the right to inspect and correct data could be a first step toward reputational justice.

Protections need to be comprehensive. If the law only burdens data brokers, large firms will just take data analysis in-house. The right to correct and inspect data must be extended into the companies proper.

Shoppers at Target, for example, should be able to find out what kind of profiling the store is doing on them. How else can they assess the risk from a massive data breach, like the one afflicting that company (and many others) in 2013? Just as hospitals and doctors must give patients a copy of their medical records, our data records need to be open to inspection and review. If small doctors' offices can handle this, so too can large corporations. And when leading firms start to take an intimate interest in their customers' and workers' health status, they should not protest the application of health privacy law standards.[15]

The rise of hacking and digital break-ins raises another critical question about data security.[16] Have the databases now so influential in our daily life been accumulated through lawful means? There is a thriving market in credit card and social security numbers on the "darknet," shadowy regions of the Internet unsurveillable by the average person or police officer. At what point will breached health, search query, or social network data show up there? And might an unscrupulous data broker try to gain a competitive edge there by buying it? To avoid a black market in hacked data (as well as to assure proper enforcement of current fair data practices law), we should require data controllers to keep records of the original source of their data, noting how it was collected, purchased, or bartered.[17]

Tracking data sources should also help individuals correct mistakes. Presently, a falsehood in a single large database can percolate into dozens of smaller ones, and it is often up to the victim to request corrections, one by one. When the follow-on users of bad data don't know where it came from, they may not believe the data subject. If they kept track of the provenance of their data, the process of correction would be easier.

Ideally, the process would be automated: the stakes of data-driven decision making are simply too high to allow mistakes to persist. Just as software updates can automatically improve the quality of a computer's performance, data updates would allow corrected information to flow through linkages to all the follow-on users of a database. Admittedly, this is probably not technically feasible *now*.[18] But regulation can prompt the development of new technology. Data controllers have created a system designed merely to maximize their own profits, not to treat data subjects decently. Just as privacy-protecting features can be designed into devices (think of the video-camera with a red light that warns you it is recording), so too can some basic safeguards be built into networked databases.

When a company builds a dossier on you, you deserve a chance to review it and correct it. When a retailer can predict a pregnant woman's due date and digital marketers can peg you as "probably bipolar" or "diabetic-concerned," those records are at least as sensitive as the average doctor visit. They should be subject to health privacy law, too.[19] Similarly, when online ad brokers are deciding whether you are going to be served offers for predatory or plain-vanilla loans, they are performing a function very similar to that of credit bureaus. They should not escape regulation simply because they do business a bit differently than the entities now targeted by the FCRA.[20]

Big Data firms also need to consider whether certain lists should even be created at all. Categories like "daughter killed in car crash," "rape victim," or "gullible elderly" may help some ghoulish marketing genius make a buck. But they also run a clear and present danger of fueling exploitive or manipulative business practices.[21] Thought leaders at the Future of Privacy Forum have explored whether that Institutional Review Boards, like the ones that must approve human subjects research at universities, should judge the appropriateness of sensitive data use. Such boards might approve uses of data that help data subjects, while delaying or blocking ones that are unnecessary, unhelpful, or worse.

## The Lawful Use of Data

Let's assume, for now, that a full transparency agenda comes to the realm of reputational information—data brokers, credit scorers, and all the algorithmic raters and rankers we've encountered so far. You can track any given bit of data about you from originator to broker to end user. You can dispute data you believe is inaccurate. If you want, you can even groom various digital versions of yourself, assuring every data monger has the latest, greatest version of your tastes, interests, and accomplishments.

Would that really allay our concerns about the new reputation economy? Probably not. First, as data use intensifies, it will be hard for persons (even with the aid of new software *and* professional help) to keep track of exactly where and how they're being characterized. Second, in many contexts, even accurate, true data can be unfairly or discriminatorily deployed.

For example, consider the credit card company that codes payments to marriage counselors as a harbinger of default (and raises cardholders' interest rates accordingly). Seeking the help of a professional for treatment should not influence decisions on terms of credit. The legal system has long recognized that tort liability can perversely undermine efficiency when, say, a person who puts a railing on a stairway finds that a plaintiff (who earlier fell off the stairway) uses the decision to put on the railing as evidence that the stairway was unduly dangerous at the time of the fall. The evidentiary rule of "subsequent remedial measures" holds that "when measures are taken that would have made an earlier injury or harm less likely to occur, evidence of the subsequent measures is not admissible to prove" negligence or culpability.[22] Those regulating our quasi-judicial system of algorithmically scored penalties should take note, to ensure that it does not end up discouraging behavior that helps individuals and improves productivity.

Moreover, it is simply not fair to compound the misery of illness with spiked interest rates. We already forbid the use of genetic information in employment decisions, because persons cannot control the genes they are born with. But note how far any individual is from responsibility for many ordinary illnesses, ranging from cancer to a broken bone to, yes, the anxiety and depression that can accompany a failing relationship. Sickness shouldn't enter into credit decisions.

Nor should it be a part of bosses' calculus, however tempting that may be for data-driven managers. Health law expert Sharona Hoffman of Case Western Reserve University has evoked the possibility of "complex scoring algorithms based on electronic health records to determine which individuals are likely to be high-risk and high-cost workers."[23] While a smart employer would never tell a worker "I'm firing you because you have diabetes," devotees of Big Data may soon be able to predict diabetes (just like Target infers pregnancy) from a totally innocuous data set (including items like eating habits, drugstore visits, magazine subscriptions, and the like). And the analyst involved (whether inside or outside the firm) could quite easily mask a diagnosis as something entirely different. Fueled by black box analytics, a firm could do the following:

a) crunch the numbers on a person's general Big Data profile (using information from data brokers, retailers, magazine subscriptions, online accounts, and other information);
b) conclude the person likely is a diabetic;
c) use another database to estimate the likely health care costs of diabetics relative to the general population; and then
d) combine b & c to conclude that the person in question is likely to be a "high cost worker"

Given the proprietary nature of the information involved, the most the firm is going to tell the fired (or unhired) worker is the end result: the data predicted that their cost to the firm was likely to be greater than their benefit. Most of the time, they need not even offer that rationale. Unexplained and unchallengeable, Big Data becomes a star chamber.[24]

Law has *begun* to address this issue in the credit context, where applicants tend to get basic, very brief rationales for adverse actions. "Explanations" like "too many revolving accounts" or "time since last account opened too short" are reason *codes*;[25] rather than explain what happened in a straightforward way, they simply name a factor in the decision. We know it was more important than other, unnamed factors, but we have little sense of how the weighing went.

While the term *code* can connote law (as in the Internal Revenue Code) or software (which involves the "coding" of instructions into machine-readable formats), it can also suggest a deliberately hidden meaning.[26] Someone sends a "coded message" in order to avoid detection, to keep third parties from understanding exactly what is going on. In algorithmic decision making, this third, mysterious aspect of code too often predominates. For example, with credit decisions, there are so many vague or conflicting reason codes that it is possible to rationalize virtually any decision.[27] Maybe you have too many accounts open, maybe you have too few—either could contribute, at any given time, to a decision to reduce a credit score or reject an application.

But what we really care about is that the data at the heart of the decision was *right*, and that it didn't include illicit or unfair considerations. It's going to take far more than reason codes to determine that. What's unfair to consider may vary from context to context. For instance, there are now many firms that don't hire people who have been unemployed for six months or longer. Legislators are beginning to address that by proposing bills that would make long-term unemployment an illicit basis for hiring decisions. But number crunchers may simply feed "length of time since last job" into their hiring models, and if that factor is weighted heavily, it could be utterly decisive. Future legislators need to take into account the ease with which big data mongers can do an end run around law designed for an analog age. For example, in the case of "time since last job," they may allow it to be up to 15 percent of a "hiring score," but no more. Just as accounting rules had to adjust to accommodate firms increasingly complex and fractional interests in other firms, laws governing credit and employment decisions need to become far more specific about the *extent to which* a forbidden ground of decision making can enter into scores meant to influence decisions.

Auditing systems also need to advance. Discovering problems in Big Data (or decision models based on it) should not be a burden we expect individuals to solve on their own. Very few of us have the time to root through the thousands of databases that may be affecting our lives. Rather, it's something that regulators should be doing, reviewing the data stores of both large firms and data brokers to find suspect data and to demand the origins of data, to assure that it is from reliable sources. In the HIPAA context, the U.S. government has already contracted with expert auditors to detect problematic data practices at hospitals and doctors' offices.[28] It could just as easily tax some of the Big Data economy (now estimated around at least $156 billion) to pay for audits of data practices outside entities covered by HIPAA.[29]

There are models for such regulation. Despite the polarized health policy landscape, the United States took a major step toward establishing a modern regulatory infrastructure for data in the Health Information Technology for Economic and Clinical Health Act

(HITECH) of 2009.[30] Many HITECH provisions help assure patients that their data will be accurate and secure, grant them access to their records, and give them the right to see who accessed their records.[31]

The wild west of online data brokers could stand to add a dose of HITECH principles into their own practices. For example, if they were required to attach a simple H (for health) into the metadata for observations recording or predicting health information, they could also filter out that information in reports and calculations performed in response to sensitive queries in the employment and insurance contexts. E-discovery and deduplication software may even be developed to remove such data without such annotation.

Privacy regulators should also require auditors to gain a deep understanding of data broker practices, so they can quickly detect and deter failures to adhere to data collection, labeling, and filtering standards. The key here is to begin separating out the many zones of life Big Data grandees are so keen to integrate in databases. Health privacy experts have already spearheaded "data segmentation for privacy" in medical records, allowing for, say, a person to segregate entries from a psychiatrist from those coming from a podiatrist. It is time for the controllers of Big Data generally to become far more careful about how they log data, to be sure its collection, analysis, and use can be influenced by public values, and not just the profit motive.

Better audit practices would also permit more substantive regulation of the private sector. As storage costs decline and cloud computing becomes ubiquitous, a decision maker can use software to default to recording the online "leads" pursued as she investigates an applicant. Anyone who has seen a search engine's "web history" knows how revealing and meticulous that documentation can be.[32]

The exact scope of the requirements will need to be worked out by administrative agencies, which will not need to reinvent the wheel. Law has long addressed the recordkeeping requirements of government agencies, carefully separating the types of searches for information that constitute forbidden ex parte contacts from the run-of-the-mill research no one expects to be recorded.

There are important objections to the proposed reputation regulation I've described so far. First, while administrative law principles of disclosing the basis of a decision are accepted for government actors, why should the private actors targeted by such legislation also be required to be open about what they are reviewing? This objection merits a layered response. Issuers of credit and insurers are pervasively regulated. As the financial crisis has demonstrated, these entities rely on government as their "ultimate risk manager."[33] After the failure of financial industry deregulation, an ever-closer intertwining of the state and the FIRE industries (finance, insurance, and real estate) is a hallmark of the Obama administration.[34] "Coming clean" on the bases of their decisions is a small price to pay for the degree of government subvention they are now receiving.

As employers, firms are subject to many antidiscrimination laws, and the fair data practices discussed above might better be incorporated into extant regulation on those grounds rather than being a freestanding privacy law. Given the extraordinary targeting of women and racial minorities online documented by Danielle Citron and other advocates of "cyber civil rights," there is already a serious civil rights case to be made against indiscriminate reliance on Internet sources.[35]

Second, why shouldn't word-of-mouth or personal recommendations be subject to the same level of review? Unlike a recommendation letter written for one or a few readers, or a phone call that is almost never heard by anyone other than the callers, Internet-based rumors and lies are frequently persistent, searchable, replicable, and accessible to any decision maker with access to the right software or database. A negative reference only hurts for as long as a job seeker keeps it on her resume; a negative comment online is almost always beyond her control. Anyone affected by such expression deserves at least some chance at discovering whether it has been considered by key decision makers.

Data brokers may break out the excuse that we've heard over and over again—that they need to keep their scoring methods secret, lest crafty consumers "game the system." For example, if schemers learn that having 4 credit cards (no more, no less) is correlated with high likelihood of paying off one's debts, they might rush out to obtain four cards in order to boost their credit score. Or those applying to be a cashier may all say they "love smiling at customers all the time," defeating the predictive power of that question in an employment personality test.

That sounds worrisome in the abstract. But it's hard to imagine thousands of aspiring deadbeats wreaking havoc by skillfully manipulating scoring algorithms. Those that *really* want to game the system are already scheming to do so, just as aspiring collegians find out as much as they can about secretive admissions tests by hiring test prep companies and counselors. Moreover, it's almost inevitable that *someone* will inadvertently disclose critical factors in decision making. Those who learn about them (or reverse engineer them) will then have an unfair advantage over others. Data scientist Cathy O'Neil has argued that easily "gameable classifiers" are inherently weak and fragile tools of modeling.[36] Modelers should be looking for predictive signals that are robust to manipulation.

Scoring companies also want to keep competitors from understanding what data they have and how they are using it. But the real basis of commercial success in Big Data–driven industries is likely the quantity of relevant data collected *in the aggregate*—something not necessarily revealed or shared via person-by-person disclosure of data held and scoring algorithms used. Moreover, however savvy absolute secrecy may be as a business strategy, it is doubtful that public policy should be encouraging it. There is little evidence that the inability to keep such systems secret would diminish innovation. Such concerns are more than outweighed by the threats to human dignity posed by pervasive, secret, and automated scoring systems. At the very least, individuals should have a meaningful form of notice and a chance to challenge predictive scores that harm their ability to obtain credit, jobs, housing, and other important opportunities.

## Spy Files

Public-sector spying also needs far better data practices. The existing privacy regime is confusing in part because each of the following groups is subject to varying requirements:

| National Security | Homeland Security | Police |
| --- | --- | --- |
| Federal Law Enforcers | State Law Enforcers | Local Law Enforcers |
| Domestic Intelligence | Government Contractors | Private Security Firms |

But as we saw in Chapter 2, it has been national policy for *over a decade* to encourage information sharing among these entities—and many more. Local police join federal agents to combat "all threats and all hazards" at fusion centers. Private data brokers gladly serve as "big brother's little helpers." Without well-funded, ethically committed, and technically expert oversight, private- and public-sector spies will pair ever more pervasive surveillance with ever more successful deflection of inquiries about it.

Despite well-publicized leaks about the NSA, much of this world remains secret. But some outrages have come to light. The ACLU has documented that "law enforcement agencies across America continue to monitor and harass groups and individuals for doing little more than peacefully exercising their First Amendment rights."[37]

Monitoring libertarians, peace activists, and Occupiers not only violates civil rights—it also wastes public resources.

Unfortunately, the political establishment has been willfully blind to well-documented abuses. In a 2014 speech on surveillance, President Obama treated the misuse of intelligence gathering as a relic of American history—something done in the bad old days of J. Edgar Hoover, and never countenanced by recent administrations.[38] But the accumulation of menacing stories—from fusion centers to "joint terrorism task forces" to a New York "demographics unit" targeting Muslims—is impossible to ignore. From Alaska (where military intelligence spied on an antiwar group) to Florida (where Quakers and antiglobalization activists were put on watch lists), activists have been considered threats, rather than citizens exercising core constitutional rights. Political dissent is a routine target for surveillance by the FBI.

The Obama administration might insist that no one has yet demonstrated that the NSA itself—the main subject of the president's speech—has engaged in politically driven spying on American citizens.[39] But the NSA is only one part of the larger story of intelligence gathering in the United States, which involves over 1,000 agencies and nearly 2,000 private companies. Moreover, we have little idea of exactly how information and requests flow between agencies.

History counsels caution. Between 1956 and 1971, the FBI's COINTELPRO (an acronym for "counterintelligence program") engaged in domestic covert action designed to disrupt groups engaged in the civil rights, antiwar, and communist movements. As Lawrence Rosenthal has observed, "History reflects a serious risk of abuse in investigations based on the protected speech of the targets," and politicians at the time responded.[40] Reviewing intelligence agency abuses from that time period, the Church Committee issued a series of damning reports in 1975–1976, leading to some basic reforms.[41] If a new Church Committee were convened, it would have to cover much of the same ground. Moreover, it would need to put in place real safeguards against politicized (or laundered) domestic intelligence gathering. Those are presently lacking. I have yet to find a case where the parties involved in any of the recent politicization of intelligence were seriously punished. Nor have I seen evidence that the victims of such incidents have received just compensation for the unwarranted intrusion into their affairs.

To advance the debate about surveillance in the United States, we need something like a Truth and Reconciliation Commission to review (and rebuke) the politicization of intelligence gathering post-9/11. Too many privacy activists have been unwilling to admit the persistence of catastrophic threats that may only be detected by spies. But the U.S. government has been even less moored to reality, unwilling to admit that a runaway surveillance state has engaged in precisely the types of activities that the Bill of Rights is supposed to prevent. Before we can even have a debate about the proper balance between liberty and security, we need to confront the many cases where misguided intelligence personnel spied on activists with neither goal in mind.

Unfortunately, the contemporary domestic intelligence apparatus is so vast as to render the judiciary incapable of fine-grained review of its decisions. They are unlikely to do much to control the alphabet soup of intelligence agencies (NSA, FBI, DHS, etc.), their state-level adjuncts, and their corporate cronies. The intelligence apparatus has fused into a "blob" on autopilot, immune to the resistance of those it engulfs, and eager to deflect attention from the economy of favors enabled by secrecy.[42]

The informality and secrecy surrounding intelligence operations also helps prevent any "critical mass" of decisions accumulating to the point where it could be questioned. A robust legal framework depends on precedent—the past, incremental distinctions between cases that give a present judge authority to interpret the legality of a contested practice. National security exceptionalism prevents all but the most extreme situations from even coming to the attention of a jurist. Moreover, even if a critical mass of cases did materialize, challenges usually evoke deference from judges fearful of tipping government's hand to terrorists.

## Transparent Citizens vs. an Opaque Government/Corporate Apparatus

America has a tradition of combining concerns about privacy with guarantees of government openness.[43] Louis Brandeis, whose Supreme Court opinions and scholarship left an indelible mark on privacy law, envisioned a world in which law could protect the private sphere from prying eyes while ensuring a robust public sphere of transparency.[44] We must build civil liberties safeguards *into the technical architecture* of our domestic intelligence network.[45] But just as important, we have to make sure that independent individuals *who are not themselves part of the intelligence apparatus* have some role in processing the staggering amounts of data that even an oversight program will generate.

Technical standards can play a crucial role in monitoring intelligence activities.[46] According to federal regulation, fusion centers are supposed to employ audit logs that record the activity taking place in the information-sharing network,[47] including "queries made by users, the information accessed, information flows between systems, and date- and time-markers for those activities."[48] Audit logs ought to be implemented at any government agency or private contractor engaged in intelligence gathering. To identify intelligence personnel who are diverging from real national security work into politicized witch hunts, someone needs to watch exactly how they are watching other people.

Unfortunately, there are now two problems with audit logs—one technical, one practical. Audit logs are not fully tamper resistant: they can be changed by personnel without a record of their alteration. This feature undermines a crucial purpose of audit logs—to aid in the detection of deliberate misuses of the system.[49] Ironically, it is exactly this type of vulnerability which has made the Snowden snafu such a problem for the NSA. The agency cannot even assess exactly what documents he copied because it lacked adequate controls to monitor who accessed what.

Immutable audit logs help solve this problem. With immutable audit logs, individual personnel cannot defeat the network's record-keeping function. This secures a permanent record of the network's activity while increasing the probative value of logs as evidence.

Agents might protest that the logs create a bureaucratic impediment to their work. Perhaps if they were required to hand-write justifications of everything they do at the time they do it, they would have a point. But when they already operate systems that silently, effortlessly record details of everyone else's communications and research, it seems odd for them to protest the same treatment for their own. A "write once, read-many" (WORM) storage drive could record all uses of the system, since it can be "designed so that data cannot be altered once it is written to disc." To assure system robustness, "records can be serialized by a system-generated counter and then given a digital signature." While such processes might have created a mountain of paperwork in the analog age, declining costs for digital storage and wiki-based records make it plausible today. As a technological matter, the cost of information storage has consistently dropped over time, and recent developments suggest even more dramatic advances in coming years.[50]

The practical problem with audit logs is that they are not reviewed nearly enough to catch the misuse of intelligence data, and penalties for misuse are rarely imposed. Part of this is a simple resource problem. Just as the Federal Trade Commission (FTC) is utterly understaffed relative to the proliferating digital threats it is supposed to regulate, the Privacy and Civil Liberties Oversight Board (PCLOB) and various internal inspectors general in the domestic intelligence apparatus are outmatched. They lack the personnel and resources to make an appreciable impact. Courts are similarly at a loss.

How many resources *should* be allocated to such oversight? Consider the development of the Human Genome Project—a program of research about as sensitive and ambitious, with as much potential for good and ill, as the Human Security Project now consuming so much of the federal budget. Key agencies funding the exploration of the genome have devoted three to five percent of that research budget to examining the "ethical, legal, and scientific" implications of their work. That funding helps us anticipate (and, ideally, preempt) misuses of genetic data, and identify better uses of it.

The Human Genome Project is, at its core, an effort to discover "what makes us tick": the fundamental biological blueprints for how human development unfolds. What we need to face up to is that pervasive surveillance, unified into massive databases by powerful corporate and government actors, is an effort to find out "what makes us tick" on a societal level. As genetics research may someday spare us from terrible diseases, constant tracking of communications and information could help prevent enormous losses of life. But when our security apparatus begins to obsess over harmless political groups, or focus undue attention on disfavored religious or ethnic groups, it evokes the Promethean allure of genetic engineering, or even the horrors of eugenics. Bioethicists studying the Human Genome Project have helped scientists identify overreaching, and develop nuanced responses to ethically complex knowledge acquisition.[51] It's time to empower ethicists, attorneys, and technical experts to identify troubling directions of our security state, and to devise policies to curb them.

If immutable audit logs of fusion centers are regularly reviewed, misconduct might be discovered, wrongdoers might be held responsible, and similar misuses might be deterred.[52] By connecting threat designations and suspicious activity reports to their instigators, such tools might also help solve another problem: data integrity and relevance. They would prevent people from appearing on watch or threat lists without supporting evidence tethered to it. That evidence would in turn be watermarked with its provenance, assuring attributions and verifiability of observations (much as citations help assure the validity of an assertion in an academic work). Such safeguards could help correct mistakes throughout the network as well.[53]

Privacy protections and security can be mutually reinforcing. For example, indiscriminate fusion center data mining of online musings casts a very wide dragnet indeed if it monitors anyone who uses the word "bomb" in postings. Proper redress mechanisms could allow the centers to drop from surveillance a theater critic who frequently judges certain plays to be a "bomb."[54] That kind of confusion may sound absurd, but remember that computer search functionalities are "dumb" in important ways. As programmer/philosopher David Auerbach has observed:

> The government may be further behind than we think; FBI director Robert Mueller admitted in the 9/11 hearings that FBI databases only searched one word at a time: "flight" or "school" but not "flight school." More recently, the cables released by

WikiLeaks at the end of 2010 each contain a handful of tags, à la Twitter. The CBC observed that one cable discussing Canada was tagged "CN" rather than "CA," designating Comoros instead of Canada, and a few cables were tagged with the nonexistent tag "CAN." It's safe to assume that these tags were also assigned manually.

The haphazardness and errors of government intelligence are not reassuring for national security, but neither are they reassuring for privacy mavens. Who knows what shortcuts are being taken in the service of expediency as surveillance data is processed? Who knows which Canadians may be classified as Comoros dissidents? Under such circumstances, it may seem quaint to complain about "profiling." Everything and everyone is being profiled all the time, often incompetently.[55]

The scholar and technologist Helen Nissenbaum has eloquently argued that privacy rights demand some basic level of information control, a "contextual integrity" afforded to data subjects rendered objects by surveillance.[56] Threats occasioned by loss of privacy can be defused once a decision maker has a fuller picture of a person unfairly categorized by the new surveillance systems. Behind any particular transformative classification—from citizen to "enemy within," from law-abiding individual to "suspect"—lies a narrative, an interpretive framework designed to "connect the dots."

At times of danger, it can be all too easy to associate a given individual with an established threat to order. Yet in the fullness of time, the accused, and citizens generally, can begin to rewrite those parts of the narrative that were erroneous and unjust. Immutable audit logs enable the tracing of history and its rewriting, as occurred during the Church Committee hearings, and more recently in the Iraq War inquiry in Great Britain.[57] They need to be a part of the state's surveillance apparatus.

## Qualified Transparency

The security state is actually *ahead* of Silicon Valley in achieving some forms of transparency. At a hearing on a proposed Google-Yahoo joint venture, former House Judiciary Committee chair John

Conyers complained that neither he nor other committee members were allowed to inspect the terms of the deal. He stated that the committee was given "more ready access to documents surrounding the President's terrorist surveillance program" than to Google's plans.[58] Journalist George Packer has also complained, calling his Amazon investigation "a reporting challenge not that much easier than covering national security and intelligence."[59] And while the Foreign Intelligence Surveillance Court offers some inspection (however cursory) of controversial government spying, we have nothing similar devoted to understanding the data gathering (and information ordering) of Silicon Valley firms. Given their role as partners or pawns of the surveillance state, we deserve better.

Companies dependent on massive Internet intermediaries should also have some basic rights, particularly when classic competition law concerns arise. For example, imagine that you own Company A, and your main competitor is the persistent (but demonstrably worse) Company B. In searches for the products you sell, you reliably end up in the top five results in the studies you've commissioned; your competitors at Company B are on the fifth or sixth pages.[60] What happens if Google purchases Company B, and immediately after the purchase, Company B appears to dominate the first page of results, and your company has been relegated to later pages? Should there be some type of remedy?

When a website's ranking suddenly tumbles dozens of places, and it has a plausible story about being targeted as a potential rival of Google, is it too much to ask for some third party to review the particular factors that led to the demotion? Changes in ranking methodology are rigorously tested and documented by firms like Google. Given how quickly a sudden drop can occur, we are not discussing an infinite variety of changes to be reviewed.[61] Nor would there necessarily be a disclosure of the entire algorithm to a third-party auditor, or even the revelation of the relevant changes in the algorithm to the party involved, much less the general public. This is highly qualified transparency.

One of the smartest thinkers in American antitrust law, Mark Patterson, has recognized that a standard arising out of the financial crisis can apply to search engines in situations like this. When credit rating agencies (CRAs like Moody's or S&P) "make material changes to rating procedures and methodologies, the SEC must now ensure that . . . the changes are applied consistently," and that the CRA "publicly discloses the reason for the change."[62] Patterson argues that search engines ought to have a similar duty of disclosure when competition law concerns arise, so that an outside arbiter can determine whether an aggrieved site really deserved a demotion, was just part of a larger algorithmic shake-up, or was specifically targeted as a business rival. Properly funded and staffed, the FTC or another agency could evaluate the claims of companies that feel unfairly singled out by a change in Google's, Amazon's, or other Internet giants' algorithms.[63]

Such inquiries do not need to be expensive, relative to the enormous cash piles accumulating at major Silicon Valley firms. In contexts ranging from privacy rights to false advertising, authorities in the United States and Europe have recognized the need for fast, flexible "quick looks" at suspect business practices. For example, in U.S. false advertising disputes, 95 percent of problematic situations are quickly resolved in a self-regulatory fashion.[64] This is not a recipe for the litigation nightmares industry advocates so frequently invoke. And given how much of internet behemoths' revenue is now being used to purchase other, smaller firms, isn't it time *some* of that surplus funded efforts to assure the competitive process is itself fair? The alternative is frightening: a few giant firms with a viselike grip over the very marketplaces where their competitors would need to succeed in order to thrive. Antitrust law flirts with irrelevance if it disdains the technical tools necessary to understand a modern information economy.[65]

Someone needs to be able to "look under the hood" and understand what is going on when companies like Foundem, Yelp, and Nextag plunge in Google results. (Haven't heard of them? Maybe they've been hidden from you.) And disclosure and auditing are not merely remedies; they may even be considered salutary extensions of current business practices. Establishing webmaster forums that allow for that type of dialogue between the ranked and the ranker has, to this point at least, seemed like a fair and responsible business practice to Google itself.[66]

If Google thought of its rankings as a kind of virtual world—one whose members have essentially accepted (via terms of service) the absolute sovereignty of the ruler of that territory—such a dialogical process would make little sense. In the digital feudalism of virtual worlds, no one has a right to question the unilateral decision of the ruler. Errors would only have meaning as lost profit opportunities, not as failures to run a competition properly. At its best, Google recognizes itself as a trusted adviser to its users rather than as a purely profit-maximizing entity.

And Google is not alone in exercising power over the Internet. Apple, Facebook, Twitter, and Amazon can also rely on opaque technologies, sometimes leaving users in the dark as to exactly why any given app, story, or book is featured at a particular time. We should expect any company aspiring to order vast amounts of information to try to keep its methods secret, if only to reduce controversy and foil copycat competitors. However wise this secrecy may be as a business strategy, it devastates our ability to truly understand the social world Silicon Valley is creating. Opacity creates ample opportunities to hide anticompetitive, discriminatory, or simply careless conduct behind a veil of technical inscrutability. Qualified transparency can address these concerns while respecting intellectual property rights.

And what should happen if something untoward is discovered? In Europe, at least, several creative approaches are now being discussed. In response to antitrust investigations, it is likely that Google will start clearly labeling which of its search results are its own properties.[67] It will also offer at least three alternatives to its own specialized properties—so, for example, links to programs at Vimeo or Hulu or other video sites might show up, in addition to Google's YouTube, when a user queries, say, "Community meowmeowbeenz." Such remedies will need to be studied and adjusted over time to assure their effectiveness.[68] Nevertheless, direct state intervention may be the only way to assure that smaller players get a fair shake at an audience. Regulators should not shy away from conducting similar inquiries at Apple's iTunes, or Amazon's digital storefronts.

Unfortunately, U.S. competition regulators have not been nearly as innovative as the Europeans. In 2012, the FTC was to determine whether Google had manipulated results so as to increase the visibility of its own services and decrease the visibility of competitors or would-be competitors. Reporters also suggested that investigators would examine how Google set advertising rates.[69] FTC staff recommended a suit against Google.[70] The agency even hired an outside litigator and an outside economist, presumably in preparation for possible litigation.[71]

But only three months after word leaked about the staff's view, the commissioners rushed to close the investigation. Did the staff change its mind? Was its draft recommendation overruled by the politically appointed commissioners?[72] If so, on what grounds? Because the decision was made behind closed doors, these questions have never been answered. In its public closing statement, the FTC spent barely two pages discussing the search bias allegations.[73]

In considering allegations of search bias, the FTC necessarily would have had to evaluate the reasons behind, and the effects of, changes to Google's algorithms. Google defended its conduct by arguing that users were better off as a result of these changes, and the FTC in the end appeared to agree. A basic question that remains unanswered is how the FTC approached this highly technical issue. The meager public record does not inspire much confidence. As the *New York Times* observed, "The FTC did not detail how it defined harm or what quantitative measures it had used to determine that Google users were better off."[74]

Nor did the agency appear to consider whether small consumer gains now from, say, an ultraclean interface of purely Google-owned or Google-affiliated results might later disserve consumers who want more diverse offerings. In response to this opacity, one public interest group has put in a FOIA request for communications between Google and the FTC. Consumer Watchdog has requested public disclosure of the staff memorandum that was reported to have recommended more robust action.[75] But because the matter was resolved without a consent decree—which would have allowed for public comment and required judicial approval—the FTC has not had to do much by way of explanation or justification for its (in)action.

The then-Director of the Bureau of Economics at the FTC responded to these concerns by assuring the *New York Times* that data came from a wide range of sources, and none of this data was taken at face value. "We kick the tires hard on all of the data we receive," he said.[76] But the four-page findings of the commission don't even give us a sense of the hypotheses the FTC tested, or even the full legal theory of the case. The comment is unintentionally revealing, however. Agencies ought to be able to "look under the hood" of highly advanced technologies like the algorithms at the heart of the Google search engine and the data they process.[77] This might involve hiring computer scientists, programmers, and other experts capable of understanding exactly how algorithms changed over time, and how directives from top management might influence what is always portrayed as a scientific, technical, and neutral process.[78] "Kicking the tires" is not a metaphor of expert analysis. Rather, it suggests a skeptical consumer trying, as best he can, to use whatever signals are available to a layperson to make an assessment ultimately beyond his competence. Until the FTC releases more information on how it assesses accusations like search bias, its investigative capacity looks little better than that of the consumers it ostensibly protects.

Admittedly, some scholars of competition law question whether the state will ever be nimble enough to perform this type of fairness inquiry in the context of search engines.[79] That's ultimately a question of resources: if antigovernment forces sufficiently defund the FTC, the Federal Communications Commission (FCC), and the Department of Justice (DOJ), of course they'll fail to keep up with the challenges of digital competition.[80]

## The First Amendment Wild Card

First Amendment scholars offer a more formidable critique. If Google were to characterize its search results as a *form* (rather than a *finder*) of media, it could invoke a First Amendment right to present information without government interference.[81] Google has already won a few cases on this ground, defeating plaintiffs who accused it of treating them unfairly under state laws.[82] For example, when a company called SearchKing claimed in an Oklahoma court in 2003 that it should have appeared more prominently in queries for "Search-King," the judge flatly rejected its arguments.[83] Since "there is no conceivable way to prove that the relative significance assigned to a given web site is false," the judge ruled that SearchKing could never demonstrate that it had been wrongly ranked by Google.[84]

Google brandished the First Amendment again in 2012, hiring two attorneys to argue that antitrust law should not apply to its search rankings. Noting that the First Amendment had even barred a lawsuit against an inaccurate mushroom encyclopedia that led an unfortunate person to eat poisonous fungi, Google argued that it had a right to "speak" any search results, for whatever reason. But antitrust law has been applied to the media in the United States— indeed, the Supreme Court has even stated that free expression and competition law are mutually reinforcing. Consider the following quote from *Associated Press v. United States* (1945), in which the newspaper association argued that it should be immune from certain aspects of competition law:

> Surely a command that the government itself shall not impede the free flow of ideas does not afford non-governmental combinations a refuge if they impose restraints upon that constitutionally guaranteed freedom. . . . The First Amendment affords not the slightest support for the contention that a combination to restrain trade in news and views has any constitutional immunity.[85]

Six years later, the Supreme Court reaffirmed that position in *Lorain Journal v. United States*[86] In *Lorain Journal*, a newspaper refused to deal with those who advertised on its new competitor, a radio station. The newspaper claimed that it had an unfettered First Amendment right to choose its own advertisers, but the Court disagreed. Media companies can communicate their messages without trampling on the Sherman Act.

How relevant is a mid-twentieth century precedent to the Internet landscape of today? Deliberately demoting search results is akin to a *Lorain*-style refusal to deal, since a significant loss of ranking amounts to a death sentence for many would-be competitors of Google. Google counters that *Lorain* is inapplicable to the search engine context because the newspaper in that case "was not excluding advertisements . . . in the exercise of some editorial judgment . . . [but rather] excluding advertisements solely because the advertisers—whatever the content of their ads—were also advertising on a competing radio station."[87] But several disputes follow that *Lorain* pattern, as complainants say Google's decisions are made only according to an economic, and not an editorial, logic. Foundem, for instance, claimed that Google was primarily (and perhaps exclusively) motivated to exclude it from search results in order to clear space for Google Shopping.[88] The search giant can only declare *Lorain Journal* inapposite by assuming what needs to be proven; namely, that there is no distinct anticompetitive *conduct* motivating the (admittedly) expressive display of search results. The First Amendment is not a "get out of jail free card" for any business with expressive dimensions.[89] And it would be deeply ironic if the First Amendment could be deployed to limit public understanding of critical Internet decision making.[90]

More forward-thinking intermediaries have recognized as much, and relinquished First Amendment defenses in the face of principled opposition to their ranking and rating schemes. Consider health insurers who have rated doctors on their websites, while acting as a small-scale physician search engine for their customers.[91] When the insurers failed to disclose the basis of the rating, many physicians sued, charging it was an unfair and deceptive practice. Some found that "excellent" rankings depended on little more than keeping insurers' cost low. The New York Attorney General's Office extracted a detailed concession from insurers promising new substantive bases for rankings, transparent databases, and opportunities for doctors to correct misleading information.[92] Insurers could have parleyed a First Amendment defense here, but opted instead to work together with the state (and the community they were ranking and rating) to produce a fairer process.

The health insurers are, of course, still free to make public declarations about any given physician. The key issue here is their taking on a role as advisers to their customers, and their *use* of inadequate data to discriminate among physicians. Just as no one has a First Amendment right to fire an employee for appearing to be sick according to a database and algorithms, the First Amendment should not limit the state's ability to assure that intermediaries are acting as honest brokers for their customers and users.

Rather than follow the health insurers' more constructive approach, Google has relied on precedents pioneered by bond raters, who characterized their ratings (AAA, AA, and so on) as opinions. Their litigation position boils down to a familiar disclaimer of responsibility: "Don't blame us if securities we rated AAA tanked—we were only offering an opinion."[93] Leading First Amendment attorney Floyd Abrams has revived those cases, brandishing them as a shield to protect credit rating agencies accused of wrongdoing during the subprime debacle. But courts are knocking holes in this constitutional armor, reasoning that free expression rights can't grow so large as to excuse fraud. If an opinion implies certain facts (such as a careful verification of creditworthiness) which in fact never occurred, those implications can be proved false.[94] Moreover, when a rating agency only issues a rating to a small group of investors, it's far from acting as an ordinary media outlet (which communicates to a broader public).[95] Rather, it's closer to an adviser, like a doctor, attorney, or accountant. And those professionals cannot simply disclaim their responsibilities to clients (or avoid malpractice lawsuits) by asserting that they are only offering opinions.

Such rulings could undermine the First Amendment protection of a Google, Apple, or Amazon, too. All those companies either now employ (or plan to deploy) some degree of personalization in their rankings of websites, apps, and products. As these algorithmic authorities get to know us better, they cultivate our business by learning more about what pleases and displeases us, and how to maintain our interest.[96] At some point, personalization becomes a relationship mutual enough to trigger the classic duties of professional advisers. If a doctor sickened a patient by recommending a medicine whose manufacturer granted him a kickback, no court would dismiss a malpractice case based on the doctor's putative right to say whatever he wanted about the proper way to treat an ailment. Similarly, intermediaries need to take on some responsibility for ordering Internet choices responsibly—if not to ranked and rated entities, then at least to their own users.[97]

## A CIA for Finance

Skeptics may doubt that any government agency can competently monitor complex Internet firms. But legislation has already set one to work on a far harder problem: assessing the *overall state* of U.S. financial markets. While a company like Google is a closed system, with standards of organization imposed from the top, finance involves transactions *between* entities. Nevertheless, the Dodd-Frank Act of 2010 empowered an Office of Financial Research (OFR) (sometimes called "The CIA of Finance") within the U.S. Department of the Treasury to improve regulation by illuminating the overall state of financial markets.[98]

Like intelligence agencies that have broad investigative powers to spot threats, the OFR collects and analyzes details of financial transactions in order to spot "systemic risk" (that is, patterns of bets that threaten to undermine the entire financial system). It can keep its analyses private, share them with other regulators, or open them to the public, within certain statutory and constitutional limits.

This is a delicate balancing act. If the OFR tries to reveal too much of the data it collects to the public at large, affected firms could bog it down in lengthy court proceedings over confidentiality. If it discloses too little, it risks being dismissed as yet another lapdog of Wall Street. But whatever its performance in detecting systemic risk, the OFR promises one benefit to future historians: permanent archives of financial decision making that might otherwise get lost in a maelstrom of business mergers, takeovers, and IT system "upgrade."

OFR analysts focused on measuring financial risk, liquidity, and the potential that the failure of a "systemically important financial institution" might spark a chain of defaults. Privy to some of the most sensitive data in financial markets, the OFR can send early warnings to financial regulators. By assessing the state of the financial system as a whole, it should provide a critical new source of knowledge to regulators long kept in the dark. The OFR is serious about its work, fully acknowledging that finance recordkeeping may have to change to promote systemic stability:

> The data simply may not exist in the form needed for monitoring purposes. In that case, the Office [must] define data requirements, evaluate the feasibility and difficulty of obtaining the data, identify the best way to fill the gap, and develop a collection strategy. If the data do exist, they may not be accessible due to confidentiality, privacy, or data-sharing limitations. The data

may be inadequate because they are not detailed enough for analysis, focused on the wrong items, too limited in scope, or of poor quality. In addition, the data may be impossible to compare or aggregate because of a lack of data standards.[99]

The last point—about data standards—is a difficult one; it has also plagued regulators in other fields, like health care. When the Obama Administration promoted the gathering and exchange of health information in 2009, many worried that the resulting data could never be aggregated and analyzed for public health purposes. But health care regulators are using an elaborate package of incentive payments to improve interoperability among electronic health record systems.

The OFR, by contrast, has no money to lure finance firms to adopt uniform standards. It can urge the various financial regulators it advises to try and nudge the sector toward some common standards. The OFR itself is now setting standards known as Legal Entity Identifiers. These would set a consistent name or number for the entities engaged in various financial transactions, and are no doubt valuable: when a large financial firm can have hundreds of ad hoc subsidiaries and "variable interest entities," regulators need to be able to quickly map who owns what.[100] But with derivatives' drafters slicing and dicing risk and reward, modern finance threatens to make basic ownership information irrelevant; if, for instance, Citibank "owns" a small firm, but has swapped the firm's net income for an interest-bearing bond, who really loses if the firm fails to generate income? And this is a very simple example: derivatives can get far more complex, with risks and rewards shifting on the basis of unforeseeable events.

Other regulators are trying to help here.[101] CFTC and SEC staff conclude "that current technology is capable of representing derivatives using a common set of computer-readable descriptions[, which] are precise enough to use both for the calculation of net exposures and to serve as part or all of a binding legal contract."[102] As with the SEC's Consolidated Audit Trail,[103] which tracks trading, the idea here is to develop methods not merely for real-time monitoring of troubling developments, but also for red-flagging the most problematic trading strategies.[104]

However ambitiously American finance regulators may set standards, their efforts are compromised by the *internationalization* of major firms, which plead that any stringent national standard for recording information may make it harder to do business overseas. They want to wait for international coordination—a process that could take decades. Or they could simply move their trading overseas.

If the proliferation of tax havens is any guide, there are plenty of places willing to bend (or end) rules to lure finance business.[105] A small, hopeful step toward improving government understanding of financial flows happened when Congress passed the Foreign Account Tax Compliance Act (FATCA). Thanks in part to a series of embarrassing investigations into tax havens by Senator Carl Levin, that law targets illicit income.[106] But there is little reason in principle why its auditing requirements could not be expanded to encompass a larger view of financial flows. Just as we need to know where shadowy data brokers' data is coming from, and where it (and the inferences drawn from it) are going to, we need to have a much better sense of where funds are flowing from, and where they (and the income they generate) is going to.

An adviser to the Tax Justice Network once said that assessing money kept offshore is an "exercise in night vision," like trying to measure "the economic equivalent of an astrophysical black hole."[107] The most fundamental tool of tax secrecy is separation: between persons and their money, between corporations and the persons who control them, between beneficial and nominal controllers of wealth. FATCA helps reconnect all those fragments. It requires foreign financial institutions (FFIs) to report financial information about accounts held by American citizens, or pay a withholding tax.[108] Congress enacted FATCA in response to the problem of international tax evasion. Too many U.S. citizens were using offshore accounts to avoid paying U.S. taxes, reminiscent of the financial firms who locate dozens of shell companies in "secrecy jurisdictions" to deflect the attention of auditors or regulators.[109] FATCA is shaping up to be a major advance in tracking global money flows.[110]

Tax havens may seem like an outlier in the global economy, a problem well outside the run of ordinary business. But tax havens are among "the most powerful instruments of globalization," critical to many business strategies.[111] Shell company networks can be structurally similar to the webs of entities used by tax evaders. FATCA requires that FFIs report both on accounts held directly by individuals and on interests in accounts held by shell entities for the benefit of U.S. individuals. It also covers foreign entities with significant United States ownership.[112] The law shifts the responsibility for reporting from the taxpayer to financial institutions. It hits those FFIs where it hurts, penalizing them monetarily if they do not report.[113] FATCA also requires participating FFIs to withhold on payments to nonparticipating FFIs, which is supposed to create a divide between compliant and noncompliant entities.[114] Isolating noncompliant firms should also be a central goal of finance regulators.

## Losing Trust in Financial Regulation

I have focused so far on the interaction between law and technology in financial regulation. But even the most technically adept government officials will accomplish little if they are not willing to impose significant penalties on firms *and persons* who violate the law. Before we place any more reliance on them, we need to contemplate some of the lessons learned in the aftermath of the global financial crisis.

Charles Ferguson, the leading documentarian of the crisis, won an Oscar for his film *Inside Job.* His acceptance speech began, "Forgive me, I must start by pointing out that three years after our horrific financial crisis caused by financial fraud, not a single financial executive has gone to jail, and that's wrong." Ferguson later followed up in his book *Predator Nation,* laying out how top executives at leading financial firms had violated basic requirements of the Sarbanes-Oxley Act and other laws,[115] and how inadequate subsequent investigations by regulatory authorities had been.[116]

Ferguson was not alone in his bleak assessment of Wall Street lawbreaking.[117] Judge Jed Rakoff accused the Department of Justice of making excuses for not criminally prosecuting top executives in an extraordinary essay in the *New York Review of Books.*[118] For example, Lanny Breuer, who was head of the DOJ's Criminal Division for much of the crisis, suggested that because there were "very sophisticated" parties on both sides of key transactions, it was too hard for prosecutors to demonstrate that one side had actually deceived the other.[119] Rakoff countered that it was the seller's duty to make sure the risks of the toxic securities were fully explained. "Given the fact that these securities were bought and sold at lightning speed," Rakoff parried, "it is by no means obvious that even a sophisticated counterparty would have detected the problems with the arcane, convoluted mortgage-backed derivatives they were being asked to purchase."[120]

High administration officials also brought up the topic of systemic risk. Attorney General Eric Holder worried that "if you do bring a criminal charge—it will have a negative impact on the national economy, perhaps even the world economy." Judge Rakoff scoffed at this "too big to jail" rationale as "apparent disregard for equality under the law"—one of cornerstones of the American justice system.[121]

A final confounding factor is the concept of mens rea (the Latin term for "guilty mind"); the requirement that to commit a crime like fraud, the defendant must intentionally or knowingly deceive others. The complexity of financial derivatives is such that anyone can say, after the fact, "Oh, I had no idea things were going to go so badly."[122] As long as the money kept rolling in, they had little reason to question exactly how it materialized.[123]

Judge Rakoff had an answer here, as well. "Willful blindness" is a "well-established basis on which federal prosecutors have asked juries to infer intent, including in cases involving complexities, such as accounting rules, at least as esoteric as those involved in the events leading up to the financial crisis."[124] Whether such ignorance was intentional, or merely wishful thinking or self-delusion, should be litigated in the open, not silently entombed in cryptic settlement agreements. One of the greatest dangers of complex and secret modeling algorithms in finance is their ability to obscure such distinctions. When a CEO can step up to the witness stand and disclaim understanding of core actions of his own firm on the grounds of their complexity, it's hard to imagine how basic legal principles of responsibility and fiduciary duty can endure.

Some finance experts argue that the modeling of transactions has become so complex that disingenuous managers can always field a phalanx of quants to hide deals' dangers. Moreover, algorithmic "control" systems, which are supposed to deter manipulation of risk models automatically, may be easier to manipulate than human experts—recall how JP Morgan Chase's London Whale traders moved the goalposts to buy time for their risky strategies.[125] But without actually reviewing the fine details of transactions, we'll never even be able to have a coherent argument about such issues.

Judge Rakoff actually tried to force such a review in one case. In 2011, he refused to accept a $285 million settlement proposed between Citigroup and the SEC regarding the bank's role in promoting suspect securities. In a scathing judgment, Rakoff accused both regulators and the regulated of making the court a mere "handmaiden to a settlement privately negotiated on the basis of unknown facts." "An application of judicial power that does not rest on facts is worse than mindless, it is inherently dangerous," cautioned the judge, especially "in any case like this that touches on the transparency of financial markets whose gyrations have so depressed our economy and debilitated our lives." Rakoff pointedly noted the irony: an enforcement process focused on bank opacity was hiding key details from all but privileged insiders. He also scoffed at the how small the proposed payment was in comparison with the bank's profits.[126]

The SEC could have used the judge's comments as leverage to urge more concessions from Citigroup. Instead, the bank and its regulators joined forces to appeal Rakoff's decision—and won in the Second Circuit Court of Appeals. As a legal matter, the higher court was probably right: administrative agencies have wide discretion to decide which cases to pursue, and which to settle.[127] Nevertheless, the Second Circuit decision ignored particularly troubling aspects of the SEC's relationship to the industry it regulates, particularly the revolving door dynamics that can turn watchdogs into lapdogs by tacitly trading current leniency for future wealth. Nor did the appellate panel consider how much of a black box the SEC can be.

For example, in 2010, a lawyer named Darcy Flynn accused top SEC management of violating federal law by destroying critical evidence gathered during investigations. Flynn had worked at the SEC for fourteen years before his bombshell accusation. During his time there, the agency had agreed (with the National Archives and Records Administration) that all of its important documents, "including case files relating to preliminary investigations," were to be stored for at least twenty-five years. But Flynn alleged that the SEC instructed investigators to destroy "documents obtained in connection with" over 17,000 matters under investigation, or MUIs.[128] Had the agency followed the law, and maintained its internal memory system properly, it might have more easily made cases against some of the most egregious financial firms.[129]

Document destruction deflects muckrakers who want to expose the cozy ties between many financial regulators and the private firms defending the targets of regulation.[130] MUIs might have illuminated troubling revolving door dynamics. The Project on Government Oversight has uncovered 789 instances of former SEC personnel announcing their intent to represent a client before the SEC within two years of leaving the agency.[131] If any were involved in MUIs related to their current employer, they may welcome the data black hole.[132]

Journalists are also routinely frustrated by finance regulators' opacity.[133] The SEC gave the *New York Times*'s William D. Cohan virtually no information on its precrisis inquiries into Goldman Sachs and Bear Stearns, despite repeated pleas and FOIA requests. Cohan has identified a series of critical events crucial to the public's understanding of the crisis. He claims that the SEC has the most revealing documents related to them, but it will not disclose them.[134] Cohan laments that decision, concluding that "if our government agencies continue to do everything in their considerable power to keep hidden information that belongs in the public realm, all the regulatory reform in the world won't end the rot on Wall Street." Without transparency, accountability is impossible. And full transparency of federal agency actions—let alone the actions of private firms—is far off. Too many regulators are underfunded, overworked, or angling for lucrative jobs from the very firms they are supposed to be regulating.[135]

That may sound like a very harsh judgment on finance regulators. But how else can we explain their sluggish response over the past six years? Formal inquiries, including the Financial Crisis Inquiry Commission and the Senate investigations mentioned earlier, have resulted in lengthy reports. These documents reveal a financial industry committed to concealing critical practices from regulators and clients. Speaking of his subcommittee's bipartisan report, Senator Carl Levin concluded, "Our investigation found a financial snake pit rife with greed, conflicts of interest, and wrongdoing."[136] No wonder Judge Rakoff was so frustrated.

Criminologist Bill Black, a bank regulator in the 1980s and early 1990s, provides another point of comparison. Like the housing bubble of the 2000s, the savings and loan (S&L) crisis of the late 1980s involved banks systematically overvaluing real estate and mortgage portfolios. In that crisis, regulators made over 10,000 referrals for potential criminal prosecution, and more than 1,400 individuals were jailed. The crisis of 2008 ballooned to over 70 times larger monetarily, and Black found the behavior of many of today's managers eerily similar to the actions of convicted S&L leaders. But there have been fewer than 100 referrals, and far fewer convictions—certainly no one near the top of a large firm has had to fear a day in jail, or even a real reduction in living standards. Black concluded that "a witches' brew of deregulation, desupervision, regulatory black holes and perverse executive and professional compensation has created an intensely criminogenic environment that produces epidemics of accounting control fraud that hyper-inflate financial bubbles and cause economic crises."[137] He has recommended intense pursuit of criminal investigations of top managers and traders with firms.

What we have seen instead is settlements. They may be a little costly, and they may provoke some embarrassing press. But some settlements are not publicly acknowledged at all.[138] For example, although federal law prohibited the FDIC from keeping its settlements secret, the agency agreed with some settling banks not to release information except in response to specific inquiries. These agreements helped bankers to avoid bad press while significantly reducing the deterrent effect that the settlements might have had on other banks.[139]

Why the lack of referrals by agencies to law enforcement? Regulators and prosecutors may have their eyes on positions in the very firms they are squaring off against. Salaries in government rarely go over $200,000 per year, while partners in the leading law firms representing Wall Street giants can enjoy seven-figure salaries and eight-figure net worths. Former prosecutors from the U.S. Attorneys Office for the Southern District of New York routinely go to work for Wall Street firms that represent big financial institutions[140] after they leave government. Few attorneys are steely (or wealthy) enough to rock a boat that has already brought so many others to lucrative private-sector shores.

### "Too Big to Fail" Meets "Too Poor to Regulate"

Another rationale for regulatory reticence is the resource differential between cash-strapped agencies and prosecutors on the one hand and the hugely wealthy financial firms on the other—a gap that has only grown as the biggest banks have acquired ever more market share. A large bank has billions of dollars at its disposal to fight off lawsuits (and to lobby for legislation and rules that tilt the playing field in its favor). The SEC's budget is less than $2 billion, and it must divide its attention among thousands of institutions and traders. Other financial regulators have even lower funding levels. The chair of the agency, Mary Jo White, testified to Congress in 2013 that its "current level of resources is not sufficient to permit the SEC to examine regulated entities and enforce compliance with the securities laws in a way that investors deserve and expect."[141] That bland assessment barely does justice to the bleak realities at resource-starved agencies, where regulators may grimly board a DC bus at 5:30 a.m. to inspect New York's masters of the universe. (Yes, Congress didn't appropriate enough money for the train, and parking in Manhattan could cost even more than the Amtrak.)[142]

The complexity of financial fraud ensures that agencies like the SEC will continue to play "catch up." Beleaguered by the complex schemes cooked up by black box finance's well-paid accountants, lawyers, traders, and managers, finance regulators triage matters by entering into settlements. Many knowledge workers feel "behind the curve" when their computers are three years out of date, but the chair of the SEC admitted in 2010 that her agency's "technology for collecting data and surveilling our markets is often as much as two

decades behind the technology currently used by those we regulate."[143] U.S. financial regulators' resources are dwarfed by the assets
of the firms (and sometimes even the individuals) they police.[144]

Overmatched and overwhelmed, finance regulators are ill-disposed
to seek costly trials. At a Banking, Housing and Urban Affairs Committee hearing in 2013, Massachusetts senator Elizabeth Warren
asked regulators representing the FDIC, the SEC, the OCC, the
CFTC, the Fed, the Treasury, and the Consumer Financial Protection Board when the last time was that they had taken a Wall Street
bank to trial.[145] No one had. Warren noted that "there are District
Attorneys and United States Attorneys out there every day squeezing ordinary citizens on sometimes very thin grounds and taking
them to trial in order to make an example, as they put it. I'm really
concerned that 'too big to fail' has become 'too big for trial.'" Senator Warren has argued that large financial institutions don't have
much incentive to follow the law if they know that they'll always be
able to negotiate a favorable settlement from regulators terrified of
bringing cases before courts.

A few months before Warren's lament, a powerful group of
legislators—the House Financial Services Committee—had voted
to slash the budgets of finance regulators. That move would endanger
their ability to even commence preliminary investigations in many
cases.[146] If budgetary concerns were the primary motive here, the
congressional representatives could have at least "empower[ed]
private actors to pursue claims on behalf of the government," as
Toledo law professor Geoff Rapp suggested in 2012.[147] But they
failed to do so. The darker possibility is that many representatives
simply want to see less financial fraud enforcement.

Even when a president publicly demands action, reasons of state
are sometimes put forward in favor of a go-slow approach. Barack
Obama's much-vaunted Foreclosure Fraud Task Force, launched in
2011, had barely been staffed by May of 2012. As stories of foreclosure fraud and other bank transgressions became harder to ignore,
leaders in the Obama administration began to leak rationales for
their failures to devote serious resources to detecting and deterring
fraud. Officials at the Department of the Treasury, for example,
characterized intensive investigations as self-defeating. They in-

sisted that the primary goal of financial regulation is to ensure the safety and soundness of the current banking system: "Look forward, not back" was a mantra. Launch too many investigations, and critical foreign investors might start to doubt the strength of the United States financial system as a whole. The administration tended to characterize those who would pursue justice as shortsighted and emotional, incapable of the cool calculation necessary to reassure skittish investors.

## Lessons from Health Fraud Enforcement

Whether financial markets really would suffer in the wake of more extensive investigations is an open question. But if we take the Obama administration at its word about the potentially catastrophic impact of *postcrisis* litigation, then the government should invest far more in *precrisis* surveillance and enforcement actions.

Admittedly, the complexity of modern finance has led some to despair of ways to detect destabilizing or potentially fraudulent behavior before it balloons into such disastrous misallocations of capital as the housing bubble. Given regulators' fragmented authority, the slow implementation of Dodd-Frank, and the pressure of budget cuts, it may seem like a lost cause to even try to monitor large financial institutions.

Yet the same might have been said in the 1990s about health care fraud. Hospitals were using increasingly sophisticated technology to overbill public programs like Medicare. Unscrupulous providers sought to make quick bucks by characterizing a fifteen-minute office visit as a thirty-minute one.[148] Some hospitals foisted complex surgeries on patients who didn't need them. Other fraudsters simply made up thousands of Medicare beneficiaries, and charged phantom doctor visits to the government using medical identity theft.

Medicare and Medicaid administrators didn't have the resources to detect many of these frauds. The agencies in charge didn't have the personnel to monitor the vast river of funds coursing through the system. Here too Congress sometimes stood in the way of robust enforcement, harshly criticizing the Department of Justice for the occasionally excessive investigation.[149] But rather than shrinking from enforcement, even in the ever more complex landscape of health-care finance, leaders opted to use specialized contractors to fight fraud and abuse.[150]

Some of the fraud detection was low-hanging fruit—for example, a computer program could red-flag a podiatrist for claiming to have cut fifteen toenails in one visit. Over time, programs have become more sophisticated. Once a contractor has access to a patient's entire history of Medicare-paid doctor visits, it's much easier to notice unusual activity. For example, if someone who's never been diagnosed with diabetes suddenly starts filling prescriptions for insulin, that may be a tipoff to a medical identity theft.

Health software is not only combating fraud, but is also rooting out waste. A doctor who fails to keep up with continuing medical education may order unduly aggressive treatments for a low-risk patient. Clinical decision support software can warn doctors about potentially dangerous drug-drug interactions, or new evidence militating against a once-preferred treatment plan. The goal here is not to automate medicine, but simply to assure that physicians have access to the most up-to-date, relevant information.

Skeptics may counter that it's easier to make a judgment about optimal medical treatment than the proper structure of a financial deal. And they may feel that financial fraud is more complicated than dubious billing and overtreatment in the health care sector. But remember that the promise of Big Data is *machine-driven pattern recognition* that doesn't depend on human expertise. Nobody at Target had to become an expert on how to diagnose pregnancy before its data scientists could develop a program for predicting due dates. The hope behind legal automation is that, with a sufficiently large data set and a sufficient record of past bad outcomes, regulators could nip problems in the bud.

That's already happening in health care. For example, when a provider's billing patterns display enough warning signs (for example, when a large number of claims are ultimately rejected, or they reveal that a doctor has performed far more of a given procedure than anyone else in his state), data-analysis contractors can spot the warning signs early enough to deploy interventions less disruptive and stigmatizing than full-scale investigation and prosecution.[151]

While spectacular "busts" may occasionally occur, in most cases more measured and calibrated interventions are sufficient.[152] Imagine if such safeguards had been in place while Ameriquest's "subprime art department" was forging W-2 forms, or AIG's Financial Products Division was piling up credit default swaps with manifestly inadequate reserves. The crisis of 2008 might have been averted, and trillions of dollars in gross national product preserved.

But, some might ask, what about financial innovation? How can algorithms based on *past* patterns of misconduct detect signs of trouble in strange new investment instruments? Here, another tactic from health law is well worth considering. Financial regulators could license new financial products. Two scholars of law and economics have proposed that firms be forbidden to sell them "until they receive approval from a government agency designed along the lines of the Food and Drug Administration, which screens pharmaceutical innovations."[153] A new "FDA for finance" could coordinate with regulators, giving early warning signs about possible abuse of a new instrument. Or it might condition approval on the security's meeting certain basic safety requirements. This is one of the ideas behind the Consumer Financial Protection Bureau's treatment of so-called "plain vanilla" mortgages, which pose much less of a regulatory and litigation risk to financial institutions than complex ones.[154]

By deploying a team of private-sector contractors at the cutting edge of the information industry, health regulators have promoted responsible billing practices and significantly increased fraud recoveries.[155] The Centers for Medicare and Medicaid Services recovered $17 for every dollar spent on health care oversight efforts in 2008.[156] Given the systemic risks posed by finance, it is likely that increased investment in law enforcement there can result in even larger gains.

Fraud, waste, and abuse in health care may at first glance seem simpler than in finance, but that's only because the average person has far more experience with medical insurance than, say, swaps or derivatives. But each field is tractable to machine learning. And we should not underestimate the complexity of health care. Opportunities for malfeasance flourish in the complex relationships between providers, employers, insurers, vendors, and patients.[157] Yet the government has learned to use data-analysis technologies to analyze these networks.[158] The Office of Financial Research set up under Dodd-Frank could be *much* more ambitious in attempting to track derivatives trades and the true overall liabilities (and interconnections) between firms. They should not be afraid to alert regulators when such liabilities appear to be too interconnected or destabilizing.

Although 50 separate states run Medicaid programs, antifraud programs appear to be unifying these once-disparate sources of data. The data miners can also compare findings of noteworthy activity in the Medicare program across states.[159] Functionality of this kind, spotting repeated patterns of mortgage fraud around the country, would have been very helpful in the run-up to the housing crisis. Just as a network of fusion centers can readily transmit suspicious patterns of criminal intelligence horizontally (to other state- or local-level agencies) or vertically (to national agencies), state Medicaid Integrity Programs both empower and are empowered by rapid data flows.[160] The Medicare-Medicaid Data Match Program breaks down the barriers between the surveillance and analysis done by each program.[161] Its successes should be a model for the entities now comprising the Financial Stability Oversight Council (FSOC), which may be able to find efficiencies (and new insights) by sharing data.

Classic deterrence theory suggests that the persistence of fraud should be countered by increasing the penalties for it, so that those caught would face jail time, large fines, or permanent exclusion from federal programs.[162] But this strategy can be risky and expensive. Proving criminal intent in a highly technical field is daunting, as Justice Department teams discovered anew in the wake of shocking acquittals in a CDO case.[163] A complementary approach is to broaden the scope of surveillance so that less intense interventions can catch nascent frauds before they metastasize, and nudge errant, suspect, or sloppy players toward better behavior. That has been the approach of the Medicare Integrity Program and other projects aimed at Medicaid providers.[164] It might be more effective in the prudent regulation of financial firms than belated and stalled efforts at prosecution and enforcement after the damage has been done. We have little to lose by trying it.

Of course, those troubled by NSA and fusion center surveillance may find any expansion of the state's investigative authority suspect. But there are key differences between the fraud detection model I'm proposing here and the sprawling domestic intelligence complex. First, unlike the ordinary citizens whose intimate details are swept into the NSA dragnet, health care providers know the terms of fraud detection, accept them as a condition of taking Medicare patients, and can challenge them in open court. Second, most of the firms I've discussed so far have already settled claims of wrongdoing. Ongoing monitoring is already built into many of these settlements. Enhancing that monitoring technologically would just make existing arrangements more effective. Third, corporations already understand that agencies enjoy significant investigatory powers.[165] Finally, we might consider finance surveillance less an *intensification* of the spying that ordinary citizens endure than a *redirection* of government nosiness toward those who really deserve it. When a digital surveillance apparatus has a hard time demonstrating that it stopped a single terrorist attack in over a decade, perhaps it should start refocusing its energies on other threats.

## A Corporate NSA

Naysayers may doubt the government's capacity to comprehensively surveil black box firms. But when the stakes are high enough, Washington is quite capable of approaching data-driven omniscience. If there is any take-home message of the parade of Snowden revelations about the NSA, it is that nearly *everything* can be recorded— even computers disconnected from the Internet, foreign leaders' medical records, or video games on a phone. Even tools that ostensibly encrypt data appear to be compromised by the agency.

The effectiveness of all this surveillance is a matter of debate. There are some black boxes that reasons of state counsel against opening. But we ought to have a reasoned debate about the *direction* of surveillance. At present, corporations and government have united to focus on the citizenry. But why not set government (and its contractors) to work on detecting more corporate wrongdoing?

Google alone has a substantial rap sheet of privacy and antitrust violations.[166] Bank scandals range from reckless bets to discrimination to laundering drug money.[167] Federal watchdogs are overwhelmed and overmatched when it comes to the Internet and finance firms, but many of their compatriots in the NSA, FBI, and DHS are wasting their time chasing after vegans, nuns, and libertarians. The budget of finance regulation is a *fraction* of what is now invested in intelligence gathering. It is time for a rebalancing.

The United States has faced two great crises in the past fifteen years: the attacks on New York and Washington in September 2001, and the near collapse of its financial system in September 2008. After 9/11, the country concluded that it had made a category mistake about the threat posed by terrorism. The government hugely upgraded its surveillance capabilities in the search for terrorists. Agencies refocused their operations on threats to domestic order. They built up a massive industry dedicated to monitoring the reputational profiles of groups and individuals. Federal agencies gather information in collaboration with state and local law enforcement officials, and with private providers of critical infrastructure, in what Congress has called the "Information Sharing Environment" (ISE).

We have not, however, seen a similar level of restructuring, reinvestment, and fortification of surveillance in the financial realm. Despite the threat to national security and order that a sudden destabilization of financial markets would pose, the United States has taken only the most tentative steps toward creating a new Information Sharing Environment for finance.[168] The Pentagon has already "simulate[d] what would happen if the world disintegrated into a series of full-fledged financial wars."[169] It should not only continue to war-game these scenarios but also implement far-reaching surveillance of markets and capital flows. It is time for a far more coordinated approach to financial instability.

The Pentagon is already investing in cybersecurity that will help all U.S. businesses, including financial ones, avoid Internet-delivered attacks. But modern financial flows are not menacing only because a computer virus could sabotage intended trades or unravel record-keeping systems. They are also, and increasingly, out of control and destabilizing when all components operate as designed. Fortunately, building early warning systems into the finance system will not be as difficult or costly as the vast antiterror apparatus.

Much of the groundwork has already been laid, both technically and legally. The NSA's domestic surveillance allowed it to "routinely examine large volumes of Americans' e-mail messages without court warrants."[170] Private communications companies gathered that data and turned it over to the government. It is part of the upward ratcheting of surveillance of ordinary citizens that is happening around the world. The question now is how to turn this surveillance to more productive ends than an ever more granular chronicling of ordinary citizens' lives. The Bush administration's 2002 National Security Strategy preamble warned that the "war against terrorism" is *a global enterprise of uncertain duration.*"[171] A "war on finance fraud and systemic risk" would be a welcome new direction for the intelligence apparatus.[172]

The migration of monetary recordkeeping to Internet-enabled computer databases can either retard or enhance the ability of regulators to detect and deter fraud and threats to financial stability.[173] In a world of unmonitored, totally encrypted capital flows, concentrated wealth could purchase power in a way that fundamentally threatens the state's ability to finance itself.[174] However, smart monitoring of electronic data flows could also help states avoid that scenario—and the varied lesser challenges to state authority that lead, on average, to hundreds of billions of dollars of illicit financial flows each year, and tens of billions more in lost tax revenue.[175] The question is whether we begin to rationalize the threat assessments of the intelligence apparatus to include financial crimes and instability— or continue to pretend that present patterns of regulation can stave off clear and present danger to social order.

## Mystery Meat of the Digital Age

Big Data technology and predictive analytics can promote public values as well as private gain. But our government now tends to confuse the latter for the former, elevating profit over the public's right to know. Having passively surrendered to for-profit firms the critical decisions we need to make about reputation, search, and finance, we are gradually losing the ability even to know *what* these decisions have been, let alone how well they are working. The result is a world that even the most celebrated muckrakers of the past might find impossible to reform.

Consider a topic as basic as food safety. Working undercover at a meatpacking plant in 1904, Upton Sinclair witnessed grotesque filth and exploitation. He rocked the industry with *The Jungle*, a novel about the plight of workers at the plant. As public outrage grew, Congress passed the Pure Food and Drug Act of 1906, which set the stage for the food and drug regulations of today.

If a would-be Sinclair tried to document today's food horror stories, there's a good chance he'd be fined, jailed, or even labeled a terrorist. In Iowa, Utah, and Missouri, undercover investigations of factory farms are illegal. Nearly every major agricultural state has proposed similar legislation. A shadowy corporate-government partnership known as the American Legislative Exchange Council (ALEC) has proposed "The Animal and Ecological Terrorism Act" to deter filming that is designed to "defame" such facilities or their owners.[176] Any violators would end up on a "terrorist registry."

Good luck finding out exactly how ALEC came to propose that law: a *Washington Post* reporter who tried to attend a gathering found that its "business meetings are not open."[177] Police escorted him away, and if he had persisted, who knows—maybe he'd have been labeled a terrorist, too. The United States has not exactly distinguished itself in its treatment of journalists. In 2012, it fell to forty-seventh in Reporters Without Borders' Press Freedom Index, well behind countries like Surinam, Mali, and Slovakia, largely due to police harassment of photographers and videographers at Occupy Wall Street protests.[178]

Like Sinclair's audience, we too are fearful of toxic food. We've also learned to be cautious about "toxic assets," hidden fees, security watch lists, and biased search engines. Most of us have developed some self-help skills: we encrypt messages, we optimize our profiles, we hunt online for credit score tips and tricks. It can feel great to outsmart a black box behemoth. But the game is constantly changing. Today's victorious strategy may be tomorrow's #totalfail; an encryption program may foil authorities one day and provoke their attention the next. Playing catch-up with the banks and the scorers and the Internet giants just reinforces their power over us. We should be challenging their rules, not trying to keep ahead of them.

The reputation, search, and finance industries profit by keeping us in the dark. And they have created a larger culture of secrecy that infects *all* industry. Even the hard-won transparency gains of Sinclair's era are slipping away. There have been many mass food poisoning incidents in the last decade, but a few years ago lobbyists gutted the Food Safety Modernization Act: a critical proposal requiring food companies to maintain records of where their ingredients came from was watered down into a mere pilot program.[179] The director of food programs at the Pew Health Group gave a simple explanation of why this system suits the shady: "It's less likely you'll be held liable if folks can't prove that you're the source of the contamination."[180] Ideology is enlisted to hide that self-serving rationale: basic, commonsense record-keeping requirements are resisted on the ostensible grounds that "big government" is strangling free enterprise. And when leading companies like Google and Goldman prosper by keeping so much of what they do "under wraps," other CEOs are quick to seize on secrecy as the key to business success.

Internet and finance firms "set the standard" for our information economy. So far, they have used their power to know the world of commerce ever more intimately. Google's cofounder, Sergey Brin, once said that "the perfect search engine would be like the mind of God."[181] As his company invests in maps, phone software, and even home management systems, its ability to see, hear, track, and sense grows. Data brokers play a similar game, piecing together ever more information about us. Wall Street aspires to know ever more, too, from flash traders angling for instant, comprehensive knowledge of trading patterns, to "expert networks" strategically located at the hubs of critical firms. Knowing more than a rival, or simply knowing it faster, is the key to vast fortunes.

But what if economic success were based less on *information advantage* and more on *genuine productivity?* Distracted from substantive judgments on what the economy *should* produce, we have been seduced by the mysterious valuations that Wall Street and Silicon

Valley place on goods and services. But their algorithmic methods, framed as neutral and objective, are predictably biased toward reinforcing certain hierarchies of wealth and attention. The next, concluding chapter will bring these biases to the foreground, while exploring a path to a more intelligible society.

# 6

# TOWARD AN
# INTELLIGIBLE SOCIETY

NOVELISTS SEE THINGS about our lives in society that we haven't noticed yet, and tell us stories about them. These prescients are already exploring black box trends.

In his story *Scroogled*, Cory Doctorow imagines a Google tightly integrated with the Department of Homeland Security. Doctorow's Google is quite willing to use its control of information to influence politics—for instance, striking fear into the hearts of Congressmen by threatening to let scandalous tidbits about them rise in the rankings of its media finders. One character observes that "the Stasi put everything about you in a file. Whether they meant to or not, what Google did is no different."[1]

Doctorow's story confronts us with a stark question: Do we permit Google to assert trade secrecy to the point that we can't even tell when a scenario like that has come to pass? When *Scroogled* was published in 2007, critics dismissed it as alarmist. But its core conceit—shadowy partnerships and power struggles between Google and the government—is already a reality. Google's ever-expanding footprint—into the home (Nest), car (Waze), space (satellite investments), and workplace (Google Enterprise), and its ability to buy data from hundreds of brokers, makes "total information awareness" by the company less a paranoid fear than a prosaic business plan.[2]

Gary Shteyngart also paints a grim picture of shadowy corporate behemoths in his dystopian *Super Sad True Love Story*, a work that has been favorably compared with *1984*. Powerless to challenge finance and homeland security giants, Shteyngart's characters scramble for places in the social pecking order by desperately competing with each other. They measure their "personality" and "sexiness" ratings with smartphone apps. Their credit scores are conveniently (and publicly) displayed at retail establishments. Like Calvinists striving to look like members of the elect, Shteyngart's characters hustle to boost their numbers. They don't worry much about what the scores signify or how they are calculated; they just want high ones. Black box rankings are a source of identity, the last "objective" store of value in a world where instability and short attention spans undermine more complex sources of the self.[3]

Globalized finance is the focus of *Union Atlantic*, Adam Haslett's cautionary tale of Wall Street. In Haslett's novel, a ruthless trader makes highly leveraged bets while his bosses and the compliance department look the other way. Corrupted by power and the high of unrestrained gambling, the trader comes to see himself as "an artist of the consequential world," the "master of conditions others merely suffered." And "suffer" is the right word—his actions leave a trail of human wreckage in their wake.[4]

In the work of seers like Doctorow, Shteyngart, and Haslett, the mutual influence of personal character and social structure is clear. Black box insiders are protected as if they are wearing a Ring of Gyges—which grants its wearer invisibility but, Plato warns us in *The Republic*, is also an open invitation to bad behavior.[5]

For those on the outside, another Platonic metaphor is apt. In the Allegory of the Cave, prisoners chained to face a stony wall watch flickering shadows cast by a fire behind them. They cannot comprehend the actions, let alone the agenda, of those who create the images that are all they know of reality. Like those who are content to use black box technology without understanding it, they can see mesmerizing results, but they have no way to protect themselves from manipulation or exploitation.[6]

## The Black Box Society

Black boxes embody a paradox of the so-called information age: Data is becoming staggering in its breadth and depth, yet often the information most important to us is out of our reach, available only to insiders. Thus the novelists' preoccupation: What kind of society does this create?

*It Creates a Rule of Scores and Bets.* Of all the reputational systems I've discussed, credit scores are by far the most regulated. Yet regulation has done little to improve them. Penalties for erroneous information on credit reports are too low to merit serious attention from credit bureaus. The fact of scoring has become a law unto itself. It encourages us to internalize certain standards and punishes us for failures. Television commercials feature tales of woe about those who let their credit scores slip, and some pitilessly equate low scores with laziness and unreliability.[7] The sponsors of these ads profit from the insecurity they both publicize and reinforce. They don't include in their moralizing the top financiers who walk away unscathed from their own companies' debts when too-risky bets don't work out.

The importance of credit reputation grows as public assistance shrinks.[8] Austerity promotes loans as a lifeline for an insecure precariat. Students who once earned state scholarships are now earning profits for government or private lenders. In our "market state" and "ownership society," *private credit* rather than *public grant* is the key to opportunity. Would-be homeowners, students, and the very poor are forced back on commercial credit to buy places to live, to prepare for careers, or even just to pay the costs of day-to-day living. By and large, private lenders are simply looking to generate more private wealth, rather than to invest long term in individuals or communities. In the paradoxical world of black box finance, those gains may be predicated on bets *against* a loan's repayment (if I've swapped away the risk of default, I may gain if the borrower fails). And when powerful actors are profiting from failure, we can probably expect a good deal more of it in the future.

*It Creates Separate and Unequal Economies.* Reputational systems for ordinary citizens and for high financiers have diverged to the point that they hardly operate in the same economy.

When a credit bureau rates a consumer, she doesn't get to consult it first about how to structure her finances for the best possible score, or lobby it to adjust its methodology so as to downplay her weaknesses and reflect her strengths. The bureau's interest lies with the firms who demand its services, not with her. But when the sponsors of structured securities need an A A A imprimatur to market their wares, they can pay $200,000 and more for their ratings. That is significant lobbying power. Furthermore, they enjoy extensive consultation from their raters on exactly how far they can push the risk envelope without adversely affecting their rating. And at least so far, when things go south, few at the top—either at the sponsors' companies or at the raters'—suffer serious financial consequences.

Compare their fates to those of the unfortunate students who are saddled for life with undischargeable debts. Students may carry their loans at rates of 7% or more, while banks access credit at less than 1%. This disparity may seem appropriate on its face; Citigroup and Goldman Sachs certainly have more assets than the average college student. But they also have more liabilities. The real reason that they are more creditworthy than a collegian is that *the government itself* implicitly or explicitly backs them.[9] There's no theoretical reason that interest rates couldn't be reduced for students and raised for banks. But students lack the backroom connections that the finance sector so richly exploits.[10]

Of course, there has to be some federal support for financial institutions—the bank runs of the Great Depression were too devastating for us to go back to 1920s-style laissez-faire. But the price of government support used to be an intricate set of regulations that strictly limited the risks banks could take. The Dodd-Frank Act of 2010 was supposed to adapt such risk regulation to the contemporary finance sector, but it is being implemented so slowly (and so incompletely) that it is hard to credit it as anything more than window dressing.[11] It promises that Congress is "doing something" while leaving enough legal loopholes to ensure that little changes.[12] And the quid pro quo between banks and government remains stacked in the banks' favor.

*It Creates Invisible Powers.* The rise of algorithmic authorities elicited widespread anxiety. In 1972, philosopher Hubert L. Dreyfus wrote a booklength treatise titled *What Computers Can't Do.*[13] Computational pioneer Joseph Weizenbaum worried that callow managers would delegate to software "tasks that demand wisdom."[14] At first, managers tried to quell concerns by emphasizing the transparency and objectivity of their systems. An algorithmically driven computer would operate dispassionately, it was argued, treating like cases alike. Avantgarde academics even advanced computation as a model for the legal system, where the jury was frequently disdained as a "black box."[15] Jurors met behind closed doors. But with algorithms, those who doubted results could look "under the hood" and see for themselves how the system worked. The disclosure requirements of patent law promoted transparency by making intellectual property protection conditional on publicly inspectable, written descriptions of claims.

In time, however, this relatively open approach was neglected; knowledgeable but unscrupulous individuals learned how to game exposed systems, and the profit advantage of informational exclusivity was too strong to resist. The less known about our algorithms—by spammers, hackers, cheats, manipulators, competitors, or the public at large—the better, went the new reasoning. Transparency was replaced by ironclad secrecy, both real and legal. The matter of legitimation was tabled.

Trade secrecy protection effectively creates a property right in an algorithm without requiring its disclosure. It also reinforces the importance of keeping algorithms secret, because once they are disclosed, they lose trade secret protection as a matter of law. Rules of state secrecy provide an even more formidable legal armamentarium when national security is at stake. This move from legitimation-via-transparency to protection-via-secrecy was the soil out of which the black box society sprang, and with it, many of the social dangers of the information age.

*It Sets Up Wasteful Arms Races and Unfair Competitions.* In more and more aspects of our lives, computers are authorized to make decisions without human intervention. Philosopher Samir Chopra and attorney Laurence White call these programs "autonomous artificial agents" (AAAs)—*agents* because they act on behalf of someone;

*artificial* because they are not organic persons or animals; and *autonomous* because they can perform actions without checking back in with the person who programmed them or set them in motion.[16]

Of course, AAAs are not new, and it's great not to have to get up to flick switches every time the dishwasher reaches a new stage of its cycle. But AAAs have infiltrated areas far more intimate and important than the mechanical. They engage in bidding wars for books on Amazon, and have transformed stock trading. They automatically gather and process certain information as you interact with apps and websites. Think back, also, to the privacy conundrums posed by Google's autocompletes. Credit scores are not the only algorithmic threat to reputation.[17]

Some progressive thinkers think the answer is "bots of our own," a digital arms race where the savvy field their own AAAs to do their bidding. But such "solutions" invariably run up against old-fashioned patterns of power and privilege. However sophisticated your bots may be, they're not going to be able to negotiate for better privacy terms for you at the most important websites. They are "take it or leave it" operations. And who is to ensure that information-gathering bots—governed by algorithms themselves—will actually stick to the terms of the "contracts" they strike in their instantaneous and unsupervised interactions online?[18]

The problems of computer-computer interaction are even deeper in search-driven finance. The day trader in Dubuque isn't going to own the computing power of the algo-trading sharpies in Manhattan. Nor will he be accessing the $300 million cable between New York and Chicago that was built for the professional traders.

Legal scholars have written penetratingly about the intertwined failures of technical and legal compliance systems in finance. They have outlined commendable ideas for changes in the current regulatory framework. Nevertheless, Wall Street deal making is now so tortuous that Disclosure 2.0 is not going to cut it. A system where financial firms are "pursuing the maximum level of profits and return on equity, without heed to systemic risk or the interests of all the stakeholders in the money grid" is a guarantee of future stagnation and crisis.[19] Moreover, better documenting endless processions of fundamentally valueless transactions is not a worthwhile aim.

## Why Is So Little Being Done?

Shadowy powers, sweetheart deals, and wasteful arms races aren't very appealing. Yet they're at the core of black box trends that seem only to accelerate with time. Why is so little being done about them? To answer that question, we need to understand why algorithmic authorities are so appealing to so many. I've hinted at the lure of the black box throughout the book, but now it's time to surface its seductions—and their limits.

*The Glamor of Rocket Science:* Eager to tout the U.S. economy as vibrant, politicians trumpet the achievements of our tech firms. But the darkness of the new Big Data economy should also give us pause about the outsized returns its top CEOs, managers, and investors are now earning. Is their market advantage attributable to genius and skill? Or does their Big Data advantage make their profits a near inevitability, potentially gleaned by any smart group of computer scientists and business experts? The mainstream media seems wedded to the "superstar" characterization, reflecting a widespread assumption that earnings inequality results from "skills-biased technological change." But merely being part of a platform with ever more data is not exactly a "skill." It instead recalls the dominance of early telephone or telegraph networks: the monopolistic power of a utility everyone must have access to in order to function in a modern society.[20]

Law developed various approaches to these utilities. The telephone company couldn't simply cut businesses off if they failed to pay rising shares of their revenues for services. Rate increases had to be plausibly connected to productive investment, or a documented rise in the firm's costs. Firms had to act in a nondiscriminatory manner, and there were limits on the degree to which they could use their privileged access to communications for their own commercial advantage.[21] My proposals in the previous chapter applied those ideas to today's reputation and search firms.

*Addicted to Speed:* High-tech firms have a parry at the ready: government is far too slow to keep up with the fast pace of change in *our* world.[22] Lobbyists for black box industries mock the capacity of government to comprehend the business practices of a Google or a Goldman.[23] But, as I showed in the previous chapter, there are clear precedents for agencies to hire private-sector expertise to assure that laws are faithfully executed. The government's successful curbing of health care fraud could serve as a model for dealing with many other kinds of skulduggery, if there were the political will for it. And the understanding.

This latter requirement is worthy of note. I was at a conference dinner talking about some basic principles of search neutrality when a Silicon Valley consultant said abruptly, "We can't code for neutrality." He meant that decisions about fair treatment of ordered sites could not be reduced to the algorithms that drive most sites' operations. When I offered some of the proposals I've made in this book, he simply repeated, with a touch of condescension: "Yes, but we can't *code* for it, so it can't be done." For him, not only the technology, but even the social practices of current operations are unalterable givens of all future policy interventions. Reform will proceed on the Silicon Valley giants' terms, or not at all. He assumed that if decisions couldn't be made at the speed of current searches, they oughtn't happen.

It is not helpful to have politicians across the political spectrum meekly submitting to this technolibertarianism—assuming that bureaucrats, and by extension themselves, are inherently incapable of influencing technical innovation. We must curb the tendency to reify the tech giants—to assume that their largely automated ways of processing disputes or handling customer inquiries are, inevitably, the way things are and must always be. Until we do, we enforce upon ourselves an unnecessary helplessness, and a self-incurred tutelage.

The arbitrariness of many forms of reputation creation is becoming clearer all the time. I will not recapitulate here the problems of discrimination (racial, political, economic, and competitive) that we examined earlier. Unfairness in today's Internet industries should be obvious by now, and is another important reason to be wary of reification. "The Internet" is a human invention, and can be altered by humans. The argument that search and reputation algorithms are what they are and must be so forever appears to carry a lot of conviction in some quarters, but it is a self-serving oversimplification and no true reflection of reality. As Google's concessions to European Union authorities in both privacy and antitrust cases show, it is possible to create a more level online playing field. But there must first be a clear recognition of the need, and then the will to act on it.[24]

Our technologies are just as much a product of social, market, and political forces as they are the outgrowth of scientific advance. They are intimately embedded in social practices that rely on human judgment. Facebook hires people to assess the appropriateness of user-shared content; it's no great burden upon the social networking behemoth to ask its human reviewers to stop algorithmic recommendations of obviously racist stories.[25] Google runs proposed algorithmic changes by human testers, who not only choose the web pages that work best, but explain *why*. Such interventions are already an essential part of the business logic of these companies; they can equally be part of their response to legal norms and obligations.[26] And when the technology really does outstrip policymakers' understanding, they can hire experts to bridge the gap. A government attorney has already hired Silicon Valley's Palantir to go after Wall Street crooks; it's time for more law enforcers to follow his lead.[27]

*Scale Fails:* In Wall Street valuations, attaining *scale* at great *speed* is critical to attracting *speculative* capital. The goal is not just a fast rate of growth, but an accelerating one. Speculators pave the way for more "committed" capital, and theoretically enable a virtuous cycle of success, recognition, and investment.[28] Platforms like Google and Facebook too accrue their power on the basis of scale. Aspiring to the same end of total information awareness, data brokers are angling to become the proprietors of the "master" profiles coveted by marketers and spies alike.

The idea is to take a few pennies each from millions of transactions, as quickly as possible. Prove that you can do that consistently, and finance capital will beat a path to your door. Capturing a small piece of everything, speedily and at very large scale, is about as close as one can get to the "free money" touted by an AIG grandee in 2007 as the holy grail of wealth accumulation.[29]

But what happens to wise judgment when businesses "scale" too fast? Mortgage securitizers didn't spend the hours it would take to review each of the hundreds of mortgages packaged into asset-backed securities. Google and Facebook are rarely willing to individualize reputational or copyright disputes. "Automated dispute resolution" at the finance and data barons leaves many out in the cold. Far more don't even try to engage, given the demoralizing experience of interacting with cyborgish amalgams of drop-down menus, phone trees, and call center staff.

There are ways to humanize these processes, via both internal reviews and external appeal rights. My proposals to that end in the previous chapter were not designed to juridify every interaction between company and customer, but to afford persons the dignity of being able to make their case to another person, with a chance at appeal to higher authorities if their complaint was treated in an unreasonable way.[30] Due process obligations have sometimes been imposed on private-sector reputation creators, occasionally even to the extent of forcing the exposure of proprietary methods. The quality of sites that rate doctors improved when regulators demanded that they reveal key data and models. Credit rating agencies would be well advised to learn from their example, and to do far more to examine the integrity of the data they use.[31]

But there will be a real cultural shift only when platforms with populations rivaling those of small countries—like Google, Facebook, Amazon, Microsoft, and Apple—adopt, either voluntarily or on compulsion, more responsive approaches to those who claim to have been harmed by them. This process is beginning outside the United States, in countries with a more advanced jurisprudential recognition of the essentially statelike characteristics of very large firms. Germany, Argentina, and Japan, for example, have all required Google to alter certain search results that defame individuals or mislead users. Institutionalizing these decisions in less formal settings than a court of law—for instance, in NGO-led arbitration panels—will be a very important step toward treating Internet users with dignity, rather than as mere algorithm fodder.[32]

*Spellbound by Speculative Capital:* Dignity and fairness are not impossible aspirations. But they cost money. The overriding reason that most finance firms resist accountability is economic: to maximize pay at the top and to continue attracting more capital. Their leaders deserve to reap some rewards from their skill and vision. However, there are also questions to be asked about exactly what these immense rewards derive from, and at what cost.

Those questions were asked when regulators and courts in the first half of the twentieth century established the concept of "reasonable rates of return" for utilities. They acknowledged the vital importance of the infrastructure on which society depends, and they validated the right to compensation for upholding that responsibility. But they limited the right of owners and administrators to hold society hostage with unreasonable demands for money, and they required as well that compensation be conditional on the provision of safe and reliable service.

Certainly banks are a vital piece of our infrastructure—QED the need for 2008's bailouts. How might the doctrine of reasonable rates of return apply to them? Where is the balance point between importance and responsibility? When do rising fees start to look like price gouging? What counts as safe and reliable service? Above all, what are these giant salaries and bonuses really *for?* What value does society derive from the work that they theoretically compensate?

For context, consider that the average Ph.D. research scientist working on a cancer treatment takes home roughly $110,000 to $160,000 a year. But a banker specializing in mergers and acquisitions is likely to realize about $2 million; his CEO, tens of millions. Top hedge fund managers make billions of dollars annually; their shadowy maneuvers are not open to public scrutiny, except on the rare occasions they catch the attention of authorities for insider trading.[33]

Some would argue that bankers make their money for taking risks. But if they are using black box techniques to risk other people's money with no personal exposure, their self-characterization as fearless captains of industry is scarcely credible. Such huge takes create inflated expectations throughout the economy the way inflated grade-curves do in schools; how can health reformers ask surgeons to accept lower salaries when their friends in finance are so much richer? The bankers' bounty fuels a derangement of value and deteriorating values.

Banks charge plenty for their vital services. Consider that late fee on your credit card; even before you incurred it, the bank had already taken a cut of every purchase you made. Consider the mysterious charges eating away at your 401(k), and the transaction costs whenever your broker buys or sells. Fee churning contributes hugely to the livelihoods of finance professionals. But how much value do those professionals really create in the process?

Not much, it would appear. The crisis of 2008 is only the most recent demonstration of how the quick "scores" of financial intermediaries drain resources *away* from Main Street investors. Former investment banker Wallace Turbeville estimates that America's "excessive wealth transfer to the financial sector is in the range of $635 billion per year."[34] A study from the New Economics Foundation (NEF) calculated that leading London bankers "destroy £7 of social value for every pound in value they generate."[35] The Kauffman Foundation concluded that an "ever-expanding financial sector is depleting the talent pool of potential high-growth company founders."[36] Why go to the trouble of developing a new product or service when you can take on much less risk, and net more money, as a financier rating and juggling investments?[37]

Whatever one thinks of their methods, at least Turbeville, NEF, and Kauffman are asking tough and necessary questions about how the world of finance interfaces with the real economy. The first step toward a realistic assessment of value in the financial sector would be to estimate what returns reflect productive contributions to the economy, and which are attributable to fee churning, accounting shenanigans, and rate rigging.[38] It would be a sobering exercise.[39]

Researcher Thomas Philippon confirms that finance firms are becoming more expensive even while they pride themselves on forcing managers in other industries to cut costs and reduce wages.[40] Macroeconomists J. Bradford DeLong and Stephen Cohen calculate that the United States experienced a 7 percent drop in manufacturing concomitant with a 7 percent expansion *in financial transactions*. When we shift labor from real engineering into financial engineering, we're effectively privileging those who shuffle *claims on productivity* over those who are actually *producing* real goods and services.[41]

This means, for example, that Wall Street has pressured pharmaceutical firms to lay off thousands of drug developers and cut R&D in favor of "core competencies," punishing Merck for investing in research and rewarding Pfizer for cutting it. The constant pressure for quarterly earnings makes each cut to scientific investment look rational at the time, but the long-range consequences are chilling—both medically for all of us and economically for the millions of Americans who are exiled from relatively prosperous sectors into low-paying service jobs, or worse. Is it any wonder that those outside finance feel like they are bickering over slices of a shrinking pie?[42]

The finance sector at present is more invested in positional competition for *buying power* than in increasing goods and services *available to buy.*[43] This is a zero-sum game in which the goal is not sustainable investment or the construction of lasting value, but complex risk-shifting that mulcts the unwary. The self-seeking might be excusable if its leading exemplars weren't so abjectly dependent on public subvention to stay afloat. Given their too-big-to-fail status, we should expect far more in the way of public service from these critical financial firms than we are currently getting.

*Makers, Takers, and Fakers:* The grand illusion of contemporary finance is that endlessly processing claims to future wealth will somehow lead to a more productive economy.[44] A similar illusion is beginning to pervade the industries of search and reputation. Intermediaries can get rich not by adding to the sum total of goods and services created, but by setting up bidding wars—for a chance to finance an investment, to appear before an audience, to qualify for an opportunity. There is good reason that these entities strive so hard to keep their methods secret: pull the curtain, and the economy's wizards look like little more than organizers of contests they'd never be able to compete in. They aren't players, but referees. In the meantime, the millions of creators whose labor is being so lucratively rated and searched and shuffled are herded into ever more competitive, global labor markets. Left to their own devices, the reputation, search, and finance sectors will continue to siphon effort out of productive innovation and into more shuffling and scrambling.[45]

We say we value "makers" over "takers" and "fakers." But we need an *intelligible* society if we want to be able to tell who's who. Internet firms are not helping us achieve that goal, thanks to clandestine deals between intermediaries and content owners. Secretly slowing down or downranking pirate sites does little to solve the underlying problems of the content industries—or the individuals they (used to) provide income to.[46] Perfect control schemes online would grant too much control to copyright holders, trampling free speech and a thriving remix culture on their way to that singular aim. But control is only one route to compensation. The recording industry itself has repeatedly (and successfully) lobbied to force composers and lyricists to accept a governmentally set compulsory license.[47] In the past, when Congress realized that new technology would lead to widespread copying, it imposed a small fee per copy—a practice known as compulsory licensing. This regime, still in place for many works, separates compensation (for works) from control (over their use).

Some say that the compulsory licensing regime can't work in the wild west of untrammeled Internet distribution. But Harvard law professor William W. Fisher has offered a detailed and compelling proposal in *Promises to Keep: Technology, Law, and the Future of Entertainment.* The Fisher plan would subsidize culture by lightly taxing the technology that leads to its uncompensated duplication. Government could also impose such fees on carriers and search engines, and distribute them to creatives.[48]

Who gets the money? Fisher wants artists to be compensated according to how often their work is actually viewed, or listened to; Dean Baker has called for "artistic freedom vouchers" that would allow taxpayers to choose ex ante whom they want to support each year. Either approach is likely to be more efficient than the current bramble of copyright law and disorderly, secret downrankings. In 2004, Fisher estimated that a fee of $6 per month on broadband subscribers would cover all the music and movie industry revenue allegedly lost due to piracy.[49]

Of course, given extreme and rising inequality, such fees will need to be capped and, hopefully, progressively keyed to income and wealth. They are probably best collected as a sliding-scale user fee. A small tax on the unearned investment income of wealthy households would also help here, just like the one imposed to help fund the Affordable Care Act. Like health care, culture has positive externalities. It deserves more support from those best able to pay for society's common needs.[50]

Unfortunately, the Recording Industry Association of America and the Motion Picture Association of America appear about as enthusiastic for a public option in entertainment as private insurers have been about it in health care. Thanks to that opposition, some might dismiss Fisher's idea as a pipe dream—nothing even remotely resembling a new tax could pass through our political system, right?[51]

But what is the alternative? The leading legislative initiative of the content industry in 2012 was the Stop Online Piracy Act (SOPA), a bill that would grant sweeping, unprecedented powers to copyright and trademark owners, deny due process to alleged infringers, and menace free expression. Like fusion centers, SOPA would accelerate surveillance by an unaccountable industry-government partnership. What does it say about our Congress that it is readier to turbocharge a police state, largely in the service of content industry oligopolists, than it is to revise and expand a venerable licensing method to support struggling journalists, artists, and musicians? Make content affordable and accessible, and the piracy problem will decline precipitously.[52]

In an increasingly self-defeating manner, contemporary American politics has privileged policing and punishment, while marginalizing the welfare state and its support for the arts and the commons. Black box interventions by carriers and search engines merely take this punitive impulse into the private sector, where it is unbalanced by the usual reporting requirements and appellate checks on law enforcement abuses.[53]

Without the adoption of digital compulsory licenses or artistic freedom vouchers, we should not be surprised if the political economy of intellectual property enforcement shifts to vertically integrated firms that use control over bottlenecks to monitor, deter, and perhaps ultimately ban content that threatens profits. SOPA ultimately failed, after provoking a powerful alliance of netizens to support basic principles of due process, free expression, and accountability online. But this battle was merely a prelude to a much more contested debate about the proper allocation of digital revenues. Like health care battles between providers and insurers, struggles between creatives and intermediaries will profoundly shape our common life. Stopping SOPA is only one small step toward preserving a fair, free, and democratic culture online.[54]

We should also be open to skepticism about technocratic solutions.[55] To work well, Fisher's proposals would rely on pervasive surveillance of what is being listened to and watched. If purely based on "number of downloads" or "number of views," they'll provoke extensive gaming. We've already seen scandals on YouTube for artists who allegedly manipulated their view count (either to gain more ad revenue or to appear more popular than they actually are). That gaming will in turn provoke countermeasures, monitoring who is viewing and liking what. Do we really want some central authority to collect all this information, merely in order to ensure that Lady Gaga gets, say, 50 times more revenue than the Magnetic Fields?

Allocating entertainment industry revenue in this way may become an instance of "modulation," an effort to monitor and exercise soft control over certain communities (here, artists).[56] We should reconsider the plasticity of institutions like compulsory license fees. Maybe there should be minimum compensation, to assure some degree of security to all artists (WPA 2.0?), and maximum gains, to discourage gaming at the high end. Perhaps the aspiration to precisely calibrate reward to "value," as measured by the number of times something is viewed or watched, fails on its own economic terms: a particularly effective film may do its "work" in one sitting. Or someone might reasonably value one experience of a particularly transcendent song over 100 plays of background music.

The larger point here is that there is not just a tension between the play of creativity and the copyright maximalism of dominant industry players. Even the most progressive reform proposals can unintentionally warp creative endeavors in one way or another. The legal establishment has more often than not tried to wall out these considerations: "We'll worry about the law and the money, and let the artists themselves figure out the creative angle." But the experience of play and creativity are at the core of the enterprise—they shouldn't be treated as "add ons" or independent of legal deliberations. We can't get cultural policy right if we fail to consider what better and worse modes of artistic creation are on the terms of creators themselves.

What if it turns out that properly calibrating risk and reward is a near-impossible task for law? I'm reminded of the insights of John Kay's *Obliquity: Why Our Goals Are Best Achieved Indirectly*, and in that spirit, let me make a side observation on the way to my point. At least in my experience, the best way of predicting whether someone would pursue a career in the arts (or as an entrepreneur) was the wealth of their spouse or family. The word is out: it's simply too risky to try and make a living as a painter, musician, actor, or poet—particularly given constant pressure for cuts to welfare benefits, food stamps, and Medicaid in the United States.

But in other countries, where the social safety net has been more generous, the possibility of failure has not been so bone-chilling. Consider the fate of J. K. Rowling, who hit "rock bottom" (in her words) while writing, and had to rely on Britain's benefits system. A few years of support allowed her to get a foothold in the literary profession—and without it, *Harry Potter* might never have been written. The implementation of the Affordable Care Act in 2014 is one bright spot for the marginally employed in the United States. Perhaps we'll find, decades hence, that the biggest impetus to artistic careers (and independent employment of all kinds) was guaranteed issue of health insurance policies via state exchanges, and subsidies to purchase them. Perhaps the health policy experts will do more to advance creativity than all the copyright policymakers combined, simply by assuring some breathing room for the inevitable throng of failures in creative industries.

I know, the tired rhetorical dichotomy between good old-fashioned American capitalism and the evils of socialism will be wheeled out against this approach. But what's more statist—a) DHS contractors busting down the doors of copyright infringers, b) an all-seeing Google/YouTube/Facebook check-in system to report on what you're watching, or c) a universal basic income that greatly reduces the need to deploy a or b? The specter of socialism becomes an ever more laughable distraction as the interpenetration of state and business in finance and law enforcement serves an ever narrower set of interests.

## On the Narrowing Divide between Government and Business

The "free markets vs. state" battles that devour American political discourse refer to a duality that is increasingly more apparent than real. Consider health care. On the one hand, that "market" is riddled with state-mandated licensure and quality regulations; on the other, even government programs like Medicare rely on private contractors that determine eligibility, deliver benefits, and profit from their delivery. Finance's patterns are similar. Even as quintessentially "market" an institution as the Chicago Board of Trade can only operate within a framework of rules. Moreover, those affected by the rules are constantly jockeying to change them or use them to their own advantage.[57] Google's corporate lobbying spend was second only to that of General Electric in 2012.[58]

We all know that market orderings are influenced by political decisions, which are influenced by the market in turn as the beneficiaries of past political decisions use moneys gained in commerce to further future political ends.[59] For example: when mortgage-backed securities began to fail after years of exploitation of subprime borrowers, U.S. financial institutions were quick to turn to the government (the president, Congress, and Federal Reserve), which moved equally quickly to protect their prestige. The government did not, however, offer the same protection to ordinary borrowers. "Banks got bailed out, we got sold out," as the protesters' refrain goes. Large financial firms then went on to leverage their financial windfall into future political advantages, as they deployed legions of lobbyists to water down the Dodd-Frank Act and its subsequent implementation.

Furthermore, elite panic over *financial* markets—in this case, the failure of overleveraged firms—was quickly characterized by key officials as an understandable and appropriate response to a mortal threat to the economy. The desperation of ordinary borrowers was met with the Kafkaesque Home Affordable Modification Program

(HAMP)—an intervention as slow and feckless as its clunky name suggests.

Many call business's influence here "capture," since industry has more power over its regulators than the regulators have over industry. But "capture" is too static a term for what is really going on. There is not a stable "Wall Street" capturing an equally inert SEC or Fed. Rather, certain parts of industry skillfully outmaneuver rivals, gain power in agencies, and change their agendas. The new regulatory environment favors certain firms and disadvantages others. The firms boosted by the new order have even more cash to influence *newer* orders. Those adept at shuttling between Washington, New York, and (now) Silicon Valley can drive an agency (and an industry) far from its original set of values, aims, and strategies.

The Yale social scientist Charles E. Lindblom suggested a better term than capture for this mutual influence and transformation: "circularity."[60] As we settle into the age of information, the revolving door between government and dominant business sectors is clearly on the rise, with unsettling implications. It is *people*, not some nameless abstraction like "industry," who've set up the rules of our black box society.[61]

The stakes are too high for us to ignore this new reality: that politicians and bureaucrats will contravene only so far the interests of a business community they aspire to join or serve. The American state, which since at least the Sherman Act of 1890 has had the job of taming monopolization, is now liable to promote the economy's biggest winners, rather than to ensure a level playing field for future competition. Furthermore, the state's immense powers of compulsion and enforcement can now be enlisted in support of the black box technologies of the search, reputation, and finance sectors. Pundits overlook real dangers to indulge a puerile fixation on the obsolete polarity between "state" and "market" solutions. This is a recipe for paralysis and worse; it is a guarantee that we will never achieve the societal ideals of security, fairness, and dignity that most of us desire, if not always in identical detail. It is time to take a fresh look at where we want to go from here, and at what gets in our way.

## The Promise of Public Alternatives

Government regulates not merely to promote private wealth, but because industry performs some essentially public functions along with its private profit-seeking ones. If we as citizens were to promote those public functions *directly*, we might begin to see some real accountability.

For example, government might commission a *public* credit scoring system, and test its predictive power against closed, proprietary services.[62] We know from experience that open-source software can function as well as—sometimes better than—proprietary algorithms, and there's no reason why this shouldn't be true of a public scoring system. Once it got fully up to speed, financial regulators could require some lenders to use the transparent system, or arrange pilot programs for its partial deployment.[63] Public credit reporting systems are used in other nations.[64] If the concept of transparent evaluative standards succeeded in consumer finance, it might come to play a larger role in reputational software generally. Furthermore, a system fully open to the scrutiny of thousands of experts invested in its success could see its errors and omissions caught and fixed more quickly (and fairly) than one understood, valued, and monitored by only a few.

Public Internet firms are another possibility. At the moment, Google and Amazon are approaching the status of book duopolists, with Google taking on the more public function of scanning, indexing, and archiving books that aren't (individually) commercially viable. Where is the Library of Congress (LOC)? Cultural theorist Siva Vaidhyanathan makes the telling point that in Google Book Search, a private firm "step[ped] into a vacuum created by incompetent or gutted public institutions." Its very existence points to what Vaidhyanathan calls a "public failure."[65] An LOC archive could provide a content base for a public book search program. Just as Medicare offers benchmarks for coverage decisions and for private insurers' payment rates (and provides access to care for those not served by private insurance markets), a public book search could both complement Google Books and assist those not served by it.[66] It would organize the vast digital database in a transparent way, allowing us at least one book recommendation system that is both comprehensible and comprehensive.

Presently, we have little sense of exactly how systems like Amazon's or Google's recommend books on topics like "obesity" (do you see books promoting or critiquing diet pills first?) or "conflict in Palestine," or "bank regulation," or "Google's antitrust problems." A public ordering would provide some opportunities for library scientists to apply venerable theories and principles to contemporary problems of filtering and ranking. An NGO like the Digital Public Library of America Foundation could add another perspective, too, if only it had access to the data driving Google's and Amazon's dominance.

The problems in finance are deeper than those in the reputation and search sectors, and deserve a more thorough response. Government should establish a more balanced reciprocity with the finance sector, exacting control in return for its implicit and explicit subsidies. Once again, the health care sector has led the way. Like the major financial firms, major hospitals are dependent on governmental support. The Medicare and Medicaid systems offer several forms of subsidy. But hospital participation in those systems is conditioned on their maintaining quality standards, providing emergency care, and submitting to extensive audits. Financial regulators merely aspire to do a small fraction of what health regulators regularly achieve.

It doesn't need to be this way. The Federal Reserve could open its low-interest "discount window" only to banks that act responsibly and that allocate capital in ways that improve productivity, rebuild infrastructure, reduce inequality, and recognize the value of all labor.[67] Congress could require agencies like the Securities and Exchange Commission and the Commodity Futures Trading Commission to create incentives for straightforward and socially valuable investment. A financial transactions tax would also deter the complex trading schemes behind some black box finance, and the volatility they engender.

Furthermore, the government could encourage citizens to reward transparency and punish unnecessary complexity, after the style of the (spontaneous) social movement to "Move Your Money" out of the big banks. It could permit post offices to offer banking services, providing a valuable low-cost option to the millions of "unbanked"

Americans.[68] This is not a radical idea: the Bank of North Dakota has offered the state's farms and businesses loans for almost a century.[69] Public banking might also provide incentives for investments in the social good. And pension plans could emphasize old-fashioned "value investing" featuring clear commitments to comprehensible business plans.[70]

Although some die-hard laissez-faire advocates vilify socially responsible investing as a form of European socialism, proposals like these have deep roots in American soil. Financial reform planners early in Franklin Roosevelt's administration envisioned agencies intended to "direct the flow of new investment in private industry" toward socially useful projects, and away from the kind of self-dealing common in the Roaring Twenties (and the more recent housing bubble).[71] Rexford Tugwell wanted a commission to "encourage or discourage the flow of capital into various industries."[72] Considering the shameful state of America's roads, bridges, and public transit today, would it be too much to ask the Fed to purchase "infrastructure bonds" to complement its vast holdings of mortgage-backed securities?[73] FDR's advisers also took a direct approach to financial stability; the corporate governance expert Adolf Berle advocated for an agency to "exercise a real control over undue expansion of groups of credit instruments."[74] His proposal is as timely now as it was then.[75]

The dynamic of circularity teaches us that there is no stable, static equilibrium to be achieved between regulators and regulated. The government is either pushing industry to realize some public values in its activities (say, by respecting privacy or investing in sustainable growth), or industry is pushing its regulators to promote its own interests.[76] Many of the black box dynamics we saw unleashed in finance arose out of failed efforts to fudge this tension—such as the credit agencies' role as a "soft" regulator, or the government's wink-wink, nod-nod (non)assurances regarding its backing of Fannie and Freddie and massive financial institutions.[77] That pattern continues to this day: the authors of Dodd-Frank say their bill solved the "too big to fail" problem, but Richard Fisher, president of the Federal Reserve Bank of Dallas, says it is all but inevitable government will bail out a massive financial firm if too many of its bets go bad.[78] Credit ratings reflect the same assumption: megabanks' risks are too complex to quantify, but the smart money assumes government will step in the moment they are in danger.

Finance experts have obsessed over matters of *structure* after the crisis: for example, how can we assure that banks are smaller, less interconnected, and better capitalized, to reduce the risk (and consequences) of failure. But questions of *substance* are far more important to building a resilient society. For example, where *should* the capital improperly invested in the MBS/CDO/CDS hall of mirrors have been allocated? Mariana Mazzucato, Geoff Mulgan, Joseph Stiglitz, and Robert Kuttner have all provided compelling answers, ranging from infrastructure and antibiotics to basic research and education. We need to heed their work. Without clear substantive answers to the question concerning finance, all we can reliably expect in the future is that capital will be allocated to whatever instruments lead to the highest fees for self-serving intermediaries.[79]

"Leaving it to the finance experts" is a recipe for decline, because the success of the finance industry bears no inevitable relationship to the long-term health of the economy. Finance can be extractive or uplifting, narrowly short-termist or focused on the infrastructural and investment needs of society as a whole. To address those needs consistently, we need a government interested in forward-thinking industrial policy, and willing to enforce its interest.[80] This attitude is currently in short supply in Washington. But the government has used its hold on the purse strings to good effect before, and it could do it again. The Chinese investment in infrastructure, education, rare earths, and green technology should be a Sputnik moment for America. It is time to commit more of our resources to enterprises likely to bear real and equitably distributed returns.[81]

Again, while these proposals will sound excessively statist to bienpensant economists, consider the alternatives. Our law enforcement apparatus has manifestly failed to deter or properly punish illegal behavior in the finance sector. The previous chapter described what it would take to fully police information advantage in the industry—as with Terry Fisher's proposal for Internet content, mass surveillance is necessary. I borrowed this model from health care, where a swarm of contractors scrutinizes billing records to detect fraud and abuse. But another health care model, designed to prevent overbilling and overtreatment, is simply to pay physicians salaries, rather than "per-procedure." Imagine if this approach were to supersede the bonus culture of Wall Street (where, for most key players, annual pay is peanuts compared to the bounty available in a banner year of spectacularly successful risks). Sure, in health care, there are worries that salary-based pay will lead to shirking. But given how destructive financial innovation has been over the past decade, maybe bankers *ought* to work less, at least until they can better prove how their sector contributes to real productivity.[82]

## Restoring Trust

For too long, we have assumed that the core aim of financial regulation is disclosure.[83] When every consumer understands the consequences of his actions, we like to believe, and when every investor has the same key data about a security as its seller, the financial playing field will finally be leveled. And in some cases, sunlight truly is the "best disinfectant."[84] But not always. "Truth" is all too apt to be told slant. And when that happens too many times, trust is unwarranted.

Lately trust issues have begun to haunt not only finance but also the leading reputation and search providers. The "rocket scientists" once adored by the precrisis media have lost some of their luster.[85] Silicon Valley giants are looking less like romantic heroes and more like "Wall Street West"—in-groups driven by lust for the quick payday. As for the finance sector itself, it is still rife with outright scandal, the most notable being the Libor-rigging debacle of 2012. Taken individually, its problems can be explained away as the work of a few bad apples; together, they suggest widespread rot. The temptation for bankers and for Silicon Valley executives alike is that even tiny manipulations of huge volumes of transactions generate easy money. The culture of speed, scale, and speculation can trample openness and honesty.

As former prosecutor Neil Barofsky summed it up in his memoir *Bailout*, "The incentives are to cheat, and cheating is profitable because there are no consequences."[86] Even a $450 million fine is about as annoying as a mosquito bite to (those in charge of) a bank with more than $50 billion in revenue.[87] Penalties in Silicon Valley are an order of magnitude more trivial. Although $22.5 million is only about four hours of revenue for Google, the FTC touted it as a record-setting fine. Facebook settled one case for $10 million.[88] The FCC once "punished" Google with a $25,000 fine. It is a broken enforcement model, and we have black boxes to thank for much of this. People can't be outraged at what they can't understand. And without some public concern about the trivial level of penalties for lawbreaking here, there are no consequences for the politicians ultimately responsible for them.

## The Limits of Black Boxes: A Hayekian Perspective

Admittedly, black boxes smooth things; they make ordinary transactions faster and more efficient. The reforms I propose would slow things down. They would incur expenses, which would likely get passed on to us. They would cost time, too. It takes an automatic algorithm milliseconds to act on a copyright complaint; it would take longer than that for people to appraise a website's claim of fair use. Credit raters would have to expend human time and judgment to spot the times when negative credit information is less credible than the person it's putting down.

I have no doubt that think tanks will offer ominous prognostications about the costs of such initiatives. (Whether they'll be as forthcoming with the identity of their sponsors remains to be seen.)[89] It's easy to forecast the loss of tens of thousands of jobs if financial transactions are taxed, or if credit bureaus are required to give a full and fair accounting of their actions. Wall Street firms have repeatedly purchased such studies and promoted them in lobbying campaigns. But, as law professor John C. Coates has shown, cost benefit analysis of regulation can be yet another misapplication of natural science methods to social scientific prediction.[90] Despite industry's predictions of doom, it is just as plausible that accountability in the reputation, search, and finance sectors would *create* jobs rather than destroy them. Accountability requires human judgment, and only humans can perform the critical function of making sure that, as our social relations become ever more automated, domination and discrimination aren't built invisibly into their code.

Another overefficiency of black boxes concerns the fact that information does not always lend itself to generalization. For example, Amar Bhidé, a professor at Tufts University with experience in finance and consulting, harshly criticizes the homogenizing impact of nationwide underwriting standards on local housing markets. He criticizes black boxes from a Hayekian perspective, exposing our giant finance firms for having faults eerily reminiscent of Communist central planners.[91]

Hayek's fundamental insight was that nobody knows everything about how goods and services in an economy should be priced, and that no one central decision maker can ever really grasp the idiosyncratic preferences, values, and purchasing power of millions of individuals.[92] That kind of knowledge, Hayek said, is *distributed.*

Today, Hayek's most vocal supporters tend to assume that he was only criticizing the state. But the finance sector is plenty concentrated, and interconnected with state power. Bhidé says that its centralization, too, is concerning, and should give way to more localized decision making. A loan officer in Phoenix, for example, would be far more likely to recognize dodgy local mortgage applicants than a high-level manager several hundred miles away. Moreover, a local bank putting its own money on the line (originating loans to keep them) would have a strong incentive to estimate clearly the potential risks and rewards of its decisions.[93]

A Hayekian critic of black box firms could take this line of reasoning even further. Why should so much of the Internet be organized by a single company, Google? Isn't its fast pace of acquiring start-ups a Promethean ambition to centralize more and more computing talent into a single firm? The same could be said with respect to Apple's tight grip over its app empire, or even the dominant provision of social networking by Facebook.[94] A committed Hayekian could easily make the case for far more aggressive antitrust enforcement in tech industries.[95]

## Black Box Endgame

In their common goals, procedures, and (increasingly) cultures, powerful alliances have developed among the reputation, search, and finance sectors. The first two deal in data, while the securities of Wall Street, ostensibly at least, appear more concrete. But the differences, while real, are less fundamental than the similarities. Ultimately, they are all in the business of information. What is money (and all its derivative forms) other than *information* about how much of our collective goods and services its owner can demand? And what are reputation and search firms establishing other than new *currencies* for allocating opportunity and attention? All these firms try to process information to score quick gains. But we should never lose sight of the fact that the numbers on their computer terminals have real effects, deciding who gets funded and found, and who is left discredited or obscure.

All rely on secrecy to protect the information on which the quick scores depend. This book could have been about many different forms of secrecy, however. Why focus on Silicon Valley and Wall Street in particular? Leading Internet and finance firms present a formidable threat to important values of privacy, dignity, and fairness. This threat, now increasingly intertwined with the power of the government, is too often obscured by self-protective black box practices and irrelevant distractions. The American political debate for the last several decades has calcified into struggles over "market forces" or "state provision." Meanwhile the agile impresarios behind reputation, search, and finance firms exploit (and create) problems that neither state nor market alone can solve.

For them, the tug-of-war between market and state has become a *pas de deux*, and the blurring of this traditional distinction lies at the core of the black box society. The "markets" described in much of this book are markets for information—about how likely someone is to click on an ad; incur medical bills; pay off a loan. Information of this kind is valuable only if it is exclusive, *and it remains exclusive only if the full power of the state can be brought to bear on anyone who discloses it without authorization.*

In 1956, the sociologist C. Wright Mills sketched the American "power elite" of that time: the corporations, the military, and the government. Mills saw these entities in rough equipoise in their Cold War setting, each with its own independent base of power (that is, the capacity to force others to do what they would not be inclined to do otherwise). Mills's division has been more and less relevant over the course of the twentieth century; after the fall of the Berlin Wall, for instance, the military's domestic power waned, while 9/11 brought with it the resurgence of a defense/intelligence/ policing complex. But his concept continues to capture attention and interest.[96]

Some social theorists have adjusted Mills's typology to take into account the rise of other important actors, such as the media. But if Mills's "triangle of power" needs updating, its quaintness derives less from the failure to include other power centers than from the separate-but-equal status that Mills attributed to its members. Twenty-first-century revolving-door dynamics present a constant temptation for public servants to "cash out" for private-sector pay-days, leaving them loath to do anything that might disrupt either their own main chance or similar opportunities for their peers and protégés.

If we are to retrieve our political process from its outmoded and self-serving rut, we must recognize the new landscape. That requires studying the "ideal role of the state in the economic and social orga-nization of a country" directly, rather than presuming it should merely get out of the way of markets.[97] This is the task of the classic social science of political economy, a method that integrates long-divided fields. Armed with that knowledge, we can take up once more the vital debate that has been so long derailed: What kind of a society do we really want?

## Toward an Intelligible Society

Capitalist democracies increasingly use automated processes to as-sess risk and allocate opportunity. The companies that control these processes are some of the most dynamic, profitable, and important parts of the information economy. All of these services make use of algorithms, usually secret, to bring some order to vast amounts of information. The allure of the technology is clear—the ancient as-piration to predict the future, tempered with a modern twist of sta-tistical sobriety.

Yet in a climate of secrecy, bad information is as likely to endure as good, and to result in unfair and even disastrous predictions. This is why the wholesale use of black box modeling, however profitable it is for the insiders who manage it, is dangerous to society as a whole. It's bad enough when innocent individuals are hurt, branded as security threats or goldbrickers or credit risks by inaccuracies that they can't contest and may not even know about. Modeling is even worse when unfair or inappropriate considerations combine with the power of algorithms to create the failures they claim to merely predict.

Moreover, when the errors are systematic enough, algorithmic control fails on its own terms. That happened most spectacularly in the crisis of 2008. Order was restored only by the infusion of hundreds of billions of dollars of government money, and even in this mammoth intervention secrecy prevailed; the identity of many of the banks involved was kept under wraps at the time.

Educated citizenship today requires more than an understanding of government, which is just the tip of an iceberg of social organization. It also demands an understanding of the companies that influence our government and culture. The firms that order the Internet and direct the flow of capital have outsized influence in Washington. For better or worse, they also increasingly determine the value and visibility of labor, companies, and investments. But they do all this in the shadows. Public options in search and finance need to be developed to create spaces not only for transparency, but for intelligibility as well. Failing that, we can count on a society ever more skewed to the advantage of black box insiders, and a populace ever more ignorant of how its key institutions actually function.

Few of us understand how our car engines work, but we can judge well enough whether they get us to our destinations safely and comfortably. We cannot so easily assess how well the engines of reputation, search, and finance do their jobs. Trade secrecy, where it prevails, makes it practically impossible to test whether their judgments are valid, honest, or fair. The designation of a person as a bad employment prospect, or a website as irrelevant, or a loan as a bad risk may be motivated by illicit aims, but in most cases we'll never be privy to the information needed to prove that. What we do know is that those at the top of the heap will succeed further, thanks in large part to the reputation incurred by past success; those at the bottom are likely to endure cascading disadvantages. Despite the promises of freedom and self-determination held out by the lords of the information age, black box methods are just as likely to entrench a digital aristocracy as to empower experts.

Open uses of technology hold a very different kind of promise. Instead of using surveillance technology against American citizens, the government could deploy it on our behalf, to monitor and contain corporate greed and waste. Public options in technology and finance would make our social world both fairer and more comprehensible. Rather than contort ourselves to fit "an impersonal economy lacking a truly human purpose," we might ask how institutions could be re-shaped to meet higher ends than shareholder value.[98] Admittedly, demands for dignity, due process, and social justice are controversial; there will always be holders of vested privilege who prefer not to share. Nevertheless, it is time for us as citizens to demand that important decisions about our financial and communication infrastructures be made intelligible, soon, to independent reviewers—and that, over the years and the decades to come, they be made part of a public record available to us all.

Black box services are often wondrous to behold, but our black box society has become dangerously unstable, unfair, and unproductive. Neither New York quants nor California engineers can deliver a sound economy or a secure society. Those are the tasks of a citizenry, which can perform its job only as well as it understands the stakes.

NOTES

ACKNOWLEDGMENTS

INDEX

# NOTES

## Book Epigraphs

Heracleitus, *On the Universe*, in *Hippocrates IV*, Loeb Classical Library 150, trans. W. H. S. Jones (Cambridge: Harvard University Press, 1931), 501.

Gerald Manley Hopkins, "That Nature is a Heraclitean Fire and of the Comfort of the Resurrection." *Poetry Foundation*. Available at http://www.poetryfoundation.org/poem/173662.

## I

### Introduction—The Need to Know

1. Harold D. Lasswell, *Politics: Who Gets What, When, How* (New York: Meridian Books, 1972).

2. Robert H. Frank and Philip J. Cook, *The Winner-Take-All Society* (New York: Penguin, 1996); David C. McClelland, *The Achieving Society* (Eastford, CT: Martino Fine Books, 2010); Hassan Masum and Mark Tovey, eds., *The Reputation Society* (Cambridge, MA: MIT Press, 2012); Jeffrey M. Berry and Clyde Wilcox, *The Interest Group Society* (Upper Saddle River, NJ: Pearson, 2008); Robert N. Bellah et al., *The Good Society* (New York: Vintage, 1992); Avishai Margalit, *The Decent Society* (Cambridge: Harvard University Press, 1996). Critiques of social order can also take this form; see, e.g., Robert B. Edgerton, *Sick Societies* (New York: Free Press, 1992).

3. Gillian Tett has described "social silences" at the core of the economy. Gillian Tett, *Fool's Gold* (New York: Free Press, 2009). Sociologist John Gaventa has focused on what is kept *off* political agendas as a "third dimension" of power, building on Antonio Gramsci's theories. John Gaventa, *Power and Powerlessness* (Champaign: University of Illinois Press, 1982). David E. Pozen, "Deep Secrecy," *Stanford Law Review* 62 (2010) 257–340.

4. Robert N. Proctor, "Agnotology: A Missing Term to Describe the Cultural Production of Ignorance (and Its Study)," in *Agnotology: The Making and Unmaking of Ignorance*, ed. Robert N. Proctor and Londa N. Schiebinger (Stanford, CA: Stanford University Press, 2008), 3.

5. Alan Greenspan, "Dodd-Frank Fails to Meet Test of Our Times," *Financial Times*, March 29, 2011; Friedrich A. Hayek, "The Use of Knowledge in Society," *American Economics Review* 35 (1945): 519–530. Of course, as Richard Bronk observes, "Hayek's analysis falls short by ignoring the role of dominant narratives, analytical monocultures, self-reinforcing emotions, feedback loops, information asymmetries and market power in distorting the wisdom of prices." Richard Bronk, "Hayek on the Wisdom of Prices: A Reassessment," *Erasmus Journal for Philosophy and Economics* 6, no. 1 (2013): 82–107.

6. Lee H. Fang, "The Invisible Hand of Business in the 2012 Election," *The Nation*, November 19, 2003, http://www.thenation.com/article/177252 /invisible-hand-business-2012-election.

7. In philosophy, the term is also polysemic. For example, if enough people simply accept the outputs of a given process as valid, *it* is a quite useful black box. Some aspects of reality are simply assumed to be true, without need for further investigation. Graham Harman stated, "We have a true black box when a statement is simply presented as raw fact without any reference to its genesis or even its author. As Latour asks, 'who refers to Lavoisier's paper when writing the formula $H_2O$ for water?'" Harman, *Prince of Networks: Bruno Latour and Metaphysics* (Melbourne: re.press, 2009), 37. One of the main purposes of this book is to raise enough questions about the results presented by leading Internet and finance firms so that they do not congeal into this kind of black box.

8. Jack Balkin, "The Constitution in the National Surveillance State," *Minnesota Law Review* 93 (2008): 1–25.

9. George Packer, "Amazon and the Perils of Non-disclosure," *The New Yorker*, February 12, 2014.

10. Arkady Zaslavsky, "Internet of Things and Ubiquitous Sensing" (Sept. 2013). *Computing Now*. Available at http://www.computer.org/portal/web /computingnow/archive/september2013.

11. April Dembosky, "Invasion of the Body Hackers," *Financial Times*, June 10, 2011.

12. Tal Zarsky, "Transparent Predictions," *Illinois Law Review* (2013): 1503–1570.

13. Bradley Keoun and Phil Kuntz, "Wall Street Aristocracy Got $1.2 Trillion in Secret Loans," *Bloomberg News*, August 22, 2011, http://www.bloomberg .com/news/2011-08-21/wall-street-aristocracy-got-1-2-trillion-in-fed-s-secret -loans.html.

14. Maxwell Strachan, "Financial Sector Back to Accounting for Nearly One-Third of U.S. Profits," *Huffington Post* (blog), March 30, 2011, http:// www.huffingtonpost.com/2011/03/30/financial-profits-percentage_n_841716 .html. Things were even better for the finance firms in the boom years.

15. Jaron Lanier, *Who Owns the Future?* (New York: Simon & Schuster, 2013). "At the height of its power, the photography company Kodak employed

more than 140,000 people and was worth $28 billion. They even invented the first digital camera. But today Kodak is bankrupt, and the new face of digital photography has become Instagram. When Instagram was sold to Facebook for a billion dollars in 2012, it employed only thirteen people." Ibid., 2.

16. Frederic Bloom, "Information Lost and Found," *California Law Review* 100 (2012): 635–690.

17. Obfuscation contributes to *complexity*, which is sometimes the natural result of modern business, but it is also, frequently, contrived for no good end. Steve Randy Waldman, "Why Is Finance So Complex?" *Interfluidity* (blog), December 26, 2011, http://www.interfluidity.com/v2/2669.html.

18. As G.K. Chesterton observed, the irremediably unknown is a mystery. We cannot solve or dissect it, but only grow wiser about it.

19. This is an old problem in law. See Grant Gilmore, "Circular Priority Systems," *Yale Law Journal* 71 (1961): 53–74.

20. Frank Partnoy and Jesse Eisinger, "What's Inside America's Banks?," *The Atlantic*, January 2, 2013.

21. Ibid.

22. Clay Shirky, "A Speculative Post on the Idea of Algorithmic Authority," *Shirky* (blog), November 13, 2009, http://www.shirky.com/weblog/2009/11/a-speculative-post-on-the-idea-of-algorithmic-authority/.

23. See Scott Patterson, *The Quants: How a New Breed of Math Whizzes Conquered Wall Street and Nearly Destroyed It* (New York: Crown Publishing, 2010).

24. Jeff Connaughton, *The Payoff: Why Wall Street Always Wins* (Westport, CT: Prospecta Press, 2013). Chapter 10 of Connaughton's book is titled "The Blob," referring to the shadowy exchange of favors among government, lobbyists, businesses, and media interests. For a theoretical and critical take on the intermixture of political and economic elites, see Hanna Fenichel Pitkin, *Attack of the Blob: Hannah Arendt's Concept of the Social* (Chicago: University of Chicago Press, 2000), 5; Janine R. Wedel, *Shadow Elite: How the World's New Power Brokers Undermine Democracy, Government, and the Free Market* (New York: Basic Books, 2009).

25. Jon Elster, *Local Justice: How Institutions Allocate Scarce Goods and Necessary Burdens* (New York: Russell Sage Foundation, 1993).

26. For an insightful account of modeling as rationalization, see Gerd Gigerenzer, *Risk Savvy: How to Make Good Decisions* (New York: Viking, 2014).

27. Ben Goldacre, *Bad Pharma: How Drug Companies Mislead Doctors and Harm Patients* (London: Fourth Estate, 2012), 3; Frank Pasquale, "Grand Bargains for Big Data: The Emerging Law of Health Care Information," *Maryland Law Review* 72 (2013): 668–772 (collecting studies on secrecy in the health context).

28. See, e.g., David Dayen, "Massive new fraud coverup: How banks are pillaging homes — while the government watches," *Salon*, at http://www.salon.com/2014/04/23/massive_new_fraud_coverup_how_banks_are_pillaging_homes_while_the_government_watches/ (Apr. 23, 2014); Yves Smith, "The Private Equity Limited Partnership Agreement Release: The Industry's Snowden Moment, Naked Capitalism," May 28, 2014, at http://www.nakedcapitalism

.com/2014/05/private-equity-limited-partnership-agreement-release-industrys
-snowden-moment.html.

29. Dave Gilson, Gavin Aronsen, Tasneem Raja, Ben Breedlove, and E.J. Fox, "An Interactive Map of the Dark-Money Universe" (June 2012). *Mother Jones*. Available at http://www.motherjones.com/politics/2012/06/interactive -chart-super-pac-election-money; Ciara Torres-Spelliscy, "Transparent Elections after Citizens United" (Mar. 2011). *Brennan Center for Justice, New York University School of Law*. Available at https://www.brennancenter.org/publication /transparent-elections-after-citizens-united.

During the debate on the Affordable Care Act, health insurers "publicly stake[d] out a pro-reform position while privately funding the leading anti-reform lobbying group in Washington." Elahe Izadi, "Exclusive: AHIP Gave More than $100 Million to Chamber's Efforts to Derail Health Care Reform," *National Journal* (blog), June 13, 2012, http://www.nationaljournal.com/blogs /influencealley/2012/06/exclusive-ahip-gave-more-than-100-million-to -chamber-s-efforts-to-derail-health-care-reform-13.

30. Shane Richmond, "Eric Schmidt: Google Gets Close to the 'Creepy Line,'" *The Telegraph*, October 5, 2010.

31. Magazines like *McClure's* paved the way for muckrakers and reformers like Brandeis. Adam Curtis, "What the Fluck?" *BBC Blog*, December 5, 2013, http://www.bbc.co.uk/blogs/adamcurtis/posts/WHAT-THE-FLUCK. Curtis also observes the need for such exposure and explanation in our day, explaining that scandals "range from the NSA [U.S. National Security Agency] and GCHQ [Britain's Government Communications Headquarters], to global banks, private equity . . . and parts of the media-industrial complex. . . . But the scandals do not join up to make a bigger picture. And our reactions are sometimes confused and contradictory—as in the case of transparency and surveillance. It is as if the scandals are part of a giant jigsaw puzzle—and what we are waiting for is someone to come along and click those pieces together to give a clear, big picture of what is happening." Ibid.

32. Robert H. Wiebe, *The Search for Order: 1870–1922* (New York: Farrar, Straus and Giroux, 1967), 132. ("They had enough insight into their lives to recognize that the old ways and old values would no longer suffice.")

33. See Trevor Potter and Bryson B. Morgan, "The History of Undisclosed Spending in U.S. Elections and How 2012 Became the Dark Money Election," *Notre Dame Journal of Law, Ethics and Public Policy* 27 (2013): 383–480.

34. The FCC was created by the Communications Act of 1934 (47 U.S.C. § 151 et seq.).

35. Robert L. Rabin, "Federal Regulation in Historical Perspective," *Stanford Law Review* 38 (1986): 1189–1326.

36. Martin Shapiro, "APA: Past, Present, Future," *Virginia Law Review* 72 (1986): 447–492.

37. Harvey J. Goldschmid, ed., Business Disclosure: Government's Need to Know (New York: McGraw-Hill, 1979); President John F. Kennedy, "Secrecy Is Repugnant," YouTube video, 5:29, from an address to newspaper publishers at the Waldorf-Astoria in New York City, April 27, 1961 (posted Dec.

2010). *4TheRecord*. Available at http://tzimnewman.blogspot.com/2010/12/jfk
-secrecy-is-repugnant-1961-speech.html. ("The very word "secrecy" is repugnant in a free and open society; and we are as a people inherently and historically opposed to secret societies, to secret oaths and secret proceedings.")

38. Rabin, "Federal Regulation in Historical Perspective."

39. Ruckelshaus v. Monsanto Co., 467 U.S. 986 (1984); Pamela Samuelson,
"Information as Property: Do *Ruckelshaus* and *Carpenter* Signal a Changing
Direction in Intellectual Property Law?," *Catholic University Law Review* 38
(1989): 365–400.

40. For background on (and critique of) the role of the "sophisticated investor" construct in finance theory, see Jennifer Taub, "The Sophisticated Investor and the Global Financial Crisis," in *Corporate Governance Failures: The
Role of Institutional Investors in the Global Financial Crisis*, ed. James P. Hawley,
Shyam J. Kamath, and Andrew T. Williams (Philadelphia: University of Pennsylvania Press, 2011), 191. (reliance "upon the sophisticated investor ignores
reality; the entities the law deems to meet the definition are largely neither
sophisticated enough to match the complexity of the instruments or lack of
data nor [are they] the actual investors who have placed their capital at risk.")

41. Rakesh Khurana, *From Higher Aims to Hired Hands: The Social Transformation of American Business Schools and the Unfulfilled Promise of Management as a Profession* (Princeton: Princeton University Press, 2009); George
F. DeMartino, *The Economist's Oath: On the Need for and Content of Professional
Economic Ethics* (Oxford, UK: Oxford University Press, 2011); Charles Ferguson, "Larry Summers and the Subversion of Economics," *The Chronicle Review*, October 3, 2010; Philip Mirowski and Esther-Mirjam Sent, eds., *Science
Bought and Sold: Essays in the Economics of Science* (Chicago: University of Chicago Press, 2002).

42. See Frederic Filloux, "Google News: The Secret Sauce," *The Guardian*, February 25, 2013.

43. Neoliberalism is a complex set of ideas, perhaps best summarized in
Philip Mirowski, *Never Let a Serious Crisis Go to Waste: How Neoliberalism Sur-
vived the Financial Meltdown* (London: Verso, 2013), 53–67. For our purposes,
the critical tenet of the neoliberal "thought collective" is that "the market
(suitably reengineered and promoted) can always provide solutions to problems seemingly caused by the market in the first place." Ibid., 64.

44. Barton Gellman, *Angler: The Cheney Vice Presidency* (New York: Penguin, 2009), 138.

45. For more, see Julian E. Zelizer, *Arsenal of Democracy* (New York: Basic
Books, 2010).

46. Dana Priest and William Arkin, *Top Secret America: The Rise of the New
American Security State* (New York: Hachette Book Group, 2011).

47. Noah Shachtman, "Pentagon's Black Budget Tops $56 Billion," *Wired*,
February 1, 2010, http://www.wired.com/2010/02/pentagons-black-budget
-tops-56-billion/.

48. Glenn Reynolds, *An Army of Davids* (Nashville, TN: Thomas Nelson,
2007); David Brin, *The Transparent Society* (Cambridge, MA: Perseus Books,
1998).

49. "2007 Electronic Monitoring and Surveillance Survey" (Feb. 2008). *American Management Association* (press release). Available at http://press.amanet .org/press-releases/177/.

50. Alexander Halavais, *Search Engine Society* (Cambridge, UK: Polity, 2008), 85; see also Adam Raff, "Search, but You May Not Find," *New York Times*, December 28, 2009, A27.

51. For a general overview of online search engines, see Jon Rognerud, *Ultimate Guide to Search Engine Optimization* (Irvine, CA: Entrepreneur Media, 2008).

52. The lack of transparency, or audits, not only provides opportunities for bias or self-serving behavior. It also undermines the validity of the "findings" driving business here. As Tim Harford has observed, "theory-free analysis of mere correlations is inevitably fragile. If you have no idea what is behind a correlation, you have no idea what might cause that correlation to break down." Tim Harford, "Big data: are we making a big mistake?," *Financial Times*, Mar. 28, 2014, at http://www.ft.com/cms/s/2/21a6e7d8-b479-11e3 -a09a-00144feabdc0.html#ixzz32xoXh98S.

53. Jamie Court and John Simpson, Letter to Google, October 13, 2008. *Consumer Watchdog*. Available at http://www.consumerwatchdog.org/resources /CWLetterToGoogle10-13-08.pdf.

54. The prescient Helen Nissenbaum warned of "eroding accountability in computerized societies." Helen Nissenbaum, "Accountability in a Computerized Society," *Science & Engineering Ethics* 2(1) (1996).

55. John Gapper, "The Price of Wall Street's Black Box," *Financial Times*, June 22, 2011.

56. George Dyson, *Turing's Cathedral: The Origins of the Digital Universe* (New York: Pantheon, 2012), 308.

57. State officials closely monitor reputational intermediaries, requiring key "doctor rating" sites to disclose the data they use and the way they analyze it. New health privacy regulations have also focused on an "accounting of disclosures" that should help patients understand how data about them is compiled and disseminated.

58. Many legal scholars have grown disillusioned with disclosure as a regulatory strategy. Omri Ben-Shahar & Carl E. Schneider, *More Than You Wanted to Know: The Failure of Mandated Disclosure* (Princeton: Princeton University Press, 2014).

59. David Brin, "The Self-Preventing Prophecy: How a Dose of Nightmare Can Help Tame Tomorrow's Perils," in *On Nineteen Eighty-Four: Orwell and Our Future*, ed. Abbott Gleason, Jack Goldsmith, and Martha C. Nussbaum (Princeton, NJ: Princeton University Press, 2005).

60. Benjamin Kunkel, "Dystopia and the End of Politics," *Dissent*, Fall 2008.

61. George Orwell, *1984* (London: Secker and Warburg, 1949); Aldous Huxley, *Brave New World* (London: Chatto & Windus, 1932).

62. *Brazil*, dir. by Terry Gilliam (1985, Universal Studios, DVD).

63. Of course, their very sophistication and precision may make them *more* menacing in some contexts. Julia Angwin, *Dragnet Nation* (New York:

Times Books, 2014). (A whistleblower told her that "the amount of data being assembled by the NSA was 'orders of magnitude' more than the world's most repressive secret police regimes, the Gestapo, the Stasi, and the KGB.")

## 2

### Digital Reputation in an Era of Runaway Data

1. John Gilliom and Torin Monahan, *SuperVision: An Introduction to the Surveillance Society* (Chicago: University of Chicago Press, 2012), 32.

2. Katy Bachman, "Big Data Added $156 Billion in Revenue to Economy Last Year," *AdWeek*, October 14, 2013, http://www.adweek.com/news/technology/big-data-added-156-billion-revenue-economy-last-year-153107 (reporting on industry estimate of "how much of the economy is driven by companies that use consumer-level data to market and retain consumers").

3. Jennifer Valentino-Devries, Jeremy Singer-Vine, and Ashkan Soltani, "Websites Vary Prices, Deals Based on Users' Information," *Wall Street Journal*, December 24, 2012, http://online.wsj.com/news/articles/SB10001424127887323777204578189391813881534.

4. "Facebook Using Offline Purchase History to Target Ads," *RT*, March 27, 2013, http://rt.com/usa/offline-facebook-ads-history-900/.

5. Charles Duhigg, "Bilking the Elderly, with a Corporate Assist" *New York Times*, May 20, 2007, http://www.nytimes.com/2007/05/20/business/20tele.html?pagewanted=all&_r=0.

6. Inside Google, "Liars and Loans: How Deceptive Advertisers Use Google," February 2011. *Consumer Watchdog*. Available at http://www.consumerwatchdog.org/resources/liarsandloansplus021011.pdf. Nathan Newman, "The Cost of Lost Privacy, Part 3: Google, the Subprime Meltdown and Antitrust Implications," *Huffington Post* (blog), July 15, 2011, http://www.huffingtonpost.com/nathan-newman/the-cost-of-lost-privacy-_3_b_893042.html. Jeff Chester, "Role of Interactive Advertising and the Subprime Scandal: Another Wake-Up Call for FTC," *Digital Destiny* (blog), August 28, 2007, http://centerfordigitaldemocracy.org/jcblog/?p=349.

7. David Anthony Whitaker, "How a Career Con Man Led a Federal Sting that Cost Google $500 Million," *Wired*, May 1, 2013, at http://www.wired.com/2013/05/google-pharma-whitaker-sting/.

8. Federal Trade Commission, *Data Brokers: A Call for Transparency and Accountability* (Washington: FTC, 2014), vii.

9. Joanne Leon, "Husband Internet Searches on Pressure Cooker and Backpack at Work. Law Enforcement Shows Up at House," *DailyKos* (blog), August 1, 2013, http://www.dailykos.com/story/2013/08/01/1228194/-Wife-searches-online-pressure-cookers-husband-a-backpack-Terrorism-task-force-shows-up-at-house. The police say the search terms included "pressure cooker bomb"; Catalano's account only mentions "pressure cookers." Even if it is the former, we should note that Google's autosuggest feature may have automatically entered the word "bomb" after "pressure cooker" while he was

typing—certainly many people would have done the search in the days after the Boston bombing merely to learn just how lethal such an attack could be. The police had no way of knowing whether Catalano had actually typed "bomb" himself, or accidentally clicked on it thanks to Google's increasingly aggressive recommendation engines. See also Philip Bump, "Update: Now We Know Why Googling 'Pressure Cookers' Gets a Visit from the Cops," *The Wire*, August 1, 2013, http://www.thewire.com/national/2013/08/government-knocking -doors-because-google-searches/67864/#.UfqCSAXy7zQ.facebook.

10. Martin Kuhn, *Federal Dataveillance: Implications for Constitutional Privacy Protections* (New York: LFB Scholarly Publishing, 2007), 178.

11. Robert Ellis Smith, *Ben Franklin's Web Site* (New York: Sheridan Books, 2004), 318–320.

12. 15 U.S.C. § 1681 et seq. (2012); Priscilla M. Regan, *Legislating Privacy: Technology, Social Values, and Public Policy* (Chapel Hill: University of North Carolina Press, 2009), 101; 15 U.S.C. § 1681a(f) (2012).

13. See 15 U.S.C. § 1681i (2012).

14. 60 Minutes, "40 Million Mistakes: Is Your Credit Report Accurate?," CBS News, Aug. 25, 2013, transcript at http://www.cbsnews.com/news/40 -million-mistakes-is-your-credit-report-accurate-25-08-2013/4/.

15. See Meredith Schramm-Strosser, "The 'Not So' Fair Credit Reporting Act: Federal Preemption, Injunctive Relief, and the Need to Return Remedies for Common Law Defamation to the States," *Duquesne Business Law Journal* 14 (2012): 170–171 (describing a "regulatory scheme that tends to favor the credit reporting industry").

16. FTC, "Marketer of Free Credit Reports Settles FTC Charges," Aug. 16, 2005, at http://www.ftc.gov/news-events/press-releases/2005/08/marketer -free-credit-reports-settles-ftc-charges. The site freecreditreport.com stated "along with your INSTANT credit report, we'll give you 30 FREE days of the Credit Check Monitoring Service at no obligation," not adequately disclosing that "after the free trial period for the credit monitoring service expired, consumers automatically would be charged a $79.95 annual membership, unless they notified the defendant within 30 days to cancel the service." *See also* EPIC Complaint and Request for Injunction, in the Matter of Experian, at http:// epic.org/privacy/experian/.

17. Daniel J. Solove, *The Digital Person: Technology and Privacy in the Information Age* (New York: New York University Press, 2004). Daniel Solove, "The ChoicePoint Settlement," *Concurring Opinions* (blog), January 30, 2006, http://www.concurringopinions.com/archives/2006/01/the_choicepoint_1 .html.

18. See Letter from Chris Jay Hoofnagle et al. to Joel Winston, Federal Trade Commission, December 7, 2004. Electronic Privacy Information Center (EPIC). Available at http://epic.org/privacy/fcra/freereportltr.html.

19. Daniel Solove, "FTC: Letting Experian Keep the Spoils," *Concurring Opinions*, Nov. 13, 2005, at http://www.concurringopinions.com/archives/2005 /11/ftc_letting_exp.html.

20. The Fair, Isaac & Co. (now known as FICO) promised scientific methods of ranking creditworthiness. After a slow start, the company grew steadily,

and its scores drive many credit decisions. Martha Poon, "Scorecards as Devices for Consumer Credit: The Case of Fair, Isaac and Company Incorporated," *Sociological Review* 55 (2007): 289; Kenneth G. Gunter, "Computerized Credit Scoring's Effect on the Lending Industry," *North Carolina Banking Institute* 4 (2000): 445; Martha Poon, "Statistically Discriminating without Discrimination" (dissertation chapter, University of California, San Diego, 2012). Available at http://www.ardis-recherche.fr/files/speakers_file_32.pdf. On predicting derogatory events, see "The FICO Score," *The Credit Scoring Site*, http://www.creditscoring.com/creditscore/fico/ (accessed February 16, 2014); Cassandra Jones Havard, " 'On The Take': The Black Box of Credit Scoring and Mortgage Discrimination," *Boston University Public Interest Law Journal* 20 (2011): 241–288.

21. Danielle Keats Citron and Frank Pasquale, "The Scored Society," *Washington Law Review* 89 (2014): 10–15.

22. Kevin Simpson, "Insurers' Use of Credit Reports Rankles Many," *Denver Post*, August 20, 2003, A1 ("Credit-scoring has been one of the components responsible for an 'alarming trend' of increased complaints to regulators over the past three years . . ."); see also Equal Employment Opportunity Commission, "EEOC Files Nationwide Hiring Discrimination Lawsuit against Kaplan Higher Education Corp.," December 21, 2010 (news release), http://www.eeoc.gov/eeoc/newsroom/release/12-21-10a.cfm.

23. For an example of weather catastrophe hurting credit scores (and the bureaus' refusal to respond), see Daniel Solove, "Hurricane Katrina and Credit Scores," *Concurring Opinions*, Oct. 10, 2005, at http://www.concurrin gopinions.com/archives/2005/10/hurricane_katri_1.html; Amy Traub, "Discredited: How Employment Credit Checks Keep Qualified Workers out of a Job," Demos (Feb., 2013), at http://www.demos.org/sites/default/files/publica tions/Discredited-Demos.pdf.

24. Brenda Reddix-Smalls, "Credit Scoring and Trade Secrecy: An Algorithmic Quagmire," *University of California Davis Business Law Journal* 12 (2011): 87–124; Havard, "On The Take," 248. ("Credit scoring if unchecked is an intrinsic, established form of discrimination very similar to redlining.")

25. For background on foreclosure fraud, see Yves Smith, *Whistleblowers Reveal How Bank of America Defrauded Homeowners and Paid for a Cover Up—All with the Help of 'Regulators'* (2013). Available at http://econ4.org/wp-content /uploads/2013/04/Naked-Capitalism-Whistleblower-Report-on-Bank-of -America-Foreclosure-Reviews-12.pdf.

26. See, e.g., Matthew Hector, "Standing, Securitization, and 'Show Me the Note,' " *Sulaiman Law Group*, http://www.sulaimanlaw.com/Publications /Standing-Securitization-and-Show-Me-The-Note.shtml (accessed February 15, 2014).

27. Jeff Harrington, "2010 Adds Its Own Terminology to Business Lexicon," *Tampa Bay Times*, December 23, 2010, http://www.tampabay.com/news /business/2010-adds-its-own-terminology-to-business-lexicon/1141681. ("Robo-sign[ing involves] a back-office system of quickly signing off on foreclosure documents like affidavits without actually doing what the affidavits say was done.")

28. See DeltaFreq, Comment to Barry Ritholtz on blog post, "Where's the Note? Leads BAC to Ding Credit Score," *The Big Picture* (blog), December 14, 2010, 11:03 a.m., http://www.ritholtz.com/blog/2010/12/note-bac-credit-score/.

29. Ibid.

30. "Credit Checks and Inquiries," *myFICO*, http://www.myfico.com/crediteducation/creditinquiries.aspx (accessed February 16, 2014).

31. Ibid. ("Generally, people with high FICO scores consistently: Pay bills on time . . . keep balances low on credit cards and other revolving credit products . . . [and] apply for and open new credit accounts only as needed.")

32. See, e.g., G. William McDonald, *Owing! 5 Lessons on Surviving Your Debt Living in a Culture of Credit* (Scottsdale, AZ: ACG Press, 2013).

33. myFICO Forums, http://ficoforums.myfico.com/ (accessed February 15, 2014).

34. "Credit Bureaus and Credit Reporting," *USA.Gov*, April 11, 2013, http://www.usa.gov/topics/money/credit/credit-reports/bureaus-scoring.shtml.

35. Carolyn Carter et al., "The Credit Card Market and Regulation: In Need of Repair," *North Carolina Banking Institute* 10 (2006): 41. (Twenty-nine percent have credit scores that differ by at least fifty points between credit bureaus; 50 to 70 percent of credit reports contain inaccurate information.)

36. Robert Pregulman, "Credit Scoring Highly Unfair," *SeattlePI*, January 28, 2002, http://www.seattlepi.com/local/opinion/article/Credit-scoring-highly-unfair-1078615.php. See also Deirdre Cummings, "Testimony in Favor of an Act Banning the Use of Socio-Economic Factors for Insurance Underwriting and Rating of Motor Vehicle Liability Insurance," *MassPirg* (blog), October 18, 2011, http://www.masspirg.org/blogs/blog/map/testimony-favor-act-banning-use-socio-economic-factors-insurance-underwriting.

37. See, e.g., Consumer Reports, "The Secret Score behind Your Auto Insurance," *MSN*, http://editorial.autos.msn.com/article.aspx?cp-documentid=435604 (accessed February 15, 2014) (noting that "insurance scores can penalize consumers who use credit reasonably"). See M. Beddingfield, "How Important Is Your Debt to Limit Ratio?" *Saving Advice*, October 11, 2008, http://www.savingadvice.com/articles/2008/10/11/102973_debt-to-limi-ratio.html.

38. Donncha Marron, "'Lending by Numbers': Credit Scoring and the Constitution of Risk within American Consumer Credit," *Economics and Society* 36 (2007): 111. For another black box analogy, see Martha Poon, "From New Deal Institutions to Capital Markets: Commercial Consumer Risk Scores and the Making of Subprime Mortgage Finance," *Accounting, Organizations and Society* 34 (2009): 654–674.

39. Theodore M. Porter, *Trust in Numbers: The Pursuit of Objectivity in Science and Public Life* (Princeton: Princeton University Press, 1996), 45 ("Numbers create and can be compared with norms, which are among the gentlest and yet most pervasive forms of power in modern democracies.").

40. See, e.g., Shawn Fremstad and Amy Traub, *Discrediting America: The Urgent Need to Reform the Nation's Credit Reporting Industry* (New York: Dēmos,

2011), 11. Available at http://www.demos.org/sites/default/files/publications /Discrediting_America_Demos.pdf.

41. Jeffrey Zaslow, "If TiVo Thinks You Are Gay, Here's How to Set It Straight," *Wall Street Journal*, November 26, 2002, http://online.wsj.com/news /articles/SB1038261936872356908.

42. Matthew Moore, "Gay Men Can Be Identified by Their Facebook Friends," *The Telegraph*, September 21, 2009, http://www.telegraph.co.uk/tech nology/facebook/6213590/Gay-men-can-be-identified-by-their-Facebook -friends.html.

43. Katie Heaney, "Facebook Knew I Was Gay before My Family Did," *BuzzFeed*, March 19, 2013, http://www.buzzfeed.com/katieheaney/facebook -knew-i-was-gay-before-my-family-did.

44. Ellen Jean Hirst, "Critics Take Aim at Data Mining after OfficeMax Addresses a Letter to Father with Line, 'Daughter Killed in Car Crash'," *Chicago Tribune*, January 21, 2014, 1.

45. Casey Johnston, "Data Brokers Won't Even Tell the Government How It Uses, Sells Your Data," *Ars Technica* (blog), December 21, 2013, http:// arstechnica.com/business/2013/12/data-brokers-wont-even-tell-the-government -how-it-uses-sells-your-data/.

46. Pam Dixon and Robert Gellman, *The Scoring of America* (San Diego: World Privacy Forum, 2014).

47. Frank A. Pasquale and Tara Adams Ragone, "The Future of HIPAA in the Cloud," *Stanford Technology Law Review* (forthcoming 2014). Available at http://papers.ssrn.com/sol3/papers.cfm?abstract_id=2298158.

48. A company called Acxiom has 1,600 pieces of information about 98 percent of U.S. adults, gathered from thousands of sources. Eli Pariser, *The Filter Bubble* (New York: Penguin, 2011), 3. At least some of them are health-indicative or health-predictive. Daniel J. Solove, *The Future of Reputation: Gossip, Rumor, and Privacy on the Internet* (New Haven, CT: Yale University Press, 2008); Natasha Singer, "You for Sale: Mapping the Consumer Genome," *New York Times*, June 16, 2012; Nicolas P. Terry, "Protecting Patient Privacy in the Age of Big Data," *UMKC Law Review* 81 (2012): 385–416.

49. Chad Terhune, "They Know What's in Your Medicine Cabinet," *BusinessWeek*, July 22, 2008.

50. Terhune, "They Know What's in Your Medicine Cabinet." While PPACA would make those gains harder for health insurers now, there are many other contexts where it is profitable to avoid doing business with a person marked as sick.

51. Intelliscript Complaint, In the Matter of Milliman, Inc. (2008) (No. C-4213), http://www.ftc.gov/os/caselist/0623189/080212complaint.pdf.

52. William W. Yu and Trena M. Ezzati-Rice, "Concentration of Health Care Expenses in the U.S. Civilian Noninstitutionalized Population," Agency for Healthcare Research and Quality Statistical Brief No. 81, 2005. Available at http://www.meps.ahrq.gov/mepsweb/data_files/publications/st81/stat81.shtml.

53. They would be "guaranteed issue" of insurance now, given the 2010 Patient Protection and Affordable Care Act (PPACA). 42 U.S.C § 1201(4), 42 U.S.C § 2702(a)–(b)(1), 42 U.S.C. § 300gg-1(a)–(b)(1) (requiring acceptance of

all applicants, but allowing limitation to certain "open or special enrollment" periods).

54. Terry, "Protecting Patient Privacy."

55. Ibid. (Those who "fill out warranty cards, enter sweepstakes, answer online surveys, agree to online privacy policies or sign up to receive e-mails from brands, they often don't realize that certain details—linked to them by name or by customer ID code—may be passed along to other companies.")

56. Lori Andrews, *I Know Who You Are and I Saw What You Did* (New York: Free Press, 2011), 70. Andrews uses the term "weblining" (an echo of the discriminatory lending practice, "redlining") to suggest how internet profiling can create new minorities who do not even know how they are being discriminated against.

57. Charles Duhigg, "How Companies Learn Your Secrets," *New York Times Magazine*, February 16, 2012, http://www.nytimes.com/2012/02/19/maga zine/shopping-habits.html?pagewanted=all.

58. Elizabeth A. Harris and Nicole Perlroth, "For Target, the Breach Numbers Grow," *New York Times*, January 1, 2014, http://www.nytimes.com/2014 /01/11/business/target-breach-affected-70-million-customers.html?_r=0.

59. Thomas R. McLean & Alexander B. McLean, "Dependence on Cyberscribes-Issues in E-Security," *8 J. Bus. & Tech. L.* (2013): 59 (discussing instances of medical information on the black market); Brian Krebs & Anita Kumar, "Hackers Want Millions for Data on Prescriptions," *Wash. Post*, May 8, 2009, at B1.

60. Misha Glenny, *DarkMarket: How Hackers Became the New Mafia* (New York: Vintage Books, 2012) 2 ("this minuscule elite (call them geeks, technos, hackers, coders, securocrats, or what you will) has a profound understanding of a technology that every day directs our lives more intensively and extensively, while most of the rest of us understand absolutely zip about it.").

61. "Experian Sold Consumer Data to ID Theft Service," *Krebs on Security*, October 20, 2013, http://krebsonsecurity.com/2013/10/experian-sold-consumer -data-to-id-theft-service/.

62. Duhigg, "How Companies Learn Your Secrets."

63. Ryan Calo, "Digital Market Manipulation," *George Washington University Law Review* (forthcoming, 2014), at http://papers.ssrn.com/sol3/papers .cfm?abstract_id=2309703&download=yes.

64. PRNewsWire, "New Beauty Study Reveals Days, Times and Occasions When U.S. Women Feel Least Attractive," October 2, 2013 (news release), http://www.prnewswire.com/news-releases/new-beauty-study-reveals -days-times-and-occasions-when-us-women-feel-least-attractive-226131921 .html.

65. Paul Ohm coined the term "database of ruin" to suggest how damaging information could accumulate about a person. Paul Ohm, "Broken Promises of Privacy: Responding to the Surprising Failure of Anonymization," *University of California at Los Angeles Law Review* 57 (2010): 1750–51.

66. Joseph Walker, "Data Mining to Recruit Sick People," *Wall Street Journal*, December 17, 2013, http://online.wsj.com/news/articles/SB10001424 05270230372210457924014055451845 8. The *Journal* tries to explain these Big

Data associations by hypothesizing that large men need minivans because they cannot fit into other vehicles. But note how easily we could also rationalize the opposite conclusion: if minivan drivers were pegged as exceptionally fit, we might hypothesize that they used the large vehicle to carry around sports equipment. We should beware post hoc rationalizations of Big Data correlations, particularly when we are unable to review the representativeness of the data processed or the algorithms used to process it.

67. Ibid.

68. Some privacy protective measures are taken with respect to search logs. But, as Nissenbaum and Toubiana observe, "Without an external audit of these search logs, it is currently impossible to evaluate their robustness against de-anonymizing attacks." V. Toubiana and H. Nissenbaum, "An Analysis of Google Log Retention Policies," *The Journal of Privacy and Confidentiality* 3, no. 1 (2011): 5. For a search query revelation that proved revealing, despite anonymization efforts, see Thomas Barbaro and Michael Zeller, "A Face Is Exposed for AOL Searcher No. 4417749," *New York Times*, August 9, 2006, A1.

69. Walker, "Data Mining to Recruit Sick People."

70. Julie Brill, "Reclaim Your Name," Keynote Address at Computers, Freedom, and Privacy Conference, June 26, 2013. Available at http://www.ftc .gov/speeches/brill/130626computersfreedom.pdf.

71. Ibid. ("One health insurance company recently bought data on more than three million people's consumer purchases in order to flag health-related actions, like purchasing plus-sized clothing, the *Wall Street Journal* reported. [The company bought purchasing information for current plan members, not as part of screening people for potential coverage.]")

72. Peter Maass, "Your FTC Privacy Watchdogs: Low-Tech, Defensive, Toothless," *Wired*, June 28, 2012, http://www.wired.com/threatlevel/2012/06 /ftc-fail/all/.

73. Charles Duhigg, "What Does Your Credit Card Company Know about You?" *New York Times*, May 17, 2009, http://www.nytimes.com/2009/05 /17/magazine/17credit-t.html?pagewanted=all. For a compelling account for the crucial role that the FTC plays in regulating unfair consumer practices and establishing a common law of privacy, see Daniel J. Solove and Woodrow Hartzog, "The FTC and the New Common Law of Privacy," *Columbia Law Review* 114 (2014): 583–676.

74. Duhigg, "What Does Your Credit Card Company Know about You?"

75. Kashmir Hill, "Could Target Sell Its 'Pregnancy Prediction Score'?" *Forbes*, February 16, 2012, http://www.forbes.com/sites/kashmirhill/2012/02 /16/could-target-sell-its-pregnancy-prediction-score/.

76. Frank Pasquale, "Reputation Regulation: Disclosure and the Challenge of Clandestinely Commensurating Computing," in *The Offensive Internet: Speech, Privacy, and Reputation*, ed. Saul Levmore and Martha C. Nussbaum (Cambridge, MA: Harvard University Press, 2010), 107–123; Frank Pasquale, "Beyond Innovation and Competition: The Need for Qualified Transparency in Internet Intermediaries," *Northwestern University Law Review* 104 (2010): 105–174.

77. Lois Beckett, "Everything We Know about What Data Brokers Know about You," *ProPublica*, March 7, 2013 (updated September 13, 2013), http://www.propublica.org/article/everything-we-know-about-what-data-brokers-know-about-you.

78. Federal Trade Commission, *Protecting Consumer Privacy in an Era of Rapid Change: Recommendations for Businesses and Policymakers* (March 2012). Available at http://www.ftc.gov/sites/default/files/documents/reports/federal-trade-commission-report-protecting-consumer-privacy-era-rapid-change-recommendations/120326privacyreport.pdf (providing list of types of data brokers).

79. Joseph Turow, *The Daily You: How the New Advertising Industry Is Defining Your Identity and Your Worth* (New Haven, CT: Yale University Press, 2012).

80. Natasha Singer, "Secret E-Scores Chart Consumers' Buying Power," *New York Times*, August 18, 2012, http://www.nytimes.com/2012/08/19/business/electronic-scores-rank-consumers-by-potential-value.html?_r=0&pagewanted=print.

81. Dixon and Gellman, *The Scoring of America*.

82. Ylan Q. Mui, "Little-Known Firms Tracking Data Used in Credit Scores," *Washington Post*, July 16, 2011, http://www.washingtonpost.com/business/economy/little-known-firms-tracking-data-used-in-credit-scores/2011/05/24/gIQAXHcWII_print.html. The firm was ChoicePoint (now a part of another, larger firm), a data broker that maintained files on nearly all Americans.

83. Many data brokers double as reputational intermediaries, offering rankings and scores that promise to simplify the data reports they can prepare about individuals. They admit their work is a black box, given the "veil of secrecy surrounding the origins of the information, how it is analyzed and who buys it." Mui, "Little-Known Firms."

84. Ibid., 79.

85. Sherry D. Sanders, "Privacy Is Dead: The Birth of Social Media Background Checks," *39 Southwestern University Law Review 243*, (2012): 264; Alexander Reicher, "The Background of Our Being: Internet Background Checks in the Hiring Process," *28 Berkeley Tech. L.J.* (2013): 153.

86. Don Peck, "They're Watching You at Work," *The Atlantic*, December 2013, 76. When work is largely done in computing environments, the assessment can be very granular. Software engineers are assessed for their contributions to open source projects, with points awarded when others use their code. E. Gabriella Coleman, *Coding Freedom: The Ethics and Aesthetics of Hacking* (Princeton, NJ: Princeton University Press, 2013) (exploring Debian open source community and assessment of community members' contributions); Stephen Baker, *The Numerati* (New York: Houghton-Mifflin, 2008), 33.

87. Mat Honan, "I Flunked My Social Media Background Check. Will You?," *Gizmodo* (July 7, 2011). Available at http://gizmodo.com/5818774/this-is-a-social-media-background-check/. ("For each [social media] internet sources, Social Intelligence scored [candidate as] either "pass" or "negative," and included comments such as "subject admits to use of cocaine as well as LSD," and "subject references use of Ketamine [another recreational drug].").

88. Solove, *The Digital Person*, 47.

89. Tom Burghardt, "Big Brother a Click Away," *Pacific Free Press*, October 10, 2010, http://www.pacificfreepress.com/news/1/7119-big-brother-a-click -away.html. See also Mickey Huff and Project Censored, *Censored 2012: The Top Censored Stories and Media Analysis of 2010–2011* (New York: Seven Stories Press, 2011), 61. The venture capital companies Google Ventures and In-Q-Tel invested in Recorded Future.

90. Peck, "They're Watching You at Work."

91. Lewis Maltby, *Can They Do That? Retaking Our Fundamental Rights in the Workplace* (New York: Portfolio, 2009), 20 (describing pervasive surveillance); Chris Bertram, "Let It Bleed: Libertarians and the Workplace," *Crooked Timber* (blog), July 1, 2012, http://crookedtimber.org/2012/07/01/let-it-bleed -libertarianism-and-the-workplace/. ("On pain of being fired, workers in most parts of the United States can be commanded to pee or forbidden to pee. They can be watched on camera by their boss while they pee.")

92. Employee consent is an affirmative defense against employee causes of action based on invasion of privacy. Larry O. Natt Gantt, II, "An Affront to Human Dignity: Electronic Mail Monitoring in the Private Sector Workplace," *8 Harv. J.L. & Tech.* (1995): 345, 375. Courts will at times not allow this defense if it goes against certain public policy interests or if a statute forbids such specific aspects of the waiver. See, e.g., Speer v. Ohio Dept. of Rehab. & Corr., 624 N.E.2d 251 (Ohio, 1993) (forbidding waiver of right to privacy in employer's bathroom).

93. William Bogard, *The Simulation of Surveillance: Hypercontrol in Telematic Societies* (Cambridge: Cambridge University Press, 1996).

94. Peck, "They're Watching You at Work."

95. Leigh Buchanan, "Unemployment Is Up. Why Is It So Hard to Find the Right Hires?" *Inc.*, June 1, 2012, http://www.inc.com/leigh-buchanan/hiring -recruiting-unemployment-wharton-peter-cappelli.html.

96. Peter Cappelli, *Why Good People Can't Get Jobs: The Skills Gap and What Companies Can Do about It* (Philadelphia, PA: Wharton Digital Press, 2012).

97. They "processed about 29 applications for every opening in 2008, up from 22 in 2007." Vanessa O'Connell, "Test for Dwindling Retail Jobs Spawns a Culture of Cheating," *Wall Street Journal*, January 7, 2009, http://online .wsj.com/article/SB123129220146959621.html?mod=googlenews_wsj; Christopher Ingraham, "Wal-Mart Has a Lower Acceptance Rate than Harvard," *Washington Post*, Mar. 28, 2014, at http://www.washingtonpost.com/blogs /wonkblog/wp/2014/03/28/wal-mart-has-a-lower-acceptance-rate-than -harvard/.

98. Barbara Ehrenreich, "Time Theft," *New Internationalist Magazine*, November 2, 2002, http://www.newint.org/features/2002/11/01/women/.

99. O'Connell, "Test for Dwindling Retail Jobs Spawns a Culture of Cheating."

100. Chris Anderson, "The End of Theory: The Data Deluge Makes the Scientific Method Obsolete," *Wired*, June 23, 2008, http://www.wired.com /science/discoveries/magazine/16-07/pb_theory.

101. Ibid.

102. Charles Tilly, *Why?: What Happens When Persons Give Reasons* (Princeton: Princeton University Press, 2008).

103. Omer Tene and Jules Polonetsky, "A Theory of Creepy: Technology, Privacy and Shifting Social Norms," *Yale Journal of Law and Technology* 16 (2014): 59–102.

104. Leon R. Kass, "The Wisdom of Repugnance," *The New Republic*, June 1997; Martha C. Nussbaum, *Upheavals of Thought: The Intelligence of Emotions* (New York: Cambridge University Press, 2001).

105. Bruce Schneier, "Will Giving the Internet Eyes and Ears Mean the End of Privacy?" *The Guardian*, May 16, 2013, http://www.guardian.co.uk /technology/2013/may/16/internet-of-things-privacy-google.

106. Danielle Keats Citron, "Technological Due Process," *Washington University Law Review* 85 (2008): 1260–1263; Danielle Keats Citron, "Open Code Governance," *University of Chicago Legal Forum* (2008): 363–368.

107. Peck, "They're Watching You at Work."

108. Lior Jacob Strahilevitz, "Less Regulation, More Reputation," in *The Reputation Society: How Online Opinions Are Reshaping the Offline World*, ed. Hassan Masum and Mark Tovey (Cambridge, MA: MIT Press, 2012), 64.

109. Associated Press, "EEOC Sues over Criminal Background Checks," *CBSNews*, June 11, 2013, http://www.cbsnews.com/8301-505123_162-57588814 /eeoc-sues-over-criminal-background-checks/.

110. Executive Office of the President, *Big Data: Seizing Opportunities, Preserving Values* (2014).

111. David Talbot, "Data Discrimination Means the Poor May Experience a Different Internet," *Technology Review*, Oct. 9, 2013, at http://www.technology review.com/news/520131/data-discrimination-means-the-poor-may-experience -a-different-internet/ (discussing work of Kate Crawford and Jason Schultz).

112. Devony B. Schmidt, "Researchers Present Findings on Online Criminal Record Websites," *The Harvard Crimson*, November 20, 2012, http://www .thecrimson.com/article/2012/11/20/research-finds-profiling/.

113. Latanya Sweeney, "Discrimination in Online Ad Delivery," *Communications of the ACM* 56 (2013): 44. She ultimately found "statistically significant discrimination in ad delivery based on searches of 2184 racially associated personal names," in that ads suggesting arrest (as in the question, Arrested?) were likely to appear in the context of names associated with blacks even when there was no actual arrest record. See generally Seeta Gangadaran, "Digital Inclusion and Data Profiling," *First Monday*, 5 (2012).

114. "Racism Is Poisoning Online Ad Delivery, Professor Says," *MIT Technology Review*, February 4, 2013, http://www.technologyreview.com/view /510646/racism-is-poisoning-online-ad-delivery-says-harvard-professor/.

115. Toon Calders & Indre Zliobaite, "Why Unbiased Computational Processes Can Lead to Discriminative Decision Procedures," in *Discrimination and Privacy in the Information Society* (Bart Custers, et al., eds.) (Heidelberg: Springer, 2013).

116. Max Nisen, "Only 2% of Google's American Workforce Is Black," *The Atlantic*, May 29, 2014, at http://www.theatlantic.com/business/archive/2014 /05/only-2-percent-of-googles-american-workforce-is-black/371805/.

117. Nathan Newman, "Racial and Economic Profiling in Google Ads: A Preliminary Investigation (Updated)," *Huffington Post* (blog), September 20, 2011, http://www.huffingtonpost.com/nathan-newman/racial-and-economic -profi_b_970451.html. (Some of Newman's work has been funded by Microsoft, a Google rival.)

118. Ibid.

119. FTC, "Spring Privacy Series: Alternative Scoring Products," March 19, 2014 (news release), http://www.ftc.gov/news-events/events-calendar/2014 /03/spring-privacy-series-alternative-scoring-products.

120. FTC chair Edith Ramirez has voiced her concerns about algorithms that judge individuals "not because of what they've done, or what they will do in the future, but because inferences or correlations drawn by algorithms suggest they may behave in ways that make them poor credit or insurance risks, unsuitable candidates for employment or admission to schools or other institutions, or unlikely to carry out certain functions." Edith Ramirez, "Privacy Challenges in the Era of Big Data: The View from the Lifeguard's Chair," Keynote Address at the Technology Policy Institute Aspen Forum, August 19, 2013. Available at http://www.ftc.gov/sites/default/files/documents/public _statements/privacy-challenges-big-data-view-lifeguard%E2%80%99s-chair /130819bigdataaspen.pdf.

121. Ibid.

122. Michael Pinard, "Collateral Consequences of Criminal Convictions: Confronting Issues of Race and Dignity," *New York University Law Review* 85 (2010): 457–534.

123. Key policymakers in the Obama administration issued a report on the issue, and stated "A key finding of this report is that big data could enable new forms of discrimination and predatory practices." Executive Office of the President, *Big Data: Seizing Opportunities, Preserving Values* (Washington, D.C., 2014), at 53.

124. Interview by Doug Henwood, Behind the News, with Sarah Ludwig, NEDAP Attorney, on *Behind the News Radio* (August 30, 2007). Available at http://www.leftbusinessobserver.com/Radio.html.

125. See generally Jerry Kang, *Implicit Bias: A Primer for Courts* (Williamsburg, VA: National Center for State Courts, 2009). Available at http://wp.jerry kang.net.s110363.gridserver.com/wp-content/uploads/2010/10/kang-Implicit -Bias-Primer-for-courts-09.pdf.

126. Cf. Loïc Wacquant, "The Punitive Regulation of Poverty in the Neoliberal Age," *OpenDemocracy*, August 1, 2011, http://www.opendemocracy.net /5050/lo%C3%AFc-wacquant/punitive-regulation-of-poverty-in-neoliberal -age. See generally Bernard E. Harcourt, *Against Prediction: Profiling, Policing, and Punishing in an Actuarial Age* (Chicago: University of Chicago Press, 2007).

127. Cf. Robert E. Goodin, "Laundering Preferences," in *Foundations of Social Choice Theory*, ed. Jon Elster and Aanund Hylland (Cambridge, UK: Cambridge University Press, 1989), 75.

128. Charles Taylor, *Philosophical Papers II: Philosophy and the Human Sciences* (New York: Cambridge University Press, 1986). Data-driven analytics promises a more scientific approach to credit allocation and marketing than narrative

histories or one-dimensional scoring. But "objective analysis" can morph into objectification, just as "more rational" credit scoring led to rationalizations of toxic subprime loans.

129. Marx W. Wartofsky, *Conceptual Foundations of Scientific Thought* (New York: Macmillan, 1968).

130. Alice Goffman, *On the Run: Fugitive Life in an American City* (Chicago: University of Chicago Press, 2014); Matt Taibbi, *The Divide* (New York: Spiegel & Grau, 2014).

131. As Charles Taylor puts it, "By 'brute data' I mean . . . data whose validity cannot be questioned by offering another interpretation or reading. . . ." Taylor, *Philosophical Papers, Vol. II*, 19.

132. Harcourt, *Against Prediction*, 156.

133. See, e.g., Floyd v. City of New York, Case No. 1:08-cv-01034-SAS-HBP (Aug. 12, 2013), 58. Available at http://ccrjustice.org/files/Floyd-Liability-Opinion-8-12-13.pdf. (The court found that "the NYPD [New York Police Department] has an unwritten policy of targeting racially defined groups for stops.")

134. William Harless, "'Ban the Box' Laws Make Criminal Pasts Off-Limits," *Wall Street Journal*, August 3, 2013, http://online.wsj.com/news/articles/SB10001424127887323997004578640623464096406.

135. Radley Balko, *Rise of the Warrior Cop: The Militarization of America's Police Forces* (New York: Public Affairs, 2013).

136. Daniel Solove, *Nothing to Hide: The False Tradeoff between Privacy and Security* (New Haven, CT: Yale University Press, 2011).

137. Gregory B. Hladky, "Arrest Exposes State's Threats List," *New Haven Register*, January 9, 2007, A1. Christine Stuart, "Reporter Arrested for Political Activism," *Connecticut News Junkie* (blog), January 5, 2007, http://www.ctnewsjunkie.com/ctnj.php/archives/entry/reporter_arrested_for_political_activism_updated_with_police_report/. Gerri Willis, "Are You on the List?," *CNN*, September 30, 2009, http://www.cnn.com/video#/video/crime/2009/09/30/willis.fusion.centers.cnn.

138. *Protecting National Security and Civil Liberties: Strategies for Terrorism Information Sharing: Hearing before the Subcomm. on Terrorism, Technology, and Homeland Security of the S. Comm. on the Judiciary*, 111th Cong. 56–57 (2009) (statement of Caroline Fredrickson, Director, Washington Office, ACLU); Lisa Rein, "Police Spied on Activists in Maryland," *Washington Post*, July 18, 2008, A1; Office of Senator Barbara Mikulski, "Senators Demand Answers," February 19, 2009 (news release), http://mikulski.senate.gov/media/pressrelease/02-19-2009-2.cfm.

139. Matthew Harwood, "Maryland State Police Spied on Nonviolent Activists and Labeled Them Terrorists," *Security Management*, October 8, 2008, http://www.securitymanagement.com/news/maryland-state-police-spied-nonviolent-activists-and-labeled-them-terrorists-004742; Rein, "Police Spied on Activists in Maryland."

140. ACLU, "Policing Free Speech" (June 2010). Available at https://www.aclu.org/files/assets/Spyfiles_2_0.pdf.

141. See, e.g., Jennifer Stisa Granick and Christopher Jon Sprigman, Op-Ed, "The Criminal N.S.A.," *New York Times*, June 28, 2013, http://www.nytimes

.com/2013/06/28/opinion/the-criminal-nsa.html?ref=opinion&_r=2&; Jennifer
Stisa Granick and Christopher Jon Sprigman, "NSA, DEA, IRS Lie about Fact
That Americans Are Routinely Spied on by Our Government: Time for a Special Prosecutor," *Forbes*, August 14, 2013, http://www.forbes.com/sites/jennifer
granick/2013/08/14/nsa-dea-irs-lie-about-fact-that-americans-are-routinely
-spied-on-by-our-government-time-for-a-special-prosecutor-2/.

142. Pam Martens, "Wall Street Firms Spy on Protestors in Tax-Funded
Center," *CounterPunch*, October 18, 2011, http://www.counterpunch.org/2011
/10/18/wall-street-firms-spy-on-protestors-in-tax-funded-center/.

143. Ibid.

144. Colin Moynihan, "Officials Cast Wide Net in Monitoring Occupy
Protests," *New York Times*, May 22, 2014, at http://www.nytimes.com/2014/05
/23/us/officials-cast-wide-net-in-monitoring-occupy-protests.html.

145. Naomi Wolf, "The Shocking Truth about the Crackdown on Occupy,"
*The Guardian*, November 25, 2011, http://www.theguardian.com/commentisfree
/cifamerica/2011/nov/25/shocking-truth-about-crackdown-occupy. Naomi Wolf,
"Revealed: How the FBI Coordinated the Crackdown on Occupy," *The Guardian*, December 29, 2012, http://www.theguardian.com/commentisfree/2012/dec
/29/fbi-coordinated-crackdown-occupy.

146. Partnership for Civil Justice Fund, "FBI Documents Reveal Secret
Nationwide Occupy Monitoring," December 22, 2012. Available at http://www
.justiceonline.org/commentary/fbi-files-ows.html.

147. Matthew Stoller, "Occupy Wall Street Is a Church of Dissent," *Naked
Capitalism* (blog), September 29, 2011, http://www.nakedcapitalism.com/2011
/09/matt-stoller-occupywallstreet-is-a-church-of-dissent-not-a-protest.html.
W. J. T. Mitchell, Bernard E. Harcourt, and Michael Taussig, *Occupy: Three
Inquiries in Disobedience* (Chicago: University of Chicago Press, 2013).

148. See essays in Susan Will, Stephen Handelman, and David C. Brotherton, eds., *How They Got Away with It: White Collar Criminals and the Financial
Meltdown* (New York: Columbia University Press, 2013).

149. "FBI Documents Reveal Secret," *Partnership for Civil Justice Fund*, December 22, 2012, http://www.justiceonline.org/commentary/fbi-files-ows.html.
Yves Smith, "Banks Deeply Involved in FBI-Coordinated Suppression of 'Terrorist' Occupy Wall Street," *Naked Capitalism* (blog), December 30, 2010, http://
www.nakedcapitalism.com/2012/12/banks-deeply-involved-in-fbi-coordinated
-suppression-of-terrorist-occupy-wall-street.html. Wolf, "Revealed."

150. Martens, "Wall Street Firms Spy on Protestors in Tax-Funded
Center."

151. Department of Homeland Security, "Secretary Napolitano Unveils
'Virtual USA' Information-Sharing Initiative," December 9, 2009 (news release), http://www.dhs.gov/news/2009/12/09/virtual-usa-information-sharing
-initiative.

152. Department of Homeland Security, "National Network of Fusion
Centers Fact Sheet." Available at http://www.dhs.gov/national-network-fusion
-centers-fact-sheet (accessed February 17, 2014).

153. Mike German and Jay Stanley, "Fusion Center Update," *ACLU* (July
2008), 12. Available at https://www.aclu.org/files/pdfs/privacy/fusion_update

_20080729.pdf; see Mark A. Randol, *The Department of Homeland Security Intelligence Enterprise: Operational Overview and Oversight Challenges for Congress*, CRS Report for Congress, RL 40602 (2010), 11 (noting that there are seventy-two fusion centers).

154. Moynihan, "Officials Cast Wide Net."

155. *Beyond ISE Implementation: Exploring the Way Forward for Information Sharing: Hearing before Intelligence, Information Sharing, and Terrorism Risk Assessment Subcomm. on Homeland Security*, 111th Cong. 18 (2009). Robert O'Harrow, Jr., "Centers Tap into Personal Databases," *Washington Post*, April 2, 2008, A1. (As fusion center officials note, "There is never ever enough information. . . . That's what post-9/11 is about.")

156. Ryan Singel, "Fusion Centers Analyzing Reams of Americans' Personal Information," *Wired*, April 2, 2008, http://www.wired.com/threatlevel/2008/04/fusion-centers/.

157. Michael German and Jay Stanley, "What's Wrong with Fusion Centers?" ACLU (December 2007), 12; see Randol, *The Department of Homeland Security Intelligence Enterprise*, 11.

158. Michael Fickes, "The Power of Fusion," *American City & County*, March 1, 2008, http://americancityandcounty.com/security/homeland/power_fusion_nsa. Matthew Harwood, "Port of Long Beach Fusion Center Opens," *Security Management*, February 9, 2009, http://www.securitymanagement.com/news/port-long-beach-fusion-center-opens-005197/.

159. Tom Monahan, "Safeguarding America's Playground," *UNLV Institute for Security Studies*, July/August 2010.

160. Some of them even attest to that inclusiveness in their names. Department of Homeland Security, "Fusion Center Locations," https://www.dhs.gov/fusion-center-locations-and-contact-information (accessed May 22, 2014). G.W. Schulz, "Homeland Security USA: Obama Wants to Hire 'Thousands' for Domestic Intel," *The Center for Investigative Reporting* (blog), March 10, 2009, http://cironline.org/blog/post/homeland-security-usa-obama-wants-hire-%E2%80%98thousands%E2%80%99-domestic-intel-486

161. Torin Monahan, *Surveillance in the Time of Insecurity* (Piscataway, NJ: Rutgers University Press, 2010), 46.

162. Ibid.

163. John Rollins, *Fusion Centers: Issues and Options for Congress*, CRS Report for Congress, RL34070 (January 2008), 21.

164. According to the CRS report, "less than 15% of fusion centers interviewed for [the report] described their mission as solely counterterrorism. In the last year, many counterterrorism-focused centers have expanded their mission to include all-crimes and/or all-hazards." Rollins, *Fusion Centers: Issues and Options*, 21.

165. Christopher Slobogin, "Surveillance and the Constitution," *Wayne Law Review* 55 (2009): 1118.

166. John Shiffman and Kristina Cooke, "Exclusive: U.S. Directs Agents to Cover Up Program Used to Investigate Americans," Reuters, August 5, 2013, http://www.reuters.com/article/2013/08/05/us-dea-sod-idUSBRE97409R20130805.

167. Quoted in Michael Coleman, "Ex-CIA, NSA Chief Defends U.S. Intelligence Gathering," *The Washington Diplomat*, August 28, 2013, http://www.washdiplomat.com/index.php?option=com_content&view=article&id=9543&Itemid=414.

168. United States Senators Tammy Baldwin, Ron Wyden, Sherrod Brown, Tom Udall, and Richard Blumenthal, Letter to the Honorable Eric Holder, August 22, 2013. Available at https://www.fas.org/irp/congress/2013_cr/nsa-dea.pdf.

169. U.S. Department of Homeland Security, *Civil Liberties Impact Assessment for the State, Local, and Regional Fusion Center Initiative* (2008), 2.

170. Rollins, *Fusion Centers: Issues and Options*, 41–42.

171. Schulz, "Homeland Security USA."

172. Examples in Danielle Keats Citron and Frank Pasquale, "Network Accountability for the Domestic Intelligence Apparatus," *Hastings Law Journal* 62 (2011): 1441–1494; Pam Martens, "Wall Street's Secret Spy Center, Run for the 1% by NYPD," *CounterPunch*, February 6, 2012, http://www.counterpunch.org/2012/02/06/wall-streets-secret-spy-center-run-for-the-1-by-nypd/.

173. Spokesperson, California Anti-Terrorism Information Center, quoted in David E. Kaplan, "Spies among Us," *U.S. News and World Report*, May 8, 2006, 40.

174. Robert Mueller, FBI Director, quoted in Stephan Salisbury, "Surveillance, America's Pastime," *The Nation*, October 4, 2010, http://www.thenation.com/article/155158/surveillance-americas-pastime.

175. "2009 Virginia Terrorism Threat Assessment" (Mar. 2009). *Virginia Fusion Center*. Available at http://rawstory.com/images/other/vafusioncenterterrorassessment.pdf. Matthew Harwood, "Fusion Centers under Fire in Texas and New Mexico," *Security Management*, March 9, 2009.

176. "MIAC Strategic Report: The Modern Militia Movement," *Missouri Information Analysis Center*, February 20, 2009, http://constitution.org/abus/le/miac-strategic-report.pdf; see Chad Livengood, "Agency Apologizes for Militia Report on Candidates," *Springfield News-Leader*, March 10, 2009.

177. T.J. Greaney, "'Fusion Center' Data Draws Fire over Assertions," *Columbia Daily Tribune*, March 14, 2009, A1.

178. Chris Jay Hoofnagle, "Big Brother's Little Helpers: How ChoicePoint and Other Commercial Data Brokers Collect, Process, and Package Your Data for Law Enforcement," *University of North Carolina Journal of International Law and Commercial Regulation* 29 (2004): 595–638.

179. Jon D. Michaels, "All the President's Spies: Private–Public Intelligence Partnerships in the War on Terror," 96 (2008): 915.

180. Solove, *The Digital Person*, 171.

181. Richard Hovel, Senior Adviser on Aviation and Homeland Security, Boeing Company, quoted in Alice Lipowicz, "Boeing to Staff FBI Fusion Center," *Washington Technology*, June 1, 2007, http://washingtontechnology.com/articles/2007/06/01/boeing-to-staff-fbi-fusion-center.aspx. ASIS International, "ASIS Foundation and Illinois Law Enforcement Create the First Private-Sector Funded Position for the Illinois Statewide Terrorism and Intelligence Fusion Center," April 21, 2009 (news release), https://www.asisonline

.org/News/Press-Room/Press-Releases/2009/Pages/FirstPrivateSectorFunded-Position.aspx. Lipowicz, "Boeing to Staff FBI Fusion Center"; "Novel Fusion Center to Boost Anti-Fraud Efforts in California," *Fraud Focus*, Summer 2008, 1. Available at http://www.insurancefraud.org/downloads/FF-Summer2008.pdf

182. Joseph Straw, "Smashing Intelligence Stovepipes," *Security Management*, http://www.securitymanagement.com/article/smashing-intelligence-stovepipes (accessed May 22, 2014).

183. Michaels, "All the President's Spies," 914–916.

184. EPIC v. NSA, 798 F. Supp. 2d 26 (D.D.C. July 8, 2011).

185. Eric Limer, "How Google Gives Your Information to the NSA," Gizmodo, June 12, 2013, at http://gizmodo.com/how-google-gives-your-information-to-the-nsa-512840958.

186. James Glanz and Andrew Lehren, "N.S.A. Spied on Allies, Aid Groups and Businesses," *New York Times*, December 20, 2013, A1.

187. Gillian E. Metzger, "Privatization as Delegation," *Columbia Law Review* 103 (2003): 1378.

188. "An impressive number of top-ranking DHS officials have already [as of 2006] abandoned public service to serve the public by working and lobbying for . . . entrepreneurial firms, moves that often are associated with a considerable increase in salary—from $155,000 per year to $934,000 in one case." John Mueller, *Overblown* (New York: Free Press, 2009), 43, citing Eric Lipton, "Former Antiterror Officials Find That Industry Pays Better," *New York Times*, June 18, 2006, A1; Eric Lipton, "Company Ties Not Always Noted in Push to Tighten U.S. Security," *New York Times*, June 19, 2006, A1. See also Paul R. Verkuil, *Outsourcing Sovereignty: Why Privatization of Government Functions Threatens Democracy and What We Can Do about It* (New York: Cambridge University Press, 2007).

189. Consider Science Applications International Corporation (SAIC). Donald L. Bartlett and James B. Steele said in their reporting on SAIC, "No Washington contractor pursues government money with more ingenuity and perseverance than SAIC . . . [and] no contractor cloaks its operations in greater secrecy." Donald L. Barlett and James B. Steele, "Washington's $8 Billion Shadow," *Vanity Fair*, March 2007 http://www.vanityfair.com/politics/features/2007/03/spyagency200703. Tim Shorrock, *Spies for Hire: The Secret World of Intelligence Outsourcing* (New York: Simon & Schuster, 2008).

190. Luke Harding, *The Snowden Files: The Inside Story of the World's Most Wanted Man* (London: Vintage, 2014).

191. Government entities mine data from social media sites for the purpose of trying to identify potential school shooters and terrorists. This type of practice, of course, comes with a high risk of false positives. Gabe Rottman, "Open Source Intelligence and Crime Prevention," *ACLU: Free Future* (blog), December 21, 2012, https://www.aclu.org/blog/technology-and-liberty-national-security-free-speech/open-source-intelligence-and-crime.

192. Hoofnagle, "Big Brother's Little Helpers."

193. Even its institutions of oversight are secretive, leaving journalists to rely on spectacular leaks like that of Edward Snowden (or well-cultivated sources, like James Bamford's at the NSA).

194. Stephen Benavides, "Outsourced Intelligence: How the FBI and CIA Use Private Contractors to Monitor Social Media," *Truthout*, June 13, 2013, http://truth-out.org/news/item/16943-outsourced-intelligence-how-the-fbi-and-cia-use-private-contractors-to-monitor-social-media.

195. Though perhaps not greater than the sum of terror threats—a question presently explored via cost-benefit analysis, but probably better addressed in scenario planning.

196. Foucault charted the classic contrast between spectacular exercises of power, and insidious biopower. Michel Foucault, *Discipline and Punish: The Birth of the Prison* (Trans. Alan Sheridan) (New York: Vintage Books, 1979). For more on the relative importance of fast and slow violence, see Rob Nixon, *Slow Violence and the Environmentalism of the Poor* (Cambridge: Harvard University Press, 2011).

197. Jathan Sadowski, "Why We Should Wash Our Hands of 'Cyber-Hygiene,'" *Slate* (blog), June 13, 2013, http://www.slate.com/blogs/future_tense/2013/06/19/cyber_hygiene_vint_cerf_s_concept_of_personal_cybersecurity_is_problematic.html.

198. Finn Brunton and Helen Nissenbaum, "Political and Ethical Perspectives on Data Obfuscation," in *Privacy, Due Process and the Computational Turn*, ed. Mireille Hildebrandt and Katja de Vries (New York: Routledge, 2013), 171; Finn Brunton and Helen Nissenbaum, "Vernacular Resistance to Data Collection and Analysis: A Political Theory of Obfuscation," *First Monday* 16, no. 5 (May 2011), http://firstmonday.org/article/view/3493/2955.

199. Adam Ostrow, "Track Who's Tracking You with Mozilla Collusion," *Mashable*, February 28, 2012, http://mashable.com/2012/02/28/mozilla-collusion/.

200. Jerry Kang, Katie Shilton, Deborah Estrin and Jeff Burke, "Self-Surveillance Privacy," *Iowa Law Review* 97 (2010): 809–848; Jonathan Zittrain, "What the Publisher Can Teach the Patient: Intellectual Property and Privacy in an Era of Trusted Privication," *Stanford Law Review* 52 (2000): 1201–1250; Latanya Sweeney, *The Data Map* (2012), http://thedatamap.org/maps.html.

201. Though some regulators are setting security standards, the leading policy response is simply to notify people that the breach occurred. Gina Stevens, *Federal Information Security and Data Breach Notification Laws*, CRS Report for Congress, RL34120 (2010).

202. Kim Zetter, "Use These Secret NSA Google Search Tips to Become Your Own Spy Agency," *Wired*, May 8, 2013, http://www.wired.com/threatlevel/2013/05/nsa-manual-on-hacking-internet/.

203. Lucas Mearian, "'Wall of Shame' Exposes 21M Medical Record Breaches," *Computerworld*, August 7, 2012, http://www.computerworld.com/s/article/9230028. Office of Civil Rights, Department of Health and Human Services, "Breaches Affecting 500 or More Individuals," http://www.hhs.gov/ocr/privacy/hipaa/administrative/breachnotificationrule/breachtool.html (accessed May 21, 2014).

204. Jonathan Dame, "Will Employers Still Ask for Facebook Passwords in 2014?," *USA Today College*, January 10, 2014, http://www.usatoday.com/story/money/business/2014/01/05/facebook-passwords-employers/4327739/.

205. In Europe, there is a "right to be forgotten" that obliges data control-lers like Google to respond if a data subject, "in the light of his fundamental rights under Articles 7 and 8 of the Charter, request[s] that the information in question no longer be made available to the general public on account of its inclusion in such a list of results," and his "rights override, as a rule, not only the economic interest of the operator of the search engine but also the interest of the general public in having access to that information upon a search relat-ing to the data subject's name," unless "the interference with his fundamental rights is justified by the preponderant interest of the general public in having, on account of its inclusion in the list of results, access to the information in question." Google Inc. v. Agencia Española de Protección de Datos (AEPD), Case C-131/12, May 13, 2014.

206. Timothy Lee, "Five Ways to Stop the NSA from Spying on You," *Washington Post Wonkblog*, June 10, 2013, http://www.washingtonpost.com/blogs /wonkblog/wp/2013/06/10/five-ways-to-stop-the-nsa-from-spying-on-you/ (recommending Tor). Bruce Schneier, "Has Tor Been Compromised?," *Schneier on Security* (blog), August 6, 2013, https://www.schneier.com/blog/archives/2013 /08/has_tor_been_co.html.

207. Julia Angwin, *Dragnet Nation* (New York: Times Books, 2014).

208. Sarah N. O'Donohue, "'Like' it or Not, Password Protection Laws Could Protect Much More than Passwords," *Journal of Law, Business, and Ethics* 20 (2014): 77, 80.

209. Peppet, "Unraveling Privacy."

210. Scott Peppet's article "Unraveling Privacy"[0] has described how in-dividual behavior can render past models of privacy protection obsolete. Scott R. Peppet, "Unraveling Privacy: The Personal Prospectus and the Threat of a Full-Disclosure Future," *Northwestern Law Review* 105 (2011): 1153–1204.

211. Nicholas Shaxson, *Treasure Islands: Tax Havens and the Men Who Stole the World* (New York, NY: Vintage Books, 2012); Hedda Leikvang, "Piercing the Veil of Secrecy: Securing Effective Exchange of Information to Remedy the Harmful Effects of Tax Havens," *Vanderbilt Journal of Transnational Law* 45 (2012): 330; David Leigh, Harold Frayman, and James Ball, "Front Men Disguise the Offshore Game's Real Players" (Nov. 2012). *International Consor-tium of Investigative Journalists.* Available at http://www.icij.org/front-men -disguise-offshore-players.

212. James S. Henry, *The Price of Offshore Revisited* (Chesham, Bucking-hamshire, UK: Tax Justice Network, 2012). Available at http://www.taxjustice .net/cms/upload/pdf/Price_of_Offshore_Revisited_120722.pdf.

213. International Consortium of Investigative Journalists and Center for Public Integrity, *Secrecy for Sale: Inside the Offshore Money Maze* (Washington, DC: Center for Public Integrity, 2013). Available at http://cloudfront-files-1 .publicintegrity.org/documents/pdfs/ICIJ%20Secrecy%20for%20Sale.pdf. The report was only possible because of a "Wikileaks"-style breach exposing the contours of labyrinthine corporate structures designed to hide income sources. We can be sure the "wealth defense industry" is redoubling its invest-ments in avoiding future leaks. Dan Froomkin, "'Wealth Defense Industry'

Protects 1% from the Rabble and Its Taxes," *Huffington Post* (blog), December 13, 2011, http://www.huffingtonpost.com/dan-froomkin/wealth-defense -industry-p_b_1145825.html.

214. Omri Marian, "Are Cryptocurrencies Super Tax Havens?," *Michigan Law Review First Impressions* 112 (2013): 38–48. Available at http://www.michigan lawreview.org/articles/are-cryptocurrencies-em-super-em-tax-havens.

215. Frank Pasquale, "Grand Bargains for Big Data: The Emerging Law of Health Information," *Maryland Law Review* 72 (2013): 682–772.

216. On the new economy as a system of social control and modulation, see Julie Cohen, *Configuring the Networked Self* (New Haven, CT: Yale University Press, 2012).

217. Letter of Thomas Jefferson to Isaac McPherson, August 13, 1813. Available at http://press-pubs.uchicago.edu/founders/documents/a1_8_8s12 .html.

# 3
## *The Hidden Logics of Search*

1. David Stark, *The Sense of Dissonance: Accounts of Worth in Economic Life* (Princeton, NJ: Princeton University Press, 2009), 1.

2. On the use and abuse of the distinction between "IRL" (in real life) and virtual spaces, see Nicholas Carr, "Digital Dualism Denialism," *Rough Type* (blog), February 20, 2013, http://www.roughtype.com/?p=2090.

3. Rotten Tomatoes, http://www.rottentomatoes.com/; "Customer Reviews," *Amazon Help.* Available at http://www.amazon.com/gp/help/customer /display.html/?nodeId=12177361. Sam Costello, "Buying Music from the iTunes Store," *About.com.* Available at http://ipod.about.com/od/buyingfromi-tunesstore/ss/buying_itunes_3.htm.

4. Philip Evans and Thomas S. Wurster, *Blown to Bits: How the New Economics of Information Transforms Strategy* (Cambridge, MA: Harvard Business Review Press, 1999); Don Tapscott, *The Digital Economy: Promise and Peril in the Age of Networked Intelligence* (New York: McGraw-Hill, 1996).

5. Economist Richard Caves once observed that "buffs, buzz, and educated tastes" tended to serve as guides to culture. Richard Caves, *Creative Industries: Contracts between Art and Commerce* (Cambridge, MA: Harvard University Press, 2000), 175. Firms like Amazon, Apple, Google, and Facebook now serve as curators of the curators, making some "buzz" of some "buffs" prominent, and hiding others.

6. Phil Simon, *The Age of the Platform: How Amazon, Apple, Facebook, and Google Have Redefined Business* (Henderson, NV: Motion Publishing, 2011). Though we commonly only refer to Google as a "search engine," it's important to note that search functionality drives our experience of all these other Internet behemoths. Whereas *reputation* is the way the world "knows" us, our *searches* are increasingly the way we "know" the world. The scare quotes connote the slippages, obfuscations, and biases that modern finance imposes on these epistemic systems.

7. On the economic impact of news aggregation, see Raquel Xalabarder, "Google News and Copyright," in *Google and the Law*, ed. Aurelio Lopez-Tarruella (The Hague, The Netherlands: Springer, 2012), 113. Some persons in the news have demanded a "right to reply" to groups of stories, which Google experimented with recognizing. Brad Stone, "Names in the News Get a Way to Respond," *New York Times*, August 8, 2007, http://www.nytimes.com/2007/08/13/technology/13google.html?_r=0.7.

8. Aaron Wall, "Google Paid Inclusion Programs: Buy a Top Ranking Today," *SEOBook* (blog), June 22, 2012, http://www.seobook.com/paid-inclusion (explaining Google's paid inclusion program, giving an example using a search for hotels, and showing how the paid results compare with the "organic" results). Pamela Parker, "Google Experimenting with 'Promoted Hotels' Ads on Hotel Finder" (June 2012). *Search Engine Land*. Available at http://searchengineland.com/google-experimenting-with-promoted-hotels-ads-on-hotel-finder-123475 (reporting on the Google Hotel Finder bidding process for advertisers who want to be "at the top of the search results"). Danny Sullivan, "Once Deemed Evil, Google Now Embraces 'Paid Inclusion'" (May 2012). *Marketing Land*. Available at http://marketingland.com/once-deemed-evil-google-now-embraces-paid-inclusion-13138 (describing the history of paid inclusion and the scope, including Google Hotel Finder, and reporting that Google does not consider its process "paid inclusion" because compensated results are marked). Danny Sullivan, "Google Blurs the Line between Paid and Unpaid Results Again" (Feb. 2010). *Search Engine Land*. Available at http://searchengineland.com/google-blurs-the-line-between-paid-unpaid-results-again-36268. ("Google has a new program that allows local businesses to get paid listings that appear within what's known as the 7-pack of local listings.")

9. Alexander Halavais, *Search Engine Society* (Cambridge, UK: Polity, 2008), 85. See also Adam Raff, "Search, but You May Not Find," *New York Times*, December 27, 2009, A27.

10. Jamie Court and John Simpson, Letter to Google, October 13, 2008. *Consumer Watchdog*. Available at http://www.consumerwatchdog.org/resources/CWLetterToGoogle10-13-08.pdf.

11. Andrew Leonard, "How Google Lost Its Cool," *Salon*, March 29, 2013, http://www.salon.com/2013/03/29/when_google_lost_its_cool/.

12. For an example of a dispute over bias, see the summary and explanation of the dispute between Google and SearchKing, in Niva Elkin-Koren and Eli M. Salzberger, *Law, Economics, and Cyberspace* (Northampton, MA: Edward Elgar Publishing, 2004), 74–75. See also Jennifer Chandler, "A Right to Reach an Audience," *Hofstra Law Review* 35 (2007): 1106–1115.

13. For a snapshot of the "bad old days," see Matthew Fagin, Frank Pasquale, and Kimberlee Weatherall, "Beyond Napster: Using Antitrust Law to Advance and Enhance Online Music Distribution," *Boston University Journal of Science and Technology Law* 8 (2002): 451–573.

14. For more on Apple's "empire," and secrecy, see Adam Lashinsky, *Inside Apple: How America's Most Admired—and Most Secretive—Company Really Works* (New York: Business Plus, 2012).

15. Albert-László Barabási, *Linked: The New Science of Networks* (Cambridge, MA: Perseus Publishing, 2002), 19 (describing increasing value of nodes in a network as it encompasses more participants).

16. Amar Bhidé, *The Venturesome Economy* (Princeton, NJ: Princeton University Press, 2008).

17. Jonathan Zittrain, *The Future of the Internet—And How to Stop It* (New Haven, CT: Yale University Press, 2009); Tim Wu, *The Master Switch* (New York: Random House, 2010).

18. Cody Lee, "Former Apple Employees Shed Light on App Review Process," *iDownload Blog*, July 4, 2012, http://www.idownloadblog.com/2012/07/04/shedding-light-on-app-review/.

19. Chris Foresman, "iPhone App Rejection Madness Still Hasn't Stopped," *Ars Technica* (blog), May 22, 2009, http://arstechnica.com/apple/2009/05/iphone-app-rejection-madness-still-hasnt-stopped/. James Montgomerie, "Whither Eucalyptus?," *James Montgomerie's World Wide Web Log*, May 21, 2009, http://www.blog.montgomerie.net/whither-eucalyptus. See also David Chartier, "iPhone App Tweetie Rejected for User Generated Content," *Ars Technica* (blog), March 10, 2009, http://arstechnica.com/apple/2009/03/iphone-app-tweetie-rejected-for-user-generated-content/. Jacqui Cheng, "NIN's iPhone App Update Finally Gets Apple's Seal of Approval," *Ars Technica* (blog), May 7, 2009, http://arstechnica.com/apple/2009/05/nins-iphone-app-update-finally-gets-apples-seal-of-approval/.

20. James Montgomerie, "Hither Eucalyptus!," *James Montgomerie's World Wide Web Log*, May 24, 2009, http://www.blog.montgomerie.net/hither-eucalyptus.

21. For a collection of ways to access public domain texts on the Internet, see Sean P. Aune, "20+ Places for Public Domain E-Books," *Mashable*, November 12, 2007, http://mashable.com/2007/11/12/public-domain-ebook-sources/.

22. Christina Bonnington and Spencer Ackerman, "Apple Rejects App That Tracks U.S. Drone Strikes," *Wired*, August 30, 2012, http://www.wired.com/dangerroom/2012/08/drone-app/.

23. Ibid.

24. Nick Wingfield, "Apple Rejects App Tracking Drone Strikes," *New York Times Bits Blog*, August 30, 2012, http://bits.blogs.nytimes.com/2012/08/30/apple-rejects-app-tracking-drone-strikes/.

25. When he finally began listing out every drone strike via Twitter, his tweets sparked sobering conversations about U.S. actions; clearly, there is an appreciative and constructive audience out there for Begley's work. Michael Kelly, "The NYU Student Tweeting Every Reported U.S. Drone Strike Has Revealed a Disturbing Trend," *Business Insider*, December 12, 2012, http://www.businessinsider.com/us-drone-tweets-reveal-double-tap-plan-2012-12.

26. Bonnington and Ackerman, "Apple Rejects App That Tracks U.S. Drone Strikes."

27. Lorenzo Franceschi-Bicchierai, "After 5 Rejections, Apple Accepts App That Tracks U.S. Drone Strikes," *Mashable*, February 7, 2014, http://mashable.com/2014/02/07/apple-app-tracks-drone-strikes/.

28. Benjamin Poynter, in an interview with *GameScenes* (transcript posted Oct. 2012). Available at http://www.gamescenes.org/2012/10/interview.html. On persuasive gaming generally, see Ian Bogost, *Persuasive Games* (Cambridge, MA: MIT Press, 2007).

29. Yves Smith, "Wired's Embarrassing Whitewash of Foxconn," *Naked Capitalism* (blog), February 8, 2012, http://www.nakedcapitalism.com/2012/02 /wireds-embarrassing-whitewash-of-foxconn.html.

30. There is a pattern here; "Sweatshop HD was removed from Apple's store because it was uncomfortable with the re-creation of a sweatshop." Tracey Lien, "The Apple Obstacle for Serious Games," *Polygon*, June 21, 2013, http://www.polygon.com/2013/6/21/4449770/the-apple-obstacle-for-serious -games.

31. To view Apple's app development guidelines, see "App Review Guidelines," *Apple Developer*. Available at https://developer.apple.com/appstore/guide lines.html. Though only registered developers can view the guidelines, the text has been posted by Leander Kahney. Leander Kahney, "Here's the Full Text of Apple's New App Store Guidelines," *Cult of Mac*, September 9, 2010, http://www.cultofmac.com/58590/heres-the-full-text-of-apples-new-app -store-guidelines/.

32. On "phoning home," see Randal C. Picker, "Rewinding Sony: The Evolving Product, Phoning Home and the Duty of Ongoing Design" (Mar. 2005). John M. Olin Law and Economics Working Paper No. 241. Available at http://www.law.uchicago.edu/files/files/241-rcp-sony.pdf.

33. Zittrain, *The Future of the Internet—And How to Stop It*, 67 (describing layers); Rob Frieden, "Apple iPhone Apps Store—Refreshing Openness or Walled Garden?," *TeleFrieden* (blog), December 18, 2008, http://telefrieden .blogspot.com/2008/12/apple-iphone-apps-storerefreshing.html.

34. For more on Apple's app ranking system, and its efforts to prevent manipulation of the rankings, see Dean Takahashi, "Apple's Crackdown on App-Ranking Manipulation: Confused Developers Caught in the Dragnet," *Venture Beat*, July 3, 2012, http://venturebeat.com/2012/07/03/apples-crackdown -on-app-ranking-manipulation/.

35. Some companies have complained that Google's malware warning system has deterred users from visiting their sites due to no fault of their own. Josh Peterson, "Websites Say Google Malware Warnings Hurting Business," *The Daily Caller*, February 18, 2013, http://dailycaller.com/2013/02/18/websites -say-google-malware-warnings-hurting-business/.

36. Yochai Benkler, *The Wealth of Networks: How Social Production Transforms Markets and Freedom* (New Haven, CT: Yale University Press, 2007). Clay Shirky, "A Speculative Post on the Idea of Algorithmic Authority" *Shirky*, November 15, 2009, http://www.shirky.com/weblog/2009/11/a-spec ulative-post-on-the-idea-of-algorithmic-authority/. For a critical view, see Oren Bracha and Frank Pasquale, "Federal Search Commission? Access, Fairness, and Accountability in the Law of Search," *Cornell Law Review* 93 (2008): 1149–1209 (critiquing Benkler). Frank Pasquale, "Assessing Algorithmic Authority," *Balkinization* (blog), November 18, 2009, http://balkin .blogspot.com/2009/11/assessing-algorithmic-authority.html (critiquing

Shirky). Amy N. Langville and Carl D. Meyer, *Google's PageRank and Beyond: The Science of Search Engine Rankings* (Princeton, NJ: Princeton University Press, 2012).

37. Tarleton Gillespie, "The Relevance of Algorithms," in *Media Technologies: Essays on Communication, Materiality, and Society*, ed. Tarleton Gillespie, Pablo J. Boczkowski, and Kirsten A. Foot (Cambridge, MA: MIT Press, 2014), 178.

38. The same spammers couldn't simply be blocked, as an ISP might do; Google merely visited sites, and could not control access to them. The spammers could also hide behind different IP addresses or otherwise conceal their identity.

39. Elizabeth Van Couvering, "Is Relevance Relevant? Market, Science, and War: Discourses of Search Engine Quality," *Journal of Computer-Mediated Communication* 12 (2007): 876.

40. Mark Walters, "How Does Google Rank Websites?" *SEOmark*. Available at http://www.seomark.co.uk/how-does-google-rank-websites/. Amy N. Langville and Carl D. Meyer, "Deeper inside PageRank," *Internet Mathematics*, 1 (2004): 335–380. Langville and Meyer, *Google's PageRank and Beyond*.

41. Siva Vaidhyanathan, *The Googlization of Everything (And Why We Should Worry)* (Berkeley: University of California Press, 2010).

42. Ibid.

43. "Trust Us—We're Geniuses and You're Not—The Arrival of Google," *Searchless in Paradise* (blog), February 19, 2013, http://feyla39.wordpress.com /page/2/. Google's current mission statement is "to organize the world's information and make it universally accessible and useful." "Company Overview," *Google*. Available at http://www.google.com/about/company/. For Google's recent dominance, see Matt McGee, "Google Now #1 Search Engine In Czech Republic; 5 Countries to Go for Global Domination" (Jan. 2011). *Search Engine Land*. Available at http://searchengineland.com/google-nunber-one-czech -republic-5-countries-left-61174. For Google's expansion into books, see Mary Sue Coleman, "Google, the Khmer Rouge, and the Public Good," Speech before the Association of American Publishers, February 6, 2006. Available at http://president.umich.edu/speech/archive/MSC_AAP_Google _address.pdf. On Google acquiring Zagat, see "Google Just Got ZAGAT Rated!" *Google Official Blog*, September 8, 2011, http://googleblog.blogspot. com/2011/09/google-just-got-zagat-rated.html.

44. "List of Mergers and Acquisitions by Google." *Wikipedia*. Available at http://en.wikipedia.org/wiki/Google_acquisitions.

45. Caitlin McGarry, "The Disappearing Web: How We're Losing the Battle to Preserve the Internet," *Tech Hive*, October 9, 2012, http://www.techhive .com/article/2011401/the-disappearing-web-how-were-losing-the-battle-to -preserve-the-Internet.html. Tom Chatfield, "The Decaying Web and Our Disappearing History," *BBC*, September 28, 2012 http://www.bbc.com/future /story/20120927-the-decaying-web.

46. Vaidhyanathan, *The Googlization of Everything*, 26. For Al Franken's criticisms of Google and other Internet companies, see Senator Al Franken, "Remarks to the American Bar Association (Antitrust Section)," March 29, 2012.

Available at http://assets.sbnation.com/assets/1033745/franken_aba_antitrust
_speech.pdf.

47. Google Reader's demise was far from a one-off—over 30 Google services have been terminated since 2008, wasting the time of users who'd invested effort in the platforms. Chris Kirk and Heather Bracy, "The Google
Graveyard," *Slate*, March 25, 2013, at http://www.slate.com/articles/technology
/map_of_the_week/2013/03/google_reader_joins_graveyard_of_dead_google
_products.html.

48. I resist simply terming it an "online world" because that is too dual-
istic. See Nathan Jurgenson, "Digital Dualism and the Fallacy of Web Objectivity," *Cyborgology* (blog), September 13, 2011, http://thesocietypages
.org/cyborgology/2011/09/13/digital-dualism-and-the-fallacy-of-web-ob
jectivity/. William Gibson, "Google's Earth," *New York Times*, September 1,
2010, A23.

49. Foundem's owners told me they were blocked, but I believe this qualified language is more appropriate, because one can only see what results
Google is sending the computer you monitor, not the entire web. When I had
a meeting at Google to discuss this issue with them, they gave some responses
that may or may not be responsive to the Raffs' concerns. I believe I am restricted from speaking about them by the terms of the nondisclosure agreement I had to sign in order to enter the building. For press coverage, see, for
example, John Lettice, "When Algorithms Attack, Does Google Hear You
Scream?" *The Register*, November 19, 2009, http://www.theregister.co.uk/2009
/11/19/google_hand_of_god/.

50. To see how Google analyzes websites for quality assurance, see "More
Guidance on Building High Quality Sites," *Google Webmaster Central Blogspot*,
May 6, 2011, http://googlewebmastercentral.blogspot.com/2011/05/more-guid
ance-on-building-high-quality.html.

51. Google Annual Form 10-K Report for 2009 (filed with United States
Securities and Exchange Commission on February 12, 2010). Available at http://
google.client.shareholder.com/secfiling.cfm?filingid=1193125-10-30774.

52. The same dynamic may be happening in dominant social networks as
well. For example, one young developer wrote a heartfelt "Letter to Mark Zuckerberg," complaining that he felt trapped by a meeting with the site's acquisition
team: he could either sell his app to the company, or risk being cut off from
customers after Facebook developed its own version. Pay-for-prominence arrangements are also worrisome because of the overbearing power of the dominant platform. Adrianne Jeffries, "Developer Has No Regrets after Angry Letter to Zuckerberg Goes Viral," *The Verge*, August 3, 2012, http://www.theverge
.com/2012/8/3/3216313/dalton-caldwell-facebook-developer-letter-mark-zuck
erberg-app-net.

53. A Google presence has become essential to many start-ups. Greg Lastowka, "Google's Law," *Brooklyn Law Review* 73 (2008): 1328. ("Fortunes are
won and lost based on Google's results pages.") Stephen Spencer, "SEO Report Card: The Google Death Sentence" (Apr. 2007). *PracticalECommerce*.
Available at http://www.practicalecommerce.com/articles/453-SEO-Report
-Card-The-Google-Death-Sentence.

54. "Foundem's Google Story" (Aug. 2009). *Search Neutrality.* Available at http://www.searchneutrality.org/eu-launches-formal-investigation/foundem-google-story.

55. "Google Faces EU Antitrust Investigation," *The New Statesman*, February 24, 2010, http://www.newstatesman.com/technology/2010/02/google-search-european. ("Google has denied the claims, arguing that Foundem struggled in its search rankings because of a lack of original content.") Charles Arthur, "Foundem Accuses Google of Using Its Power to Favour Own Links," *The Guardian*, November 30, 2010, http://www.theguardian.com/technology/2010/nov/30/google-foundem-ec-competition-rules. ("Google says it 'de-indexed' the company because much of its content—about 87%—was copied from other sites. . . .") "Defendant Google's Reply Memorandum," KinderStart v. Google, No. C-06-2057 (N.D. Cal. 2006), 17.

56. See Danny Sullivan, "Google Launches 'Universal Search' & Blended Results" (May 2007). *Search Engine Land.* Available at http://searchengineland.com/google-20-google-universal-search-11232. For more on how Google has entered the vertical search market and integrates its vertical search services into "universal search," see Damian Ryan and Calvin Jones, *Understanding Digital Marketing* (London: Kogan Page, 2012), 90.

57. Alex Goldman and PJ Vogt, "How Google is Killing the Best Site on the Internet," *On the Media*, June 2, 2014, at http://www.onthemedia.org/story/27-how-google-killing-best-site-internet/.

58. Oren Bracha, "Standing Copyright Law on Its Head? The Googlization of Everything and the Many Faces of Property," *Texas Law Review* 85 (2007): 1799–1870; Field v. Google, 412 F. Supp. 2d 1106 (D. Nev. 2006).

59. Greg Sterling, "Vertical vs. Horizontal Search Engines," *Search Engine Journal*, January 17, 2007, http://www.searchenginejournal.com/vertical-vs-horizontal-search-engines/4274/.

60. Donald MacKenzie, *An Engine, Not a Camera: How Financial Models Shape Markets* (Cambridge, MA: MIT Press, 2008).

61. Vaidhyanathan, *The Googlization of Everything*, 58–64.

62. "Commitments in Case COMP/C-3/39.740— Foundem and Others" (Apr. 2013), 5–7. Available at http://ec.europa.eu/competition/antitrust/cases/dec_docs/39740/39740_8608_5.pdf (response to European Commission preliminary assessment of antitrust case). For some caution about this type of remedy, see David A. Hyman and David J. Franklyn, "Search Neutrality and Search Bias: An Empirical Perspective on the Impact of Architecture and Labeling" (Sept. 2013). Illinois Program in Law, Behavior and Social Science Paper No. LE13-24; Univ. of San Francisco Law Research Paper No. 2013-15. Available at http://papers.ssrn.com/sol3/papers.cfm?abstract_id=2260942. Mark Patterson, "Search Engine Objectivity," *Concurring Opinions* (blog), November 23, 2013, http://www.concurringopinions.com/archives/2013/11/search-engine-objectivity.html.

63. Federal Trade Commission, "Google Agrees to Change Its Business Practices to Resolve FTC Competition Concerns in the Markets for Devices Like Smart Phones, Games and Tablets, and in Online Search," January 3, 2013 (news release), http://ftc.gov/opa/2013/01/google.shtm.

64. According to the Google website, their "advertising programs, which range from simple text ads to rich media ads, help businesses find customers, and help publishers make money off of their content. We also provide cloud computing tools for businesses that save money and help organizations be more productive." "Our Products and Services," *Google*. Available at http://www.google.com/about/company/products/.

65. Ellen P. Goodman, "Stealth Marketing and Editorial Integrity," *Texas Law Review* 85 (2006): 83–89; Federal Trade Commission Staff, *Dot Com Disclosures: Information about Online Advertising* (Washington, DC: Federal Trade Commission, 2000). Available at http://www.ftc.gov/os/2000/05/0005dotcom staffreport.pdf. With regard to hyperlinks that "lead to disclosures," the link should be "obvious," appropriately labeled, and well-situated. Ibid., 1–2.

66. Laurianne McLaughlin, "The Straight Story on Search Engines," *ComputerWorld*, June 25, 2002, http://www.computerworld.com.au/article /27204/straight_story_search_engines/. ("Despite our misgivings, the situation is not completely hopeless. There's always Google. Not only does Google deliver exceptionally relevant matches, but it's also the best of the bunch at identifying ads.")

67. Steven Levy, *In the Plex: How Google Thinks, Works, and Shapes Our Lives* (New York: Simon & Schuster, 2010); John Battelle, *The Search: How Google and Its Rivals Rewrote the Rules of Business and Transformed Our Culture* (New York: Portfolio, 2005); Randall Stross, *Planet Google* (New York: Free Press, 2008).

68. Levy, *In the Plex: How Google Thinks, Works, and Shapes Our Lives.*

69. John Koetsier, "Search Expert Danny Sullivan Asks FTC to Review Google's New Paid Ad Policies," *Venture Beat*, June 10, 2012, http://venturebeat .com/2012/06/10/ftc-review-google-paid-inclusion-policies/.

70. Andrew Sinclair, "Regulation of Paid Search Listings," *Boston University Journal of Science and Technology Law* 10 (2004): 146–170; Acting Associate Director, FTC, Heather Hippsley, Letter to Search Engine Companies about Paid Placement Search Engines, June 27, 2002. *Keytlaw*. Available at http://www.keytlaw.com/FTC/Rules/seplacementltr.htm.

71. The Chinese search engine Baidu has aggressively demanded "pay for play." Chi-Chu Tschang, "The Squeeze at China's Baidu," *Bloomberg Businessweek*, December 30, 2008, http://www.businessweek.com/stories/2008-12-30/the -squeeze-at-chinas-baidu.

72. Danny Sullivan, "Once Deemed Evil, Google Now Embraces 'Paid Inclusion'" (May 2012). *Marketing Land*. Available at marketingland.com/once -deemed-evil-google-now-embraces-paid-inclusion-13138.

73. Danny Sullivan, "Google's Broken Promises and Who's Running the Search Engine?" (Nov. 2013). *Marketing Land*. Available at http://marketingland .com/google-broken-promises-65121.

74. Matthew Ingram, "Giants behaving badly: Google, Facebook and Amazon show us the downside of monopolies and black-box algorithms," *GigaOm*, at http://gigaom.com/2014/05/23/giants-behaving-badly-google -facebook-and-amazon-show-us-the-downside-of-monopolies-and-black-box -algorithms/ (May 23, 2014); Derek Muller, "The Problem with Facebook," YouTube video, 7:00, posted by "2veritasium," January 14, 2014, https://www

.youtube.com/watch?v=l9ZqXlHl65g (arguing that "creators want to reach fans but their posts are being throttled to force them to pay to be seen").

75. For more on EdgeRank, see Chris Treadaway and Mari Smith, *Facebook Marketing: An Hour a Day* (Indianapolis: Sybex/Wiley, 2012), 43–44, 233–234.

76. Josh Constine, "Facebook Now Lets U.S. Users Pay $7 to Promote Posts to the News Feeds of More Friends," *TechCrunch*, October 3, 2010, http://techcrunch.com/2012/10/03/us-promoted-posts/. Casey Johnston, "Is Facebook 'Broken on Purpose' to Sell Promoted Posts?" *Ars Technica* (blog), November 4, 2012, http://arstechnica.com/business/2012/11/is-facebook-broken -on-purpose-to-sell-promoted-posts/.

77. On "murketing," see Rob Walker, *Buying In: What We Buy and Who We Are* (New York: Random House, 2009).

78. Sergey Brin and Lawrence Page, "The Anatomy of a Large-Scale Hy-pertextual Web Search Engine," in Seventh International World-Wide Web Conference, April 14–18, 1998, Brisbane, Australia, Appendix A. Available at http://ilpubs.stanford.edu:8090/361/.

79. Goodman, "Stealth Marketing and Editorial Integrity."

80. Ibid.

81. Konrad Lischka, "Blaming the Algorithm: Defamation Case High-lights Google's Double Standard," *Spiegel*, September 10, 2012. ("A Google spokesperson," in defending the decision not to intervene with search results, said the offensive results "are the algorithmic result of several objective fac-tors, including the popularity of search terms.") David Auerbach, "Filling the Void," *Slate*, November 19, 2013, http://www.slate.com/articles/technology /bitwise/2013/11/google_autocomplete_the_results_aren_t_always_what_you _think_they_are.html.

82. For an overview of the Wulff case, see Stefan Niggemeier, "Autocom-pleting Bettina Wulff: Can a Google Function Be Libelous?" *Spiegel*, Septem-ber 20, 2012, http://www.spiegel.de/international/zeitgeist/google-auto complete-former-german-first-lady-defamation-case-a-856820.html. See also "Google Refuses Order to Take Down Defamatory Auto Complete Search Results," *Japan Real Estate Commentary* (blog), October 22, 2012, http://japan realestatecommentary.blogspot.com/2012/10/google-refuses-court-orders-to -take.html. Note that in each case, Google, like the rating agencies discussed earlier, blamed *public interpretation of the result* rather than taking responsibility for it.

83. "Autocomplete," *Google*. Available at https://support.google.com/web search/answer/106230. (It also specifies that Autocomplete cannot be turned off.)

84. Evgeny Morozov, "Don't Be Evil," *The New Republic*, July 30, 2011, http://www.newrepublic.com/article/books/magazine/91916/google-schmidt -obama-gates-technocrats.

85. Evan McMorris-Santoro, "Search Engine Expert: Rick Santorum's New Crusade against Google Is Total Nonsense" (Sept. 2011). *Talking Points Memo*. Available at http://2012.talkingpointsmemo.com/2011/09/search-en gine-expert-rick-santorums-new-crusade-against-google-is-total-nonsense

.php?ref=fpb. James Grimmelmann, "Don't Censor Search," *Yale Law Journal* 117 (2007) (pocket part 48).

86. A 2005 Google statement on Google bombing explained that "we're also reluctant to alter our results by hand in order to prevent such items from showing up. Pranks like this may be distracting to some, but they don't affect the overall quality of our search service, whose objectivity, as always, remains the core of our mission." Marziah Karch, "Google Bombs Explained." *About. com.* Available at http://google.about.com/od/socialtoolsfromgoogle/a/google bombatcl.htm. Eventually, though, Google did correct the Bush Google bomb. Danny Sullivan, "Google Kills Bush's Miserable Failure Search and Other Google Bombs" (Jan. 2007). *Search Engine Land.* Available at http://searchengineland.com/google-kills-bushs-miserable-failure-search-other -google-bombs-10363.

87. James Grimmelmann, "Some Skepticism about Search Neutrality," in *The Next Digital Decade*, eds. Berin Szoka and Adam Marcus (Washington, DC: TechFreedom, 2011), 435–461 (discussing four types of manual intervention).

88. The site, http://www.jewwatch.com/, is an obvious hate site.

89. David Segal, "A Bully Finds a Pulpit on the Web," *New York Times*, November 26, 2010 (noting how a dubious eyeglass seller rose to the top of many results pages thanks to numerous critical reviews linking to or mentioning it).

90. See "Google Search Ranking of Hate Sites Not Intentional" (Apr. 2004). *Anti-Defamation League.* Available at http://www.adl.org/rumors/google _search_rumors.asp. ("The ranking of Jewwatch and other hate sites is in no way due to a conscious choice by Google, but solely is a result of this automated system of ranking.") "ADL Praises Google for Responding to Concerns about Rankings of Hate Sites" (Apr. 2004). *Anti-Defamation League.* Available at http://archive.adl.org/PresRele/Internet_75/4482_75.htm. ("Google has placed text on its site that gives users a clear explanation of how search results are obtained.")

91. "An Explanation of Our Search Results," *Google.* Available at http://www.google.com/explanation.html. ("If you recently used Google to search for the word 'Jew,' you may have seen results that were very disturbing. We assure you that the views expressed by the sites in your results are not in any way endorsed by Google. We'd like to explain why you're seeing these results when you conduct this search.") But see Eric Goldman, "Demise of Search Engine Utopianism," *Yale Journal of Law and Technology* 8 (2006): 533.

92. Craig Timberg, "Could Google Tilt a Close Election?," *Washington Post*, March 29, 2013, at http://www.washingtonpost.com/opinions/could-google -tilt-a-close-election/2013/03/29/c8d7f4e6-9587-11e2-b6f0-a5150a247b6a _story.html (reporting on the experiments of Robert Epstein).

93. Jonathan Zittrain, "Facebook Could Decide an Election Without Anyone Ever Finding Out," *The New Republic*, June 3, 2014, at http://www.newrepublic.com/article/117878/information-fiduciary-solution-facebook-digital -gerrymandering.

94. Mary Anne Ostrom, "Google CEO Eric Schmidt to Stump for Obama," *San Jose Mercury News*, October 20, 2008 http://www.mercurynews

.com/google/ci_10769458 (noting that Google's CEO openly supported Obama).

95. See Chris Crum, "Is Google Showing Political Bias with Search Results?" (Feb. 2009). *Web Pro News*. Available at http://www.webpronews.com/is -google-showing-political-bias-with-search-results-2009-02.

96. Michelle Malkin, "Google News: Not So Fair and Balanced," *Michelle Malkin*, February 5, 2005, http://michellemalkin.com/2005/02/05/google-news -not-so-fair-and-balanced/.

97. Tom Zeller, Jr., "A New Campaign Tactic: Manipulating Google Data," *New York Times*, October 26, 2006, http://www.nytimes.com/2006/10 /26/us/politics/26googlebomb.html?_r=0. See also Ira S. Nathenson, "Internet Infoglut and Invisible Ink: Spamdexing Search Engines with Meta Tags," *Harvard Journal of Law & Technology* 12 (1998): 43–148.

98. Joshua Rhett Miller, "Unlike Bush's 'Google Bomb,' Google Quickly Defuses Obama's," *Fox News*, January 30, 2009 http://www.foxnews.com/story /0,2933,485632,00.html.

99. Ibid.

100. Frank Pasquale, "Rankings, Reductionism, and Responsibility," *Cleveland State Law Review* 54 (2006): 114–140.

101. Brian McDowell, "Between the Lines of Google Search Algorithm Improvements," *Conductor* (blog), September 6, 2011, http://www.conductor .com/blog/2011/09/between-the-lines-of-googles-search-algorithm-improve ments/.

102. Daniel Crane, "Search Neutrality as an Antitrust Principle," *George Mason Law Review* 19 (2012): 1199–1210.

103. Google once offered a "right of reply" feature on some Google News stories. See Brad Stone, "Names in the News Get a Way to Respond," *New York Times*, August 13, 2007, http://www.nytimes.com/2007/08/13/technology /13google.html?_r=0. One can imagine a more public-spirited company adopting in the US a change that has been forced in Europe: offering some individualized response to those particularly hard hit by search results. The "right to be forgotten," vindicated by a top European court, offers individuals a chance not to have one damaging incident or characterization dominate important reports about them.

104. For more on Twitter as a tool to search for news and updates, see Mark Levene, *An Introduction to Search Engines and Web Navigation*, 2nd ed. (Hoboken, NJ: John Wiley & Sons, 2010), 351.

105. "FAQs about Trends on Twitter," *Twitter Help Center*. Available at https://support.twitter.com/groups/31-twitter-basics/topics/111-features/articles /101125-about-trending-topics (accessed May 23, 2014). "Subscribe" may be too strong a word here; many people "follow" thousands of accounts, but really only consult a small subset of them, via a list. Since many lists are private, only Twitter really know who's being closely watched—though metrics of Retweets and Favorites may help other firms, like Klout, get some handle on a person's true level of salience and influence.

106. Tarleton Gillespie, "Can an Algorithm Be Wrong? Twitter Trends, the Specter of Censorship, and Our Faith in the Algorithms around Us," *Culture*

*Digitally* (blog), October 19, 2011, http://culturedigitally.org/2011/10/can-an
-algorithm-be-wrong/.

107. Gilad Lotan, "Data Reveals That 'Occupying' Twitter Trending Topics Is Harder Than It Looks," *Social Flow* (blog), October 12, 2011, http://
giladlotan.com/?p=7120244374 (discussing the many challenges faced by those
attempting to trend). Gillespie, "Can an Algorithm Be Wrong?"

108. Sean Garrett, Twitter post, October 1, 2011, 6:00 p.m., https://twitter
.com/SG/status/120302135597473794. For more on the controversy between
Twitter and Occupy Wall Street, and information on the Twitter algorithms,
see Laura Sydell, "How Twitter's Trending Algorithm Picks Its Topics," *National Public Radio*, December 7, 2011, http://www.npr.org/2011/12/07/143013503
/how-twitters-trending-algorithm-picks-its-topics.

109. "To Trend or Not Trend . . ." *Twitter Blog*, December 8, 2010, http://
blog.twitter.com/2010/12/to-trend-or-not-to-trend.html. Gillespie, "Can an
Algorithm Be Wrong?"

110. Christina Chaey, "Silenced by Twitter, Thunderclap Returns with a
Bang on Facebook," *Fast Company*, June 20, 2012, http://www.fastcompany.
com/1840874/silenced-twitter-thunderclap-returns-bang-facebook.html.

111. Tarleton Gillespie, "Can an Algorithm Be Wrong?" *Limn* (blog),
http://limn.it/can-an-algorithm-be-wrong/. Accessed May 23, 2014.

112. Ibid.

113. See Robert W. McChesney, *Digital Disconnect: How Capitalism Is Turning the Internet against Democracy* (New York: The New Press, 2013).

114. Its position is particularly interesting, because it had another way of
deflecting liability even if it were held to be a speaker. Had it characterized its
autosuggestions as a mere opinion, it could well have consistently tried to
maintain its position as a First Amendment speaker.

115. For more on regulation of "conduits" under First Amendment law, see
Jim Chen, "Conduit-Based Regulation of Speech," *Duke Law Journal* 54
(2005): 1359–1456.

116. Eugene Volokh and Donald Falk, "First Amendment Protection for
Search Engine Search Results," *Journal of Law, Economics and Policy* 8 (2012):
883–900.

117. Frank Pasquale, "Asterisk Revisited: Debating a Right of Reply on
Search Results," *Journal of Business and Technology Law* 3 (2008): 61.

118. Vaidhyanathan, *The Googlization of Everything*, 183.

119. Danny Sullivan, "Google Now Personalizes Everyone's Search Results" (Dec. 2009). *Search Engine Land*. Available at http://searchengineland.com
/google-now-personalizes-everyones-search-results-31195.

120. We should also entertain reconceptualizing our participation in digital platforms as work, since it is often unavoidable, laborious, and value generating. Kevin Kelly, *What Technology Wants* (New York: Viking, 2010), 331
("each time we click a link we strengthen a node somewhere in the supercom-
puter's mind, thereby programming . . . it"); Trebor Scholz, ed., *Digital Labor:
The Internet as Playground and Factory* (New York: Routledge, 2013); Jaron
Lanier, *Who Owns the Future?* (New York: Simon & Schuster, 2013); Jessica
Weisberg, "Should Facebook Pay Its Users?," *The Nation*, January 14, 2014

(quoting manifesto "WE WANT TO CALL WORK WHAT IS WORK SO THAT EVENTUALLY WE MIGHT REDISCOVER WHAT FRIEND-SHIP IS").

121. Eli Pariser, *The Filter Bubble* (New York: Penguin, 2011).

122. Ibid., 6–7.

123. Fortunately, one has written a work of fiction to suggest what could go wrong. Shumeet Baluja, *The Silicon Jungle: A Novel of Deception, Power, and Internet Intrigue* (Princeton, NJ: Princeton University Press, 2011).

124. Cathy O'Neil, "When Accurate Modeling Is Not Good," *Mathbabe* (blog), December 12, 2012, http://mathbabe.org/2012/12/12/when-accurate-modeling-is-not-good/ (analyzing the work of a casino CEO concerned with predictive analytics).

125. Evgeny Morozov, *The Net Delusion: The Dark Side of Internet Freedom* (New York: PublicAffairs, 2011); Senator Dick Durbin, Letter to Mark Zuckerberg, February 2011. Available at http://www.durbin.senate.gov/public/index .cfm/files/serve?File_id=ec32a7a8-4671-4ab9-b5f4-9c0b9736deae. ("Facebook does not allow democracy and human rights activists in repressive regimes to use Facebook anonymously.")

126. On a cost-per-impression or cost-per-click basis. For a full account of digital advertising, see Joseph Turow, *The Daily You: How the New Advertising Industry Is Defining Your Identity and Your Worth* (New Haven, CT: Yale University Press, 2012).

127. John O'Connor et al., "Electronic Marketing and Marketing Communications," in *Marketing Communication: New Approaches, Technologies, and Styles*, ed. Allan J. Kimmel (New York: Oxford University Press, 2005).

128. For example, see Geoffrey Manne and Joshua Wright, "Google and the Limits of Antitrust: The Case against the Antitrust Case against Google," *Harvard Journal of Law and Public Policy* 34 (2011): 181.

129. For a recent account in this vein, see Deborah Perry Piscione, *Secrets of Silicon Valley* (New York: Palgrave Macmillan, 2013).

130. Doc Searls, *The Intention Economy: When Customers Take Charge* (Boston: Harvard Business Review Press, 2012), 188.

131. For a fuller exposition of the ideas in this and the next paragraph, see Frank Pasquale, "Privacy, Antitrust, and Power," *George Mason Law Review* 20 (2013): 1009–1024.

132. For an account of the rise of consumer welfare as antitrust's standard (and the problems this has caused), see Barak Orbach, "How Antitrust Lost Its Goal," *Fordham Law Review* 81 (2013): 2253–2278.

133. Paul Ohm, "The Rise and Fall of Invasive ISP Surveillance," *University of Illinois Law Review* (2009): 1425 (describing the many commercial pressures leading firms to "monetize behavioral data at the expense of user privacy").

134. Viktor Mayer-Schönberger and Kenneth Cukier, *Big Data: A Revolution That Will Transform How We Live, Work, and Think* (New York: Houghton Mifflin Harcourt, 2013).

135. Elizabeth Gudrais, "Googling Google," *Harvard Magazine*, November-December 2007, 16. Given that the vast majority of web searchers are looking only for a rapid, relevant response, it is unlikely that privacy concerns could

actually lead to significant market share shifts. They have not, to date, despite numerous privacy controversies raised by dominant firms.

136. Task Force on Competition Policy and Antitrust Laws, House Committee on the Judiciary, *Internet Nondiscrimination Principles for Competition Policy Online*, 110th Cong. (2010).

137. Google uses enough electricity "to power a city of 100,000 to 200,000 people." James Glanz, "Google Details and Defends Its Use of Electricity," *New York Times*, September 9, 2011, B1.

138. Stross, *Planet Google*. Note also the number of start-ups the company has purchased. Evelyn M. Rusli, "For Google, a New High in Deal-Making," *New York Times Deal Book* (blog), October 27, 2011, http://dealbook.nytimes.com /2011/10/27/google-hits-new-ma-record/.

139. Frank Pasquale, "Internet Nondiscrimination Principles: Commercial Ethics for Carriers and Search Engines," *University of Chicago Legal Forum* (2008): 263–300; Rusli, "For Google, a New High in Deal-Making."

140. Nathan Newman, "If Microsoft Can't Compete with Google, Who Can?" *Huffington Post* (blog), August 2, 2011, http://www.huffingtonpost.com /nathan-newman/if-microsoft-cant-compete_b_916000.html.

141. David Goldman, "Microsoft's Plan to Stop Bing's $1 Billion Bleeding," *CNN Money*, September 20, 2011, http://money.cnn.com/2011/09/20/technology /microsoft_bing/index.htm. For Quaero's budget, see William D. Bygrave and Andrew Zacharakis, *Entrepreneurship* (Hoboken, NJ: John Wiley & Sons, 2011), 350.

142. James Pitkow et al., "Personalized Search," *Communications of the ACM* 45 (2002): 50 (discussing methods of personalizing search systems); Elinor Mills, "Google Automates Personalized Search," *CNET*, June 28, 2005, http://www.news.com/Google-automates-personalized-search/2100 -1032_3-5766899.html (reporting that Google launched a new version of its personalized search that monitors previous searches to refine future results).

143. Robert K. Merton, "The Matthew Effect in Science: The Reward and Communication Systems of Science," *Science* 59 (1968): 56–63 (inspired by Matthew 25:29: "For unto every one that hath shall be given" more).

144. Google's terms of service have prohibited any action that "interfere[s] with Google's services." "Terms of Service" (Mar. 2012). *Google*. Available at http://www.google.com/accounts/TOS. Repeated queries to the service necessary to gather data on its operations may well violate these terms.

145. Ibid. The TOS would proscribe both the automatic data collection and the use of a nonapproved "interface" for accessing Google's database, regardless of the exact means. ("You may not copy, modify, distribute, sell, or lease any part of our Services or included software.")

146. Chris Lake, "Ben Edelman on Affiliate Marketing Fraud," *Econsultancy* (blog), November 4, 2008, http://econsultancy.com/uk/blog/2908-ben -edelman-on-affiliate-marketing-fraud (prepared testimony for subsequently canceled congressional hearing) (arguing that "Google's restrictions on export and copying of advertisers' campaigns . . . hinder competition in Internet advertising"); Ben Edelman, "PPC Platform Competition and Google's 'May

Not Copy' Restriction" (Jun. 2008*). Ben Edelman*. Available at http://www.
benedelman.org/news/062708-1.html.

147. Battelle, *The Search*, 8. Due to trade secrecy, it is impossible for policymakers to discover how much of the intermediary's success is due to its employees' inventive genius, and how much is due to the collective contributions
of millions of users to the training of the intermediary's computers.

148. See Stross, *Planet Google*.

149. Steve Lohr, "Drafting Antitrust Case, F.T.C. Raises Pressure on
Google," *New York Times*, October 12, 2012, http://www.nytimes.com/2012/10
/13/technology/ftc-staff-prepares-antitrust-case-against-google-over-search
.html?pagewanted=all&_r=0. "Google said in a statement on Friday, 'We are
happy to answer any questions that regulators have about our business." In the
past it has said many times that "competition is a click away.'"

150. For information on the 2013 Governing Algorithms conference, as
well as links to the talks, discussion papers, and responses, see Governing Algorithms, "Conference updates," on the Welcome! page. Available at http://
governingalgorithms.org/.

151. A pioneer of artificial intelligence described this process in more general terms: "In order for a program to improve itself substantially it would
have to have at least a rudimentary understanding of its own problem-solving
process and some ability to recognize an improvement when it found one.
There is no inherent reason why this should be impossible for a machine."
Marvin L. Minsky, "Artificial Intelligence," *Scientific American* 215 (September 1966): 260.

152. Martin Ford, *The Lights in the Tunnel* (Acculant Publishing, 2009),
60–62.

153. The more we understand the underlying dynamics here, the more we
can apply scholarly insights on the proper balance between public and provide
provision of infrastructure. Brett Frischmann, *Infrastructure: The Social Value
of Shared Resources* (New York: Oxford University Press, 2013).

154. Gar Alperovitz and Lewis C. Daly, *Unjust Deserts* (New York: New
Press, 2009).

155. Tom Slee, *No One Makes You Shop at Walmart* (Toronto: BTL Books,
2006).

156. Indeed, a Walmart board member has indicated that the company
considers Google a serious competitor. Steve Lohr, "Just Googling It Is Striking Fear into Companies," *New York Times*, November 6, 2005, http://www
.nytimes.com/2005/11/06/technology/06google.html?pagewanted=all&_r=0.

157. Mark Ames, "Revealed: Apple and Google's wage-fixing cartel involved dozens more companies, over one million employees," *Pando Daily*,
March 22, 2014, at http://pando.com/2014/03/22/revealed-apple-and-googles
-wage-fixing-cartel-involved-dozens-more-companies-over-one-million
-employees/.

158. On YouTube, at least, Content Partners have been "contractually pro-
hibited from revealing how much they earn from the ads running on their
YouTube channels," so it is difficult to judge how well they are being treated.
Ben Austen, "The YouTube Laugh Factory: A Studio System for Viral Video,"

*Wired,* December 16, 2011, http://www.wired.com/magazine/2011/12/ff_you tube/all/.

159. On the barriers to organization of digital labor, see Scholz, *Digital Labor.*

160. Lawrence Lessig, *Remix: Making Art and Commerce Thrive in the Hybrid Economy* (New York: Penguin, 2008), 128.

161. James Galbraith, *The Predator State* (New York: Free Press, 2008), xix.

162. Thomas Piketty, *Capital in the Twenty-First Century* (Cambridge: Harvard University Press, 2014): 571.

163. Turow, *The Daily You.*

164. Jerry Kang, "Race.Net Neutrality," *Journal on Telecommunications and High Technology Law* 6 (2007): 9–10.

165. Ibid. See also Jack Balkin, "Media Access: A Question of Design," *George Washington Law Review* 76 (2008): 933.

166. "Complaint of McGraw-Hill Companies, Inc.," McGraw-Hill Companies, Inc. v. Google Inc., No 05-CV-8881 (S.D.N.Y. 2005); "Complaint of the Author's Guild," The Author's Guild v. Google Inc., No 05-CV-8136 (S.D.N.Y. filed Sept. 20, 2005); Siva Vaidhyanathan, "The Googlization of Everything and the Future of Copyright," *University of California Davis Law Review* 40 (2007): 120 (arguing that the Google Library Project threatens the very foundation of copyright law); Emily Anne Proskine, "Google's Technicolor Dreamcoat: A Copyright Analysis of the Google Book Search Library Project," *Berkeley Technology Law Journal* 21 (2006): 217–219 (discussing Google Library Project).

167. For a general discussion, see Hannibal Travis, "Google Book Search and Fair Use: iTunes for Authors, or Napster for Books?," *University of Miami Law Review* 61 (2006): 87.

168. Katie Hafner, "Libraries Shun Deals to Place Books on Web," *New York Times,* October 22, 2007, A1.

169. Frank Pasquale, "Breaking the Vicious Circularity: Sony's Contribution to the Fair Use Doctrine," *Case Western Reserve University Law Review* 55 (2005): 777.

170. For more on the ever-rising cable rates, see Igor Greenwald, "The Cable Bill's Too High. Here's Why," *Forbes,* January 15, 2013, http://www.forbes.com /sites/igorgreenwald/2013/01/15/the-cable-bills-too-high-heres-why/.

171. Giancarlo F. Frosio, "Google Books Rejected: Taking the Orphans to the Digital Public Library of Alexandria," *Santa Clara Computer and High Technology Law Journal* 28 (2011): 81.

172. Floora Ruokonen, *Ethics and Aesthetics: Intersections in Iris Murdoch's Philosophy* (Finland: University of Helsinki, Department of Philosophy, 2008), 37–38. Available at https://helda.helsinki.fi/bitstream/handle/10138/21816 /ethicsan.pdf?sequence=1.

173. This analogy is inspired by Nick Carr, *The Big Switch: Rewiring the World, from Edison to Google* (New York: W.W. Norton & Company, 2013).

174. For other utility comparisons, see Rebecca MacKinnon, *Consent of the Networked* (New York: Basic Books, 2012). See also Lanier, *Who Owns the Future?*

175. Wu, *The Master Switch*; Charles Monroe Haar and Daniel William Fessler, *The Wrong Side of the Tracks* (New York: Simon & Schuster, 1986), 109–140; Jim Rossi, "The Common Law 'Duty to Serve' and Protection of Consumers in an Age of Competitive Retail Public Utility Restructuring," *Vanderbilt Law Review* 51 (1998): 1242–1250; Herbert Hovenkamp, "Regulatory Conflict in the Gilded Age: Federalism and the Railroad Problem," *Yale Law Journal* 97 (1988): 1087; Sallyanne Payton, "The Duty of a Public Utility to Serve in the Presence of New Competition," in *Applications of Economic Principles in Public Utility Industries,* ed. Werner Sichel and Thomas G. Gies (Ann Arbor: University of Michigan Press, 1981): 121, 139–144.

176. Hovenkamp, "Regulatory Conflict in the Gilded Age," 1044–1054; Joseph D. Kearney and Thomas W. Merrill, "The Great Transformation of Regulated Industries Law," *Columbia Law Review* 98 (1998): 1323, 1331–1333; Joseph William Singer, "No Right to Exclude: Public Accommodations and Private Property," *Northwestern University Law Review* 90 (1996): 1283.

177. On the historical origins of the law of common callings, see generally Haar and Fessler, *The Wrong Side of the Tracks,* 55–108; David S. Bogen, "The Innkeeper's Tale: The Legal Development of a Public Calling," *Utah Law Review* (1996): 51–92; Charles K. Burdick, "The Origin of the Peculiar Duties of Public Service Companies," *Columbia Law Review* 11 (1911): 514–531.

178. Haar and Fessler, *The Wrong Side of the Tracks,* 109–140, 141–193; Rossi, "The Common Law 'Duty to Serve,'" 1244–1260; Gustavus H. Robinson, "The Public Utility Concept in American Law," *Harvard Law Review* 41 (1928): 277. The regulatory model that consolidated at the turn of the twentieth century has undergone a fundamental transformation during the recent decades of "deregulation." See Joseph D. Kearney and Thomas W. Merrill, "The Great Transformation of Regulated Industries Law," *Columbia Law Review* 98 (1996):1323–1409. In most industries these changes meant a new paradigm of regulation rather than no regulation at all. Ibid., 1323–1330.

179. Wu, *The Master Switch.*

180. Christopher S. Yoo, "Deregulation vs. Reregulation of Telecommunications: A Clash of Regulatory Paradigms," *Journal of Corporation Law* 36 (2011): 847–868.

181. Bracha and Pasquale, "Federal Search Commission?," 1149.

182. Frank Pasquale, "Beyond Innovation and Competition," *Northwestern University Law Review* 104 (2010): 105.

183. Zittrain, *The Future of the Internet—And How to Stop It,* 67 (describing layers).

184. Their growth is provoking monopolization in adjacent realms, too. For example, a large cable company may plead to regulators that its only way to bargain with firms as massive as Google and Facebook is to maximize its own size and subscriber base. As Susan Crawford has exhaustively demonstrated, broadband companies are heading toward less competition rather than more as incumbent players carve up markets. Susan Crawford, *Captive Audience* (New Haven, CT: Yale University Press, 2012).

185. Pasquale, "Internet Nondiscrimination Principles: Commercial Ethics for Carriers and Search Engines," 263 (discussing ClearWire deal); Frank

Pasquale, "Search, Speech, and Secrecy: Corporate Strategies for Inverting Net Neutrality Debates," *Yale Law and Policy Review Inter Alia* 29 (2010): 25–33. Available at http://ylpr.yale.edu/inter_alia/search-speech-and-secrecy-corporate -strategies-inverting-net-neutrality-debates.

186. The scholars who developed the idea of "co-opetition" praise it as a new pattern of business interaction. Adam M. Brandenburger and Barry Nalebuff, *Co-Opetition: A Revolution Mindset That Combines Competition and Cooperation* (New York: Currency Doubleday, 1997). When looked at less from the perspective of managers than that of customers, different perspectives emerge.

187. David Weinberger, *Everything Is Miscellaneous* (New York: Holt Paperbacks, 2007). For a contemporary account of when YouTube broke onto the scene, see Scott Kirsner, "Now Playing: Your Home Video," *New York Times*, October 27, 2005, C1.

188. See generally, Eugene C. Kim, "YouTube: Testing the Safe Harbors of Digital Copyright Law," *Southern California Interdisciplinary Law Journal* 17 (2007): 139; Amir Hassanabadi, "Viacom v. YouTube—All Eyes Blind: The Limits of the DMCA in a Web 2.0 World," *Berkeley Technology Law Journal* 26 (2011): 405.

189. Tim Wu, "Tolerated Use" (May 2008). Columbia Law and Economics Working Paper No. 333. Available at http://papers.ssrn.com/sol3/papers.cfm ?abstract_id=1132247.

190. Hassanabadi, "Viacom v. YouTube."

191. Partners "are contractually prohibited from revealing how much they earn from the ads running on their YouTube channels," so it is difficult to judge how well they are being treated. Ben Austen, "The YouTube Laugh Factory: A Studio System for Viral Video," *Wired*, December 16, 2011, http:// www.wired.com/magazine/2011/12/ff_youtube/all/. See also John Carr, "I Want My Net TV!," *Information Today*, June 2008, at 1. ("YouTube has a revenue sharing program, but 'the process is opaque, requires [a nondisclosure agreement], and there is no reporting on what views are monetized.'")

192. Frank Pasquale, "A 'Content Loss Ratio' for Cable Companies?" *Madisonian* (blog), January 4, 2010, http://madisonian.net/2010/01/04/a-content -loss-ratio-for-cable-companies/; William W. Fisher, *Promises to Keep* (Stanford, CA: Stanford University Press, 2004).

193. Frank Pasquale, "Digital Cultural Wars," *Boston Review*, January 18, 2012, http://www.bostonreview.net/frank-pasquale-sopa-pipa-free-internet.

194. Vaidhyanathan, *The Googlization of Everything*, 18, 32–36. See also Niggemeier, "Autocompleting Bettina Wulff."

195. Julie Samuels and Mitch Stoltz, "Google's Opaque New Policy Lets Rightsholders Dictate Search Results," *Electronic Frontier Foundation*, Deeplinks Blog, August 10, 2012, https://www.eff.org/deeplinks/2012/08/googles -opaque-new-policy-lets-rightsholders-dictate-search-results.

196. Vaidhyanathan, *The Googlization of Everything*, 36–37.

197. For more on the relationship between Vevo and YouTube, see Jemima Kiss, "Vevo Boss Nic Jones: 'We're at the Pointy End of Labels' Activities,'" *The Guardian*, May 19, 2013, http://www.guardian.co.uk/media/2013/may/19 /vevo-nic-jones.

198. "An Explanation of Our Search Results," *Google*.

199. Samuels and Stoltz, "Google's Opaque New Policy Lets Rightsholders Dictate Search Results."

200. When Google discovers that a website is compromised with malware, it has used nonprofit, third-party mediators to explain to the stigmatized site what is wrong and how to fix it. But it is not clear whether sites demoted for alleged infringement can avail themselves of such help. Sullivan, "The Pirate Update: Google Will Penalize Sites Repeatedly Accused of Copyright Infringement." Google has linked websites affected with malware to "Stopbadware.org," which "is led by Harvard Law School's Berkman Center for Internet and Society and Oxford University's Internet Institute." Jeremy Kirk, "Google Irks Web Site Owners over Malware Alerts," *Info World*, January 11, 2007, http://www.info world.com/d/security-central/google-irks-web-site-owners-over-malware -alerts-839.

201. Jeffrey Rosen, "Google's Gatekeepers," *New York Times Magazine*, November 30, 2008, http://www.nytimes.com/2008/11/30/magazine/30google-t .html?partner=rss&emc=rss&pagewanted=all.

202. Bruce Ackerman and Ian Ayres, "A National Endowment for Journalism," *The Guardian*, February 12, 2009, http://www.theguardian.com /commentisfree/cifamerica/2009/feb/12/newspapers-investigative-journal ism-endowments. Jacob Weisberg, "The New Hybrids: Why the Debate about Financing Journalism Misses the Point," *Slate*, February 21, 2009, http://www.slate.com/articles/news_and_politics/the_big_idea/2009/02 /the_new_hybrids.html (describing the "sorry predicament of the newspaper industry").

203. "All the News That's Free to Print: Is Charity the Newspaper Industry's Last, Best Hope?" *The Economist*, July 21, 2009, http://www.economist. com/node/14072274; Steve Waldman, *The Information Needs of Communities: The Changing Media Landscape in a Broadband Age* (Washington, D.C.: Federal Communications Commission, 2011).

204. Bob Garfield, *The Chaos Scenario* (Nashville, TN: Stielstra Publishing, 2009), 10; Tim Arango, "Broadcast TV Faces Struggle to Stay Viable," *New York Times*, February 28, 2009, A1.

205. "66% of those ages 18–29 own smartphones." Lee Rainie, "Smart-phone Ownership Update" (Sept. 2012*). Pew Research Internet Project*. Available at http://pewInternet.org/Reports/2012/Smartphone-Update-Sept-2012.aspx. Evan Hark, "Will Spotify Become the Most Popular Music Service Behind iTunes?" (Jul. 2011). *Wall St. Cheat Sheet*. Available at http://wallstcheatsheet .com/stocks/will-spotify-become-the-most-popular-music-service-behind -itunes.html/.

206. Leslie Marable, "False Oracles: Consumer Reaction to Learning the Truth about How Search Engines Work—Results of an Ethnographic Study," *Consumer WebWatch*, June 30, 2003, 5. Available at http://www.kruse.co.uk /contextreport.pdf.

207. Jim Edwards, "Google Is Now Bigger Than Both the Magazine and the Newspaper Industries," *Business Insider*, November 12, 2013, http://www .businessinsider.com/google-is-bigger-than-all-magazines-and-newspapers

-combined-2013-11. If current trends continue, it will be greater than both combined.

208. Glenn Reynolds, *An Army of Davids: How Markets and Technology Empower Ordinary People to Beat Big Media, Big Government and Other Goliaths* (Nashville, TN: Thomas Nelson, Inc., 2007).

209. Jane Hamsher, "Has Google Destroyed the 4th Estate?," *ByteGeist* (blog), October 4, 2012, http://bytegeist.firedoglake.com/2012/10/04/has-google-destroyed-the-4th-estate/. Craig Timberg, "Web Sites Lose to Google, AOL in Race for Obama, Romney Campaign Ads," *Washington Post*, October 4, 2012, http://articles.washingtonpost.com/2012-10-04/business/35498725_1_web-sites-online-ads-aim-ads.

210. Vaidhyanathan, *The Googlization of Everything*; Jeff Jarvis, *What Would Google Do?* (New York: Harper Business, 2009); Stephen Baker, *The Numerati* (New York: Houghton Mifflin, 2008); Ian Ayres, *Super Crunchers* (New York: Bantam, 2007). Jarvis's title, WWGD, evokes the evangelical maxim What Would Jesus Do (WWJD), which suggests his own attitude toward the company.

211. Lanier, *Who Owns the Future?*

212. Alexis C. Madrigal, "How Google Builds Its Maps—and What It Means for the Future of Everything," *The Atlantic*, September 6, 2012, http://www.theatlantic.com/technology/archive/2012/09/how-google-builds-its-maps-and-what-it-means-for-the-future-of-everything/261913/. But note Matt Yglesias on how this ultimately helped Apple, and the fundamental lesson: nobody gets displaced, it's just a clash of titans over market share. Matthew Yglesias, "A Great iOS Google Maps Product Vindicates Apple's Strategy," *Slate MoneyBox* (blog), December 13, 2012, http://www.slate.com/blogs/moneybox/2012/12/13/ios_google_maps_if_it_s_great_thank_apple_s_strategy.html.

213. Labor experts have sharply criticized Amazon's labor practices both online (at its Mechanical Turk platform) and its warehouses. Trebor Scholz, ed., *Digital Labor: The Internet as Factory and Playground* (New York: Routledge, 2013).

214. Norman Solomon, "If Obama Orders the CIA to Kill a U.S. Citizen, Amazon Will Be a Partner in Assassination," *Alternet*, February 12, 2014, http://www.alternet.org/print/news-amp-politics/if-obama-orders-cia-kill-us-citizen-amazon-will-be-partner-assassination.

215. On the Verizon/Google framework, see Pasquale, "Search, Speech, and Secrecy: Corporate Strategies for Inverting Net Neutrality Debates."

216. David Amerland, "Google Takes Sides in Fight against Piracy," *Digital Journal*, August 17, 2012, http://digitaljournal.com/article/331014.

217. Langdon Winner, "Technology as Forms of Life," in *Readings in the Philosophy of Technology*, ed. David M. Kaplan (New York: Rowman & Littlefield, 2004), 103.

218. Greg Lastowka, *Virtual Justice: The New Laws of Online Worlds* (New Haven, CT: Yale University Press, 153) (discussing whether "virtual societies are premised on owner- user relationships similar to those between lords and vassals in feudal societies"); Bruce Schneier, "Feudal Security," *Schneier Blog*

(Dec. 3, 2012), at https://www.schneier.com/blog/archives/2012/12/feudal_sec
.html.

219. David Golumbia, *The Cultural Logic of Computation* (Cambridge, MA:
Harvard University Press, 2009).

220. Wu, *The Master Switch*, 83, 312, 314; Robert Lee Hale, *Freedom through
Law* (New York: Columbia University Press, 1952).

221. Lanier, *Who Owns the Future?* (describing the inequality generated by
the new digital economy).

222. Hale, *Freedom through Law*, 541.

# 4

## *Finance's Algorithms: The Emperor's New Codes*

1. Hernando de Soto, *The Other Path* (New York: Harper & Row, 1989).

2. Hernando de Soto and Karen Weise, "The Destruction of Economic
Facts," *Bloomberg Businessweek*, April 28, 2011, http://www.businessweek.com
/magazine/content/11_19/b4227060634112.htm.

3. As leading firms obsessed over short-term profit opportunities, one
economist half-jokingly concluded that finance's core competencies were
"finding fools for counterparties," evading regulations, and "disguising
gambling as hedging." Robert Waldmann, quoted in "What Are the Core
Competences of High Finance?" *Grasping Reality with Both Invisible Hands:
Fair, Balanced, and Reality-Based: A Semi-Daily Journal*, May 19, 2012, http://
delong.typepad.com/sdj/2012/05/what-are-the-core-competences-of-high
-finance.html.

4. Elaborate rules govern transactions ranging from home sales to stock
trading. Programs follow steps in mathematicized procedures, and use complex
pattern recognition techniques to analyze massive data sets. Scott Patterson,
*The Quants: How a New Breed of Math Whizzes Conquered Wall Street and Nearly
Destroyed It* (New York: Crown Business, 2011), 251.

5. Few people fully grasp the impact of credit scoring. You may think
that the late fee for paying a credit card bill is merely $35 or so. But if it re-
duces your credit score, the price could be far steeper. For instance, consider
someone who took out a $500,000, thirty-year fixed-rate mortgage in 2010
with a credit score of about 765. At some point, he might accidentally miss a
payment on a credit card, and his score might drop to, say, 690. Neither of
these is a bad score, but at that time, those with scores above 760 could expect a 4.52 percent rate (resulting in $2,539 monthly mortgage payments),
while those scoring below 700 would probably end up with a 4.91 percent
rate, at $2,657 per month. That's $128 extra per month—and over the full
term of a thirty-year mortgage, a total cost of $46,080 over the life of the
loan. Rates on other credit would also be higher. So the *real impact* of a late
payment could be well over $50,000—the typical *annual income* in the United
States in 2012.

6. I borrow the term "cyborg finance" from Tom C.W. Lin, "The New
Investor," *University of California at Los Angeles Law Review* (2013): 678.

7. Andrew W. Lo, "Reading about the Financial Crisis: A Twenty-One-Book Review," *Journal of Economic Literature* 50 (2012): 151–178; Andrew Ross Sorkin, *Too Big to Fail: The Inside Story of How Wall Street and Washington Fought to Save the Financial System—and Themselves* (New York: Penguin, 2010).

8. Jeremy Gogel, "'Shifting Risk to the Dumbest Guy in the Room'—Derivatives Regulation after the Wall Street Reform and Consumer Protection Act," *Journal of Business and Securities Law* 11 (2010): 1–52.

9. Ibid. See also Robert Stowe England, *Black Box Casino: How Wall Street's Risky Shadow Banking Crashed Global Finance* (Santa Barbara, CA: Praeger, 2011).

10. Tom Frost, "The Big Danger with Big Banks," *Wall Street Journal*, May 16, 2012, A15.

11. Stephen Davidoff, "Did Going Public Spoil the Banks?" *New York Times*, August 22, 2008, http://query.nytimes.com/gst/fullpage.html?res=9C03 E7DF1639F931A1575BC0A96E9C8B63; Claire Hill and Richard Painter, "Berle's Vision beyond Shareholder Interests: Why Investment Bankers Should Have (Some) Personal Liability," *Seattle University Law Review* 33 (2010): 1173–1199.

12. Jeff Madrick, *Age of Greed: The Triumph of Finance and the Decline of America, 1970 to the Present* (New York: Vintage, 2011); Joseph E. Stiglitz, *Freefall: America, Free Markets, and the Sinking of the World Economy* (New York: W.W. Norton, 2010); Hedrick Smith, *Who Stole the American Dream* (New York: Random House, 2012).

13. The language of finance is specialized. To define the term "derivative," we should begin with the word "security," which is an instrument representing some level of financial value. Broadly speaking, such instruments are categorized as either debt securities (such as bonds) or equity securities (such as stocks). A bond gives its owner a right to regular interest payments and return of the principal at the end of a given time period. Shares of stock are fractional claims to ownership of a business. They sometimes pay dividends, and their value can rise or fall based on the value of the business.
There is a third type of security—contracts known as derivatives. These include futures and options, which give counterparties (the contracting parties) certain rights in the future in exchange for cash payments, or assumptions of duties. Their value is "derived" from the value of underlying (or reference) asset(s). The seller of the derivative may agree to pay the buyer in case of some triggering event. Or the derivative may require a certain action.

14. Cheryl Strauss Einhorn, "The Shadow War at AIG," *Investment Dealers' Digest*, September 6, 1993, 14.

15. Gregory J. Millman, *The Vandal's Crown* (New York: The Free Press, 1995). Comptroller of Currency Eugene Ludwig described derivatives as "something quite new," a development in "financial technology" comparable to the "discovery of fire." April 2010 Senate Report, S. REP. 111–176, The Restoring American Financial Stability Act of 2010, at 41 (April 29, 2010), 43. Warren Buffett has called them financial "weapons of mass destruction."

16. Philippe Jorion, *Big Bets Gone Bad: Derivatives and Bankruptcy in Orange County—The Largest Municipal Failure in U.S. History* (San Diego, CA: Academic Press, 1995).

17. Frank Partnoy, *F.I.A.S.C.O.: Blood in the Water on Wall Street* (New York: Penguin, 1997).

18. Terry Carter goes into more of the legal details in the article "How Lawyers Enabled the Meltdown: And How They Might Have Prevented It," *ABA Journal* (January 2009): 34–39.

19. Simon Johnson and James Kwak, *13 Bankers: The Wall Street Takeover and the Next Financial Meltdown* (New York: Pantheon Books, 2010), 9.

20. Jennifer Taub, "The Sophisticated Investor and the Global Financial Crisis," in *Corporate Governance Failures: The Role of Institutional Investors in the Global Financial Crisis*, ed. James P. Hawley, Shyam J. Kamath, and Andrew T. Williams (Philadelphia: University of Pennsylvania Press, 2011), 191 ("reliance upon the sophisticated investor ignores reality; the entities the law deems to meet the definition are largely neither sophisticated enough to match the complexity of the instruments or lack of data nor the actual investors who have placed their capital at risk").

21. Adam J. Levitin and Susan M. Wachter, "Explaining the Housing Bubble," *Georgetown Law Journal* 100 (2012): 1254.

22. The protocols by which the resulting aggregates paid out were defined by complex ratings and prioritizings. Christopher L. Peterson, "Predatory Structured Finance," *Cardozo Law Review* 28 (2007): 2209; Eamonn K. Moran, "Wall Street Meets Main Street: Understanding the Financial Crisis," *North Carolina Banking Institute* 13 (2009): 38–39. (CDOs are "used to purchase asset-backed instruments, such as MBSs or CMOs with various ratings and projected returns. CDOs . . . are constructed from a portfolio of hundreds or thousands of fixed-income assets, such as actual loans or bonds.")

23. Ibid.

24. Donald MacKenzie, "Unlocking the Language of Structured Securities," *Financial Times*, August 19, 2010.

25. Ibid.

26. Ashwin Parameswaram, "How to Commit Fraud and Get Away With It: A Guide for CEOs," *Macroresilience* (Dec. 4, 2013) ("the more complex the algorithm, the more opportunities it provides to the salespeople to 'game' and arbitrage the system in order to commit fraud").

27. Michael W. Hudson, *The Monster* (New York: Times Books, 2010), 3, 7. Ameriquest has a long history in housing market controversies. Jennifer Taub, *Other People's Houses* (New Haven: Yale University Press, 2014).

28. Ibid., 163.

29. Like the stealthy assassins of martial arts lore, the NINJA loans were sneaked into mortgage-backed securities. In theory, large enough mortgage pools would spread out the risk of such loans so much that it wouldn't matter. But the risk ended up being more like a toxic salad: one bad leaf can make a very large bowl entirely unpalatable or dangerous.

30. Linda E. Fisher, "Target Marketing of Subprime Loans: Racialized Consumer Fraud and Reverse Redlining," *Journal of Law and Policy* 18 (2009):

121–155; Baher Azmy, "Squaring the Predatory Lending Circle: A Case for States as Laboratories of Experimentation," *Florida Law Review* 57 (2005): 295–405.

31. Suzanne McGee, *Chasing Goldman Sachs* (New York: Crown Publishing, 2010), 285.

32. Timothy Sinclair, *The New Masters of Capital* (Ithaca, NY: Cornell University Press, 2005); Elizabeth Devine, "The Collapse of an Empire? Rating Agency Reform in the Wake of the 2007 Financial Crisis," *Fordham Journal of Corporate and Financial Law* 16 (2011): 177–202.

33. Devine, "Collapse of an Empire?," 181–185.

34. Ibid., 181.

35. Ibid.

36. Ibid.

37. Outsourcing judgment to rating agencies had many of the same deficiencies of a larger project of technocratic privatization, described in Jon Michaels, "Privatization's Pretensions," *University of Chicago Law Review* 77 (2010): 717–780.

38. Jonathan M. Barnett, "Certification Drag: The Opinion Puzzle and Other Transactional Curiosities," *Journal of Corporation Law* 33 (2007): 95–150.

39. John Quiggin has cataloged other problems with rating agencies, particularly an apparent bias toward private (and against public) investment. John Quiggin, "Discredited," *Crooked Timber* (blog), October 20, 2008, http://crookedtimber.org/2008/10/20/discredited/.

40. U.S. Senate Subcommittee on Investigations, Committee on Homeland Security and Governmental Affairs, *Wall Street and the Financial Crisis: Anatomy of a Financial Collapse* (Apr. 2011), 6. Available at http://hsgac.senate.gov/public/_files/Financial_Crisis/FinancialCrisisReport.pdf.

41. Just one of the rating agencies had rated nearly 45,000 mortgage-related securities as AAA between 2000 and 2007. Financial Crisis Inquiry Commission, *The Financial Crisis Inquiry Report* (Jan. 2011), xxv (hereafter cited as *FCIC Report*). Available at http://fcic-static.law.stanford.edu/cdn_media/fcic-reports/fcic_final_report_full.pdf.

42. Roger Lowenstein, "Triple-A Failure," *New York Times*, April 27, 2008, www.nytimes.com/2008/04/27/magazine/27Credit-t.html?pagewanted=all&_r=0. The CRA forecast in June 2006 that only 4.9 percent of the underlying pool of mortgages would suffer losses. Given this imprimatur, tranches of it sold briskly. But in less than a year, 13 percent were delinquent, and by early 2008, 27 percent were delinquent.

43. Will Davies, "The Tyranny of Intermediaries" (Feb. 2013). Available at https://www.academia.edu/5236421/The_Tyranny_of_Intermediaries.

44. John Cassidy, "Burning Down the House of S&P," *The New Yorker*, February 5, 2013; Lorraine Woellert and Dawn Kopecki, "Moody's, S&P Employees Doubled Ratings, E-Mails Say," *Bloomberg*, October 22, 2008, http://www.bloomberg.com/apps/news?pid=newsarchive&sid=a2EMlP5s7iMo. Note that S&P disclaimed its motto of "objectivity" as "puffery" in a lawsuit filing in 2013. Order Denying Defendant's Motion to Dismiss, United States

v. S&P, July 16, 2013. Available at http://online.wsj.com/public/resources/doc uments/sandpdismisso717.pdf.

45. S&P Corrected Answer and Demand for Jury Trial, September 3, 2013, para. 140. Available at http://online.wsj.com/public/resources/documents /090313sandp.pdf. ("S&P admits that, during 2004, S&P Ratings considered potentially incorporating the Equation referenced in Paragraph 139 into a new version of the LEVELS model that would be called LEVELS 6.0, avers that the incorporation of the Equation into the proposed model produced results that were deemed to be insufficiently reliable for incorporation into any actual S&P Ratings model, and otherwise denies the allegations in Paragraph 140 [of the government complaint].")

46. Roberta Romano, "Does the Sarbanes-Oxley Act Have a Future?" *Yale Journal on Regulation* 26 (2009): 239 ("section 404 . . . requires management to certify the adequacy of its internal controls and the outside auditor to attest to management's certification").

47. Alison Frankel, "Sarbanes-Oxley's lost promise: Why CEO's haven't been prosecuted," *Reuters*, July 27, 2012, at http://blogs.reuters.com/alison -frankel/2012/07/27/sarbanes-oxleys-lost-promise-why-ceos-havent-been -prosecuted/ (explaining that subcertifications insulate top executives from false certification charges); Walter "Trey" Stock, "United States v. Scrushy and its Impact on Criminal Prosecutions Under the Certification Requirements of Sarbanes-Oxley," *Texas Wesleyan Law Review*: 13 (2006).

48. Michael Hudson, "Countrywide Protected Fraudsters by Silencing Whistleblowers, Say Former Employees," *Center for Public Integrity*, September 22, 2011, http://www.publicintegrity.org/2011/09/22/6687/countrywide -protected-fraudsters-silencing-whistleblowers-say-former-employees.

49. Eileen Foster, "Obama Administration Needs to Tap, Not Stiff-Arm, Wall Street Whistleblowers," *Rolling Stone* (blog), August 9, 2012, http://www .rollingstone.com/politics/blogs/national-affairs/the-obama-administration -needs-to-tap-not-stiff-arm-wall-street-whistleblowers-20120809.

50. Ibid.; see also Emily Flitter, "Countrywide Whistleblower Sees No Change in Financial Sector," Reuters, April 26, 2012. Available at http://www .reuters.com/article/2012/04/26/us-usa-banks-whistleblowers-idUSBRE 83P1CY20120426.

51. Michelle Conlin and Peter Rudegeair, "Former Bank of America Workers Allege It Lied to Home Owners," Reuters, June 14, 2013. Available at http://www.reuters.com/article/2013/06/14/us-bankofamerica-mortgages -idUSBRE95D10O20130614.

52. Hudson, *The Monster*.

53. Bob Ivry, "Woman Who Couldn't Be Intimidated by Citigroup Wins $31 Million," *Bloomberg*, May 31, 2012, http://www.bloomberg.com/news/2012 -05-31/woman-who-couldn-t-be-intimidated-by-citigroup-wins-31-million .html.

54. *FCIC Report*, 19.

55. Scott Patterson, *The Quants*, 8, 93–94.

56. Erik F. Gerding, "Code, Crash, and Open Source: The Outsourcing of Financial Regulation to Risk Models and the Global Financial Crisis,"

*Washington Law Review* 84 (2009): 134; Kenneth Bamberger, "Technologies of Compliance: Risk and Regulation in a Digital Age," *Texas Law Review* 88 (2010): 669.

57. A CDS is essentially a promise to pay on behalf of a debtor in case the debtor fails to pay. (It is called a "swap" because the two parties to the transaction swap the risk that one party will be unlucky enough to be relying on a defaulting debtor.) You might be thinking: that sounds a lot like insurance—and aren't insurers regulated? For the gory details on why CDSes escape many of these strictures, see M. Todd Henderson, "Credit Derivatives Are Not 'Insurance,'" *Connecticut Insurance Law Journal* 16 (2009): 1–58.

58. Michael Simkovic, "Secret Liens and the Financial Crisis of 2008," *American Bankruptcy Law Journal* 83 (2009): 253–296.

59. Andrew G. Haldane, "The Dog and the Frisbee." Speech delivered at the Federal Reserve Bank of Kansas City's 366th Economic Policy Symposium, Jackson Hole, Wyoming, August 31, 2012 (on manipulability of Basel II and III capital requirements).

60. CDSes played a major role in promoting the leverage that led to the financial crisis. A firm invested in mortgage-backed securities might need to maintain an "equity cushion" in order to cover its losses if the securities declined in value. But if it purchased a CDS to cover those losses, its equity cushion could be deployed elsewhere. Both investors and regulators might be particularly impressed by a CDS underwritten by AIG, one of the most highly regarded firms in the United States at the time. Other CDSes were even shakier. Moreover, it was hard to keep track of where the credit risk lay, because, as Stephen Lubben notes, "many credit default swaps were assigned to new protection buyers without the prior consent of the seller," even though the ISDA Master Agreement governing such deals forbids this. Stephen J. Lubben, "Credit Derivatives and the Future of Chapter 11," *American Bankruptcy Law Journal* 81 (2007): 415.

61. As the Financial Crisis Inquiry Commission majority report observed, some derivatives, such as CDS's, did not require the seller to put up reserves or hedge their exposure. The value of the underlying assets "insured" for outstanding CDS grew from $6.4 trillion at the end of 2004 to $58.2 trillion at the end of 2007. Because investment banks were not subject to the same capital requirements as commercial and retail banks, they were able to rely on their internal—faulty—risk models in determining capital requirements. Predictably, the investment banks increased their leverage to extraordinary levels, sometimes as high as 40:1. The investment banks were able to hide the extent of their leverage by selling assets right before the reporting period and subsequently buying them back. The Financial Crisis Inquiry Commission, *Financial Crisis Inquiry Report*, February 25, 2011. Available at http://www.gpo.gov/fdsys/pkg/GPO-FCIC/pdf/GPO-FCIC.pdf.

62. William K. Sjostrom, Jr., "The AIG Bailout," *Washington and Lee Law Review* 66 (2009): 943–994; *FCIC Report*, 351–354 (noting that most of the firm's funds were locked into regulated insurer subsidiaries which could not put their own funds toward the parent firm's obligations).

63. Thus insured, they could free up precious capital to begin the leverage process again.

64. Gretchen Morgenson, "Behind Insurer's Crisis, Blind Eye to a Web of Risk," *New York Times*, September 28, 2008, http://www.nytimes.com/2008 /09/28/business/28melt.html?pagewanted=all&_r=0. AIG, *2006 Annual Report* (Form 10-K) 94 (March 1, 2007). Available at http://idea.sec.gov/Archives /edgar/data/5272/000095012307003026/y27490e10vk.htm. ("The likelihood of any payment obligation by AIGFP under each [CDS] transaction is remote, even in severe recessionary market scenarios.")

65. Roddy Boyd, *Fatal Risk: A Cautionary Tale of AIG's Corporate Suicide* (Hoboken, NJ: John Wiley & Sons, Inc., 2011).

66. As of July 1, 2008, AIG had about $17.6 billion in cash and cash equivalents available to meet the needs of its operations, despite its potential need to pay out far more in case credit events triggered its CDS counterparties' right to demand payment. Sjostrom, "The AIG Bailout."

67. Sjostrom, "The AIG Bailout."

68. *FCIC Report.*

69. *FCIC Report.*

70. "Bank Regulators Cutting the Red Tape and Screwing the Rest of Us," *Investment Mercenaries* (blog), September 1, 2011, http://investmentmercenaries .blogspot.com/2011/09/bank-regulators-cutting-red-tape-and.html.

71. Watters v. Wachovia Bank, 550 U.S. 1 (2007).

72. A majority of the Financial Crisis Inquiry Commission (FCIC) concluded that OTS "ignored its responsibilities under the European Union's Financial Conglomerates Directive (FCD)—responsibilities the OTS had actively sought." *FCIC Report.* Note that in 2004 and 2005, several large financial institutions tried to get out from under both state law (via federal preemption) and EU law (by obtaining assurances that U.S. regulatory bodies would be their primary supervisory entities). The *FCIC Report* criticized OTS's enabling of this development.

73. "FASB: Here Comes Mark to Fantasy Accounting!," *Socio-Economics History Blog*, April 3, 2009, http://socioecohistory.wordpress.com/2009/04/03 /fasb-here-comes-mark-to-fantasy-accounting/.

74. Arthur E. Wilmarth, Jr., "Citigroup: A Case Study in Managerial and Regulatory Failures," *Indiana Law Review* 47 (forthcoming 2014).

75. "Understanding Corporate Networks—Part 2: Control without Voting," *OpenCorporates* (blog), October 31, 2013, http://blog.opencorporates.com /2013/10/31/understanding-corporate-networks-part-2-control-without -voting/.

76. Graham Harman, *Prince of Networks: Bruno Latour and Metaphysics* (Melbourne: re.press, 2009), 32.

77. William W. Bratton and Adam J. Levitin, "A Transactional Genealogy of Scandal: From Michael Milken to Enron to Goldman Sachs," *Southern California Law Review* 86 (2013): 783–868.

78. Simkovic, "Secret Liens and the Financial Crisis of 2008."

79. James K. Galbraith, "Tremble, Banks, Tremble," *The New Republic*, July 9, 2010, http://www.tnr.com/article/economy/76146/tremble-banks-tremble.

80. Matt Taibbi, "Invasion of the Home Snatchers: How Foreclosure Courts Are Helping Big Banks Screw Over Homeowners," *Rolling Stone*, November

10, 2010, http://www.rollingstone.com/politics/news/matt-taibbi-courts -helping-banks-screw-over-homeowners-20101110.

81. Mike Konczal, "Foreclosure Fraud for Dummies," *Rortybomb*, Oct. 8, 2010, at http://rortybomb.wordpress.com/2010/10/08/foreclosure-fraud-for -dummies-1-the-chains-and-the-stakes/.

82. Christopher L. Peterson, "Two Faces: Demystifying the Mortgage Electronic Registration System's Land Title Theory," *William and Mary Law Review* 53 (2011): 111–162.

83. Ibid.

84. Dustin A. Zacks, "Robo-Litigation," *Cleveland State Law Review* 60 (2013): 867–912; Dale A. Whitman, "A Proposal for a National Mortgage Regis- try: MERS Done Right," *Missouri Law Review* 78 (2013); Nolan Robinson, "Note: The Case Against Allowing Mortgage Electronic Registration Systems, Inc. (MERS) to Initiate Foreclosure Proceedings," *Cardozo Law Review* 32 (2011).

85. As Simon Head has observed, "The Wall Street machine was able to achieve the speed that it did only by automating . . . complex judgments that should have been subject to painstaking, time-consuming analysis." Simon Head, *Mindless: Why Smarter Machines are Making Dumber Humans* (New York: Basic Books, 2014), 82.

86. Donald MacKenzie, "What's in a Number?" *London Review of Books* 30, no. 18 (September 25, 2008): 11–12. Available at http://www.lrb.co.uk/v30/n18 /donald-mackenzie/whats-in-a-number.

87. The advantage of this system is that it allowed for diverse estimates of prices even if actual borrowing weren't going on. Some Libor rates (such as eleven-month loans) are thinly traded.

88. U.S. Commodity Futures Trading Commission, "CFTC Orders Bar- clays to Pay $200 Million Penalty for Attempted Manipulation of and False Reporting Concerning LIBOR and Euribor Benchmark Interest Rates," June 27, 2012 (news release). Available at http://www.cftc.gov/PressRoom/PressRe leases/pr6289-12.

89. U.S. Commodity Futures Trading Commission, "CFTC Orders the Royal Bank of Scotland plc and RBS Securities Japan Limited to Pay $325 Mil- lion Penalty to Settle Charges of Manipulation, Attempted Manipulation, and False Reporting of Yen and Swiss Franc LIBOR," February 6, 2013 (news re- lease). Available at http://www.cftc.gov/PressRoom/PressReleases/pr6510-13.

90. Ibid.

91. Matthew Leising, Lindsay Fortado, and Jim Brunsden, "Meet ISDA- fix, the Libor Scandal's Sequel," *Bloomberg Businessweek*, April 18, 2013, http:// www.businessweek.com/articles/2013-04-18/meet-isdafix-the-libor-scandals -sequel.

92. Matt Taibbi, "Everything Is Rigged: The Biggest Price-Fixing Scan- dal Ever," *Rolling Stone*, April 13, 2013, http://www.rollingstone.com/politics /news/everything-is-rigged-the-biggest-financial-scandal-yet-20130425#ixzz 2pRbVN1ew.

93. Frank Partnoy and Jesse Eisinger, "What's Inside America's Banks?," *The Atlantic*, January 2, 2013, http://www.theatlantic.com/magazine/archive /2013/01/whats-inside-americas-banks/309196/.

94. Asjylyn Loder, Stephanie Bodoni, and Rupert Rowling, "Oil Manipulation Inquiry Shows EU's Hammer after Libor," *Bloomberg*, May 22, 2013, http://www.bloomberg.com/news/2013-05-23/oil-manipulation-inquiry -shows-eu-s-hammer-after-libor.html.

95. There is a kind of magic here, but not genius. As Clive Dilnot once observed of dodgy credit default swaps and tax schemes, "There is no great financial acumen in hiding liabilities. . . . *The Producers* were more inventive, the stock-exchange games of the 1920s more complex." Clive Dilnot, "The Triumph—and Costs—of Greed," *Real-World Economics Review* 49 (2009): 46.

96. Justin Baer et al., "'Fab' Trader Liable in Fraud: Jury Finds Ex-Goldman Employee Tourre Misled Investors in Mortgage Security," *Wall Street Journal*, August 2, 2013, http://online.wsj.com/news/articles/SB10001424127887323681 9045786418432844500004.

97. E. J. Dionne, Jr., "How Wall Street Creates Socialists," *Truthout*, April 28, 2010, http://www.truthout.org/ej-dionne-jr-how-wall-street-creates-so-cialists58971.

98. The case Tourre was embroiled in helps illustrate the point. Lawrence Cunningham, "Goldman's $550 Million SEC Settlement," *Concurring Opinions* (blog), July 15, 2010, http://www.concurringopinions.com/archives/2010 /07/goldmans-550-million-sec-settlement.html. ("In a bruising Consent to a Final Judgment in the federal case against it, Goldman acknowledges [that its] marketing circular said the reference portfolio was "selected by" the independent firm, ACA Management LLC, when in fact Paulson & Co. Inc., an interested party, played a role in that selection.") Cora Currier, "13 Reasons Goldman's Quitting Exec May Have a Point," *ProPublica*, March 14, 2012, http:// www.propublica.org/article/13-reasons-goldmans-quitting-exec-may-have-a -point. Shahien Nasiripour, "Goldman Sachs Values Assets Low, Sells High to Customers as Senate Panel Alleges Double Dealing," *Huffington Post*, April 14, 2011, http://www.huffingtonpost.com/2011/04/14/goldman-sachs-values-asse _n_849398.html.

99. Kayla Tausche, "Wall Street into Snapchat, and Regulators Are on Alert," *CNBC*, July 30, 2013, http://www.cnbc.com/id/100924846.

100. For example, since a "simple fixed/floating interest-rate swap contract . . . has zero value at the start," it "is considered neither an asset nor a liability, but is an 'off-balance-sheet' item." Carol J. Loomis, "Derivatives: The Risk That Still Won't Go Away (Fortune 2009)," *CNN Money*, May 20, 2012, http://features.blogs.fortune.cnn.com/2012/05/20/derivatives-the-risk-that -still-wont-go-away-fortune-2009/.

101. Bill Davidow, "Why the Internet Makes It Impossible to Stop Giant Wall Street Losses," *The Atlantic*, May 18, 2012, http://www.theatlantic.com /business/archive/2012/05/why-the-internet-makes-it-impossible-to-stop-giant -wall-street-losses/257356/.

102. Loomis, "Derivatives."

103. Gretchen Morgenson and Joshua Rosner, *Reckless Endangerment: How Outsized Ambition, Greed, and Corruption Created the Worst Financial Crisis of Our Time* (New York: Times Books, 2011); Bethany McLean and Joe Nocera, *All the Devils Are Here: The Hidden History of the Financial Crisis* (New York:

Portfolio Books, 2010). This willful obliviousness to risk was compounded by the "greater fool" logic of the daisy chain transactions documented by Eisinger and Drucker: even if credit risk *were* to clearly manifest, holders of CDOs assumed there'd always be someone else willing to take on the risk. Jake Bernstein and Jesse Eisinger, "Banks' Self-Dealing Super-Charged Finanical Crisis," Pro Publica, August 26, 2010, at http://www.propublica.org/article/banks-self-dealing-super-charged-financial-crisis.

104. Jaron Lanier, *You Are Not a Gadget: A Manifesto* (New York: Alfred A. Knopf, 2010), 96.

105. U.S. Senate Permanent Subcommittee on Investigations, *JPMorgan Chase Whale Trades: A Case History of Derivatives Risks and Abuses* (2013), 8. ("In the case of the CIO VaR, after analysts concluded the existing model was too conservative and overstated risk, an alternative CIO model was hurriedly adopted in late January 2012, while the CIO was in breach of its own and the bankwide VaR limit. The CIO's new model immediately lowered the SCP's VaR by 50%, enabling the CIO not only to end its breach, but to engage in substantially more risky derivatives trading. Months later, the bank determined that the model was improperly implemented, requiring error-prone manual data entry and incorporating formula and calculation errors.")

106. Ibid. By contrast, in health care, the "aviation model" of safety has been taken seriously by a number of providers, with encouraging results. Lucian Leape et al., "What Practices Will Most Improve Safety?: Evidence-Based Medicine Meets Patient Safety," *Journal of the American Medical Association* 288 (2002) 501, 504; James Reason, "A Systems Approach to Organizational Error," *Ergonomics* 38 (1995): 1708–1721; Richard L. Cook, *How Complex Systems Fail* (Chicago: University of Chicago Press, 1998).

107. Intelligence Squared U.S., "Break Up the Big Banks" (October 16, 2013). Available at http://intelligencesquaredus.org/images/debates/past/transcripts/101613%20big%20banks.pdf.

108. Adair Turner et al., eds., *The Future of Finance: The LSE Report* (London: London School of Economics and Political Science, 2010).

109. Gillian Tett, *Fool's Gold: How the Bold Dream of a Small Tribe at J.P. Morgan was Corrupted by Wall Street Greed and Unleashed a Catastrophe* (New York: Free Press, 2009).

110. Arthur E. Wilmarth, Jr., "Turning a Blind Eye: Why Washington Keeps Giving In to Wall Street," *University of Cincinnati Law Review* 81 (2013): 1283–1446; Haley Sweetland Edwards, "He Who Makes the Rules," *Washington Monthly*, March/April 2013, http://www.washingtonmonthly.com/magazine/march_april_2013/features/he_who_makes_the_rules043315.php?page=all (exploring how "lobbyists and conservative jurists in the shadowy, Byzantine rule-making process" can eviscerate Dodd-Frank).

111. Lawrence E. Mitchell, *The Speculation Economy: How Finance Triumphed over Industry* (San Francisco: Berrett-Koehler Publishers, Inc., 2007); Greta R. Krippner, *Capitalizing on Crisis: The Political Origins of the Rise of Finance* (Cambridge, MA: Harvard University Press, 2011).

112. Joe Nocera, *A Piece of the Action: How the Middle Class Joined the Money Class* (New York: Simon & Schuster, 1994).

113. Doug Henwood, *Wall Street: How It Works and for Whom* (New York: Verso, 1997).

114. Lynne Dallas, "Short-Termism, the Financial Crisis, and Corporate Governance," *Journal of Corporation Law* 37 (2011): 264.

115. This paragraph and the next two rely on the diagram that is part of Matthew Philips and Cynthia Hoffman, "What Really Happens When You Buy Shares," *Businessweek*, January 6, 2013. ("A transaction that used to be straightforward can now take an almost infinite variety of paths.")

116. Scott Patterson, *Dark Pools: The Rise of the Machine Traders and the Rigging of the U.S. Stock Market* (New York: Crown Business, 2012), 202 (traders are "exploiting the 'latency' of the system, a measurement of the time it takes for information to move from place to place").

117. Algorithmic trading refers to the use of computers to place orders on equities markets while using algorithmic codes to decide the specific aspects of the order, such as the timing, price, and quantity, all without any human intervention. Nathan D. Brown, "The Rise of High Frequency Trading: The Role Algorithms, and the Lack of Regulations, Play in Today's Stock Market," *Appalachian Journal of Law* 11 (2012): 209–230. Algorithmic codes are typically proprietary and secret. Ibid., 222.

118. Brody Mullins, Michael Rothfeld, Tom Mcginty and Jenny Strasburg, "Traders Pay for an Early Peek at Key Data," *Wall Street Journal*, June 12, 2013, at http://online.wsj.com/news/articles/SB10001424127887324682204578 515963191421602.

119. Ibid., 209–210; Tor Brunzell, "High-Frequency Trading—To Regulate or Not to Regulate—That Is the Question," *Journal of Business and Financial Affairs* 2 (2013), http://www.omicsgroup.org/journals/high-frequency-trading -to-regulate-or-not-to-regulate-that-is-the%20question-does-scientific-data -offer-an-answer-2167-0234.1000e121.pdf (discussing the common arguments proponents of high-frequency trading make supporting its use). There are a range of algorithmic trading strategies; high-frequency trading (HFT) describes one subset of these strategies. David Golumbia, "High-Frequency Trading: Networks of Wealth and the Concentration of Power," *Social Semiotics* 23 (2013): 278–299.

120. HFT often involves "very high order amounts; rapid order cancellation; a flat position at the end of the trading day; extracting very low margins per trade; and trading at ultra-fast speeds." Andrew J. Keller, "Robocops: Regulating High Frequency Trading after the Flash Crash of 2010," *Ohio State Law Journal* 73 (2012): 1459.

121. Matthew O'Brien, "High-Speed Trading Isn't About Efficiency—It's About Cheating," *The Atlantic*, February 8, 2014. Available at http://www.the atlantic.com/business/archive/2014/02/high-speed-trading-isnt-about-effi-ciency-its-about-cheating/283677/; Charles Schwab and Walt Bettinger, "Statement on High-Frequency Trading," April 3, 2014. Available at http://www.aboutschwab.com/press/issues/statement_on_high_frequency_trading.

122. Robert Hiltonsmith, *The Retirement Savings Drain: The Hidden and Excessive Costs of 401(k)s* (New York: Dēmos, 2012). Available at http://www.demos .org/sites/default/files/publications/TheRetirementSavingsDrain-Final.pdf.

123. Martin Smith, "The Retirement Gamble," *Public Broadcasting Service*, at April 23, 2013 ("Assume you are invested in a mutual fund, he says, with a gross return of 7 percent, but that the mutual fund charges you an annual fee of 2 percent.

Over a 50-year investing lifetime, that little 2 percent fee will erode 63 percent of what you would have had. As Bogle puts it, 'the tyranny of compounding costs' is overwhelming.").

124. Adair Turner, "What Do Banks Do? Why Do Credit Booms and Busts Occur and What Can Public Policy Do about It?," in *The Future of Finance*, 40.

125. Wallace Turbeville, "Cracks in the Pipeline, Part Two: High Frequency Trading," *Dēmos*, March 8, 2013, http://www.demos.org/publication /cracks-pipeline-part-two-high-frequency-trading. Sal Arnuk and Joseph Saluzzi, *Broken Markets: How High Frequency Trading and Predatory Practices on Wall Street Are Destroying Investor Confidence and Your Portfolio* (Upper Saddle River, NJ: FT Press, 2012).

126. Report of the Staffs of the CFTC and SEC to the Joint Advisory Committee on Emerging Regulatory Issues, *Findings Regarding the Market Events of May 6, 2010* (September 2010). Available at http://www.sec.gov/news /studies/2010/marketevents-report.pdf.

127. Ibid.

128. See ibid., 79. ("It has been hypothesized that these delays are due to a manipulative practice called 'quote-stuffing,' in which high volumes of quotes are purposely sent to exchanges in order to create data delays that would afford the firm sending these quotes a trading advantage.") Note also the disastrous $440 million loss of Knight Capital in August 2012, which was traced to IT/ software issues at the firm that took nearly an hour to fix—losing the firm $440 million in the meantime. Dan Olds, "How One Bad Algorithm Cost Traders $440m," *The Register*, August 3, 2012, http://www.theregister.co.uk/2012/08/03 /bad_algorithm_lost_440_million_dollars/. Stephanie Ruhle, Christine Harper, and Nina Mehta, "Knight Trading Loss Said to Be Linked to Dormant Software," *Bloomberg Technology*, August 14, 2012, http://www.bloomberg.com/news /2012-08-14/knight-software.html. Korean exchanges faced a smaller crash in late 2013.

129. For example, McCabe observes, a "Chicago-New York cable will shave about 3 milliseconds off . . . communication time." Thomas McCabe, "When the Speed of Light Is Too Slow: Trading at the Edge," *Kurzweil Accelerating Intelligence* (blog), November 11, 2010, http://www.kurzweilai.net/when-the -speed-of-light-is-too-slow.

130. This story opens Michael Lewis, *Flash Boys* (New York: W.W. Norton, 2014), 15. Economic sociologists have also studied Spread Networks. Donald Mackenzie et al., "Drilling Through the Allegheny Mountains: Liquidity, Materiality and High-Frequency Trading" (Jan., 2012), at http://www.sps.ed .ac.uk/__data/assets/pdf_file/0003/78186/LiquidityResub8.pdf.

131. Ibid. A. D. Wissner-Gross and C. E. Freer, "Relativistic Statistical Arbitrage," *Physical Review E 056104-1* 82 (2010): 1–7. Available at http://www .alexwg.org/publications/PhysRevE_82-056104.pdf.

132. Keller, "Robocops," 1468.

133. Ibid.

134. Ibid.

135. See Matt Prewitt, "High-Frequency Trading: Should Regulators Do More?," *Michigan Telecommunications and Technology Law Review* 19 (2012): 148 (discussing "spoofing" and other deceptive HFT tactics).

136. See Andrew Saks McLeod, "CFTC Fines Algorithmic Trader $2.8 Million for Spoofing in the First Market Abuse Case Brought by Dodd-Frank Act, and Imposes Ban," *Forex Magnates*, July 22, 2013, http://forexmagnates.com /cftc-fines-algorithmic-trader-2-8-million-for-spoofing-in-the-first-market -abuse-case-brought-by-dodd-frank-act/ (discussing "spoofing").

137. See Prewitt, "High-Frequency Trading." Another article that describes "spoofing" pretty well is by Robert C. Fallon, writing for *Lexology*. Robert C. Fallon, "High Frequency Trader 'Spoofs' and 'Layers' His Way to Penalties from U.S. and British Regulators," *Lexology*, July 30, 2013, http://www.lexology .com/library/detail.aspx?g=c6f66fb4-e220-47be-896a-7352984c9622.

138. "Strobing" is a HFT strategy in which the same order is sent and canceled many times to create the appearance of liquidity. The Commodity Futures Trading Commission considers this a form of "spoofing." See Robert Fallon, "CFTC's Final Rule on Disruptive Trading Clarifies Disruptive Trading Practices" *Dodd-Frank.com*, May 24, 2013, http://dodd-frank.com/cftc -disruptive-trading-practices-strobing-and-spoofing/ (including that "strobing" is prohibited "spoofing").

139. "Smoking" is an HFT scheme that exploits slow traders by offering attractive limit orders, then quickly revising these prices to take advantage of an unsuspecting slow trader's market order. Prewitt, "High-Frequency Trading," 148.

140. "Last second withdrawal" refers to the strategy of canceling orders at the final second of a call procedure. See Brunzell, "High-Frequency Trading—To Regulate or Not to Regulate."

141. Graham Bowley, "Computers That Trade on the News," *New York Times*, December 23, 2010, http://www.nytimes.com/2010/12/23/business /23trading.html?ref=technology.

142. Edward Tenner, "Wall Street's Latest Bubble Machines," *The Atlantic*, December 27, 2010, http://www.theatlantic.com/business/archive/2010/12 /wall-streets-latest-bubble-machines/68547/.

143. Felix Salmon and Jon Stokes, "Algorithms Take Control of Wall Street," *Wired*, December 27, 2010, http://www.wired.com/magazine/2010/12 /ff_ai_flashtrading/.

144. Billionaire Pete Peterson has endowed a think tank, the Peterson Institute, to buttress a Beltway consensus about the debt-induced fragility of public finances. Automated trading billionaire Thomas Peterffy has also engaged in a campaign to stop "socialism" in the United States.

145. Legal changes pushing workers and companies into "defined contribution" rather than "defined benefit" or public pension plans have fueled the growth of the financial sector. James W. Russell, *Social Insecurity: 401(k)s and the Retirement Crisis* (Boston: Beacon Press, 2014); Robin Blackburn, *Banking on Death* (London: Verso, 2004).

146. Peter Boone and Simon Johnson describe how a "doomsday cycle" of privatized gains and socialized losses continues to this day. Peter Boone and Simon Johnson, "Will the Politics of Global Moral Hazard Sink Us Again?," in *The Future of Finance*. See also Paul De Grauwe and Yuemei Ji, "Strong Government, Weak Banks," CEPS Policy Brief No. 305, November 25, 2013, http://www.ceps.eu/ceps/dld/8646/pdf (and note how those "earning" the most at banks want them weak; a strong institution would do more to limit their pay).

147. Associated Press, "10-Year Treasury Yield Rises from Near Record Low," May 18, 2012. Available at http://bigstory.ap.org/content/10-year-treasury-yield-rises-near-record-low.

148. John Kay, "It's Madness to Follow a Martingale Betting Strategy in Europe," *Financial Times*, November 22, 2011, http://www.ft.com/intl/cms/s/o/ofd87462-14fe-11e1-a2a6-00144feabdco.html#axzz2NZ6LQwOn.

149. Stephen Mihm, "The Black Box Economy," *The Boston Globe*, January 27, 2008, http://www.boston.com/bostonglobe/ideas/articles/2008/01/27/the_black_box_economy/?page=full.

150. William K. Black, *The Best Way to Rob a Bank Is to Own One: How Corporate Executives and Politicians Looted the S&L Industry* (Austin: University of Texas Press, 2005); see also Kenneth Harney, "FBI Cracks Down on Growing Mortgage Fraud," *U-T San Diego*, July 31, 2005, http://www.utsandiego.com/uniontrib/20050731/news_1h31harney.html.

151. Lynn A. Stout, "Derivatives and the Legal Origin of the 2008 Credit Crisis," *Harvard Business Law Review* 1 (2011): 13.

152. Yves Smith and Tom Adams, "FCIC Report Misses Central Issue: Why Was There Demand for Bad Mortgage Loans?," *Huffington Post*, January 31, 2011, http://www.huffingtonpost.com/thomas-adams-and-yves-smith/fcic-report-misses-centra_b_816149.html.

153. Mike Konczal, "An Interview on Off-Balance Sheet Reform," *Rortybomb* (blog), April 30, 2010, http://rortybomb.wordpress.com/2010/04/30/an-interview-on-off-balance-sheet-reform/; Mike Konczal, "An Interview with Jane D'Arista on the Volcker Rule," *Rortybomb* (blog), April 30, 2010, http://rortybomb.wordpress.com/2010/04/30/an-interview-with-jane-darista-on-volcker-rule/.

154. Alireza Gharagozlou, "Unregulable: Why Derivatives May Never Be Regulated," *Brooklyn Journal of Corporate, Financial and Commercial Law* 4 (2010): 269–295 (exploring "various methods of regulating financial derivative contracts, including (a) regulation by judicially created case law, (b) regulation as gambling, (c) regulation as insurance, (d) regulation as securities, (e) regulation via a clearinghouse and (f) oversight by a super financial regulator").

155. Nassim Nicholas Taleb, *Black Swan* (New York: Random House, 2007).

156. Nomi Prins, *Other People's Money: The Corporate Mugging of America* (New York: New Press, 2004). Nomi Prins, *It Takes a Pillage: Behind the Bailouts, Bonuses and Backroom Deals from Washington to Wall Street* (Hoboken, NJ: Wiley, 2009).

157. For example, Yves Smith describes a structure that catalyzed $533 in funding for subprime mortgages for every dollar invested in it. Yves Smith, *ECONned: How Unenlightened Self Interest Undermined Democracy and Corrupted Capitalism* (New York: Palgrave Macmillan, 2010), 261.

158. Thorvaldur Gylfason, "Mel Brooks and the Bankers," *Vox EU*, August 17, 2010, http://economistsview.typepad.com/economistsview/2010/08/mel -brooks-and-the-bankers.html. John K. Galbraith, "In Goldman Sachs We Trust," in *The Great Crash of 1929* (New York: Houghton Mifflin Harcourt, 1954), 43–66.

159. Frank Pasquale, "The Economics Was Fake, but the Bonuses Were Real," *Concurring Opinions* (blog), December 19, 2008, http://www.concurring opinions.com/archives/2008/12/only_the_bonuse.html.

160. Roben Farzad, "AIG May Not Be as Healthy as It Looks," *Bloomberg Businessweek*, April 26, 2012, http://www.businessweek.com/articles/2012-04 -26/aig-may-not-be-as-healthy-as-it-looks (discussing U.S. Treasury depart-ment decision to allow AIG, Ally, and Citibank to "claim operating losses from previous years to eliminate taxes on current income"—an allowance which "typically does not apply to bankrupt or acquired companies").

161. See generally Golumbia, "High-Frequency Trading."

162. Amar Bhidé, *A Call for Judgment: Sensible Finance for a Dynamic Econ-omy* (New York: Oxford University Press, 2010). See also Meredith Schramm-Strosser, "The 'Not So' Fair Credit Reporting Act: Federal Preemption, Injunctive Relief, and the Need to Return Remedies for Common Law Defa-mation to the States," *Duquesne Business Law Journal* 14 (2012): 169.

163. For historical accounts of corrupt or conflicted practices, see Gal-braith, *The Great Crash of 1929*; Fred Schwed, *Where Are the Customers' Yachts?* (New York: Wiley, 2006); Henwood, *Wall Street: How it Works*; Robert Kuttner, *The Squandering of America: How the Failure of Our Politics Undermines Our Prosperity* (2010), 112, 231.

164. Satyajit Das, *Traders, Guns and Money: Knowns and Unknowns in the Dazzling World of Derivatives* (Great Britain: FT Press, 2006), 144.

165. Daniel Carpenter, *Reputation and Power: Organizational Image and Pharmaceutical Regulation at the FDA* (Princeton, NJ: Princeton University Press, 2010), 20.

166. Quoted in Brian McKenna, "How Will Gillian Tett Connect with the Natives of the U.S. Left?," *CounterPunch*, March 4, 2011, http://www.counter punch.org/2011/03/04/how-will-gillian-tett-connect-with-the-natives-of-the -us-left/.

167. Consider, for instance, the cutting analysis from Erik Banks's pre-scient *The Failure of Wall Street*, which describes "financial controllers and au-ditors who don't understand the nature of the business they are meant to be 'independently monitoring,'" and trading desks which have little sense of "what kind of credit risks they are exposed to." Erik Banks, *The Failure of Wall Street: How and Why Wall Street Fails—And What Can Be Done about It* (New York: Palgrave Macmillan, 2004).

168. Bruno Latour, *Reassembling the Social: An Introduction to Actor-Network-Theory* (New York: Oxford University Press, 2005), 245.

169. Benjamin Kunkel, "Forgive Us Our Debts," *London Review of Books* 34, no. 9 (May 10, 2012): 23–29. Available at http://www.lrb.co.uk/v34/n09/benjamin -kunkel/forgive-us-our-debts.

170. Michael Hudson, *The Bubble and Beyond: Fictitious Capital, Debt Defla-tion, and Global Crisis* (Dresden: Islet, 2012).

171. Matt Taibbi, *Griftopia: A Story of Bankers, Politicians, and the Most Audacious Power Grab in American History* (New York: Spiegel & Grau, 2010).

172. Alan D. Morrison, *Investment Banking: Institutions, Politics, and Law* (New York: Oxford University Press, 2008).

# 5

## Watching (and Improving) the Watchers

1. Frank Pasquale, "Reputation Regulation: Disclosure and the Challenge of Clandestinely Commensurating Computing," in *The Offensive Internet: Speech, Privacy, and Reputation*, ed. Saul Levmore and Martha C. Nussbaum (Cambridge, MA: Harvard University Press, 2010), 107–123; Oren Bracha and Frank Pasquale, "Federal Search Commission: Access, Fairness, and Accountability in the Law of Search," *Cornell Law Review*, 93 (2008): 1149–1210.

2. Stephen Breyer, *Breaking the Vicious Circle: Toward Effective Risk Regulation* (Cambridge, MA: Harvard University Press, 1993), 70 (complaining that Carter-era "interagency regulatory liaison group" had inadequate staff and support, and pointing to other nations' coordinating mechanisms as models).

3. Preston Thomas, "Little Brother's Big Book: The Case for a Right of Audit in Private Databases," *CommLaw Conspectus* 18 (2009): 155–198 (weighing "the various components of a right of audit, suggesting those that are truly central to establishing an effective right").

4. Archon Fung, Mary Graham, and David Weil, *Full Disclosure: The Perils and Promise of Transparency* (New York: Cambridge University Press, 2007).

5. Former FTC Chairman Jon Leibowitz admitted as much, conceding that "we all agree that consumers don't read privacy policies" even though they've been a cornerstone of his agency's enforcement strategy. Jon Leibowitz, Chairman, Federal Trade Commission, "Introductory Remarks at the FTC Privacy Roundtable" (Dec. 2009). Available at http://www.ftc.gov/speeches/lei bowitz/091207privacyremarks.pdf . As law professor Fred H. Cate observes, this is "a remarkable acknowledgement from the U.S. federal agency that has probably done the most to promote [privacy policies]." Fred H. Cate, "Protecting Privacy in Health Research: The Limits of Individual Choice," *California Law Review* 98 (2010): 1772.

6. Margaret Jane Radin, *Boilerplate: The Fine Print, Vanishing Rights, and the Rule of Law* (Princeton, NJ: Princeton University Press, 2013), 116.

7. M. Ryan Calo, "Against Notice Skepticism in Privacy (and Elsewhere)," *Notre Dame Law Review* 87 (2012): 1027–1072.

8. Daniel J. Solove, "Introduction: Privacy Self-Management and the Consent Dilemma," *Harvard Law Review* 126 (2013): 1880–1903 (critiquing consent theories of privacy).

9. Mark A. Lemley, "Terms of Use," *Minnesota Law Review* 91 (2006): 469 ("No one reads [many of these] forms of contract anyway . . ."); Yannis Bakos, Florencia Marotta-Wurgler, and David R. Trossen, "Does Anyone Read the Fine Print? Consumer Attention to Standard Form Contracts," *Journal of Legal Studies* 43 (2014): 1–35.

10. Timothy J. Muris, Chair, Federal Trade Commission, "Protecting Consumers' Privacy: 2002 and Beyond." Remarks at the Privacy 2001 Conference (Oct. 2001). Available at http://www.ftc.gov/public-statements/2001/10/protecting-consumers-privacy-2002-and-beyond (describing futility of notices).

11. Alexis C. Madrigal, "Reading the Privacy Policies You Encounter in a Year Would Take 76 Work Days," *The Atlantic*, March 1, 2012, http://www.theatlantic.com/technology/archive/2012/03/reading-the-privacy-policies-you-encounter-in-a-year-would-take-76-work-days/253851/.

12. "Facebook Settles FTC Charges That It Deceived Consumers by Failing to Keep Privacy Promises," *Federal Trade Commission*, November 29, 2011. Available at http://www.ftc.gov/opa/2011/11/privacysettlement.shtm.

13. I borrow the term "lords of the cloud" from Jaron Lanier. Lanier, *You Are Not a Gadget* (New York: Alfred A. Knopf, 2011), xiii.

14. Casey Johnston, "Data Broker Won't Even Tell the Government How It Uses, Sells Your Data." *Ars Technica* (blog), December 21, 2013, http://arstechnica.com/business/2013/12/data-brokers-wont-even-tell-the-government-how-it-uses-sells-your-data/.

15. Standards of data access in health care are a critical part of the rollout of electronic health record subsidies. Eligible providers who receive government subsidies (or who merely want to avoid penalties after 2015) provide patients with digital files containing health information (including test results, medication lists, illnesses, and allergies), upon request, and provide clinical summaries for patients for each office visit. Frank Pasquale, "Grand Bargains for Big Data: The Emerging Law of Health Information," *Maryland Law Review* 72 (2013): 682–772.

16. Woodrow Hartzog, "Chain-Link Confidentiality," *Georgia Law Review* 46 (2012): 657–704.

17. Though anyone with a smartphone controls data about others, the requirements would not apply to everyone, of course. Regulation might begin by focusing on for-profit corporations possessing 5,000 or more unique records to be subject to certain transparency and disclosure requirements.

18. Though we should not underestimate the ingenuity of developers' devoted to correcting misinformation. See, e.g., Brian Fung, "Retwact: A Tool for Fixing Twitter's Misinformation Problem," *Atlantic*, April 30, 2013, http://www.theatlantic.com/technology/archive/2013/04/retwact-a-tool-for-fixing-twitters-misinformation-problem/275418/.

19. For a sense of the rigors of health privacy law with respect to data transfers, see Frank Pasquale and Tara Adams Ragone, "The Future of HIPAA in the Cloud," *Stanford Technology Law Review* (forthcoming, 2015).

20. Note that the FCRA itself must also be expanded, given the many exceptions and loopholes it contains. For a sense of the legal landscape here, see Richard Fischer, *The Law of Financial Privacy* (New York: LexisNexis, 2013), 1-133 to 1-135 (describing obligations of users of credit reports).

21. Ryan Calo, "Digital Market Manipulation," *George Washington Law Review* (forthcoming 2014). Draft available at http://papers.ssrn.com/sol3/papers.cfm?abstract_id=2309703.

22. Federal Rules of Evidence, Rule 407, 88 Stat. 1932 (2011 edition).

23. Sharona Hoffman, "Employing E-Health: The Impact of Electronic Health Records on the Workplace," *Kansas Journal of Law and Public Policy* 19 (2010): 409–432. Indeed, this may be happening now (but don't expect bosses to reveal these predictive methods to employees—it might hurt morale).

24. Kate Crawford and Jason Schultz, "Big Data and Due Process: Toward a Framework to Redress Predictive Privacy Harms," *Boston College Law Review* 55 (2014): 93–128.

25. Both legislation and regulation shaped the rise of the reason codes by effectively determining that release of the *top four* factors affecting a credit score in the case of adverse action would generate enough "reason-giving" to make discriminatory action evident. 15 U.S.C. § 1681g(f)(1)(c) (2012). The Fair Credit Reporting Act requires that consumers receive some account of why their credit reports might have led to a denial of credit. Under the FCRA, whenever a creditor takes an "adverse action" against a consumer, that creditor is required to provide the consumer with a notice explaining that action. 15 U.S.C. § 1681m(a) (2012); 15 U.S.C. § 1681a(k) (2012). An adverse action might also include a denial, cancellation, increased charge, reduction, or change in insurance or an adverse employment decision. § 1681a(k); see also Julie J.R. Huygen, "After the Deal Is Done: Debt Collection and Credit Reporting," *Air Force Law Review* 47 (1999): 102–103. In *Safeco Insurance Company of America v. Burr*, the U.S. Supreme Court, considering insurance rates, determined that the term "adverse action" in the FCRA "speaks to a disadvantageous rate even with no prior dealing; the term reaches initial rates for new applicants." 551 U.S. 47, 63 (2007).

26. Lawrence Lessig, *Code: And Other Laws of Cyberspace* (New York: Basic Books, 2000).

27. In 2006, the Eastern District Court of Pennsylvania, in *Pettineo v. Harleysville National Bank and Trust Company*, introduced the "general transparency test" to determine if the creditor's language in a rejection is adequate. The court stated, "Notice provisions of the ECOA and its implementing regulations do not require that the notification letter be narrowly tailored to fit the specific instance of a denied application." Pettineo v. Harleysville National Bank and Trust Co., No. Civ. A. 05-4138, 2006 WL 241243, at *3 (E.D. Pa. Jan. 31, 2006). And in *Aikens v. Northwestern Dodge, Inc.*, the court reached a similar decision. No. 03-C-7956, 2006 WL 59408 (N.D. Ill. Jan. 5, 2006). In *Higgins v. JC Penney, Inc.*, plaintiff argued that rejection on the basis of "type of bank accounts" and the "type of credit references" were not specific enough. The *Higgins* court reasoned that the statements were not ambiguous because they resembled some of those listed in the regulation. 630 F. Supp. 722, 725 (E.D. Mo. 1986).

28. Office of Inspector General, Department of Health and Human Services, *Fiscal Year 2008 Annual Performance Report* (2008), 2. Available at http://oig.hhs.gov/publications/docs/budget/FY2008_APR.pdf.

29. Frank Pasquale, "Industrial Policy for Big Data," Technology Academics Policy,

30. American Recovery and Reinvestment Act of 2009 (ARRA), Pub. L. No. 111-5, 123 Stat. 115; Mark Faccenda and Lara Parkin, "Meaningful Use—

What Does It Mean to You?," *Health Lawyer* 23, No. 3 (2011): 10–19 (citing ARRA, Title IV, Subtitles A and B).

31. Frank Pasquale, "Grand Bargains for Big Data." About $30 billion in subsidies were appropriated for this purpose. "CMS Medicare and Medicaid EHR Incentive Programs Milestone Timeline," *Centers for Medicare and Medicaid Services* (November 15, 2010). Available at https://www.cms.gov/EHRIn centivePrograms/Downloads/EHRIncentProgtimeline508V1.pdf. Bob Brown, "What Is a 'Certified EHR'?," *Journal of Health Care Compliance* 12, No. 1 (2010): 31–67. See generally Nicolas P. Terry, "Certification and Meaningful Use: Reframing Adoption of Electronic Records as a Quality Imperative," *Indiana Health Law Review* 8 (2011): 45–70 (examining meaningful use as the condition for receiving EHR subsidy funds).

32. Cloud computing transfers "application software and server-based databases to centralized, large data centers." Jared A. Harshbarger, "Cloud Computing Providers and Data Security Law," *Journal of Technology Law and Policy* 16 (2011): 230–231.

33. David A. Moss, *When All Else Fails: Government as the Ultimate Risk Manager* (Cambridge, MA: Harvard University Press, 1999).

34. Richard A. Posner, *A Failure of Capitalism: The Crisis of '08 and the Descent into Depression* (Cambridge, MA: Harvard University Press, 2009); Andrew Ross Sorkin, *Too Big to Fail: The Inside Story of How Wall Street and Washington Fought to Save the Financial System—and Themselves* (New York: Viking Penguin, 2009).

35. Danielle Keats Citron, "Cyber Civil Rights," *Boston University Law Review* 89 (2009): 61–126.

36. Cathy O'Neil, "Let Them Game the Model," *MathBabe* (blog), February 3, 2012, http://mathbabe.org/2012/02/03/let-them-game-the-model/. Even if gaming persists, it, too, can be addressed by regulation. Tal Z. Zarsky, "Law and Online Social Networks: Mapping the Challenges and Promises of User-Generated Information Flows," *Fordham Intellectual Property, Media, and Entertainment Law Journal* 18 (2008): 780.

37. The American Civil Liberties Union has posted stories of police surveillance and obstruction of First Amendment–protected activity in over half the states. ACLU, *Spying on First Amendment Activity—State by State*, December 19, 2012. Available at https://www.aclu.org/files/assets/spying_on_first _amendment_activity_12.19.12_update.pdf.

38. Barack Obama, Remarks by the President on Review of Signals Intelligence, January 17, 2014. Available at http://www.whitehouse.gov/the-press -office/2014/01/17/remarks-president-review-signals-intelligence.

39. Some advocates assure us that "if the NSA ever does start blackmailing people, the information will come out because you can't blackmail someone without talking to him." Eric Posner, "The NSA's Metadata Program Is Perfectly Constitutional," *Slate*, December 30, 2013, http://www.slate.com/arti cles/news_and_politics/view_from_chicago/2013/12/judge_pauley_got_it _right_the_nsa_s_metadata_program_is_perfectly_constitutional.2.html. But no monitoring system should rely on individuals to risk embarrassment, condemnation, jail, or worse, to report wrongdoing.

40. Lawrence Rosenthal, "First Amendment Investigations and the Inescapable Pragmatism of the Common Law of Free Speech," *Indiana Law Journal* 86 (2011): 37.

41. For an insightful account of the Church Committee investigation, see Frederick A. O. Schwarz, Jr., and Aziz Z. Huq, *Unchecked and Unbalanced: Presidential Power in a Time of Terror* (New York: The New Press, 2011), 32–52 (describing the Church Committee's exposure of hundreds of abuses of domestic intelligence gathering, under the leadership of Idaho Senator Frank Church).

42. See Hanna Fenichel Pitkin, *The Attack of the Blob: Hannah Arendt's Concept of the Social* (Chicago: University of Chicago Press, 1998), 6–7. ("The real-world problem that Arendt intended her concept of the social to address . . . concerns the gap between our enormous, still-increasing powers and our apparent helplessness to avert the various disasters—national, regional, and global—looming on our horizon.")

43. Marc Rotenberg, "Privacy and Secrecy after September 11," in *Bombs and Bandwidth: The Emerging Relationship between Information Technology and Security*, ed. Robert Latham (New York: The New Press, 2003), 138–139.

44. See generally Danielle Keats Citron, "Mainstreaming Privacy Torts," *California Law Review* 98 (2010): 1805–1852.

45. See Danielle Keats Citron, "Technological Due Process," *Washington University Law Review* 85 (2008): 1305–1306.

46. David Singh Grewal, *Network Power: The Social Dynamics of Globalization* (New Haven, CT: Yale University Press, 2009), 21.

47. Criminal Intelligence Systems Operating Policies, 28 C.F.R. 20.23 (2013). Although federal regulation requires audit logs, evidence suggests that existing fusion centers do not comply with this requirement. *Protecting National Security and Civil Liberties: Strategies for Terrorism Information Sharing: Hearing before the Subcomm. on Terrorism, Technology, and Homeland Security of the S. Comm. on the Judiciary*, 111th Cong. 46 (2009) (statement of Zoë Baird, President, Markle Foundation).

48. Markle Task Force on National Security in the Information Age, "Implementing a Trusted Information Sharing Environment: Using Immutable Audit Logs to Increase Security, Trust, and Accountability" (New York: Markle Foundation, 2006), 1. Available at http://research.policyarchive.org/15551.pdf [hereinafter Markle Task Force].

49. Ibid., 2.

50. Reform suggestions are from Markle Task Force report. Ibid., 2. See also Viktor Mayer-Schönberger, *Delete: The Virtue of Forgetting in the Digital Age* (Princeton, NJ: Princeton University Press, 2011), 65, 71.

51. National Human Genome Research Institute, *Review of the Ethical, Legal and Social Implications Research Program and Related Activities* (1990–1995), at http://www.genome.gov/10001747 (noting rationale for the ELSI program, including worries that "mapping and sequencing the human genome would have profound implications for individuals, families, and society. . . . and concern that information would be gained that might result in anxiety, stigmatization and discrimination.").

52. Even John Poindexter, proponent of the controversial data-mining proposal called "Total Information Awareness," embraced the use of immutable audit logs. Shane Harris, *The Watchers: The Rise of America's Surveillance State* (New York: Penguin, 2010), 190. (John Poindexter "proposed an 'immutable audit trail,' a master record of every analyst who had used the TIA [Total Information Awareness] system, what data they'd touched, and what they'd done with it . . . to spot suspicious patterns of use. . . . Poindexter wanted to use TIA to watch the watchers.")

53. Jeff Jonas and Jeff Rosenzweig have argued the "no fly" database should provide "tethering and full attribution of data to allow corrections to propagate through the system." Paul Rosenzweig and Jeff Jonas, "Correcting False Positives: Redress and the Watch List Conundrum," *Heritage Foundation Legal Memorandum*, June 17, 2005, 1. Available at http://s3.amazonaws.com/thf _media/2005/pdf/lm17.pdf.

54. There are several examples of the overly broad "dragnet" in which e-mail surveillance can result. See, e.g., Harris, *The Watchers*, 112 (describing how Condoleezza Rice and William Cohen were included as "persons of interest" based on "Operation Able Danger").

55. David Auerbach, "The Stupidity of Computers," *n+1 Magazine*, July 5, 2012, http://nplusonemag.com/the-stupidity-of-computers. See also Xeni Jardin, "U.S. Drones Could Be Killing the Wrong People Because of Metadata Errors," *BoingBoing*, February 10, 2014, http://boingboing.net/2014/02/10/us -drones-could-be-killing-the.html; John Bowman, "Database: Text of Canadian Cables in Wikileaks," *CBC News*, December 2, 2010, http://www.cbc.ca /m/touch/news/story/1.918412.

56. Helen Nissenbaum, "Privacy as Contextual Integrity," *Washington Law Review* 79 (2004): 155.

57. For more on the Church Committee investigation, see Schwarz and Huq, *Unchecked and Unbalanced: Presidential Power in a Time of Terror*, 32–52.

58. House Judiciary Committee, *Competition on the Internet*, 110th Cong., July 15, 2008, 5:16–5:20 (video; opening remarks by the committee chair, John Conyers).

59. George Packer, "Amazon and the Perils of Nondisclosure," *New Yorker*, February 12, 2014, http://www.newyorker.com/online/blogs/books/2014/02 /the-perils-of-non-disclosure.html.

60. I don't even raise the possibility of the site owner knowing whether it is in the top-five results generally, because, in an era of personalization, only Google can know that. At present, we can only hope for relatively good sampling of sites.

61. Of course, if Google were hell bent on avoiding scrutiny, it would respond to a "sudden drop" trigger by dropping companies gradually. A trusted third party should be able to note those trends, too, and recommend appropriate countermeasures. See, for example, Frank Pasquale, "Beyond Innovation and Competition: The Need for Qualified Transparency in Internet Intermediaries," *Northwestern University Law Review* 104 (2010): 105–174. And to the extent large Internet or finance firms recalcitrantly avoid or evade the regulatory measures proposed in this chapter, the more extensive proposals discussed in my concluding chapter should become more compelling.

62. Patterson, "Manipulation of Product Ratings: Credit-Rating Agencies, Google, and Antitrust," *Competition Policy International*, April 17, 2012, https://www.competitionpolicyinternational.com/manipulation-of-product-ratings-credit-rating-agencies-google-and-antitrust/ (internal quotation marks omitted).

63. The rise of "computer assisted reporting" should also boost journalistic efforts here. Nicholas Diakopoulos, *Algorithmic Accountability Reporting: On the Investigation of Black Boxes* (New York: Tow Center for Digital Journalism, 2014).

64. Seth Stevenson, "How New Is 'New'? How Improved is 'Improved'?" *Slate*, July 13, 2009, http://www.slate.com/articles/business/ad_report_card/2009/07/how_new_is_new_how_improved_is_improved.html.

65. Joshua Hazan, "Stop Being Evil: A Proposal for Unbiased Google Search," *Michigan Law Review* 111 (2013): 791 (arguing that "Google's conduct does in fact violate § 2 of the Sherman Act and § 5 of the FTC Act"). Nathan Newman, "Search, Antitrust, and the Economics of the Control of User Data," August 13, 2013, 1. Available at http://papers.ssrn.com/sol3/papers.cfm?abstract_id=2309547 ("what is largely missed in analyses defending Google from antitrust action is how that ever expanding control of user personal data and its critical value to online advertisers creates an insurmountable barrier to entry for new competition"). Benjamin Edelman, "Bias in Search Results?: Diagnosis and Response," *Indian Journal of Law and Technology* 7 (2011): 16–32, 30.

66. Search engines rank websites at least in part by algorithmically processing signals from the site (such as the number of links to it, the number of links to those links, whether users have clicked on the site when it was ranked in search results previously, etc.). Let's say that, for whatever reason, Google's technology fails to pick up on all the signals relating to a given website. The webmaster for the site might complain, and may well get a response.

67. Mark Patterson, "Search Engine Objectivity," *Concurring Opinions* (blog), November 23, 2013, http://www.concurringopinions.com/archives/2013/11/search-engine-objectivity.html; Greg Sterling, "EU Antitrust Chief Says Google Settlement Essentially Done," *Search Engine Land*, March 18, 2014.

68. David A. Hyman and David J. Franklin, "Search Neutrality and Search Bias: An Empirical Perspective on the Impact of Architecture and Labeling," Illinois Program in Law, Behavior and Social Science Paper No. LE13-24, May 8, 2013. Available at https://papers.ssrn.com/sol3/papers.cfm?abstract_id=2260942. The study was funded indirectly, in part, by Microsoft.

69. Jeff Bliss and Sara Forden, "Google Antitrust Probe Said to Expand as FTC Demands Information," *Bloomberg*, August 13, 2011, http://www.bloomberg.com/news/2011-08-12/google-probe-expands-as-ftc-demands-information.html.

70. See, for example, Sara Forden and Jeff Bliss, "Google Antitrust Suit Said to Be Urged by FTC Staffers," *Bloomberg*, October 13, 2012, http://www.bloomberg.com/news/2012-10-12/google-antitrust-suit-said-to-be-urged-by-ftc-staffers.html.

71. Allen Grunes, "Is There a Basis in Antitrust Law for Requiring 'Neutral' Search Results?," *Antitrust and Competition Policy Blog*, May 21, 2012,

http://lawprofessors.typepad.com/antitrustprof_blog/2012/05/is-there-a-basis
-in-antitrust-law-for-requiring-neutral-search-results-comments-of-allen
-grunes-.html.

72. The company had friends in high places, including Senator Ron Wyden. Declan McCullagh, "Senator Blasts Leaks in FTC's Google Investigation," *CNET*, January 9, 2013, http://news.cnet.com/8301-13578_3-57563103 -38/senator-blasts-leaks-in-ftcs-google-investigation/. Google was the fourth-largest donor to Wyden's campaign committee from 2007 to 2012. Center for Responsive Politics, "Data Available for Ron Wyden," *OpenSecrets*. http://www .opensecrets.org/politicians/contrib.php?cycle=2012&type=I&cid=N00007724 &newMem=N&recs=20 (accessed February 12, 2014).

73. Google, "Commitments in Case COMP/C-3/39.740." Available at http://ec.europa.eu/competition/antitrust/cases/dec_docs/39740/39740_8608 _5.pdf.

74. See Edward Wyatt, "Critics of Google Antitrust Ruling Fault the Focus," *New York Times*, January 6, 2013, http://www.nytimes.com/2013/01/07 /technology/googles-rivals-say-ftc-antitrust-ruling-missed-the-point.html.

75. See Stephen Shankland, "Watchdog Seeks FTC Staff Opinion on Google Antitrust Case," *CNET*, January 8, 2013, http://news.cnet.com/8301 -1023_3-57562841-93/watchdog-seeks-ftc-staff-opinion-on-google-antitrust -case/.

76. Wyatt, "Critics of Google Antitrust Ruling Fault the Focus."

77. See Pasquale, "Beyond Innovation and Competition," 105.

78. Elizabeth Van Couvering, "Is Relevance Relevant? Market, Science, and War: Discourses of Search Engine Quality," *Journal of Computer-Mediated Communication* 12 (2007): 866–887.

79. Daniel A. Crane, "Search Neutrality as a Neutrality Principle," *George Mason Law Review* 19 (2012): 1199–1210.

80. Thomas Frank, *The Wrecking Crew: How Conservatives Ruined Government, Enriched Themselves, and Beggared the Nation* (New York: Henry Holt, 2008).

81. Jennifer Chandler, "A Right to Reach an Audience: An Approach to Intermediary Bias on the Internet," *Hofstra Law Review* 35 (2007): 1095–1138.

82. Langdon v. Google, 474 F. Supp. 2d 622 (D. Del. 2007); Kinderstart .com LLC, v. Google, Inc., No. C 06-2057 JF (RS), 2007 WL 831806 (N.D. Cal. Mar. 16, 2007); Search King v. Google Technologies, No. CIV-02- 1457-M, 2003 WL 21464568, at *4 (W.D. Okla. May 27, 2003).

83. Dahlia Lithwick, "Google-Opoly: The Game No One but Google Can Play," *Slate*, January 29, 2003. Available at http://www.slate.com/articles /news_and_politics/jurisprudence/2003/01/googleopoly_the_game_no_one _but_google_can_play.html.

84. *Search King*, 2003 WL 21464568, at *4.

85. Associated Press v. United States, 326 U.S. 1, 20 (1945) (internal quotes omitted).

86. Lorain Journal Co. v. United States, 342 U.S. 143, 155 (1951). ("The publisher claims a right as a private business concern to select its customers and to refuse to accept advertisement from whomever it pleases. . . . [But the]

right claimed by the publisher is neither absolute nor exempt from regulation. Its exercise as a purposeful means of monopolizing interstate commerce is prohibited by the Sherman Act.")

87. Eugene Volokh and Donald M. Falk, "Google: First Amendment Protection for Search Engine Search Results," *Journal of Law, Economics and Policy* 8 (2012): 883–900.

88. James Temple, "Foundem Takes On Google's Search Methods," *SF Gate*, June 26, 2011, http://www.sfgate.com/business/article/Foundem-takes -on-Google-s-search-methods-2366725.php.

89. On how a low Google ranking can spell disaster for many firms, see Spencer, "SEO Report Card: The Google Death Sentence." For more on the relation between antitrust law and First Amendment law, see Wayne Overbeck and Genelle Belmas, *Major Principles of Media Law* (Boston: Wadsworth, 2010), 508–510; Christopher L. Sagers, "The Legal Structure of American Freedom and the Provenance of the Antitrust Immunities," *Utah Law Review* (2002): 927–972.

90. Mark Patterson, "Additional Online Search Comments," *Antitrust and Competition Policy Blog*, May 23, 2012, http://lawprofessors.typepad.com/anti trustprof_blog/2012/05/additional-online-search-comments-by-mark-patter son.html. Of course, I can't verify Foundem's claims independently—the black box nature of search algorithms makes that impossible. But even if one thinks Google's rationale for Foundem's exclusion is more plausible—i.e., that other offerings were far better than Foundem's—we cannot simply take Google's word for it.

91. Sometimes the results would be presented like a search engine results page. In other situations, doctors were presented alphabetically, but with stars indicating a "quality rating," much like the starred ratings restaurants receive from reviewers. Health insurer Wellpoint even hired a restaurant rating firm to help it. Note that Google has also gotten into this business, buying Zagat.

92. Frank Pasquale, "Grand Bargains for Big Data."

93. As the 10th Circuit said in *Jefferson Cty. School District v. Moody's*, the ratings agencies are often considered members of the media, and "at least in situations . . . where a media defendant is involved . . . a statement on matters of public concern must be provable as false before there can be liability under state defamation law."

94. James Grimmelmann, "The Structure of Search Engine Law," *Iowa Law Review* 93 (2007): 1–60; James Grimmelmann, "Speech Engines," *Minnesota Law Review* 98 (2014): 874.

95. Frank Pasquale, "From First Amendment Absolutism to Financial Meltdown?" *Concurring Opinions* (blog), August 22, 2007, http://www.concur-ringopinions.com/archives/2007/08/from_first_amen.html#. Ben Hallman, "S&P Lawsuit First Amendment Defense May Fare Poorly Experts Say," *Huffington Post*, February 4, 2013, http://www.huffingtonpost.com/2013/02/04/sp -lawsuit-first-amendment_n_2618737.html. Alison Frankel, "Will CDO Investors' Deal Boost Litigation against Ratings Agencies?," Reuters (blog), April 29, 2013, http://blogs.reuters.com/alison-frankel/2013/04/29/will-cdo-investors -deal-boost-litigation-against-rating-agencies/.

96. Ibid.

97. Jack Balkin, "Information Fiduciaries in the Digital Age," *Balkinization*, March 5, 2014, at http://balkin.blogspot.com/2014/03/information-fiduciaries-in-digital-age.html.

98. Jennifer Taub, "Great Expectations for the Office of Financial Research," in *Will It Work? How Will We Know? The Future of Financial Reform*, ed. Michael Konczal (New York: Roosevelt Institute, 2011).

99. Office of Financial Research, *2013 Annual Report* (Dec. 2013), 72. Available at http://www.treasury.gov/initiatives/ofr/about/Documents/OFR_AnnualReport2013_FINAL_12-17-2013_Accessible.pdf.

100. See, for example, Office of Financial Research, *Policy Statement on Legal Entity Identification for Financial Contracts* (Nov. 2010). Available at http://www.treasury.gov/initiatives/Documents/OFR-LEI_Policy_Statement-FINAL.PDF.

101. CFTC and SEC Staff, *Joint Study on the Feasibility of Mandating Algorithmic Descriptions for Derivatives.*

102. U.S. Securities and Exchange Commission (SEC) and the U.S. Commodity Futures Trading Commission (CFTC), "Joint Study on the Feasibility of Mandating Algorithmic Descriptions for Derivatives," April 7, 2011. Available at http://www.sec.gov/news/studies/2011/719b-study.pdf. Unfortunately, after considering the vagaries of accounting, securitization, and credit rating described above, it is difficult to credit the SEC's optimism here. Just as the FDIC's hypothetical resolution of Lehman "amused many by its naïveté," the staff appears to be promoting an aspiration as a likely achievement. Stephen J. Lubben, "Resolution, Orderly and Otherwise: B of A in OLA," *University of Cincinnati Law Review* 81 (2012): 485–486. ("The Federal Deposit Insurance Corporation [FDIC or Corporation], keen to demonstrate its competency to wield the new powers given it under Dodd–Frank, rushed to produce a hypothetical resolution of Lehman that amused many by its naïveté.") Harry Surden, "Computable Contracts," *University of California Davis Law Review* 46 (2012): 629–700.

103. See, for example, U.S. Securities and Exchange Commission, "SEC Approves New Rule Requiring Consolidated Audit Trail to Monitor and Analyze Trading Activity," July 18, 2011 (news release), http://www.sec.gov/news/press/2012/2012-134.htm.

104. They will face resistance. One witness called by House Republicans characterized OFR monitors as "Soviet-style central planners." Nassim N. Taleb, "Report on the Effectiveness and Possible Side Effects of the Office of Financial Research (OFR)," http://financialservices.house.gov/UploadedFiles/071411nassim.pdf. Accessed February 15, 2014.

105. Alain Deneault, *Offshore: Tax Havens and the Rule of Global Crime* (New York: The New Press, 2011).

106. Foreign Account Tax Compliance Act (FATCA) in 2010 as part of the Hiring Incentives to Restore Employment Act, Pub. L. No. 111–147, 124 Stat. 71 (2010) (codified at 26 U.S.C. §§ 1471–1474). The law is effective as of 2014.

107. James S. Henry, *The Price of Offshore Revisited* (Chesham, Buckinghamshire, UK: Tax Justice Network, 2012), 3. Available at http://www.taxjustice.net/cms/upload/pdf/Price_of_Offshore_Revisited_120722.pdf

108. Itai Grinberg, "Beyond FATCA: An Evolutionary Moment for the International Tax System" (Jan. 2012), 3, 23. Available at http://papers.ssrn.com /sol3/papers.cfm?abstract_id=1996752.

109. J. Richard (Dick) Harvey, Jr., "Offshore Accounts: Insider's Summary of FATCA and Its Potential Future," *Villanova Law Review* 57 (2012): 474. The overall goal was to "deter and identify patterns suggestive of the use of offshore accounts to evade tax on domestic income earned by closely held businesses." Ibid., 487.

110. Leigh Goessl, "Swiss Government Weakens Bank Secrecy to Give U.S. Officials Info," *Digital Journal*, May 30, 2013, http://digitaljournal.com /article/351155. David Voreacos et al., "Swiss Banks Said Ready to Pay Billions, Disclose Customer Names," *Bloomberg*, October 24, 2011, http://www.bloom berg.com/news/2011-10-24/swiss-banks-said-ready-to-pay-billions-disclose -customer-names.html.

111. Ronen Palan, Richard Murphy, and Christian Chavagneux, *Tax Havens: How Globalization Really Works* (Ithaca, NY: Cornell University Press, 2010), 272; Raymond Baker, *Capitalism's Achilles Heel: Dirty Money and How to Renew the Free-Market System* (Hoboken, NJ: John Wiley & Sons, Inc., 2005).

112. 26 U.S.C. §§ 1471(c)(1).

113. Grinberg, "Beyond FATCA," 24.

114. Ibid.

115. Charles H. Ferguson, *Predator Nation: Corporate Criminals, Political Corruption, and the Hijacking of America* (New York: Crown Publishing, 2012).

116. Ferguson lays out the following "reasonable list of prosecutable crimes committed during the financial crisis, and the aftermath period by financial services firms: securities fraud, accounting fraud, honest services violations, bribery, perjury and making false statements to federal investigators, Sarbanes-Oxley violations (certifying false accounting statements), RICO offenses and criminal antitrust violations, federal aid disclosure regulations (related to Federal Reserve loans), personal conduct offenses (many forms: drug use, tax evasion, etc)." Ibid., 190.

117. See, for example, Susan Will, Stephen Handelman, and David C. Brotherton, eds., *How They Got Away with It: White Collar Criminals and the Financial Meltdown* (New York: Columbia University Press, 2013).

118. Jed S. Rakoff, "The Financial Crisis: Why Have No High-Level Executives Been Prosecuted?" *New York Review of Books*, January 9, 2014, http:// www.nybooks.com/articles/archives/2014/jan/09/financial-crisis-why-no -executive-prosecutions/?pagination=false.

119. Breuer later left the Department for a job rumored to pay $4 million a year, at one of DC's top law firms, which counted many top banks among its clients. Mark Karlin, "Lanny Breuer Cashes In after Not Prosecuting Wall Street Execs," *Buzzflash*, March 28, 2013, http://www.truth-out.org/buzzflash /commentary/item/17885-lanny-breuer-cashes-in-after-not-prosecuting-wall -street-execs-will-receive-approximate-salary-of-4-million-dollars. For a general treatment of the problem of the revolving door and its worsening over the past two decades, see Lawrence Lessig, *Republic, Lost: How Money Corrupts Congress and How to Stop It* (New York: Hatchette Book Group, 2011).

120. Rakoff, "The Financial Crisis."

121. Ibid.

122. As law professor Kenneth Bamberger has explained, "automated systems—systems that governed loan originations, measured institutional risk, prompted investment decisions, and calculated capital-reserve levels— shielded irresponsible decisions, unreasonably risky speculation, and intentional manipulation, with a façade of regularity." Kenneth A. Bamberger, "Technologies of Compliance: Risk and Regulation in a Digital Age," *Texas Law Review* 88 (2010): 669–740.

123. Ashwin Parameswaran, "How to Commit Fraud and Get Away with It," *Macroresilience* (blog), December 4, 2013, http://www.macroresilience.com /2013/12/04/how-to-commit-fraud-and-get-away-with-it-a-guide-for-ceos/.

124. Rakoff, "The Financial Crisis."

125. Parameswaran, "How to Commit Fraud."

126. U.S. SEC v. Citigroup Global Mkts. Inc., 827 F. Supp. 2d 328, 332 (S.D.N.Y. 2011). Bill Singer, "Judge Rakoff Rejects SEC's 'Contrivances' in Citigroup Settlement," *Forbes*, November 29, 2011, http://www.forbes.com/sites /billsinger/2011/11/29/judge-rakoff-rejects-secs-contrivances-in-citigroup -settlement/.

127. A preliminary opinion (later affirmed) stated that Judge Rakoff had no "authority to demand assurance that a voluntary settlement reached between an administrative agency and a private party somehow reflects the facts that would be demonstrated at a trial." U.S. SEC v. Citigroup Global Markets, Inc., 673 F.3d 158, 166 (2d Cir. 2012). As Adrian Vermeule has observed in another context, the sheer size and complexity of the American bureaucracy makes it impossible for hundreds of federal judges to fully understand, let alone police, precisely how tens of thousands of federal enforcement officials decide to apply the law. Adrian Vermeule, "Our Schmittian Administrative Law," *Harvard Law Review* 122 (2009): 1095–1150.

128. Matt Taibbi, "Is the SEC Covering Up Wall Street Crimes?," *Rolling Stone*, August 17, 2011, http://www.rollingstone.com/politics/news/is-the-sec -covering-up-wall-street-crimes-20110817?print=true.

129. For example, agency critics like Harry Markopolos have berated it for years for failing to catch Bernie Madoff earlier; the (now-deleted) MUI file about him might have led to some accountability for the individuals who failed to follow up on complaints about Madoff. Harry Markopolos, *No One Would Listen: A True Financial Thriller* (Hoboken, NJ: John Wiley & Sons, Inc., 2010). Past bad behavior can contextualize current accusations. But such a process would also prove embarrassing to the agency itself. Undoubtedly, in some of those cases, materials related to an MUI could raise questions about why personnel involved failed to launch a full-fledged enforcement action.

130. Finance journalists chronicle a superclass shuttling from beltway to bourse and back. Taibbi, "Is the SEC Covering Up Wall Street Crimes?"; Yves Smith, "Sleaze Watch: NY Fed Official Responsible for AIG Loans Joins AIG as AIG Pushes Sweetheart Repurchase to NY Fed," *Naked Capitalism* (blog), March 22, 2011, http://www.nakedcapitalism.com/2011/03/sleaze-watch-ny -fed-official-responsible-for-aig-loans-joins-aig-shortly-before-aig-pitches -sweetheart-repurchase-to-ny-fed.html.

131. Project on Government Oversight (POGO), "POGO Database Tracks Revolving Door between SEC and Wall Street," May 13, 2011 (news release), http://www.pogo.org/about/press-room/releases/2011/fo-fra-20110513.html #sthash.HzMuYDLu.dpuf. Citizens for Responsibility and Ethics in Washington, the Center for Public Integrity, the Center for Effective Government, Public Citizen, and other watchdogs have also documented troubling revolving-door dynamics.

132. Erik F. Gerding, "The Dangers of Delegating Financial Regulation to Risk Models," *Banking and Financial Services Policy Report* 29, no. 4 (2010): 1–8.

133. William D. Cohan, "Why Are the Fed and SEC Keeping Wall Street's Secrets?," *Bloomberg*, April 1, 2012, http://www.bloomberg.com/news/2012-04 -01/why-are-the-fed-and-sec-keeping-wall-street-s-secrets-.html.

134. William D. Cohan, "A Bomb Squad for Wall Street," *New York Times Opinionator* (blog), January 21, 2010, http://opinionator.blogs.nytimes.com /2010/01/21/a-bomb-squad-for-wall-street/.

135. Simon Johnson and James Kwak, *13 Bankers: The Wall Street Takeover and the Next Financial Meltdown* (New York: Pantheon, 2010), 94; Center for Responsive Politics, "Report: Revolving Door Spins Quickly between Congress, Wall Street," *OpenSecrets Blog*, June 3, 2010),http://opensecrets.org/news /2010/06/report-revolving-door-spins-quickly.html.

136. "U.S. Senate Investigations Subcommittee Releases Levin-Coburn Report on the Financial Crisis," April 13, 2011 (news release), http://www.levin .senate.gov/newsroom/press/release/us-senate-investigations-subcommittee -releases-levin-coburn-report-on-the-financial-crisis.

137. "'Disappointing and Inspiring': Warren, Johnson, Black, and More React to FinReg," *Next New Deal* (blog), June 25, 2010, http://www.nextnew deal.net/disappointing-and-inspiring-warren-johnson-black-and-more-react -finreg.

138. The FDIC included "no press release" clauses in over 200 settlements related to bank failures accompanying the financial crisis. E. Scott Reckard, "FDIC Begins to Reveal Settlements Related to Financial Crisis," *Los Angeles Times*, March 19, 2013, http://articles.latimes.com/2013/mar/19/business/la-fi -fdic-settlements-20130319.

139. E. Scott Reckard, "In Major Policy Shift, Scores of FDIC Settlements Go Unannounced," *Los Angeles Times*, March 11, 2013, http://articles.latimes .com/2013/mar/11/business/la-fi-fdic-settlements-20130311.

140. Kara Scannell, "Law: The Inner Circle," *Financial Times*, May 21, 2013. The revolving door spun in the 1980s, too, but the financial rewards of private practice (relative to staying in government) have increased since the S&L debacle.

141. *Testimony on SEC Budget: Hearing before the House Subcommittee on Financial Services and General Government* (May 7, 2013) (statement of Mary White, Chair, SEC). Ben Protess, "White Makes Case for Bigger SEC Budget," *DealBook* (blog), May 7, 2013, http://dealbook.nytimes.com/2013/05/07/white -makes-case-for-bigger-s-e-c-budget.

142. Ryan Chittum, "The Regulators on the Bus: A *Times* Story Shows the Resources Gap between Regulators and Wall Street," *Columbia Journalism Re-*

*view*, May 4, 2011, http://www.cjr.org/the_audit/the_regulators_on_the_bus
_sec_cftc.php.

143. SEC chair Mary Schapiro, "Opening Statement at the SEC Open
Meeting—Consolidated Audit Trial," May 26, 2010. Available at http://www
.sec.gov/news/speech/2010/spch052610mls-audit.htm.

144. For income figure: compare SEC budget and Paulson's fortune, de-
scribed in Gregory Zuckerman, *The Greatest Trade Ever: The Behind-the-Scenes
Story of How John Paulson Defied Wall Street and Made Financial History* (repr.,
New York: Crown Business, 2010) (on Paulson's shorting of CDOs based on
RMBSes); see also David Rothkopf, *Power, Inc.: The Epic Rivalry between Big
Business and Government—And the Reckoning That Lies Ahead* (New York: Far-
rar, Straus and Giroux, 2012) (comparing the relative discretionary spending
power of firms and governments).

145. Ryan Grim, "Wall Street Blocked Elizabeth Warren from Her Consumer Protection Board and This Is What They Got," *Huffington Post Politics*,
February 17, 2013, http://www.huffingtonpost.com/2013/02/17/wall-street
-warren-video_n_2707016.html.

146. See Ben Protess, "U.S. Regulators Face Budget Pinch as Mandates
Widen," *DealBook* (blog), May 3, 2011, http://dealbook.nytimes.com/2011/05
/03/u-s-regulators-face-budget-pinch-as-mandates-widen/?ref=todayspaper.

147. Geoffrey Christopher Rapp, "Mutiny by the Bounties: The Attempt
to Reform Wall Street by the New Whistleblower Provisions of the Dodd-
Frank Act," *Brigham Young University Law Review* (2012): 124.

148. Leemore Dafny and David Dranove, "Regulatory Exploitation and
Management Changes: Upcoding in the Hospital Industry," *Journal of Law
and Economics* 52 (2009): 223–250. ("Billing –for services not rendered" is a
scheme wherein a bill is deliberately submitted for payment even though no
medical service was actually provided. "Upcoding," in contrast, is a scheme
wherein the health care providers submits a bill using a procedure code that
yields a higher payment than the code for the service that was truly rendered.)
Federal Bureau of Investigation, *Financial Crimes Report to the Public: 2010–2011*.
Available at http://www.fbi.gov/stats-services/publications/financial-crimes-re-
port-2010–2011. It is important to distinguish these two schemes, which are
committed deliberately, with inadvertent errors in coding for which "there are
no comprehensive statistics." Jessica Silver-Greenberg, "How to Fight a Bogus
Bill," *The Wall Street Journal*, February 18, 2011.

149. For example, see Thomas L. Greaney and Joan H. Krause, *"United
States v. Krizek: Rough Justice under the Civil False Claims Act,"* in *Health Law
and Bioethics: Cases in Context*, ed. Sandra H. Johnson, Joan H. Krause, Richard
S. Saver, and Robin Fretwell Wilson (New York: Aspen, 2009), 187, 199–200.

150. Alice G. Gosfield, *Medicare and Medicaid Fraud and Abuse* (New York:
Thomson West, 2012), § 1:4.

151. Ibid.

152. For the "bust" model, see U.S. Department of Justice, Office of Public
Affairs, "Dallas Doctor Arrested for Alleged Role in Nearly $375 Million Health
Care Fraud Scheme," February 28, 2012 (news release), http://www.justice.gov
/opa/pr/2012/February/12-crm-260.html.

153. See Eric Posner and E. Glen Weyl, "An FDA for Financial Innovation: Applying the Insurable Interest Doctrine to 21st Century Financial Markets," *Northwestern University Law Review* 107 (2013): 1307–1358. (The agency would approve financial products if they satisfy a test for social utility that focuses on whether the product will likely be used more often for insurance than for gambling. Other factors may be addressed if the answer is ambiguous.") Saule T. Omarova, "License to Deal: Mandatory Approval of Complex Financial Products," *Washington University Law Review* 90 (2012), 63.

154. Todd Zywicki, "Plain Vanilla through the Back Door," *Volokh Conspiracy* (blog), September 12, 2013, http://www.volokh.com/2013/09/12/cfpb -plain-vanilla-back-door/.

155. Sara Kay Wheeler, Stephanie L. Fuller, and J. Austin Broussard, "Meet the Fraud Busters: Program Safeguard Contractors and Zone Program Integrity Contractors," *Journal of Health and Life Sciences Law* 4 (2011): 1–35 (citing 42 C.F.R. §§ 421.100 (FIs), 421.200 (carriers), 421.210 (DMERCs) and describing the functions of each); see also Centers for Medicare and Medicaid Services, *Medicare Program Integrity Manual* § 1.3.6 (2009); 42 C.F.R. § 421.304 (describing the function of Medicare Integrity Program Contractors).

156. Office of the Inspector General, *Fiscal Year 2008 Annual Performance Report* (Washington, DC: Department of Health and Human Services, 2008), 2. Available at http://oig.hhs.gov/publications/docs/budget/FY2008_APR.pdf.

157. Rebecca S. Busch, *Healthcare Fraud: Auditing and Detection Guide* (Hoboken, NJ: John Wiley & Sons, 2012), 52 (discussing "15 layers of fragmentation" in health care). Robert Radick, "Claims Data and Health Care Fraud: The Controversy Continues," *Forbes*, September 25, 2012, http://www.forbes.com/sites /insider/2012/09/25/claims-data-and-health-care-fraud-the-controversy-con tinues. "New Technology to Help Fight Medicare Fraud," *Fierce HealthIT*, June 22, 2011 (news release), http://www.fiercehealthit.com/press-releases/new -technology-help-fight-medicare-fraud.

158. Gosfield, *Fraud & Abuse*, § 6:13.

159. Ibid.

160. Ibid.

161. See Office of the Inspector General, *The Medicare-Medicaid (Medi-Medi) Data Match Program* (Washington, DC: Department of Health and Human Services, 2012). Available at https://oig.hhs.gov/oei/reports/oei-09-08 -00370.asp.

162. See 18 U.S.C. § 1347; 18 U.S.C. § 24; Medicare-Medicaid Anti-Fraud and Abuse Amendments, Pub. L. No. 95-142 (1977).

163. "An initial burst of optimism by federal officials when they began examining [financial fraud] . . . slowly gave way to frustration over how to prove criminal intent." John Eaglesham, "Financial Crimes Bedevil Prosecutors," *Wall Street Journal*, December 6, 2011, C1.

164. "State Medicaid Fraud Control Units: Data Mining," 76 Fed. Reg. 14637 (proposed Mar. 17, 2011) (to be codified at 42 C.F.R. pt. 1007). Divisions within OIG (such as the Office of Audit Services, Office of Investigations, and Office of Evaluation and Inspections) can also undertake data analysis. 5 U.S.C. App. 3 § 2(2)(B). See also Government Accountability Office, GAO-

11-592, *Medicare Integrity Program: CMS Used Increased Funding for New Activities But Could Improve Measures of Program Effectiveness* (2011). Available at http://www.gao.gov/assets/330/322183.pdf (analyzing CMS use of its funding).

165. See, e.g., Endicott Johnson Corp. v. Perkins, 317 U.S. 501 (1943); Oklahoma Press Pub'g Co. v. Walling, 327 U.S. 186 (1946); FTC v. Crafts, 355 U.S. 9 (1957); U.S. v. Morton Salt, 338 U.S. 632, 652 (1950).

166. Scott Cleland, "Google's Global Antitrust Rap Sheet." Available at http://googleopoly.net/wp-content/uploads/2013/05/Googles-Global-Antitrust-Rap-Sheet-Copy.pdf. Scott Cleland, "Google's Privacy Rap Sheet." Available at http://www.googleopoly.net/GooglePrivacyRapSheet.pdf.

167. Cora Currier and Lena Groeger, "A Scorecard for This Summer's Bank Scandals," *ProPublica*, August 21, 2012, http://www.propublica.org/special/a-scorecard-for-this-summers-bank-scandals.

168. These include the work of the Money Laundering Threat Assessment Working Group (including agencies within the Department of the Treasury, Department of Justice, Department of Homeland Security, the Federal Reserve, and the United States Postal Service), "U.S. Money Laundering Threat Assessment" (Dec. 2005). Available at http://www.treasury.gov/resource-center/terrorist-illicit-finance/Documents/mlta.pdf. United Nations Office for Drug Control and Crime Prevention, "Financial Havens, Banking Secrecy and Money-Laundering," 1998, 57. Available at http://www.cf.ac.uk/socsi/whoswho/levi-laundering.pdf.

169. Eric J. Weiner, *The Shadow Market: How a Group of Wealthy Nations and Powerful Investors Secretly Dominate the World* (New York: Scribner, 2010), 13; Kevin D. Freeman, *Secret Weapon: How Economic Terrorism Brought Down the U.S. Stock Market and Why It Can Happen Again* (New York: Regnery, 2012).

170. See James Risen and Eric Lichtblau, "E-Mail Surveillance Renews Concerns in Congress," *New York Times*, June 16, 2009, http://www.nytimes.com/2009/06/17/us/17nsa.html?pagewanted=all.

171. *National Security Strategy of the United States of America* (2002), 1. Available at http://nssarchive.us/?page_id=32.

172. See also Aziz Z. Huq and Christopher Muller, "The War on Crime as Precursor to the War on Terror," *International Journal of Law, Crime, and Justice* 36 (2008): 215–229.

173. *See* Matt Krantz, "Computerized Stock Trading Leaves Investors Vulnerable," *USA Today*, July 9, 2010, http://www.usatoday.com/money/markets/2010-07-09-wallstreetmachine08_CV_N.htm.

174. Max Weber has defined state authority as a "monopoly on the legitimate use of force." Max Weber, "Politics as a Vocation" Speech delivered at Munich University (1918), in *From Max Weber: Essays in Sociology*, H. H. Gerth and C. Wright Mills eds. and trans. (New York: Routledge, 1958), 77, 78.

175. Baker, *Capitalism's Achilles Heel*, 186–191; see also Hilaire Avril, "Political Elites Ensure Continuing Flight of Dirty Money," *IPS*, September 16, 2009, http://www.ipsnews.net/africa/nota.asp?idnews=48460 (interviewing Raymond Baker, and describing a definitive study of "illicit financial flows from developing countries [estimated at] a trillion dollars a year").

176. Richard A. Oppel, Jr., "Taping of Farm Cruelty Is Becoming the Crime," *New York Times*, April 6, 2013, http://www.nytimes.com/2013/04/07/us /taping-of-farm-cruelty-is-becoming-the-crime.html.

177. Dana Milbank, "ALEC Stands Its Ground," *Washington Post*, December 4, 2013, http://www.washingtonpost.com/opinions/dana-milbank-alec-stands -its-ground/2013/12/04/ad593320-5d2c-11e3-bc56-c6ca94801fac_story.html.

178. Reporters Without Borders, *World Press Freedom Index* (2013). Available at http://fr.rsf.org/IMG/pdf/classement_2013_gb-bd.pdf.

179. Elizabeth Dwoskin, "Your Food Has Been Touched by Multitudes," *Bloomberg Businessweek*, August 25, 2011, http://www.businessweek.com/maga zine/your-food-has-been-touched-by-multitudes-08252011.html.

180. Ibid.

181. James B. Rule, "The Search Engine, for Better or Worse," *New York Times*, March 18, 2013, http://www.nytimes.com/2013/03/19/opinion/global /the-search-engine-for-better-or-for-worse.html?pagewanted=all. The aspi- ration to divine omniscience recalls Gloucester's lament about omnipotence: "As flies to wanton boys are we to th' gods, / They kill us for their sport." Wil- liam Shakespeare, *King Lear*, Act 4, Scene 1, 36–37.

# 6

## *Toward an Intelligible Society*

1. Cory Doctorow, "Scroogled" (September 17, 2007). Available at http:// blogoscoped.com/archive/2007-09-17-n72.html.

2. As cyberlaw expert James Boyle has observed, science fiction writers are among "the best social theorists of the information age." James Boyle, "A Politics of Intellectual Property: Environmentalism for the Net?," *Duke Law Journal* 47 (1997): 88.

3. Gary Shteyngart, *Super Sad True Love Story* (New York: Random House, 2010).

4. Adam Haslett, *Union Atlantic* (New York: Anchor, 2011), 162.

5. Plato, *Republic: Book II.* In *Five Great Dialogues*, ed. Louise Ropes Loo- mis, trans. Benjamin Jowett (New York: Walter J. Black, 1942), 253, 484.

6. Plato, *The Republic of Plato.* 2nd ed. Ed. and trans. Allan Bloom (New York: Basic Books, 1968) 193–194. As Douglas Rushkoff puts it, "The less involved and aware we are of the way our technologies are programmed and program us, the more narrow our choices will become." Douglas Rushkoff, *Program or be Programmed* (Boston: Soft Skull Press, 2010), 148–149. See also Danah Boyd, *It's Complicated: The Social Lives of Networked Teens* (New Haven, CT: Yale University Press, 2014) ("Developing Wisdom" about online life "requires active learning.").

7. Creditreport.com ad (June 1, 2013). Available at https://www.youtube .com/watch?v=EaobwbtWvWQ. ("My score's not great. It's 580. So creditors think I'm lazy.")

8. Andy Kroll, "Dark Money," *Mother Jones*, January 23, 2014, http://www .motherjones.com/category/secondary-tags/dark-money.

9. See Simon Johnson and James Kwak, *13 Bankers: The Wall Street Takeover and the Next Financial Meltdown* (New York: Pantheon, 2010), 135; Anat Admati and Martin Hellwig, *The Bankers' New Clothes* (Princeton, NJ: Princeton University Press, 2013).

10. Chris Gentilviso, "Elizabeth Warren Student Loans Bill Endorsed by Several Colleges, Organizations," *Huffington Post*, May 24, 2013, http://www.huffingtonpost.com/2013/05/24/elizabeth-warren-student-loans-bill_n_3329735.html.

11. Ryan Cooper, "Dodd Frank's Death by a Thousand Cuts," *Political Animal* (blog), March 4, 2013, http://www.washingtonmonthly.com/political-animal-a/2013_03/dodd_franks_death_by_a_thousan043346.php.     Gary Rivlin, "Wall Street Fires Back," *The Nation*, May 20, 2013, 11; Davis Polk, *Dodd-Frank Progress Report* (April 2013). Available at http://www.davispolk.com/files/Publication/900769d7-74f0-474c-9bce-0014949f0685/Presentation/PublicationAttachment/3983137e-639b-4bbc-a901-002b21e2e246/Apr2013_Dodd.Frank.Progress.Report.pdf. J. P. Morgan Chase's "London Whale" debacle proved that extraordinarily risky trades were still going on at major banks as of 2012. And had things gone worse for the firm, it is unclear what would have been different in 2012 than in 2008, in terms of policymaker reaction to massive losses. U.S. Senate Permanent Subcommittee on Investigations, *JPMorgan Chase Whale Trades: A Case History of Derivatives Risks and Abuses* (2013). Available at http://www.hsgac.senate.gov/download/report-jpmorgan-chase-whale-trades-a-case-history-of-derivatives-risks-and-abuses-march-15-2013.

12. Murray Edelman, *The Symbolic Uses of Politics* (Urbana: University of Illinois Press, 1964).

13. Hubert L. Dreyfus, *What Computers Can't Do* (Cambridge: MIT Press, 1972)[0].

14. Joseph Weizenbaum, *Computer Power and Human Reason: From Judgment to Calculation* (San Francisco: W. H. Freeman, 1976), 227.

15. Julius Stone, *Legal System and Lawyers' Reasonings* (Stanford, CA: Stanford University Press, 1964), 37–41 (observing that "experiments are proceeding in the use of electronic computers as aids to legal memory, analysis and thought," but cautioning against misuse or overuse of them).

16. Samir Chopra and Laurence F. White, *A Legal Theory for Autonomous Artificial Agents* (Ann Arbor: University of Michigan Press, 2011).

17. Christopher Steiner, *Automate This: How Algorithms Came to Rule Our World* (New York: Portfolio/Penguin, 2012).

18. Anish Puaar, "Fed Fears Increase in Runaway Algos," *The Trade News*, September 19, 2012, http://www.thetradenews.com/news/Regions/Americas/Fed_fears_increase_in_runaway_algos.aspx. Woodrow Hartzog, "Chain-Link Confidentiality," *Georgia Law Review* 46 (2012): 657–704.

19. Kenneth A. Bamberger, "Technologies of Compliance: Risk and Regulation in a Digital Age," *Texas Law Review* 88 (2010): 669–740; Erik F. Gerding, "The Outsourcing of Financial Regulation to Risk Models and the Global Financial Crisis: Code, Crash, and Open Source," *Washington Law Review* 84 (2009): 127–198. Quote from Suzanne McGee, *Chasing Goldman Sachs: How the*

*Masters of the Universe Melted Wall Street Down . . . And Why They'll Take Us to the Brink Again* (New York: Crown Business, 2011), 306.

20. For other utility comparisons, see Rebecca MacKinnon, *Consent of the Networked: The Worldwide Struggle for Internet Freedom* (New York: Basic Books, 2013). See also Jaron Lanier, *Who Owns the Future?* (New York: Simon & Schuster, 2013).

21. Susan Crawford, *Captive Audience: The Telecom Industry and Monopoly Power in the New Gilded Age* (New Haven, CT: Yale University Press, 2013).

22. As Paul Woolley observes, "The shortening of investment horizons has been a feature of capital markets over the past two decades." Paul Woolley, "Why Are Financial Markets So Inefficient and Exploitative—And a Suggested Remedy," in *The Future of Finance: The LSE Report*, ed. Adair Turner et al. (London: London School of Economics and Political Science, 2010), 133.

23. William Scheuerman, *Liberal Democracy and the Social Acceleration of Time* (Baltimore, MD: The Johns Hopkins University Press, 2004).

24. Yunchee Foo, "Google Makes New Concessions to EU Regulators: Paper," Reuters. July 27, 2012. Available at http://www.reuters.com/article/2012/07/17/us-eu-google-idUSBRE86G08T20120717.

25. For examples of obviously inappropriate "related stories," see Michael Kranish, "Facebook Draws Fire on Related Stories Push," *Boston Globe*, May 4, 2014, at http://www.bostonglobe.com/news/nation/2014/05/03/facebook-push-related-articles-users-without-checking-credibility-draws-fire/rPae4M2LlzpVHIJAmfDYNL/story.html.

26. Adrian Chen, "Inside Facebook's Outsourced Anti-Porn and Gore Brigade, Where 'Camel Toes' Are More Offensive Than 'Crushed Heads,'" *Gawker* (blog), February 16, 2012, http://gawker.com/5885714/inside-facebooks-outsourced-anti+porn-and-gore-brigade-where-camel-toes-are-more-offensive-than-crushed-heads. Adrian Chen, "Facebook Release New Content Guidelines, Now Allows Bodily Fluids," *Gawker* (blog), February 16, 2012, http://gawker.com/5885836/facebook-releases-new-content-guidelines-now-allows-bodily-fluids. On Google's use of humans in changing its algorithms, see Rob D. Young, "Google Discusses Their Algorithm Change Process," *Search Engine Journal*, August 26, 2011, http://www.searchenginejournal.com/google-discusses-their-algorithm-change-process/32731/.

27. Quentin Hardy, "Unlocking Secrets, if Not Its Own Value," *New York Times*, May 31, 2014, at http://www.nytimes.com/2014/06/01/business/unlocking-secrets-if-not-its-own-value.html?_r=0.

28. William Janeway, *Doing Capitalism in the Innovation Economy: Markets, Speculation, and the State* (New York: Cambridge University Press, 2012).

29. Philip Coggan, *Paper Promises: Debt, Money, and the New World Order* (New York: PublicAffairs, 2012), 181.

30. Mathews v. Eldridge, 424 U.S. 319 (1976); Goss v. Lopez, 419 U.S. 565 (1975).

31. For examples of reputational accountability in the health context, see Frank Pasquale, "Grand Bargains for Big Data: The Emerging Law of Health Information," Maryland Law Review (2013): 701.

32. In the German case, the plaintiffs claimed that autocomplete suggested links to fraud and Scientology when their names were put into Google's search engine. The Court held that Google must remove defamatory autocomplete results after being notified. "Top German Court Orders Google to Alter Search Suggestions" (May 13, 2013). Available at http://www.dw.de/top-german-court-orders-google-to-alter-search-suggestions/a-16811219. The Argentina case dealt with a complaint that suggested searches lead users to anti-Semitic sites. The court ordered Google to alter the suggestion function and to erase "highly discriminatory" sites from the results page. Danny Goodwin, "Argentina Court: Google Must Censor Anti-Semitic Search Results, Suggestions" (May 20, 2011) *Search Engine Watch*. Available at http://searchenginewatch.com/article/2072754/Argentina-Court-Google-Must-Censor-Anti-Semitic-Search-Results-Suggestions. Kadhim Shubber, "Japanese Court Orders Google to Censor Autocomplete, Pay Damages," *Wired*, April 16, 2013, http://www.wired.co.uk/news/archive/2013-04/16/google-japan-ruling.

33. Les Leopold, *How to Make a Million Dollars an Hour: Why Hedge Funds Get Away with Siphoning Off America's Wealth* (Hoboken, NJ: John Wiley & Sons, Inc., 2013); Danielle Kucera and Christine Harper, "Traders' Smaller Bonuses Still Top Pay for Brain Surgeons, 4-Star Generals," *Bloomberg News*, January 13, 2011, http://www.bloomberg.com/news/2011-01-13/traders-smaller-bonuses-still-top-pay-for-brain-surgeons-4-star-generals.html. Justin Fox, "Just How Useless Is the Asset-Management Industry?" *Harvard Business Review* (blog), May 16, 2013, http://blogs.hbr.org/fox/2013/05/just-how-useless-is-the-asset-.html.

34. Wallace C. Turbeville, "A New Perspective on the Costs and Benefits of Financial Regulation: Inefficiency of Capital Intermediation in a Deregulated System," *Maryland Law Review* 72 (2013): 1179. ("By inferring that the historical increase in financial sector share of GDP is attributable to the value diverted from capital intermediation, the excessive wealth transfer to the financial sector is in the range of $635 billion per year.") See also John Quiggin, "Wall Street Isn't Worth It," *Jacobin*, November 14, 2013, https://www.jacobinmag.com/2013/11/wall-street-isnt-worth-it/. ("The financial services sector as a whole accounts for more than 20 percent of US GDP, and this share has grown by around 10 percentage points since the 1970s. . . . Is the financial sector making a contribution to society commensurate with its returns? The evidence is overwhelmingly against this proposition.")

35. New Economics Foundation, *A Bit Rich: Calculating the Real Value to Society of Different Professions* (2009). Available at http://dnwssx4l7gl7s.cloudfront.net/nefoundation/default/page/-/files/A_Bit_Rich.pdf.

36. Jeffrey Hollender, "The Cannibalization of Entrepreneurship in America" (June 2011). *Jeffrey Hollender Partners*. Available at http://www.jeffreyhollender.com/?p=1622. Paul Kedrosky and Dane Stangler, "Financialization and Its Entrepreneurial Consequences" (Mar. 2011). Kansas City, MO: Kauffman Foundation Research Series. Available at http://www.kauffman.org/~/media/kauffman_org/research%20reports%20and%20covers/2011/03/financialization_report_32311.pdf.

37. See William K. Black, discussing WaMu's accounting practices, for an example of how things can go wrong when a "sure thing" is expected. *Examining Lending Discrimination Practices and Foreclosure Abuses: Hearing before the Senate Committee on the Judiciary*, 112th Cong. 41 (2012) (prepared testimony of William K. Black). Available at http://www.gpo.gov/fdsys/pkg/CHRG-112shrg74142/pdf/CHRG-112shrg74142.pdf.

38. For an example of such a project, see Richard L. Sandor, *Good Derivatives: A Story of Financial and Environmental Innovation* (Hoboken, NJ: John Wiley & Sons, Inc., 2012).

39. J. Bradford DeLong, *The End of Influence: What Happens When Other Countries Have the Money* (New York: Basic Books, 2010), 146–147.

40. Thomas Philippon, "Has the U.S. Finance Industry Become Less Efficient?" (Dec. 2011). NYU Working Paper No. 2451/31370. Available at http://papers.ssrn.com/sol3/papers.cfm?abstract_id=1972808.

41. DeLong, *The End of Influence*, 146–147. John LaMattina, "Why Should Wall Street Dictate the Level of Pharma R&D Spending?" *Drug Truths*, October 18, 2011, http://johnlamattina.wordpress.com/2011/10/18/why-should-wall-street-dictate-the-level-of-pharma-rd-spending/. Brian Vastag, "Scientists Heeded Call but Few Can Find Jobs," *Washington Post*, July 8, 2012, A14.

42. Raghuram G. Rajan, *Fault Lines: How Hidden Fractures Still Threaten the World Economy* (Princeton, NJ: Princeton University Press, 2010), 30; James K. Galbraith, *Inequality and Instability: A Study of the World Economy Just before the Great Crisis* (New York: Oxford University Press, 2012).

43. Dean Baker, "TARP Repayment and Legalized Counterfeiting," *Real-World Economics Review Blog*, December 14, 2010, http://rwer.wordpress.com/2010/12/14/tarp-repayment-and-legalized-counterfeiting/.

44. Geoff Mulgan, *The Locust and the Bee: Predators and Creators in Capitalism's Future* (Princeton, NJ: Princeton University Press, 2013).

45. This dynamic is clearest in finance. Gautam Mukunda, "The Price of Wall Street's Power," *Harvard Business Review* (June, 2014).

46. Astra Taylor, *The People's Platform* (New York: Metropolitan Books, 2014).

47. For more on the use of compulsory licenses historically and today, see Timothy A. Cohan, "Ghost in the Attic: The Notice of Intention to Use and the Compulsory License in the Digital Era," *Columbia Journal of Law and the Arts* 33 (2010): 499–526.

48. William W. Fisher, *Promises to Keep: Technology, Law, and the Future of Entertainment* (Stanford, CA: Stanford University Press, 2004), 199–259. On the UK television licensing fee, see "What Does Your Licence Fee Pay For?" *TV Licensing.* Available at http://www.tvlicensing.co.uk/check-if-you-need-one/topics/what-does-your-licence-fee-pay-for-top13/.

49. Dean Baker, "The Reform of Intellectual Property," *Post-Autistic Economics Review* 32 (2005): article 1. Available at http://www.paecon.net/PAEReview/development/Baker32.htm. Fisher, *Promises to Keep*, 221–222.

50. For more on the ACA's tax increase on the wealthy, see Maximilian Held, "Go Forth and Sin [Tax] No More," *Gonzaga Law Review* 46 (2010–2011): 737.

51. Frank Pasquale, "Single-Payer Music Care?" *Concurring Opinions* (blog), March 22, 2006, http://www.concurringopinions.com/archives/2006/03/viva_la_france.html.

52. "Who Owns the Media?" *Free Press.* Available at http://www.freepress.net/ownership/chart. For more on SOPA, see Brent Dean, "Why the Internet Hates SOPA," *Computer Crime and Technology in Law Enforcement* 8 (2012): 3.

53. Bernard E. Harcourt, *The Illusion of Free Markets: Punishment and the Myth of Natural Orders* (Cambridge, MA: Harvard University Press, 2012).

54. Cavan Sieczkowski, "SOPA Is Dead: Lamar Smith Withdraws Bill from the House," *International Business Times*, January 20, 2012, http://www.ibtimes.com/sopa-dead-lamar-smith-withdraws-bill-house-398552.

55. Evgeny Morozov, *To Save Everything, Click Here: The Folly of Technological Solutionism* (New York: Public Affairs, 2013).

56. Julie Cohen, *Configuring the Networked Self* (New Haven, CT: Yale University Press, 2012).

57. Harcourt, *The Illusion of Free Markets*, 179–180; G. Richard Shell, *Make the Rules or Your Rivals Will* (Philadelphia: G. Richard Shell Consulting, 2011).

58. Tom Hamburger and Matea Gold, "Google, once disdainful of lobbying, now a master of Washington influence," *Washington Post*, Apr. 12, 2014, at http://www.washingtonpost.com/politics/how-google-is-transforming-power-and-politicsgoogle-once-disdainful-of-lobbying-now-a-master-of-washington-influence/2014/04/12/51648b92-b4d3-11e3-8cb6-284052554d74_story.html.

59. See, e.g., Harcourt, *The Illusion of Free Markets;* James K. Galbraith, *The Predator State: How Conservatives Abandoned the Free Market and Why Liberals Should Too* (New York: Free Press, 2008); G. Richard Shell, *Make the Rules or Your Rivals Will* (New York: Crown Business, 2004).

60. Charles E. Lindblom, *Politics and Markets: The World's Political Economic Systems* (New York: Basic Books, 1977).

61. Janine R. Wedel, *Shadow Elite: How the World's New Power Brokers Undermine Democracy, Government, and the Free Market* (New York: Basic Books, 2009); Frank Pasquale, "Reclaiming Egalitarianism in the Political Theory of Campaign Finance Reform," *University of Illinois Law Review* 45 (2008): 599–660.

62. See Michael Abramowicz, "Perfecting Patent Prizes," *Vanderbilt Law Review* 56 (2003): 115–236.

63. Here, again, the health sector is ahead of reputation, search, and finance firms, adopting a raft of pilot programs via the Affordable Care Act. Atul Gawande, "Testing, Testing," *The New Yorker*, December 14, 2009, http://www.newyorker.com/reporting/2009/12/14/091214fa_fact_gawande?currentPage=all.

64. Nicola Jentzsch, *Financial Privacy: An International Comparison of Credit Reporting Systems* (Berlin: Springer-Verlag, 2007), 62.

65. Siva Vaidhyanathan, *The Googlization of Everything (And Why We Should Worry)* (Berkeley: University of California Press, 2010).

66. Harvard University Library director Robert Darnton's proposal for a "Digital Public Library of America" is one model. Robert Darnton, "Can We

Create a Digital National Library?," *New York Review of Books*, October 28, 2010, 4.

67. Timothy A. Canova, "The Federal Reserve We Need," *The American Prospect* 21, no. 9 (October 2010). Available at http://prospect.org/article/federal -reserve-we-need.

68. David Dayen, "The Post Office Should Just Become a Bank," *The New Republic*, Jan. 28, 2014, at http://www.newrepublic.com/article/116374/postal -service-banking-how-usps-can-save-itself-and-help-poor.

69. Jason Judd and Heather McGhee, *Banking on America* (Washington, D.C.: Demos, 2010).

70. Move Your Money Project. Available at http://www.moveyourmoney-project.org/.

71. Henry T. C. Hu, "Too Complex to Depict? Innovation, 'Pure Information,' and the SEC Disclosure Paradigm," *Texas Law Review* 90 (2012): 1601–1715.

72. Bernard Sternsher, *Rexford Tugwell and the New Deal* (New Brunswick, NJ: Rutgers University Press, 1964).

73. For details, see Canova, "The Federal Reserve We Need."

74. Joel Seligman, *The Transformation of Wall Street: A History of the Securities and Exchange Commission and Modern Corporate Finance* (New York: Aspen, 2003), 40–41.

75. Nathaniel Popper, "Banks Find S&P More Favorable in Bond Ratings," *New York Times*, August 1, 2013, A1.

76. Galbraith, *The Predator State*. The book casts a harsh light on corporate and government malfeasance. It also provides some positive recommendations that should guide progressives.

77. Matthew Stoller, "Review of 'Capitalizing on Crisis,' by Greta Krippner," *Observations on Credit and Surveillance*, February 16, 2014. ("In the 1970s, politicians got tired of fighting over who would get what, and just turned those decisions over to the depoliticized market. This is known as 'financialization.' Then political leaders didn't have to say 'no' anymore to any constituency group, they could just say 'blame the market.'")

78. Richard Fisher, in an interview with Russ Roberts, "Richard Fisher on Too Big to Fail and the Fed" (Dec. 2013). *Econ Talk*. Transcript of interview available at http://www.econtalk.org/archives/2013/12/richard_fisher.html.

79. Fresh thinking in finance recognizes the importance of this substantive turn. See, e.g., Ann Pettifor, *Just Money: How Society Can Break the Despotic Power of Finance* (London: Commonwealth Publishing, 2014); Mary Mellor, *The Future of Money: From Financial Crisis to Public Resource* (New York: Pluto Press, 2010); Mariana Mazzucato, *The Entrepreneurial State: Debunking Public vs. Private Sector Myths* (New York: Anthem Press, 2013).

80. Todd Woody, "You'd Never Know He's a Sun King," *New York Times*, May 9, 2010, BU1; "Vice Fund Manager Finds Plenty of Virtue in Sin Stocks," *Middletown Press*, August 24, 2010, http://www.middletownpress.com/articles /2010/08/24/business/doc4c732f5c49a1d717896087.txt.

81. Mark Kinver, "China's 'Rapid Renewables Surge,'" *BBC News*, August 1, 2008, http://news.bbc.co.uk/2/hi/science/nature/7535839.stm.

82. Moreover, overwork has been documented among many in the industry. Kevin Roose, *Young Money: Inside the Hidden World of Wall Street's Post-Crash Recruits* (New York: Grand Central Publishing, 2014); Karen Ho, *Liquidated: An Ethnography of Wall Street* (Durham, NC: Duke University Press, 2009).

83. See, e.g., Regina F. Burch, "Financial Regulatory Reform Post-Financial Crisis: Unintended Consequences for Small Businesses," *Penn State Law Review* 115 (2010–2011): 443. See generally Thomas J. Schoenbaum, "Saving the Global Financial System: International Financial Reforms and United States Financial Reform, Will They Do the Job?," *Uniform Commercial Code Law Journal* 43 (2010): 482.

84. Louis Brandeis, "What Publicity Can Do," *Harper's Weekly*, December 20, 1913. Reprinted in *Other People's Money and How the Bankers Use It* (New York: Frederick A. Stokes, 1914), 92 ("Sunlight is said to be the best of disinfectants . . ."); Eric W. Pinciss, "Sunlight Is Still the Best Disinfectant: Why the Federal Securities Laws Should Prohibit Soft Dollar Arrangements in the Mutual Fund Industry," *Annual Review of Banking and Financial Law* 23 (2004): 863–889.

85. Clive Dilnot, "The Triumph—and Costs—of Greed," *Real-World Economics Review* 49 (2009): 52.

86. Neil Barofsky, *Bailout: An Inside Account of How Washington Abandoned Main Street While Rescuing Wall Street* (New York: Free Press, 2012).

87. James B. Stewart, "Calculated Deal in a Rate-Rigging Inquiry," *New York Times*, July 13, 2012.

88. Jon Mitchell, "Google Gets the Biggest FTC Privacy Fine in History—and Deserves It," *Read Write*, July 10, 2012, http://readwrite.com/2012/07/10/google-gets-the-biggest-ftc-privacy-fine-in-history-and-deserves-it#awesm=~ovx13R50AmMHx1. David Kravets, "Millions Will Flow to Privacy Groups Supporting Weak Facebook Settlement," *Wired*, July 13, 2012, http://www.wired.com/threatlevel/2012/07/groups-get-facebook-millions/.

89. Ken Silverstein, "Think Tanks in the Tank?," *The Nation*, June 10, 2013, 18; George F. DeMartino, *The Economist's Oath: On the Need for and Content of Professional Economic Ethics* (New York: Oxford University Press, 2011).

90. John C. Coates IV, "Cost-Benefit Analysis of Financial Regulation: Case Studies and Implications," *Yale Law Journal* 124 (forthcoming, 2014); Matteo Marsili, "Toy Models and Stylized Realities," *European Physics Journal* 55 (2007): 173 ("Computational . . . approaches [to modeling] have been very useful in physics because the knowledge of microscopic laws constrains theoretical modeling in extremely controlled ways. This is almost never possible for socioeconomic systems.").

91. Amar Bhidé, *A Call for Judgment: Sensible Finance for a Dynamic Economy* (New York: Oxford University Press, 2010).

92. Friedrich A. Hayek, "The Use of Knowledge in Society," *American Economics Review* 35 (1945): 519–530.

93. Bhidé, *A Call for Judgment*.

94. MacKinnon, *Consent of the Networked*; Anupam Chander, "Facebookistan," *North Carolina Law Review* 90 (2012): 1807–1844.

95. For the strange career of neoliberal approaches to antitrust law, see Robert Van Horn and Philip Mirowski, "Reinventing Monopoly," in *The Road from Mount Pèlerin*, ed. Philip Mirowski and Dieter Plehwe (Cambridge, MA: Harvard University Press, 2009), 219 ff.

96. C. Wright Mills, *The Power Elite*. New ed. (New York: Oxford University Press, 2000). First published 1956.

97. Thomas Piketty, *Capital in the Twenty-First Century* (Cambridge: Harvard University Press, 2014), 574.

98. Pope Francis, *Evangelii Gaudium (Apostolic Exhortation)*, November 24, 2013, para. 55. Available at http://w2.vatican.va/content/francesco/en/apost _exhortations/documents/papa-francesco_esortazione-ap_20131124_evangelii -gaudium.html.

# ACKNOWLEDGMENTS

This book is based on ten years of research covering law, technology, and social science. Several institutions have provided a refuge from the usual pressure toward academic specialization. Under the leadership of Jack Balkin, Laura Denardis, Eddan Katz, and Margot Kaminski, Yale's Information Society Project has hosted conferences that influenced my thought on reputation and search. Princeton's Center for Information Technology Policy hosted me as a Visiting Fellow, and has been a leader in promoting privacy and technological accountability. When I began teaching at Seton Hall University, mentors like Kathleen Boozang, Charles Sullivan, and John Jacobi supported wide-ranging intellectual interests.

The University of Maryland has also proven to be a community of scholars unafraid to challenge conventional wisdom. I have learned a great deal from my colleagues in the Association of Professors of Political Economy and Law (APPEAL) (particularly Martha Mc-Cluskey, Jennifer Taub, and Zephyr Teachout) about the interactions between law and economics. To the extent this book makes any contribution to the theory and practice of social justice, it is inspired by the lifelong commitments of scores of colleagues at the four law schools where I have taught. Nadia Hay, Susan McCarty, and David Vibelhoer offered expert assistance in the preparation of the manuscript for publication.

Looking further back, I want to acknowledge the contribution of several mentors: Bill Eskridge, Glyn Morgan, Peter Schuck, and Ruella Yates. At various points, they gave me a lasting gift—the sense that I was saying something worth listening to. As I edited the manuscript, Eve Golden offered a wealth of helpful suggestions. I also thank my editor at Harvard Press, Elizabeth Knoll, who encouraged me to bridge traditionally disconnected fields. The work of Oren Bracha, Danielle Keats Citron, Catherine Corman, Lawrence Joseph, John Davis Malloy, Tara A. Ragone, and Simon Stern has also inspired me.

On a personal note, this book is dedicated to the memory of my mother and father. Despite suffering many depredations of the black box society, they were always there for me. Their values animate this work. As Richard Powers' novel *Gain* suggests, personal and corporate histories can interact in unexpected ways.

Finally, I offer deep gratitude to my partner, Ray. His creativity, playfulness, resilience, and determination inspire me daily. His support and encouragement for this project and so many others, have never been in doubt. I could only dive into the wreck of contemporary political economy because I am sustained by the love and laughter of our home.

# INDEX